Global Phenomenologies of Religion

The Study of Religion in a Global Context

Series editors

Satoko Fujiwara	Katja Triplett	Alexandra Grieser
Executive Editor	Series Editor	Managing Editor
University of Tokyo	Leipzig University	Trinity College Dublin

The series, published in association with the International Association for the History of Religions, encourages work that is innovative in the study of religions, whether of an empirical, theoretical or methodological nature. This includes multi- or inter-disciplinary studies involving anthropology, philosophy, psychology, sociology and political studies. Volumes will examine the continuing influence of postcolonial, decolonial and intercultural dynamics, as well as contemporary responses from intersectional studies. They will also address the relevance and application of more recent approaches such as cognitivist, as well as ones concerned with aesthetic culture – art, architecture, media, performance and sound.

Published
Philosophy and the End of Sacrifice
Disengaging Ritual in Ancient India, Greece and Beyond
Edited by Peter Jackson and Anna-Pya Sjödin

The Relational Dynamics of Enchantment and Sacralization
Changing the Terms of the Religion Versus Secularity Debate
Edited by Peik Ingman, Terhi Utriainen, Tuija Hovi and Måns Broo

Translocal Lives and Religion
Connections between Asia and Europe in the Late Modern World
Edited by Philippe Bornet

Forthcoming
Religion as Relation
Studying Religion in Context
Edited by Peter Berger, Marjo Buitelaar and Kim Knibbe

Global Phenomenologies of Religion
An Oral History in Interviews

Edited by
Satoko Fujiwara, David Thurfjell and Steven Engler

SHEFFIELD UK   BRISTOL CT

Published by Equinox Publishing Ltd.

UK: Office 415, The Workstation, 15 Paternoster Row, Sheffield, South Yorkshire S1 2BX

USA: ISD, 70 Enterprise Drive, Bristol, CT 06010

www.equinoxpub.com

First published 2021

ISBN-13   978 1 78179 914 7   (hardback)
          978 1 78179 915 4   (paperback)
          978 1 78179 916 1   (ePDF)
          978 1 80050 044 0   (ePub)

British Library Cataloguing-in-Publication Data

A catalogue record for this book is available from the British Library.

Library of Congress Cataloging-in-Publication Data

Names: Fujiwara, Satoko, 1963- editor. | Thurfjel, David, editor. | Engler, Steven, editor.
Title: Global phenomenologies of religion : an oral history in interviews /
    edited by Satoko Fujiwara, David Thurfjel and Steven Engler.
Description: Bristol, CT : Equinox Publishing Ltd., 2021. | Series: The study of religion in
    a global context | Includes bibliographical references and index. | Summary:
    "This volume investigates how the phenomenology of religion was accepted and
    developed in different national contexts. It consists of interviews with senior
    scholars, who are experts on the development of the phenomenology of religion
    in their countries, along with commentary and analysis"— Provided by publisher.
Identifiers: LCCN 2020048092 (print) | LCCN 2020048093 (ebook) | ISBN 9781781799147
    (hardback) | ISBN 9781781799154 (paperback) | ISBN 9781781799161 (pdf) |
    ISBN 9781800500440 (epub)
Subjects: LCSH: Religion—Philosophy—Miscellanea. |
    Religion—Research—Miscellanea. | Phenomenology—Research—Miscellanea.
    | Interviews. | Globalization—Religious aspects.
Classification: LCC BL51 .G669 2021 (print) | LCC BL51 (ebook) | DDC 210—dc23
LC record available at https://lccn.loc.gov/2020048092
LC ebook record available at https://lccn.loc.gov/2020048093

Typeset by JS Typesetting Ltd, Porthcawl, Mid Glamorgan

Contents

Contents

Introduction

The Contested Legacies of Phenomenologies of Religion

SATOKO FUJIWARA, DAVID THURFJELL AND STEVEN ENGLER

Purposes of This Book: Why Now?

Phenomenology of religion is dead; long live phenomenology of religion! We are not evoking dynastic succession here – or the zombie-like return of an approach that many consider dead and buried. We mean to underline a key finding of this book: the coexistence of divergent discourses. Most scholars identify with the first part of the statement that began this paragraph, but many identify with the second.

The narrative of the passing of an era – the fading away of phenomenology of religion – is a common one. To choose just one example, Steffen Führding writes, "Since the decline of the phenomenology of religion as a guiding paradigm that provided common grounds for the Study of Religion in the 1960s, theories and methods have become diverse – a process which began in the 1970s at the latest" (Führding 2017, 1). Führding suggests that the 1960 IAHR conference in Marburg "initiated ... the decline of the phenomenology of religion" (ibid., 8–9). The voices collected here as a series of interviews present a less tidy picture, both in terms of historical moments and in terms of divergent developments in different parts of the globe. Taken as a whole, this book helps to fill in and reassess details of the historical trajectory of phenomenology of religion (henceforth PoR).

All three of us belong to the post-PoR generations. Though educated in different corners of the world – Japan, Sweden and Canada – we all started our careers after the obsolescence – general but far from complete – of PoR. We learned to see it as something that appealed to older generations.

So why this book, and why now? It is not an attempt to rehabilitate or reboot PoR. Nor is it another tirade accusing PoR of essentialism and

1

religionism. It offers a different way of looking at the past, current and future trajectory of the study of religion. Instead of arguing that the study of religion has progressed (or declined), we let contemporary witnesses present their own views. The resulting chorus of voices – with its many points of dissonance – casts light on the academic processes that formed the current generations of scholars of religion. In that sense, this book is intended to serve as a case study of the non-linear or spasmodic theoretical development of our discipline.

What is PoR?

Some readers may not be familiar with the term "PoR". Others may wonder precisely what this book means by the term. As editors we do not provide any definition of "PoR". A main ambition of this book is to show the differing meanings that scholars ascribe to this notion, without imposing any meaning by ourselves. If "PoR" turns out to have one common, agreed-upon definition, that would be an empirical finding of this project, not an editorial presumption or imposition. But, as will become evident, we found no such agreement.

PoR has been one of the most disputed branches of the study of religion, not least because it is directly related to our discipline's identity. To define PoR – one way or another – would be to take sides in these formative disputes, something that we have tried to avoid. Instead we asked each of our witnesses – interviewees belonging to more senior generations – to tell us how they define it.

Notwithstanding this ambition, an initial sketch may be useful in order to help readers orient themselves to the topic of the book. Here is a very brief explanation, reviewing how "PoR" is defined in the largest and most popular encyclopaedia of the study of religion. We do not endorse this particular view, but it has the advantages of being clear and of reflecting common understandings in our discipline.

Douglas Allen starts his article "Phenomenology of Religion" in the *Encyclopedia of Religion* by acknowledging that there is no single, clear-cut definition of PoR because "The term has become very popular and is used by numerous scholars who share little if anything in common" (Allen 2005, 7086). Accordingly, instead of providing a simple definition, Allen classifies uses of the term into four groups. The first includes "works in which *phenomenology of religion* is used in the vaguest, broadest, and most uncritical of ways" and often only means "an investigation of the phenomena of religion". The second includes works in which PoR refers to "the comparative study and the classification of different types of religious phenomena". The third embraces works by "numerous scholars" who "identify the phenomenology religion as a specific branch, discipline, or method within *Religionswissenschaft*". The fourth consists of "scholars whose phenomenology of religion is influenced by philosophical phenomenology" (ibid., 7086–7087).

Allen then names major phenomenologists of religion: Max Scheler (1874–1928), W. Brede Kristensen (1867–1953), Rudolf Otto (1869–1937), Gerardus van der Leeuw (1890–1950), Friedrich Heiler (1892–1967), C. Jouco Bleeker (1898–1983), Mircea Eliade (1907–1986) and Ninian Smart (1927–2001). He further identifies a set of characteristics of PoR:

> its identification as a comparative, systematic, empirical, historical, descriptive discipline and approach; its antireductionist claims and its autonomous nature; its adoption of philosophical phenomenological notions of intentionality and *epoché*; its insistence on the value of empathy, sympathetic understanding, and religious commitment; and its claim to provide insight into essential structures and meaning.
>
> (Allen 2005, 7093)

In our view, not all scholars will regard the above eight names as representatives of PoR and this is a consequence of disagreement over the meaning of PoR. Some may exclude Scheler. Others may include P. D. Chantepie de la Saussaye (1848–1920), Geo Widengren (1907–1996) and Åke Hultkrantz (1920–2006), all of whom Allen categorizes under the second group. Still others may think that Raffaele Pettazzoni should be added. Who appears in such lists depends on such factors as which characteristics of PoR are prioritized, the particular reception of different authors, and the vagaries of translations. The definition of PoR is further complicated by the fact that most of the characteristics that Allen lists have been matters of controversy, enthusiastically supported by some and vehemently criticized by others. Some such controversies developed among scholars of religion (i.e. for whom *Religionswissenschaft* is a discipline) and they remained limited to that disciplinary context. Others have extended further afield. For example, some PoR-scholars' emphasis on a turn towards inner religious experience is related to debates over the disciplinary location of the study of religion: is it part of the humanities or social sciences; or does it have one foot in the natural sciences? And, of course, these debates resonate with the philosophical literature on phenomenology and on discussions of phenomenology as an approach in other disciplines (e.g. medical anthropology).

To further help readers get a sense of the landscape, here is a brief sketch of some of the main characteristics that are often associated with PoR. As the terms themselves are defined differently by different scholars, we again refer to Allen, because he serves as a prominent example, not because we recommend his take on these terms over others.

- **Antireductionism:** the insistence that "investigators approach religious data as phenomena that are fundamentally and irreducibly religious", with a correlated criticism of "the reductions of religious data to fit nonreligious perspectives, such as those of sociology, psychology, or economics", based on the view that such reductionism "destroy[s] the specificity, complexity and irreducible intentionality of religious phenomena" (Allen 2005, 7094).
- **Autonomy:** "the identification of phenomenology of religion as an autonomous discipline and approach", which "utilizes a specific method of understanding that is commensurate with the religious nature of the subject matter" (ibid., 7094). The term "*sui generis*" has often been employed to qualify this autonomous nature, though that term has other related meanings.
- **Intentionality:** the nature of the "structure of religious consciousness", "religious experience" or "religious meaning". All of these point to "the transcendent sacred". While reductionist approaches negate "the unique intentionality of religious phenomena", phenomenologists try to capture "the intentional characteristics of religious manifestations" as given in immediate religious experience (ibid., 7094).
- *Epoché:* as a methodological commitment, to "suspend all personal preconceptions as to what is 'real'" in the attempt to "describe the meaning of religious phenomena as they appear in the lives of religious persons". It can also more widely refer to the suspension of all value judgments (ibid., 7095). This basic stance is often signalled by the term "bracketing".
- **Empathy, sympathetic understanding:** as a methodological commitment, "to place [oneself] within the religious 'life-world' of others and to grasp the religious meaning of the experienced phenomena" (ibid., 7095).
- **Insight into essential structures and meaning:** to aim at "intuiting, interpreting and describing the essence of religious phenomena". Also called "eidetic vision" (ibid., 7095–7096).

Allen also says that PoR "emerges as both a major field of study and an extremely influential approach" (ibid., 7086) and that "some of the vocabulary of philosophical [Husserlean] phenomenology and, in several cases, some of its methodology have influenced the phenomenology of religion" (ibid., 7089). However, even such seemingly basic assessments of PoR are not shared by all scholars of religion.

Encyclopaedia articles like Allen's and textbook descriptions are helpful for providing an initial framework for understanding. But this sort of generic description of PoR would not be particularly helpful if we were to actually look for phenomenologists in the field. On the one hand, many supposedly PoR elements – neutrality, sympathetic understanding, classification and so on – are common to a wide variety of approaches. They are held by many scholars who do not see themselves as, and are not seen by others as, practising PoR. On the other hand, as the interviews in this book illustrate, not all scholars associated with PoR work with all of these characteristics. We could start by taking the above list of characteristics as an initial family-resemblance approach to understanding the nature of PoR. However, as readers will see, it is a particularly unruly and divided family. In sum, there is no single set of elements that characterizes PoR. Particular historical, national and regional contexts have led scholars of religion to perceive or construct PoR as an approach or stance in different ways. That recognition was the initial impetus for this book. As a result, in our view, it is more productive to listen to historical witnesses than to start by presenting one view or another of the "true" nature of PoR.

Backgrounds

In preparing this volume, we started with two related hypotheses. PoR has declined, over the last half-century, from a place of prominence in the meta-theoretical landscape of our discipline to a moribund state. And a majority of scholars of religion, if they think about PoR at all, hold a negative view of it. By and large, the interviews collected in this book support these two hypotheses.

However, they also paint a more interesting and complicated picture, in four senses. First, they reveal a greater range of meanings of PoR than we expected. (We anticipate that readers will have the same eye-opening experience.) Second, this polyphony of meanings reflects not just individual points of view but divergent national histories and discourses. Third, PoR has been more than just a theoretical and methodological position or approach: it has served, and continues to serve, a symbolic role in meta-theoretical debates. It stands in for various sets of issues that are both valued and criticized. Interesting differences arise here. Compare, for example, the generation gap illustrated by the interview from Sweden with the multi-generational consistency of PoR's rhetorical place in Canadian meta-theoretical debates, as discussed in that chapter's commentary. Fourth, certain accepted "facts" about the history of PoR turn out to be far from straightforward (see, for example, the chapter on the Netherlands).

The study of religion has been called a "child of the Enlightenment" (Mensching 1948, 8, 39f). Since the 1990s, more attention has been paid to its Romantic heritage (Kippenberg 1997). Either way, its history tends to be presented with a triumphalist and emancipatory narrative. The study of religion emerged as it separated itself from theology. In the beginning, the separation was incomplete. But secular, critical approaches have gradually superseded religionist approaches over many decades, ridding the discipline of theological legacies, one after another.

There is certainly some degree of truth to this view. However, it is simplistic to posit a linear view of progress, as if the disciplinary identity of the study of religion were a symptom or side-effect of processes of disenchantment, rationalization or secularization in modernity. Relations between theology and the study of religion are more complex for several reasons: for example, theoretical and methodological overlap; national variations in past and present relations between the two (see e.g. Engler 2006); and the presence of a third, competing meta-theoretical and epistemic stream in our discipline, Perennialism (Sedgwick 2004). The risk of bias is most prominent in the guiding trope that a scientific and/or critical study of religion is the result of a reflexive self-purging of theology's impurities: the substitution of reason for faith. Most scholars of religion who seek coherent and methodological rigorous approaches do not rely on this trope, if only because they just get on with their business, spending little or no time reflecting on their discipline's identity and allegiances. But we should remain alive to the Orientalist overtones of this stance, to its correlation with imaginary fault lines between rational, scientific West/North and emotional, faith-rooted East/South. To the extent that such stereotypes are seen as applying to differences between Western European/North American scholars of religion and those in the rest of the world, it is impossible to foster a viable international identity for the study of religion (see Kim 2019).

With this in mind, this book problematizes not PoR itself but prevalent oversimplified views of the history of the study of religion. It does so by presenting perspectives from ten different countries. Precisely because PoR has been so contested, it provides a useful vantage point from which to compare national variations in the development of the study of religion. After all, PoR is the one approach, method or theory that has claimed to be uniquely proper to the study of religion; and for this very reason it has been heavily criticized by other scholars of religion. In part, then, this book is about more than PoR. It is an international mosaic of answers to the question, "What does it mean to study religion?"

Methods

In addition to its exclusive focus on PoR, this book is different from other books on the history of the study of religion in that it consists of interviews. The interviews were given by scholars from ten countries, all belonging to the PoR generation (born around the 1930s and 1940s).[1] The interviewers are younger scholars of religion from those same countries. To date, the history of the discipline has been written primarily by single authors (Sharpe, Kippenberg, Stausberg, etc.). Even in collections, each contribution is generally written by a single author on one national or regional context (Alles 2008).[2] Single authors' historical narratives tend to be highly coherent, rightly emphasizing comprehensibility, and they also come across as "success stories", emphasizing themes of progress and implicitly (sometimes explicitly) comparing local developments favourably to the situation in other disciplines or countries. Given that reflections on the past are necessarily constructive – never conveying pure historical facts alone – a collection of interviews, or dialogues, helps to reveal a more complex reality. It does so both because of the plurality of voices speaking from different perspectives, and because we hear more from participants, not from observers seeking to produce consolidated, unitary accounts. This approach also provided more space for women's voices. As with most academic disciplines, the study of religion has been dominated and its history primarily narrated by male scholars. This is even more so with PoR. How women scholars view and are engaged in PoR has almost entirely been invisible in preceding studies. Given this gender bias and the historical – as opposed to revisionary – focus of this book, it inevitably replicates that male dominance to some extent. That said, there is significant participation by women: the interviewer and interviewee in the UK, the interviewer and one of the two interviewees in Japan, the interviewer in Germany, and several of the voices brought into the commentary on the Canadian situation are women. All interviewees were conscious of women's perspectives.

This book is multi-voiced, but it is also multi-layered. Each interview is followed by a commentary by its interviewer, which aims to clarify the national, academic and other contexts of the interview. The interview is

---

1. Some of the interviewees are in their seventies but regard themselves as belonging to the post-PoR generation.
2. The 2nd edition of the *Encyclopedia of Religion* includes a set of national/regional overviews, and the journal *Religion* has published many surveys of the study of religion in different countries and parts of the world. Again, single-authorship is almost universal.

a primary source and the commentary is a secondary source. Yet, many of the commentaries offer more than basic contextualization. The interviewees, being scholars of religion, also reflect on the history of PoR in their own ways. Interviewers add additional observations and reflections from their own standpoints, not always harmonizing with those of the interviewees.

Consisting largely of transcriptions of spoken language, the book offers a "lived history" of PoR, covering more than half a century, with many concrete anecdotes. It vividly discloses the personalities of the interviewees. Though the interviewers know the interviewees personally or through their works, many unexpected surprises arose during the interviews. On the one hand, we see more clearly the extent to which the critical studies of the past few decades have subalternized the PoR generation. On the other hand, many interviewers were surprised when their interviewees, widely held to be devout followers of PoR, did not identify themselves as such. This raises important historiographic questions. Were there actually that many "phenomenologists of religion" in the twentieth century? Have critical studies of religion been attacking straw dolls?

The selection of ten countries was designed to let underrepresented countries come to the fore. James L. Cox's *A Guide to the Phenomenology of Religion: Key Figures, Formative Influences and Subsequent Debates* (2006) is the most comprehensive history of the PoR available. It extensively describes Dutch, British, African and North American developments, but it has no chapters on PoR in Scandinavia or Germany. German scholars appear only as precursors of PoR, and well-known German phenomenologists such as F. Heiler and G. Mensching are completely missing. Still less does the book mention the Italian situation and Asian developments. Therefore, we have collected interviews from all these countries and regions: Sweden, Finland, Germany, Italy, Japan and South Korea. And as for the order of chapters, we have placed these six countries first, and then Canada, the USA, the UK and, finally, the Netherlands. We offer some comments on PoR in India, Latin America and Africa later in this Introduction.

It is notable that almost all recent contributions to PoR chapters of major textbooks and methodological/theoretical books are written by Anglophone scholars rather than by Dutch or German scholars, even though the books are co-authored by various international scholars (Ryba 2006; Allen 2005, 2009; Spickard 2011; Cox 2017).[3] Even in a German

---

3. The "Phenomenology" chapter in the 2nd edition of the *Routledge Handbook of Research Methods in the Study of Religion* (forthcoming) is by Kalpana Ram. She is an Indian immigrant to Australia who does fieldwork in South India.

textbook the chapters on R. Otto and F. Heiler are written by Anglophone authors (Michaels 2010). Readers of our book will learn from its German and Dutch chapters why this is so.

Common Questions for Interviews ...

The interviews were conducted in a semi-structured style. The interviewers all began with the following common set of questions, supplementing them as they felt appropriate:

1 How did you define PoR when you began your career? How do you define it now? Do you see yourself as a phenomenologist?
2 When was PoR born/introduced in your country? Who introduced/started it? In which universities and which departments was it prominent?
3 When was PoR most popular? Among whom? Why did it become popular?
4 Were there academic exchanges with PoR scholars in other countries?
5 Were there academic exchanges with phenomenological scholars in other disciplines? E.g,, sociologists (Peter Berger-like phenomenologists, or ethnomethodologists), philosophers, anthropologists (Geertzian interpretivists).
6 Do you think there is any connection/correlation between phenomenologists of religion (in your country or in general) and their religious affiliations (not just the tag of "religionists")?
7 When did PoR decline/fall out of favour in your national context? What do you think the causes were? What kind of criticisms were brought forward against PoR in your country?
8 What did PoR bring to the study of religion, after all? What kind of accomplishments did PoR achieve?
9 Have PoR exerted any influence upon public education? Or upon any other system of society?
10 Do you think Cognitive Science of Religion is completely different from PoR? Or do you see similarities?
11 Is there a reason to reevaluate PoR now, or a path to doing so?
12 How far do you agree/disagree with the historical descriptions and evaluations of PoR given by Eric Sharpe (*Comparative Religion: A History*) and by James Cox (*A Guide to the Phenomenology of Religion*)?
13 What are the important books/articles to know the history of PoR in your country?

The interviews took place during 2016–2018. Many were face to face; some were by telephone or email. Details on when and how each interview was conducted are given in each chapter.

... and Answers: At a Glance

In order to ease understanding, we present a preliminary summary of how each interviewee explained the rise (and fall) of PoR in his/her national context (all quotes are from the interviews). This is only a signpost, and readers can skip it if they prefer diving into the first-hand text.

The Swedish interviewee Ulf Drobin (Chapter 1) opposes Cox's view that PoR traces (at least in part) its origin to Husserl. He and other Nordic scholars see PoR as a taxonomic tool in the empirical, historical study of religions, a discipline that should be devoid of normative truth-claims.[4] Nor should PoR be confused with the "school of thought" represented by Otto, van der Leeuw and Eliade. Drobin argues that PoR "has attempted to define the various things that appear in the world of religion and to compile a general list of concepts which contains these. Such a compilation is necessary in order to make a comparison of different religions. ... [PoR] neither entails a certain theoretical perspective nor a standpoint on the truthfulness of religious claims." Nevertheless, contrary to the interviewer's assumption that anti-Eliadeans are anti-essentialist and anti-sui-generist, Drobin has no hesitation in identifying the essence of religion as the "mystery of life", an "existentialistic" definition that is not a part of PoR.

According to Drobin, non-theological Swedish PoR developed along with the history of religion as textual and philological studies, starting with the Religion Department at the faculty of the humanities at Stockholm University in the early twentieth century. Hultkrantz and Widengren were key figures, and they played a major role in the re-orientation of the International Association for the Study of Religions (IAHR) after its 1960 Marburg Congress.

However, even this (self-proclaimed) neutral PoR failed to survive, declining rapidly since the 1990s. Drobin attributes this change to the secularization (loss of personal religious commitments) of scholars of religions: "Could it not be the case that these scholars, who obviously are not themselves religious, simply lack the ability to empathize with religious experience and therefore replace it with materialistic reasoning?"

---

4.   Åke Hultkrantz described PoR as "a classification device" (1966, 134).

On the other hand, the interviewer draws attention to institutional and social changes in academia, not least increased pressure to engage in socially relevant and short-term research.

The Finnish co-authors Veikko Anttonen and Teuvo Laitila (Chapter 2) point to other causes for the trajectory of Nordic, empirical PoR in Finland. They trace the beginning of Finnish PoR to Uno Holmberg-Harva (1882–1949), who explored the ancient religion of peoples belonging to the Uralic and Finno-Ugric language family. Harva's *Der Baum des Lebens* (1922) was a comparative study of the symbolism of what Eliade called *axis mundi*. Remarkably, this was an independent innovation of Harva's. Anttonen argues that "Harva's ethnography was not about the existential situation of an individual *homo religiosus*, but rather about a collectively shared tradition of a folk making up an ethnos." Harva's early attempt was followed by "regional phenomenology", led by Lauri Honko and Juha Pentikäinen. "As for Finland ... scholars in the field have classified, identified, and compared types, forms, functions, and structures of religious representations not so much on a worldwide scale, but rather within the boundaries of a limited geographic area." Honko organized an influential study conference of the IAHR in Turku in 1973 to discuss current methodological issues, including the future of PoR.

Nevertheless, regional phenomenology ceased appealing to Anttonen and other Finnish scholars in the 1990s. Anttonen regards the change as caused not by external pressures but by excitement aroused by the encounter with cognitive science. Other scholars also came to draw on a wide array of methodological choices. At the same time, PoR was updated by scholars at the University of Helsinki who integrated elements of continental philosophy, such as Merleau-Pontian phenomenology of perception and Gadamerean hermeneutics.

PoR was especially prominent in Germany, centred on Marburg where Otto, Heiler and Mensching worked successively. However, a radical revolution took place in as early as 1972, in which year Mensching was voted out as Chair of the German Association for the History of Religion. The interviewees for Chapter 3, Peter Antes and Hubert Seiwert – both educated in West Germany in the 1960s – were involved in that revolution and have been key younger scholars critical of the older generation.

Antes recalls that he was taught nothing of PoR at his university (Freiburg) in the 1960s. He presumes that the older generation of scholars were sanguine about empirically-ungrounded methods such as empathy because they were part of a homogeneous social group: "I think that this homogeneity reflects embedded thought structures that explain why these scholars reached such similar results." Seiwert remembers how dissatisfied he was with the study of religion as a student at the University of Bonn in the midst of the student movement of 1968. What was at stake among students across disciplines were methodological issues, especially the dispute between Frankfurt-School Critical Theory and the Critical Rationalism of Popper: "Given the theoretical standard of these discussions, religious studies were plainly undertheorized. My teachers simply could not understand these methodological discussions or at least would not respond to the problems discussed."[5]

By contrast, Italian scholars of religion, since the time of Pettazzoni, have often discussed PoR, as represented by Eliade and German scholars, albeit in negative terms. PoR has been an indispensable rival, against which they have constantly constructed and maintained their own academic identity. Thus, while some outsiders subsume Pettazzoni under PoR, the Italian interviewee Giovanni Casadio (Chapter 4), argues:

> Paradoxically enough, the standard image we have of Pettazzoni in Italy is that of a stout supporter of historicism and an unyielding adversary of phenomenology and hermeneutics. This representation of Pettazzoni as a full-fledged historicist is shared by Eliade who, as is well-known, positioned himself in the middle ground between the Dutch and German phenomenologists and historical and social reductionists.

For Casadio, two factors shaped these negative attitudes towards PoR:

> Catholicism (phenomenology of religion originated against the background of Protestant liberal theology) and Historicism, two conceptions of the world and man within history that look and are opposite but share some basic elements, including a deep distrust toward the irrational and emotional components of life and history.

Even Ugo Bianchi, who was "[a]mong the disciples of Pettazzoni the only one who has not harboured an utterly negative attitude toward phenomenology", firmly rejected "the psychological, emotional and somewhat irrational components of religious phenomena".

---

5.   To add another witness, after the two interviews, the interviewer and one of the editors (Fujiwara) visited Martin Kraatz, a good friend of Heiler, to fill in the story of Marburg. Surprisingly, Kraatz said that no scholar in Marburg saw him/herself as doing PoR, not even Heiler. As far as he recalls, Heiler did not talk about PoR, and it is unclear how he defined it. No "Heilerian school" was formed, and no scholar of Marburg carried on the Heilerian approach. A symmetrical case is the marginal role of a key critic of PoR, Kurt Rudolph, who started teaching in Marburg in the 1980s. Although Rudolph is mentioned in Sharpe's *Comparative Religion* as an important scholar, he exerted no influence in Marburg, according to Kraatz.

Yet, for the interviewer, what many Italian historians of religions were doing in the Roman School actually had much in common with PoR. This may hold true even with the prominent historian, Carlo Ginzburg: "an Eliadian influence on his conception of shamanism – which in turn informs his most renowned work about the European Sabbath (Ginzburg 1991) – is easily recognizable, in spite of the author's overt dislike of Eliade's methods".

Japan exemplifies a very different reception of PoR. While in all the aforementioned countries, van der Leeuw was accused of having led PoR in the wrong direction, there are Leeuw-lovers in Japan, particularly at Tohoku University. According to interviewee Toshimaro Hanazono (Chapter 5), Teruji Ishizu – who presumably introduced PoR to Japan in the 1930s – criticized van der Leeuw because he did *not* place sufficient emphasis on eidetic vision: "[Ishizu] was rather critical of van der Leeuw, … saying that he had ended up creating a typology and failed to exercise phenomenological reduction to reach the eidetic vision of religion, which is the ultimate goal of PoR."

These Japanese scholars expected philosophy – continental and, above all, German – to provide theories and methodologies to ground their study of religion. Being aware that the Husserlian vocabulary employed by van der Leeuw was a mere afterthought, some attempted to refine Leeuwean PoR with a more fully philosophical phenomenology. Hanazono recalls: "Japanese scholars expected PoR to be, above all, a study of the essence or essential features of religion. Accordingly, many works on PoR became theoretical." He argues that Japanese scholars did not confine PoR to classification because they were hindered from creating a universal taxonomy, due both to the lack of first-hand materials on ancient or indigenous religions and to disadvantages in mastering ancient languages.

Nevertheless, what scholars of religion at Tohoku University actually do has never been solely speculative. Rather, their research resembles what later came to be called the study of lived religion. For example, Masahiro Kusunoki attempted to identify "the nature of 'common people-ness' of popular beliefs", in contrast to the Eliadean search for the archaic man as essential *homo religiosus*. It was an inductive study based on his intensive local fieldwork. Hanazono hesitates to label himself or any of his fellow scholars as practitioners of PoR.

On the other hand, the second interviewee for Chapter 5, Yoshiko Oda, radically switched from the Kyoto School philosophy of religion to the history of religions while she studied at the University of Chicago. In contrast to the popular image of the Chicago school of the history of religions as an American development of essentialistic and existentialistic PoR, she recalls learning about diversity and community-based social aspects of religion in Chicago. For her, it was the Kyoto School that had Protestant-like preconceptions of religion.

In South Korea, PoR has also been seen as a search for meanings not taxonomy. In the case of the interviewee Chin-Hong Chung (Chapter 6) – the first scholar to teach PoR in Korea – this was not motivated by interest in philosophy. PoR enabled him to expand the study of religion beyond a collection of the history of individual "world religions". Referring to his early experiences of battlefields, he says that he came to ask what religion is: "my concern has always been about the more general understanding of the phenomenon called 'religion'". Only PoR could answer his question because "in PoR, you pursued meanings through an encounter with the phenomenon itself, while other fields in the study of religion pursued understandings through historical approaches". Furthermore, he found that Eliade's *Patterns in Comparative Religion* had advanced PoR because "the book questioned the background experiences behind the phenomena that are encountered, and tried to understand the humans who were the subjects of those experiences".

Thus Chung summarized PoR as "an exploration of the grammar needed to read 'religion in culture'", holding that "questions about religion start from 'what is religion', and shift towards 'why is it called religion', then finally end with 'who had experiences from which this kind of question cannot help but emerge?'" In addition, he defends PoR as a matter of "art" and calls it "imagination of culture" or "imagination of human beings". He argues, "If the quest for meaning is the final expectation of commentary work [i.e. textual studies], it inevitably ends with imagination."

However, Chung found it challenging to spread PoR among Korean scholars. He recalls: "In the Korea of the early 1970s, PoR was regarded as a new trend in religious studies; but in the 1980s, opinions of PoR at SNU [Seoul National University] changed dramatically." According to him, "the atmosphere of religious studies that I experienced was not entirely free" in the 1950s and 1960s, and "I, who claimed to be a scholar of PoR, could not find a niche". PoR became acceptable among Korean scholars only in the 1970s, but Western criticisms of PoR and Eliade soon followed.

Chapter 7, on Canada, has two interviewees, one from Québec and one from English Canada. The editors of this book had greatest difficulty in finding an interviewee for English Canada. For some, PoR has been neglected in Canada; for others it remains prevalent. This suggests that there is no common understanding of PoR in Canada, even though one of the most famous Canadian scholars of religion, Wilfred Cantwell Smith, falls under PoR according to James Cox and Eric Sharpe. (See Earle Waugh's interview for a divergent perspective.) In addition, since many scholars of religion working in English Canada were trained in the USA, it is doubtful whether there is a distinctly English-Canadian PoR. The interviewee, Earle H. Waugh was educated at the University of Chicago. So was William Closson James, another Canadian scholar who is said to practise PoR.

Waugh's view of PoR has some distinctive characteristics. He (Waugh) categorizes earlier PoR as "philosophical phenomenology" and calls the Chicago School of the history of religions, Eliade, J. M. Kitagawa and Jonathan Smith, "philosophical". By "philosophy" he seems to refer to an attempt to identify universal structures:

> Philosophical phenomenology is a rigid kind of activity, where you focus on the structures of consciousness and you emphasize what fits into those structures. That approach to phenomenology restricted the field. It shut down discussion. It was not adapted to the multi-dimensional aspects of religiosity.

Instead, Waugh practices "existential phenomenology", which is to "look at the experience of how people perceive their encounter with religion". For example:

> In the field, when I went into a Sufi group, my attitude towards them was, "you are a novel and important expression of religion, so tell me how you understand your world, how do you understand the reality of this world to be coming to you, and how do you inter-relate with it?" So it was a very existential kind of study.

It is notable that Waugh calls the taxonomical aspect of PoR "philosophical" and contrasts it with the *Verstehen* aspect of PoR. The dichotomy within European PoR is sharply reversed here.

In contrast to English Canada, a uniquely *québecoise* perspective, *religiologie*, emerged in the 1960s and continues to be influential today. Interviewee Louis Rousseau explains *religiologie*'s indebtedness to PoR, points to *québecois*, national and international debates provoked by its emergence, and notes key works in the movement. He concludes that this book's "project of mapping national epistemological fields could serve as a starting point for more rigorous work".

The first American interviewee, Charles H. Long (Chapter 8), traced the history of PoR from Chantepie de la Saussaye to Eliade in an influential

1967 chapter. Looking back now, he says, "I was never concerned to ever write a paper or teach a course on phenomenology, because for me, it was just a part of the apparatus of making sense that this was something to study when you study religion." He also prefers not using the word "phenomenology" because "it gives a sense that it's some big, abstract theory". He holds that there was no tension in Chicago between PoR and the history of religions – despite the fact that, in the 1960s, both Eliade and he wrote about that tension.

Long's PoR is clearly different from Nordic PoR, especially in how he understands the term "phenomenon". The Swedish interviewee, Drobin identifies "phenomena" as "simply such things which *de facto* exists in the so-called reality". According to this usage, one can talk about "social phenomena" as well as about "religious phenomena". On the other hand, Long argues that "phenomenon" is "what appears": "it was *about* the appearances that human beings have in the normality of their lives. And it moves one away from the notion that every form of datum in the world is the result of human agency, that the appearances occur because there is something other than human agency."

Ivan Strenski shares the taxonomy-*Verstehen* dichotomy of PoR, and notes that the taxonomical part was modelled after natural "science". But he downplays taxonomical PoR, being "so tedious and dry". He argues that, compared with the "scientific" taxonomical version of PoR, Smartean PoR "has much to recommend itself". For the latter, "[t]o take the phenomenological perspective on religion is to chart the interacting parts that, taken together as a universe of rules, may explain what happens in other parts of a religious territory". In other words, "Understanding is about seeing how things hang together." Having an artistic temperament, Smart described religion "as being like tapestries where you had different threads emerging and interwoven, and so forth". Strenski regards this analogy as "a powerful insight to phenomenology".

In the United Kingdom, PoR has been a key concept not only in the study of religion but also in religious education, which is compulsory in all state-funded schools. Ninian Smart represented PoR in both, and the interviewee Denise Cush (Chapter 9) has observed its development in both. She points to differences between PoR's rise and, especially, fall in the two areas. According to Cush, the PoR that entered schools was a "somewhat watered-down version". PoR has offered a method, or, a general approach to multi-faith religious education as opposed to Christianity-centred, theological religious education, by "methodological agnosticism and empathy" and "various tools that you could use *across* religions". As such, school PoR was free from the Husserlian eidetic vision, and therefore, was resistant to criticisms of academic PoR as essentialist.

Likewise, Cush argues for the autonomy of both religious studies and religious education not because she believes in the *sui generis* nature of religion but because the study of religion is overly West-centric in other disciplines:

> There's a paper going around from the Church of England that says religious studies/religious education is a mixture of theology, sociology and philosophy. And my response was, "No, it's not. It really isn't. It is religious studies, which has its own identity as a discipline." ... One problem is that theology, sociology and philosophy tend to be very "Western" in both content and methods.

Cultural and academic trends that now seem to have very different backgrounds converged in England in the 1970s. When PoR became popular at that time, "through them [Smart and Sharpe] came across the Dutch phenomenologists, van der Leeuw and Kristensen, who were more influential at that point in British phenomenology". At the same time "Youth culture was looking to the Beatles going to India, Hinduism and Buddhism were coming into the culture and we wanted to know about them."

As seen from these interviews, opinions are sharply divided on Dutch PoR, above all, regarding van der Leeuw. Some say he promoted "good PoR", some "bad PoR". The interviewee from the Netherlands, Jan Platvoet (Chapter 10), argues that van der Leeuw is nothing but a phantom created and imagined by foreign scholars. According to Platvoet, it is simply wrong to assume that there is a Dutch "school" of PoR, a circle of scholars gathering around van der Leeuw, who is a direct heir of de la Saussaye, and further that the school has been the mainline of the Dutch study of religion, with Waardenburg as its restorer. Van der Leeuw used Husserlian vocabulary "only because it was intellectually fashionable", and the title of *Einführung in die Phänomenologie der Religion* was actually coined by Heiler (who, as claimed in note 5, did not identify with PoR). Furthermore, even as simple taxonomical works, the PoR of Dutch scholars was guided by an explicitly theological agenda. As a result, the following generation of scholars completely abandoned PoR in any form, as early as the beginning of the 1970s. It was this post-PoR generation who employed methodological agnosticism. Having been influenced by Wilfred Cantwell Smith, Jacques Waardenburg came up with the idea of neo-phenomenology, but his Dutch colleagues considered his aim of "understanding the subjective meaning of religion" to offer little useful leverage: it was "unexceptional and unobjectionable". None was convinced of the need to formulate a new approach for the aim, according to Platvoet.

As these overviews illustrate, the interviews collected in this book reveal a wide variety of conceptions of PoR and of its value. Views vary between scholars and between countries. Though the narrative of decline is largely supported, PoR remains alive and well, in the views of a minority of scholars. For our overall assessment of findings and implications, see the Afterword of this book.

PoR in Other Parts of the World

PoR is, of course, found beyond the ten countries represented in the chapters of this book. Limitations of space prevented our including more interviews. A fuller account of PoR's international dimension would require a sequel at least as large. As our last contribution to the retelling of the history of PoR, we offer a few thoughts on PoR elsewhere, in order to acknowledge, however selectively, that unavoidable limitation.

Several Indian scholars, working in Europe and North America, have done relevant work.[6] Here is an excerpt from the unedited transcription of Giovanni Casadio's interview for Chapter 4 of this book:

> The Indian (Tamil, of Roman and British education) Jesuit Mariasusai Dhavamony (1926–) considered himself a historian of religions as well as a phenomenologist. Consequently, he defined his approach as "historical phenomenology of religion", a discipline that he taught at the Pontifical Gregorian University in Rome from 1966 until his retirement. His presentation is very clear, precise and didactic as typical of Jesuit scholarship. Let us sum up his account with a few paraphrases and citations (from Dhavamony 1973, 3-27). Phenomenology of religion presents a systematic view of religious phenomena. It does not try to compare religions to each other as complex units but selects similar facts and phenomena from different religions, bringing them together and studying them in groups. Historical phenomenology tries "to understand the modes of religious behaviours, institutions and beliefs contained in myths, rituals, conceptions of High Gods, etc.". With regard to the accusation moved by historicist scholars against the phenomenology's claim to grasp the essence of

---

6. In South Asia, although the term "PoR" is not used, the influence of Wilfred Cantwell Smith upon their disciplinary identity is recognized by the Bangladesh scholars of the Department of World Religions and Culture at the University of Dhaka. Joseph T. O'Connell, "a humble follower" of Smith who taught at the University of Toronto, played a major role in the establishment of the department (Sayem 2016, 174–175).

religious phenomena, he states that phenomenology of religions intends to understand only "the essence of the religious phenomenon, taken in the empirical sense of the invariable structure of a phenomenon that underlies every religious fact". Nonetheless, he denies that religious structures are "completely historically conditioned", underlining that meanings are universal and common to many analogous phenomena. In the end, phenomenology with the help of typology (the study of types), morphology (the study of forms, patterns, structures and configurations), the principle of epoché (suspension of preconceived judgment in order to let the phenomenon speak for itself), and empathy ("reproductive experiencing" of a religious act on the basis of one's own personal experience), will be able to grasp "the inner meaning of a religious phenomenon as it is lived and experienced by religious men", in other words a religious phenomenon in its "specific aspect of religiousness".

The Indian-born but educated in USA (Harvard) scholar of Hindu and comparative religion Arvind Sharma (1940–) travelled and taught throughout the Anglosphere, from Australia to Canada, where he succeeded Wilfred Cantwell Smith (1916-2000) to the Birks Chair of Comparative Religion. He is a prolific (perhaps too prolific) author of (popularly written) academic books on important classical topics in contemporary religious studies, including women studies in world religions. As I know through a personal communication, he still enthusiastically shares the method and the approach of his mentor Smith, controversial promoter of an approach to the study of religion based on the dynamic dialectic between cumulative tradition and personal faith – an approach that is basically dialogical and in the last analysis theological. Smith's perspective was clearly phenomenological; this is demonstrated by his stress on empathy and his pronounced hostility towards every kind of reductionism. Sharma, who defines himself a "comparatively religious Hindu", adopted the phenomenological approach of his master, the Presbyterian minister Smith, as is evident in his textbook on phenomenology of religion, where he pleads for "a religious way of studying religion" (Sharma 2001, 263), and in his many educational books where he introduces the concept of "reciprocal illumination" to describe the mutual enlightenment that can occur when a comparison is made between one tradition and another, one method and another, or between a tradition and a method (Sharma 2005).

It is also noteworthy that one of the two English translations of G. Mensching's works, *Structures and Patterns of Religion*, was published in India in 1976 (the other was published by the University of Alabama Press in 1971). It was co-translated by Hans-J. Klimkeit, Mensching's successor at the University of Bonn, and by V. Srinivasa Sarma, who translated other German books on Indian literature into English around that time. Mensching's lack of popularity – as evidenced by the lack of translations in Western countries – may reflect in part his Nazi connections.

PoR's situation in Latin America reinforces this volume's findings. It is a marginal perspective though championed by a few scholars; it varies both by country and in terms of views of what constitutes PoR; and it ranges across the study of religion, theology, philosophy and psychology (for overviews, see Duran, Scannone and Silva 2003; Walton 2004). German scholar Hermann Brandt argues that "while in Europe the study of religion bids farewell to the phenomenology of religion, Latin America welcomes it with open arms" (2006, 132). He notes, however, the prominence of under-theorized uses of "PoR" and of an implicit Christian bias.

There are works on PoR throughout the region: e.g. Argentina (Croatto 2002; Scannone 2005), Chile (Doerr-Zegers and Velásquez 2012), Colombia (Ramírez 2015; Arboleda Mora and Castrillón López 2015) and Mexico (Cabrera 2002; Moreno Romo 2011). The academic study of religion, as a discipline, is present in only some Latin American countries and still struggles to establish itself (Engler et al. 2009). Philosophical interest in phenomenology has been strongest in Mexico (Zirión Quijano 2003; Xolocotzi Yáñez 2009).[2] Scholars from Spain have written valuable introductions to PoR that are influential in Spanish-speaking Latin America (e.g. Martín Velasco 2017 [1978]; de Sahagún 1999), and work from Spain is sometimes published in Latin American journals (e.g. García-Alandete 2009). Spanish works often take a Christian theological perspective (e.g. Escudero Torres 2002; Duch 2005; Ferrer Arellano 2013). Spanish philosopher Xavier Zubiri has developed a distinct approach to PoR that has influenced debates in Latin America (Solari 2014; see www.zubiri. net). Spanish- and Portuguese-language scholars in Latin America draw on translations published in Spain and Portugal, as well as throughout Latin America (e.g. de la Saussaye, Duméry, Eliade, Heidegger, Husserl, Otto, Ries, van der Leeuw and Widengren). Mexican philosopher Maria Zambrano's highly original work emphasized reason's mediating role in relating human experience to the sacred, with an emphasis on intuition and the phenomenology of dreams (Zambrano 1973 [1955], 1992 [1960]; see López Saénz 2013). Argentinian anthropologist and philosopher Rodolfo Kusch argued for a phenomenology of popular and indigenous knowledges. For Kusch, the attempt to resuscitate indigenous modes of thinking cannot begin with "a philosophical attitude still entangled in a Comtean system of a hundred years ago, or with a phenomenology

---

7.   The website of the Circulo Latinoamericano de Fenomenologia – https://clafen. org – gives a useful sense of Mexican and international developments, including information on two conferences that have run since the early 2000s: the Coloquio Latinoamericano de Fenomenología and the Coloquio Internacional de Fenomenología y Hermenéutica.

studied only so as to be repeated in the university classroom" (2010 [1970], 2); see Cullen 1984).

The situation in Brazil is linguistically distinct but illustrative.[8] Relevant work in the small but growing discipline of the study of religion tends to focus on more robust, classic PoR (e.g. Dreher 2003; Cruz 2009; Josgrilberg 2012). Eduardo Gross has emphasized that the trajectory and status of PoR in Brazil reflect complex relations of complementarity and competition between the study of religion and theology (2018). Antônio Gouvêa Mendonça argued that "the development of the study of religion ... will depend on the distinction between essence and forms of religion" (Mendonça 1999, 87). He suggested that philosophical PoR could serve as a bulwark against four pernicious tendencies in the study of religion: the imposition of theological agendas, superficially descriptive work, resistance to models of research in the empirical sciences, and a narrow hermeneutical focus on texts (Mendonça 2001, 190, 193). Van der Leeuw, Otto and Eliade have been especially influential in Brazil; Ninian Smart, James Cox and James Spickard are practically unknown. Religious aspects of Husserl's work have come to the fore with the recent Portuguese translation of two works by Italian philosopher, Angela Ales Bello (2016, 2019). Brazilian PoR has been prominent in the area of psychology (Holanda 2004, 2017; Freitas and Vilela 2017).

Cox addressed the development of PoR in Africa in the twentieth century. He introduced his discussion of British scholars of PoR, working in Africa, with some remarks on two African theologians, E. Bolaji Idowu and John S. Mbiti (Cox 2006, 157). Lately, two college textbooks on PoR by Eastern African scholars were published in the 2010s (Kasomo 2010; Sakali 2013). The books are entirely pedagogical and model the practical use of PoR, in a step by step manner. For example:

> Activity. Find a place where you can be alone. Perform epoché. Allow the phenomena to strike your consciousness in its suspended condition. Do this for at least twenty minutes without losing concentration. Write a five-page essay summarizing what you experienced. Include in your essay an analysis of how your mind organized the phenomena.
>
> (Kasomo 2010)[9]

> Activity. Follow the procedure in a project of epoché, but for shorter intervals, for 14 days. Keep a daily diary in which you name the phenomena

---

8. The editors thank the following Brazilian scholars for email exchanges that informed this paragraph: Adriano F. Holanda, Eduardo R. Cruz, Roberlei Panasiewicz, Leonildo S. Campos and Davison Schaeffer.
9. The Kasomo volume has no page numbers. The two books share identical passages at points.

perceived, describe relationships between them as they strike your consciousness, and list any processes involved. At the end of the two weeks, write a summary of what you learned from the experience.

(Kasomo 2010)

While both authors state that PoR is a method of "the science of religion" (Kasomo 2010; Sakali 2013, 65), they also emphasize the *sui generis* nature of religion and its study:

> Religion is human phenomenon. Nothing religious, therefore, can be ultimately alien to human experience. Religion, moreover, forms one component among others comprising the whole of human activity and understanding. The study of this component forms a discipline in its own right and should not be subsumed under other academic studies within the human sciences.
>
> (Kasomo 2010; Sakali 2013, 3)

Notably, instead of claiming such anti-reductionism as a universal axiom, they relate it to the colonial context of Africa, referring to Harold Turner (1981).

> Harold Turner argues that the tendency to reduce religious experience to social scientific explanations has been particularly prevalent in Africa. This has occurred partly as a result of attitudes of western superiority displayed in accounts by nineteenth-century explorers, ethnographers, and missionaries.
>
> (Kasomo 2010; Sakali 2013, 48)

Although neither book acknowledges or cites Cox, it is likely that they are, in part, the outcomes of Cox's dissemination of PoR in Eastern Africa during his appointment at the University of Zimbabwe around 1990.

Satoko Fujiwara is Professor of the Department of Religious Studies, Faculty of Letters/Graduate School of the Humanities and Sociology, at the University of Tokyo. She received a PhD in the History of Religions from the Divinity School of the University of Chicago. She is Secretary General of the International Association for the History of Religions (2020–). Her publications include "The Reception of Otto and *Das Heilige* in Japan: In and Outside the Phenomenology of Religion" *Religion*, 47(4), 2017 and "Japan" in *Religious Studies: A Global View*, edited by Gregory D. Alles (Routledge, 2008).

David Thurfjell is Professor in the Study of Religions at Södertörn University, Stockholm. His research circles around themes pertaining to Shi'ite and Pentecostal revivalism, religion as a means of social mobilisation and the discourse surrounding religion and secularity in northern Europe. Among his publications are the monographs *Living Shi'ism* (Brill, 2006), *Faith and Revivalism in a Nordic Romani Community* (Tauris, 2011) and *Godless People* (Norstedts, 2015).

Steven Engler is Professor of Religious Studies at Mount Royal University in Calgary. He studies religions in Brazil, as well as theories and methodology in the study of religion/s. See http://stevenengler.ca

Acknowledgements

The editors would like to thank the anonymous reviewers of this Introduction and the individual chapters for sharing their time and expertise, and for their helpful suggestions.

This work was supported by JSPS KAKENHI Grant Number JP16H03354.

References

A comprehensive bibliography is available from www.l.u-tokyo.ac.jp/religion/resources/phenomenology_of_religion.pdf

Ales Bello, Angela. 2016. *Edmund Husserl: pensar Deus, crer em Deus*. Translated by Aparecida Turolo Garcia, Márcio Luiz Fernandes. São Paulo: Paulus.

Ales Bello, Angela. 2019. *O sentido do sagrado: da arcaicidade à dessacralização*. São Paulo: Paulus.

Allen, Douglas. 2005. "Phenomenology of Religion." In *Encyclopedia of Religion*, 2nd edition, vol. 10, edited by Lindsay Jones, 7086–7101. Detroit, MI: Macmillan.

Allen, Douglas. 2009. "Phenomenology of Religion." In *The Routledge Handbook of the Study of Religion*, edited by John R. Hinnells, 203–224. London and New York: Routledge.

Alles, Gregory D. (ed.). 2008. *Religious Studies: A Global View*. New York: Routledge.

Arboleda Mora, Carlos, and Luis Alberto Castrillón López. 2015. "Experiencia originaria de Dios, desinstitucionalización y deconstrución de las religiones." *Escritos* (Medellín) 23(50): 83–108.

Brandt, Hermann. 2006. "As ciências da religião numa perspectiva intercultural: a percepção oposta da fenomenologia da religião no Brasil e na Alemanha." *Estudos Teológicos* 46(1): 122–151.

Cabrera, Isabel. 2002. *Fenomenología y religión*. Madrid: Trotta Editorial.

Cox, James L. 2006. *A Guide to the Phenomenology of Religion*. London: T. & T. Clark International.

Cox, James L. 2017. "The Phenomenology of Religion." In *Religion, Theory, Critique: Classic and Contemporary Approaches and Methodologies*, edited by Richard King, 401–412. New York: Columbia University Press.

Croatto, José Severino. 2002. *Experiencia de lo Sagrado y Tradiciones Religiosas: Estudio de Fenomenología de la Religión*. Estella: Editorial Verbo Divino.

Cruz, Raimundo José Barros. 2009. "Rudolf Otto e Edmund Husserl: considerações acerca das origens do método da fenomenologia da religião." *Horizonte: Revista de Estudos de Teologia e Ciências da Religião* 7(15): 122–141.

Cullen, Carlos. 1984. "Fenomenología y sabiduría popular." In *Sabiduría popular, símbolo y filosofía. Diálogo internacional en torno de una interpretación latinoamericana*, edited by Juan Carlos Scannone, 27–43. Guadalupe: Buenos Aires.

de Sahagún Lucas Hernández, Juan. 1999. *Fenomenología y Filosofía de la Religión*. Madrid: Biblioteca de Autrores Cristianos.

Dhavamony, Mariasusai. 1973. *Phenomenology of Religion*. Rome: Universitá Gregoriana Editrice.

Doerr-Zegers, Otto, and Óscar Velásquez. 2012. "Análisis fenomenológico-hermenéutico de la experiencia religiosa en el mito y en la locura." *Actas Españolas de Psiquiatría* 40(Supl. 2): 66–72.

Dreher, Luís H. (ed.). 2003. *A essência manifesta: a fenomenologia nos estudos interdisciplinares da religião*. Juiz de Fora: UFJF.

Duch, Lluís. 2005. *Fenomenología y filosofía de la religión*. Madrid: Biblioteca de Autrores Cristianos.

Duran Casas, Vicente, Juan Carlos Scannone and Eduardo Silva (eds). 2003. *Problemas de filosofia de la religion desde America Latina. De la experiencia a la reflexion*. Bogota: Siglo del Hombre Editores.

Engler, Steven. 2006. "Religious Studies in Canada and Brazil: Pro-pluralism and Anti-theology in Context." *Studies in Religion/Sciences Religieuses* 35(3–4): 445–471.

Engler, Steven, Anatilde Idoyaga Molina, Renée de la Torre, Pablo Barrera Rivera and Sylvia Marcos. 2009. "Religious Studies in Latin America." In *Religious Studies: A Global View*, edited by Gregory D. Alles, 269–300. New York: Routledge.

Escudero Torres, Esteban. 2002. *Creer es razonable: fenomenología y filosofía de la religion*. Valencia: Siquem.

Ferrer Arellano, Joaquín. 2013. *Filosofía y Fenomenología de la Religión: Cristianismo y Religiones*. Madrid: Ediciones Palabra.

Freitas, Marta Helena de, and Paula Rey Vilela. 2017. "Leitura fenomenológica da religiosidade: implicações para o psicodiagnóstico e para a práxis clínica Psicológica." *Phenomenological Studies - Revista da Abordagem Gestáltica* 23(1): 95–107.

Führding, Steffen. 2017. "Introduction: Theory, Method, Hannover and the Study of Religion." In *Method and Theory in the Study of Religion: Working Papers from Hannover*, edited by Steffen Führding, 1–26. Leiden: Brill.

García-Alandete, Joaquín. 2009. "Sobre la experiencia religiosa: aproximación fenomenológica." *Folios* (Bogotá) n.s. 30: 115–126.

Ginzburg, Carlo. 1991 [1989]. *Ecstasies: Deciphering the Witches' Sabbath.* Translated by Raymond Rosenthal. Chicago, IL: University of Chicago Press.

Gross, Eduardo, 2018. "Phenomenology and Hermeneutics in Brazilian Religious Studies." *Open Theology* 4: 246–257.

Holanda, Adriano Furtado (ed.). 2004. *Psicologia, Religiosidade e Fenomenologia.* Campinas: Átomo.

Holanda, Adriano Furtado. 2017. "Fenomenologia e psicologia da religião no Brasil: fundamentos, desafios e perspectivas." *Revista Pistis & Praxis: Teologia e Pastoral* 9(1): 131–151.

Hultkrantz, Åke. 1966. "An Ecological Approach to Religion." *Ethnos* 31/1–4: 131–151.

Josgrilberg, Rui de Souza. 2012. "Hermenêutica fenomenológica e a tematização do sagrado". In *Linguagem da Religião desafios métodos e conceitos centrais*, edited by Paulo Augusto de Souza Nogueira, 31–67. São Paulo: Paulinas.

Kasomo, Daniel W. 2010 *Phenomenology of Religion Made Simple.* Saarbrücken: LAP Lambert Academic Publishing.

Kim, Chae Young. 2019. "Modest Reflections on the Ambiguous Future of the Study of Religion/s." *Religion* 50/1: 83–89.

Kippenberg, Hans. 1997. *Die Entdeckung der Religionsgeschichte. Religionswissenschaft und Moderne.* Munich: C. H. Beck.

Kusch, Rodolfo. 2010 [1970]. *Indigenous and Popular Thinking in América*, translated by María Lugones and Joshua M. Price. Durham, NC: Duke University Press.

López Saénz, Maria Carmen. 2013. "Aproximación fenomenológica a la razón mediadora de Zambrano. Intuición y creación." *Revista de Filosofía* 38(2): 35–59.

Martín Velasco, Juan. 2017 [1978]. *Introducción a la fenomenología de la religión.* Madrid: Trotta Editorial.

Mendonça, Antônio Gouvêa. 1999. "Fenomenologia da experiência religiosa." *Numen: Revista de Estudos e Pesquisa da Religião* 2(2): 65–89.

Mendonça, Antônio Gouvêa. 2001. "Comentários sobre um texto prévio de Luís Dreher – UFJF. Ciência(s) da religião: Teoria e pós-graduação no Brasil." In *A(s) ciência(s) da religião no Brasil: Afirmação de uma área acadêmica*, edited by Faustino Teixeira, 179–196. São Paulo: Paulinas.

Satoko Fujiwara, David Thurfjell and Steven Engler

Mensching, Gustav. 1948. *Geschichte der Religionswissenschaft*. Bonn: Universitäts-Verlag.

Michaels, Axel hrsg. 2010. *Klassiker der Religionswissenschaft: Von Friedrich Schleiermacher bis Mircea Eliade*. Munich: C. H. Beck.

Moreno Romo, Juan Carlos. 2011. "Filosofía, deconstrucción, fenomenología y religión en la crisis de nuestro mundo transmoderno." *Escritos* (Medellín) 19(43): 285–313.

Ramírez Z., Alberto. 2015. "Fenomenología y Teología de la Liberación: el giro teológico en la teología de América Latina." *Cuestiones Teológicas* 42(97): 229–249.

Ryba, Thomas. 2006. "Phenomenology of Religion." In *The Blackwell Handbook of the Study of Religion*, edited by Robert A. Segal, 91–121. Oxford: Blackwell.

Sakali, Ferdnand. 2013. *Phenomenology of Religion: An Introduction*. Saarbrücken: LAP Lambert Academic Publishing.

Sayem, Md. Abu. 2016. "The Nature of the Academic Study of Religion in Dhaka University and the Role of Professor Joseph T. O'Connell." *Argument* 6: 163–182.

Scannone, Juan Carlos. 2005. *Religión y nuevo pensamiento: Hacia una filosofía de la religión para nuestro tiempo desde América Latina*. México: Anthropos Editorial.

Sedgwick, Mark. 2004. *Against the Modern World: Traditionalism and the Secret Intellectual History of the Twentieth Century*. Oxford: Oxford University Press.

Sharma, Arvind. 2001. *To the Things Themselves. Essays on the Discourse and Practice of the Phenomenology of Religion*. Berlin: Walter de Gruyter.

Sharma, Arvind.2005. *Religious Studies and Comparative Methodology: The Case for Reciprocal Illumination*. Albany, NY: Suny Press.

Sharpe, Eric. 1998. *Comparative Religion. A History*, 2nd edn. London: Duckworth.

Solari, Enzo. 2014. "Zubiri sobre la religion." *Franciscanum* 161(56): 51–98.

Spickard, James V. 2011. "Phenomenology." In *The Routledge Handbook of Research Methods in the Study of Religion*, edited by Michael Stausberg and Steven Engler, 333–345. New York: Routledge.

Turner, Harold. 1981. "The Way Forward in the Religious Study of African Primal Religions." *Journal of Religion in Africa* 12(1): 1–15.

Walton, Roberto J. 2004. "Problemas de filosofía de la religión desde América Latina: desde la experiencia a la reflexión." *Revista Portuguesa de Filosofia* 60(4): 1041–1050.

Xolocotzi Yáñez, Ángel. 2009. *Fenomenología viva*. México: Fomento Editorial.

Zambrano, Maria. 1973 [1955]. *El hombre y lo divino.* Ciudad de México: Fondo de Cultura Económica.

Zambrano, Maria. 1992 [1960]. *Los sueños y el tiempo.* Madrid: Ediciones Siruela.

Zirión Quijano, Antonio. 2003. *Historia de la fenomenología en* México. Morelia: Jitanjáfora.

Semantic Confusions and the Mysteries of Life

An Interview with Ulf Drobin (Sweden)

DAVID THURFJELL

Ulf Drobin was born in 1935. He is a Swedish historian of religion who, through his teaching and research, has been instrumental in forming the profile of the History of Religions department at Stockholm University. He started his university studies in the beginning of the 1960s. After studies in the German language and thereafter in the Scandinavian languages – including modern and old Icelandic – he specialized in the field of History of Religions and got his doctoral degree under the supervision of Åke Hultkrantz from the same university in 1983. In 1986 he was appointed Associate Professor at the department and he continued to teach there until his retirement in 2011. Drobin's empirical specialties are comparative Indo-European studies, Old Norse religion, Buddhism and indigenous traditions. He has also taken a wide interest in questions related to the theories and methods of the comparative study of religion in general and Indo-European studies in particular. It is this theoretical interest that is most reflected in his publications. The collection of articles that constitute his doctoral dissertation *Om teori och empiri i religionshistorisk forskning* (On theory and empirical data in History of Religions research) constitute prominent examples here, as do the monographs *Folklore and Comparative Religion* (1983), *Psychology, Philosophy, Theology and Epistemology* (1982) and *Indogermanische Religion und Kultur? Eine Analyse des Begriffes indogermanisch* (1980).

Keywords: phenomenology of religion, history of religions, Sweden, Geo Widengren, Åke Hultkrantz

Introduction

The Department of Comparative Religion at Stockholm University was founded in 1913 and its professorial chair was first held by Torgny Segerstedt, who later was to become one of Sweden's most profiled anti-fascist publishers. After Segerstedt left it in 1917, the chair and the department developed its profile through the work of several renowned scholars. The Islamic studies scholar and psychologist of religion Tor Andrae (1885–1947) was one of these: he held the chair for a couple of years in the 1920s. Another one was Ernst Arbman (1891–1959), who held the chair between 1937 and 1958. Arbman was primarily an Indologist but he also had a deep interest in Old Norse and Saami religions as well as in the psychology of religion and the comparative study of indigenous peoples. Åke Hultkrantz (1920–2006) became Arbman's student and successor. He took over the chair in 1958 and continued Arbman's work on indigenous traditions, specializing in the ethnographic study of native American traditions until his retirement in 1986. After this, the chair passed on to Louise Bäckman (b. 1926) who specialized in Saami studies, and thereafter to the Buddhologist and Tibetologist Per-Arne Berglie (born 1944) (Drobin 2016).

Ulf Drobin was a close associate and colleague of Åke Hultkrantz, Louise Bäckman and Per-Arne Berglie. As the following interview will illustrate, Drobin is a firm believer in the neutrality of the concept of Phenomenology of Religion (PoR) as a system for classification of religious phenomena and in its necessity for the scientific studies in religion. In line with Hultkrantz (1970) and several other prominent Scandinavian historians of religion – like William Brede Kristensen (1867–1953) and Geo Widengren (1907–1996) – he also criticizes all attempts to make PoR a matter of philosophical or theological positioning or concern (see Tucket 2016; Widengren 1969, 1972). It is worth mentioning that the History of Religions department at Stockholm University, from its beginning, has been eager to uphold a non-theological profile. Unlike the case at many other Swedish universities, from the early twentieth century religion was studied at Stockholm University from a historical perspective within the faculty of humanities and without connections to either Christian academic theology or to the Church as an institution. This situation still holds today. An early theoretical contribution from the department, that can be seen as an outcome of this explicitly non-theological ambition, was the formulation of analytical concepts that were not laden with Christian connotations. A prominent example here is the system of concepts of the soul which was developed by Arbman and Hultkrantz (Drobin 2016).

The following interview was conducted in Ulf Drobin's home in Stockholm, Sweden on 23 January 2018. Before the interview, I had, at Ulf Drobin's request, sent him a copy of James Cox's book *A Guide to the Phenomenology of Religion* in order to convey an idea of what had informed my own understanding of the topic of our conversation. This explains why this book is explicitly mentioned on several occasions in the interview. As the reader will note, a big part of the conversation is spent on trying to bring some order to the confusion about what it is that actually constitutes PoR, and to discuss the origin of the many perceived misconceptions surrounding this concept.

David Thurfell: What would be your definition of PoR?

Ulf Drobin: Well, in the field of History of Religions it has been necessary to systematically study the content of religions, i.e. the phenomena that are included in these: notions about the realm of the afterlife, concepts about the soul and so on. In order to do this, you need to define these phenomena: what is a spirit? What is a concept of a soul? What is a belief in an afterlife? And so on. PoR has attempted to define the various things that appear in the world of religion and to compile a general list of concepts which contains these. Such a compilation is necessary in order to make a comparison of different religions. If you do not have a concise definition of what, for instance, a notion of the afterlife is, well, then you cannot study such a phenomenon scientifically or conduct comparative research on religions. It would be like a mathematician who does not know what the numbers stand for – calculations would be impossible. It is the same thing with our discipline, if you don't know the basic concepts you cannot work with comparative religion.

I see.

The important thing here is that PoR neither entails a certain theoretical perspective nor a standpoint on the truthfulness of religious claims. Some phenomenologists of Religion are religious, others are not, but this is of no crucial significance for their research. You do not have to hold a certain view of the existential questions in order to grasp the meaning of the basic notions in the world of religion. A scholar's personal worldview usually does not affect the results of his or her work as a phenomenologist of Religion. Of course, it is possible that the personal ideas of a scholar sometimes will shine through. Some scholars may hold a positive attitude to religion and ascribe a certain value to it, while others may think of it as a delusion. If we exemplify this with some important Swedish phenomenologists of religion, I know that Carl Martin Edsman had a religious agenda while Geo Widengren did not, and neither did Åke Hultkrantz. I cannot, however, say that this is something that is possible to detect from the work of these scholars or from the way they practised History of Religions. Such preferences do not necessarily mean anything for the scholarly results and principally they should not. Rather they are to be seen as personal opinions.

So, PoR is not a perspective that is connected to the personal worldview or religiosity of the scholar.

No, definitely not.

I think it is quite common that PoR is associated with an Eliadean perspective. I suppose many would say that there is a line stretching from Rudolf Otto (1869–1937), through Gerardus van der Leeuw (1890–1950) and Mircea Eliade (1907–1986) and that PoR is the pro-religionist school of thought that these scholars represent.

If that is the case it is an unfortunate mistake. Because this school of thought has nothing to do with PoR. It is possible to apply a number of differing perspectives in the study of religions, but these perspectives have nothing to do with the basic notion of PoR.

On the Relation to Husserl's Philosophical Phenomenology

But would you not agree that there is a connection between PoR and the epistemological position of the scholar? In his book *An Introduction to the Phenomenology of Religion* James Cox seems to suggest this. Do you agree with the description of PoR that he presents?

No, I strongly disagree with what he writes. Cox suggests that Edmund Husserl (1859–1938) has been of great importance for PoR and his presentation takes this as its point of departure. This is a fatal mistake. Husserl and the philosophical phenomenology does not have a connection to PoR proper. Husserl's scholarly contribution is philosophical and epistemological and that is something rather different from what we are dealing with here. Cox's description is highly mistaken. This makes him partly responsible for some of the misunderstandings concerning the meaning of PoR that are now spreading. Without reason, PoR has been mixed up with philosophy. But it is incorrect to categorize PoR as a discipline that is based on certain philosophical assumptions, it is a grave mistake to do so.

Interesting. Can we discuss how this misunderstanding has arisen then? Perhaps we can start with the word "phenomenology".

Yes, the word phenomenology is central here. There is this saying that you should be careful of what you say since it might come "true". Some words are bound to be misunderstood, and the word "phenomenon", it seems, has an unrivalled position in this regard. The word "phenomenon" has a multilayered philosophical meaning, but it also has the very commonplace and everyday meaning of factual things, that is, such things that de facto exists. In late Latin we have the word phaenomenon which comes from the Greek φαινόμενον which means "that which shows itself", in other words "that which presents itself to our consciousness". This word is in its turn related to φαίνω, "to appear or make present". Phenomena, hence, are simply such things which de facto exists in the so-called reality. It is this common place and everyday meaning of the word that PoR is based on. The word refers to the phenomena that have to do with religion, in other words, the things that constitute its content, nothing else.

As you understand, this is something rather different than the epistemological and philosophical perspectives that Husserl represents. The historian of religion who works with PoR does not necessarily adhere to a specific philosophical approach. There is nothing in PoR as such that unites the scholars who work with it around a specific world view, definitely not. The level of philosophical training is of course varied among historians of religion, but that is a different matter. PoR, unlike Husserl's philosophical phenomenology, is not a philosophical perspective, it is not a metaphysical viewpoint and it is not a theory of religion. There are no such connections and there never were.

I see, but some, for instance Cox, still present PoR as linked to Husserl's philosophical perspective. How do you think this has become the case?

Well, I think it is the word phenomenon that has led to these problems and misunderstandings. The word itself can both signify a complex philosophical notion and the everyday notion of something that de facto exists.

And the understanding of the word that is relevant for PoR is the latter, simply the components of religion, that which de facto exists.

Yes, but then it is of course possible to have different beliefs concerning what exists. A believer may think there is a reality behind notions of gods and spirits and so on, and an atheist may think there is not, but it is not that type of differences I am talking about here. The important thing is that being religious is in no way a criterion for being a phenomenologist of religion. Neither is there an idea that it would be beneficial to be a believer or any such thing. It is completely open in this regard, and it always was. Cox's confusion with Husserl's phenomenology is based on the mixing up of these two possible meanings of the word phenomenon. I think it is simply this semantic confusion that lies at the root of this. He has been tricked by the word phenomenon, associated it to Husserl and thus drawn this faulty conclusion.

But is it really only the word phenomenon that we are talking about here? Are there not a number of other concepts in PoR that appear to be taken from the vocabulary of Husserlian phenomenology? Take, for instance, *eidetic vision* or *epoché*?

Well, it may be the case that there are some shared notions, but that does not mean that phenomenologists of religion are some kind of Husserlians, definitely not.

So, how should we then construe the fact that Gerardus van der Leeuw or Mircea Eliade use these concepts?

These are common philosophical concepts that almost have become a part of the academic language in general. That is the simple explanation. Their choice of words does not tie them to Husserl but is a part of the general academic vocabulary of their time.

The Epistemology of PoR

I think what you say about the confusion with Husserl is clear. But I am not so sure about your claim that there is no epistemology or philosophical perspective connected to PoR. Let me try to formulate a critique of this statement to which you can then respond.

That will be fine.

OK, one critique against the idea of philosophical neutrality in PoR, takes its point of departure in what has been labelled the linguistic turn of the humanities and social sciences. This, then, was a postmodern theoretical change of perspective that became influential during the latter half of the twentieth century. One basic idea was that our language and its concepts, though we might think of them as neutral and descriptive, actually are imbued with theoretical assumptions that in their turn mirror the power relations that permeate society.

Stop right there! It is obvious that a person's values and opinions influence the way he or she thinks, but the ideal of science is to lay such personal opinions aside as much as possible and to strive for objectivity. In PoR this means to portray that which can be seen in the religion described. It is of course difficult to completely avoid a certain bias, but one should not develop a creed of some sort or try to win adherents for this or that position. If you do that you have clearly crossed the border of what is acceptable for a phenomenologist of religion. What you believe and think in private is of course a completely different matter.

But the critique I am thinking of is not primarily theological or focused on whether the scholars are believers or not. Rather it is a political critique somewhat similar to Edward Said's famous critique of Orientalism from the 1960s. Said, as you know, meant that the categories of Orientalism hid a political agenda.

That the people described were less developed than the western world and so on, yes of course.

So, what do you say about the critique of the notion of religion that is formulated in the same spirit? That is, the critique that this word, just like the notion of the Orient, says more about the researchers who use it than about the people whose practices it is meant to describe.

I suppose it is possible to find examples where this is a relevant critique, but as a general assessment of PoR it is not valid in my opinion.

Some scholars, like for instance Talal Asad (2003), Fiona Bowie (2006), Timothy Fitzgerald (2000) and Tomoko Masuzawa (2005), have suggested that religion as a universal category is a western construction created on the blueprint of Christianity and Judaism and that the very word "religion" is difficult to translate outside of the Judeo-Christian world.

Yes, but I do not share that critique. People have always known that there are many differing religions and this idea is nothing that has arisen from Christianity or from other so called higher religions. Religion is a part of human behaviour and there are no peoples that entirely lack religion.

I suppose that these scholars would claim that it is the overarching category of religion that is problematic. What we call religion consists of a number of human behaviours and ideas, but when these are lumped together to form a category – religion – there is a risk that this creates misunderstandings about other cultures. Take Japan as an example: Swedish students discover that Japanese religion is syncretistic since people there are both Shinto and Buddhist at the same time. From a European perspective this appears strange. But it appears in that way because the implicit model for how normal religion is supposed to be is based on a Christian model where syncretism is anomalous.

I think this type of critique is valid to some extent when it comes to political ideas and opinions about people in other parts of the world. But I disagree when it comes to the History of Religions. To begin with only a rather limited number of historians of religion hold a Christian belief or call themselves Christian. There are a few of course but it is not the common picture. On the contrary, since the beginning the explicit ambition has been to study other religions without taking a Christian point of view as one's point of departure. Historians of religion have endeavoured to avoid looking at other religions through a Christian lens. And furthermore, it is the work of historians of religion that has made it possible to understand Christianity from a different viewpoint than the confessional one that previously prevailed. The main point of History of Religions is to *not* translate into Christian categories but to approach the world of religion and its content – the religious phenomena – in all parts of the globe without such bias. Furthermore, this approach has deepened our knowledge of Christianity. So, it is actually the opposite of what these critics claim. Postcolonial ideas may be fancy these days, but they do not have much to do with the History of Religions.

The Position of PoR Today

I understand. The reason I bring this up is because my picture is that a majority of historians of religion today would somewhat distance themselves from PoR and that one explanation for this is the notion that PoR entails an essentialist approach.

But the case is the complete opposite! No one can be a historian of religions without basic knowledge of PoR.

It is important that we are clear with what we mean now, because PoR that I think they distance themselves from, is PoR as it is portrayed by Cox.

If that is the case it is definitely very saddening, because Cox's position is very misleading and not common at all.

Well, here I think our views of what the situation is like today differ. I have tried to follow some of the international discussions in our discipline over the last twenty years and my impression is that the dominating picture of PoR is quite close to what Cox, perhaps mistakenly, represents. My guess is that your definition of PoR is rather marginalized today, at least among scholars of religion in general. So, the question becomes: what it is these scholars distance themselves from when they say that they do not want to use the term PoR to designate their own research.

I think this reflects some kind of postcolonial and superficial arguments that have come in and which thrive in the fringes of our discipline.

That is possible. But if you look at the sessions of the international conferences of History of Religions and the Study of Religions, the word PoR is not that present lately.

Of course not, because that would be too banal. Since everyone has to be a phenomenologist of religion that would not be a good way to profile yourself. Being a phenomenologist of religion is not what makes a scholar's perspective and approach distinguishable from that of others. Then it is of course important to clarify what conferences it is we are talking about here. There are lots of conferences happening and some of them attract lay people who are not trained historians of religion and who may have all kinds of opinions.

Yes, that is true. I was primarily thinking of the conferences of the IAHR and the EASR. These are organizations fronted by scholars like Peter Antes, Michael Pye and Einar Thomassen. These are all important and influential historians of religion. But conferences aside, I also think that James Cox's book is something of a standard piece in the curriculum when students are being introduced to PoR nowadays.

Where is that book a standard piece in the curricula?

Primarily in the anglophone world, I would guess.

Well, in that case it only shows how wrong things have gone in the US.

What do you think is the reason behind this development?

I think certain postcolonial ideas have become so influential that they have started to dissolve science, both in the USA and in other places. If this is the case it is deeply disturbing and depressing, that such a disintegration of knowledge is allowed to happen. But these are the currents that we can see in the world today.

Yes, I suppose you are right that postmodern ideas may have contributed here. There has been a trend for the last forty years to criticize previous generations of scholars, like for instance Eliade. Do you think that this has happened in a way that throws out the baby with the bathwater?

Yes, I do. You see, it is easy to turn to these postmodern ideas when you don't know anything for real. People think they have discovered the essence of everything and feel great satisfaction with their presumed ability to debunk the work of previous generations, but actually they don't have any real knowledge at all. This is a tendency that we can see in our time and that is very strong, not least within the sphere of politics. It is a catastrophically destructive process. One prominent example is found in these climate deniers like

Donald Trump and his supporters in the US. Trump has many supporters on the climate issue, and this is despite the fact that he has no knowledge of climate theory or of the extensive research that has been conducted in that field. It would be wrong to say that these Trump-supporters now have brought new and valuable scientific data to the table and that we therefore happily can stop worrying about the climate. If they try to throw out the PoR that I represent, then they are just like one of those climate deniers. It is a current of shallowness that is strong in American society today and from there it reaches out to other parts of the world as well.

I think many share your worries about this development, but perhaps the criticism here lies on a different level. Everyone agrees that you have to learn languages, that you have to study and work hard, but the core of the criticism is that the concepts themselves are not neutral and that they bring with them implicit ideas which are not necessarily true. It has been pointed out that the discipline of History of Religions was born in a certain cultural context and in a specific era, namely that of European Protestant culture during the colonial period. The critics claim that the basic perspectives and notions of the discipline reflect the context from which they sprang.

That is, if you excuse me for saying it, pure nonsense! This critique belittles the Study of Religions, and more than that, it could lead to its complete dissolution.

But if my observation that PoR is something many scholars would disassociate themselves from is true, then the question would be why this is so. From what you have said, I understand that one explanation may be that they distance themselves because they do not know what phenomenology actually is. Another explanation has to do with the impact of certain postmodern language-oriented philosophical trends in the academic world, trends that can also be discerned in politics as well as in society at large.

Yes.

I think that there are, in addition to these, some other explanations. One is the influx of sociological theory in the History of Religions as a discipline. History of Religions in Sweden has changed from a strictly historical, language-anchored and philological discipline to a more social-scientific discipline focused on contemporary issues. Languages and the study of texts are increasingly marginalized in this process. Another explanation could be the anglification of academic discourse in Sweden. Theoretical influences come here almost exclusively from the English-speaking world nowadays. This makes us more prone to follow theoretical trends from the US and Britain than we used to. Ideas from these countries affect us very quickly while French and German scholarship has much less impact.

Yes, here we definitely have a new situation. For me German was the first foreign language, and English and French second to that.

PoR and Essentialism

So, you have a point about the impact of postmodern currents, and these have primarily reached Sweden from the anglophone world. Perhaps these have also entailed that the discipline, as you put it, has become shallower. There is one more, perhaps mistaken, critique of PoR that we must discuss, namely the idea that religion exists *sui generis* and critiques of this view. Can we speak a little about this?

Yes, in that case we should start by clarifying what we mean with some of the concepts. This discussion depends on what we mean by *sui generis*. The Latin words literally mean something "of its kind" and it is of course obvious that religion is something that can be distinguished as separate from other phenomena and hence something that exists *sui generis*. For me this is an obvious banality, religion is religion just like tennis is tennis. Tennis is also something that exists *sui generis*, obviously.

The main point of the critique I think is that the idea that religion is something *sui generis* is linked to the notion that there is an essence and a core in it. The *sui-generis* position is thereby connected to an essentialist understanding of religion which, according to the critics, is problematic.

Yes, but I do not agree entirely with their critique.

Would you say that it is possible to identify a core or an essence in religion as a phenomenon?

Yes, I think I would. And if I am to say something about existential questions I would say that religion, for me, is something that, on an aesthetic level, relates to the mystery of life. This is something that every thinking human being faces and which, at the end of the day, is unable to grasp. It concerns the universe, and our very existence. The fact that we at all exist is on a fundamental level incomprehensible and beyond the reach of what science and the human intellect are able to explain.

Would you say that this mystery is the essence of religion? Certain famous historians and phenomenologists of religion would certainly say so, Rudolf Otto and Eliade for instance.

Yes, and I entirely share their view in this matter. Because life is a phenomenon that cannot be explained, it is a very tangible mystery for all thinking human beings. To state this does not necessarily mean that you are religious in a more conventional sense; it only means that you recognize the fact that being and existence in itself is a mystery.

So, would you agree that PoR and History of Religions, as you define these, are built on the premise and idea that the essence in all religion is the relation that humans have to the holy and these existential questions?

Yes, I agree with this statement. It is the feeling of awe before life itself, or before the sight of heaven – where does heaven end? – and so on, all such simple questions. These are the existential questions that we find in religion everywhere.

But what then is your response to the critique of this idea that religion, on its deepest level, has to do with deep existential dimensions of life? I am now thinking of the critique that this idea was formulated by historians of religion at about the same time that Protestant theologians – Schleiermacher and others – formulated the idea that the core of Christianity is that experienced mystery of life. Some critics would claim that the idea was influenced by the ideo-historical context in which it was formulated, namely Protestant Europe and the tension between Romanticism and Enlightenment that characterized the nineteenth century. By placing the essence of religion in the domain of inner experiences, these theologians escaped the scientific and historicist critic of, for instance, the genesis of the biblical texts. For the phenomenologists of religion, similarly, this way of thinking became a way to defend religion against the advances of modernism. This is the contextual backdrop in which History of Religions appeared. Some have even labelled some of the classical phenomenologists of religion "religionists" in order to highlight this, by this I think they mean that they assented to the mystical wisdom of religions in general without connecting this to one specific religious tradition. Swedish historian of religion Nathan Söderblom (1866–1931) is a prominent example of such a religionist, I suppose. On his deathbed he is supposed to have said that "I know that God exists and I can prove it in history." As a theologian and a bishop in the Church of Sweden he also represented a type of liberal dialogue-oriented Protestantism that resembled his scholarly position as a historian of religion.

Yes, Nathan Söderblom was of course confessional and bound to the Christian church in his work. But metaphysical and existential problems are not limited to Christianity. They are equally real for all humans. Life is a mystery, and that is true for every reflecting person.

I suppose you are right about that. But the question is whether this, the mystery of existence, constitutes the core in all religions. If you claim that it does, don't you then implicitly say that, for instance, religious rules surrounding food, or ideas of how power-relations are to be organized within a family, or regulations surrounding ritual purity and impurity, that all such things are secondary outer layers that supposedly surround a deeper core which has to do with this existential mystery? Is that really a reasonable claim?

Well, I mean, who can say what is the true core of anything? Obviously, there are many cores in religion. Perhaps I should say that in my own personal idea, the essence of all religion is the mystery of existence. But it is of course true that many other things are important as well. When it comes to ideas about life in the hereafter, for instance, it is certainly reasonable to think that it is the metaphysical experience of life's mystery that gives rise to the belief that there is life after death, a belief that certainly can be most comforting for those who hold it. But, of course, there are many cores. Most aspects of human life have been expressed in and through religion, so naturally it is very difficult to pinpoint one thing only as its essence, but at least the existential mystery has a very central position.

Yes, of course. Just let me linger on this topic with one more example. Graham Harvey is a historian of religion who has studied a number of indigenous peoples in the world. He has one story where he asks an elderly and learned Maori man to tell him what the purpose of religion is. The Maori man responds that its utmost purpose is to "do violence with impunity". So, for this man, it seems, religious actions have a juridical function, their foremost meaning is related to penal codes and laws. He does not say that his religion has to do with his inner feelings of the mystery of life. Probably he has such feelings, but he does not identify these as the core of his religion. If someone from another tradition had been asked, probably something else had been put forth as the core, and if a third person had been asked probably yet another something. If we then take Eliade, or perhaps Rudolf Otto may be an even clearer example, when he says that religion in its essence circles around the *mysterium tremendum et fascinans* and that religion is something that exists in all human cultures, then he identifies a core, and in relation to that core the statement of Graham Harvey's Maori becomes sort of an anomaly. Or perhaps one would have to say that there is an experience of a *mysterium tremendum* and existential questions that hide behind the talk of impunity and violence. But such a position could be criticized for homogenizing religion as a cultural phenomenon, and perhaps also for being a too be-nevolent an interpretation of it. I suppose some would even say that the talk of mysteries and existential questions is a mystification that functions as smokescreens to cover the power structures that actually are at play.

This last thing I completely disagree with. Of course, religion is used to wield power of differing sorts, that is obvious if we look at religious organizations and all the things they do. But if we are now talking about existential questions, that is a different issue altogether.

But would you not say then that there is a philosophical understanding of what religion is, that is implicit in PoR?

To cut to the heart of the matter, it is obvious for all thinking human beings that life is a mystery. But this idea is not a part of PoR as such. PoR is, as I said before, a list of concepts related to religious phenomena. You do not have to be a phenomenologist or historian of religion to understand this with the mystery of existence, that is clear to all thinking people.

I understand, but I would think that many historians or other scholars of religion today would not agree so easily with the statement that the essence of all religion is an existential mystery.

In that case, they are completely detached from religion. The existential mystery is a core in all religion, but it is also a core in all thinking people.

The Development of the Discipline

Even if you think that it is negative, would you agree with the observation that many contemporary scholars tone down the existential essence of religion and rather focus on other things, such as cognitive structures, power structures or sociological perspectives?

Yes, this may very well be the case, and they can do all these things, but then they lack understanding of what religion as such is about. It is obvious that religion is of great importance socially and sociologically and for human life in general on a thousand different levels, but if they think that they can seek the truth about religion only in social interactions and power play between people, well then they have not taken into consideration that which makes religion differ from other types of human ideas. If it really is religion you want to talk about, then you cannot remove the existential perspective, because that is what fundamentally makes religion into religion, isn't it? It is evidently a part of the essence of religion and if you think that you can remove it, well, then I think that you have de facto ceased to be a historian of religion. It makes no sense to remove the most important element in the world of religion and then keep calling yourself a historian of religion.

Perhaps what has happened is simply that the perspective that you express here has been marginalized in the scholarly study of religion. That
many historians of religion – and by this, I mean those who hold positions
in the universities and publish in academic history-of-religion journals –
do not share the idea that the existential mystery is the essential core in
religion.

Yes, maybe this is the case.

**Would you say, then, that these scholars are less interested in what you
would call religion.**

Yes, I would actually. Perhaps they feel that they have become more scientific
if they disregard that side, or that they can become more convincing by keep-
ing quiet about it. Perhaps they are completely uninterested in the holiness
– or, shall we say, mystery – aspect. Perhaps they want to show themselves
as down-to-earth scholars who have a scientific approach in the conventional
sense of the word. This is perhaps understandable, but it means that they
disregard something that is of utmost importance in the world of religions
and that they do so for reasons which remain unclear.

**It is this shift of scholarly focus that we want to elucidate and explore
with this publication. Before, most scholars thought along the same lines
as you and now they seek to be earth-bound and scientific in the conventional sense. As you see it, this means that they abandon the core and the
very point of our discipline. The question then is, why did this happen?
Why was the perspective abandoned?**

Could it not be the case that these scholars, who obviously are not themselves religious, simply lack the ability to empathize with religious experience
and therefore replace it with materialistic reasoning? The inability to empathize with religious sentiments entails that they become uninterested in
the holiness- or mystery-aspects and, as a consequence, they disregard of
something very important in religion without arguing why.

When do you think this shift began?

Well, it is relatively late. Secularization has reached far, and I suppose the historians of religions also want to be secularized, scientific and so on. The public
spirit surrounding these matters has changed, so I suppose this is something
that is spreading more and more. The ideal of the natural sciences is breaking
through also within the History of Religions. One way of expressing this is to
say that History of Religions, as a discipline, has become secularized. But this
has happened on false premises, because the existential questions concern
all humans. So, I would not say that it is a particularly flattering development
for our discipline.

So, for you the disappearance or fading away of the existential mystery perspective is the same as the fading away of the History of Religions as a discipline?

Yes, it would be, in that case. But I sure hope that History of Religions will not fade away, and I have not noticed any such tendencies, so I don't think so. Religions will probably not disappear, so History of Religions should not do that either. But I do believe that the historians of religion have become more explicitly secularized. These tendencies within the discipline reflect trends that we can see in society at large. And if they now want to get rid of the very notion of religion, or of the level of existential meaning in it, then this is something that I have to consider as very negative. Not just for the historians of religion but for knowledge and thinking in general. I think that History of Religions has made an important contribution by mapping and clarifying this type of thinking. I also see this focus on the overarching concepts as an expression of a general tendency towards shallowness and triviality. It is a kind of attitude in which it is believed that you do not need a deeper knowledge about the subject matter. But PoR is built on the opposite attitude, it is about laboriously acquiring extensive knowledge.

If this now is the case, how can we reverse the development? What do we need to do?

I think we have to be a bit old fashioned and study PoR with all that it entails in order to acquire real knowledge. We have to go through the hardships of studying and learning languages to do this. There are no shortcuts here, I am afraid. And we cannot close down the discipline of History of Religions. Because knowledge about religions is a very important aspect of knowledge about life itself, in other words, about the life of human beings under different circumstances. If I take Buddhism and Old Norse religion, which are the traditions I myself have focused especially on, we find meaningful knowledge that says something about what life has meant for people on a general level: knowledge about how we, as humans, have thought about the big questions that face each and every one of us. It would be a tragedy if we were to lose that.

Thank you for taking the time to talk with me about this.

Thank you.

Commentary

The interview with Ulf Drobin revolves around two themes: the first is the meaning and definition of PoR, and the second is the pros and cons of an essentialist understanding of religion. For Drobin, as he makes clear in the interview, these two topics are not necessarily related. For him, PoR is about the non-theoretical definition and compiling of religious phenomena, whereas as essentialist view of religion, as something that in its core pivots around the mystery of existence, is his personal understanding but also, as he puts it, a perspective without which the discipline of History of Religions would be dissolved. As I understand it, the conversation is characterized by a partly frustrating and partly intriguing mutual attempt to correct misunderstandings, to find some kind of common ground and to bridge our differing viewpoints. To a certain extent, the conversation – and the linguistic confusion that characterizes it – may in itself serve as an illustration of the generational gap within which PoR – as a perspective or a conceptual foundation for all research in our discipline – risks getting lost.

Ulf Drobin and I came into this conversation with quite divergent ideas about both the definition and the present status of PoR in Sweden. Ulf Drobin has his experience of direct contact and collaboration with Widengren and Hultkrantz and some of the other the great representatives of the twentieth-century Swedish History of Religions. For him, PoR represents the unchallenged legacy of these scholars and the foundation of our discipline. I belong to a later generation and received my training from another university, that of Uppsala. My teachers – Jan Bergman (1933–1999), Kaarina Drynjeva (born 1941), Anders Hultgård (born 1936) and some others – are the now elderly disciples of Geo Widengren who, when I started my PhD programme in 1997, were approaching their retirement. I got my undergraduate and PhD training in a time when the academic landscape was changing in Sweden and in many other countries in Europe. At this time, the Swedish academic world was both broadened – with a massive expansion of new universities and colleges – and streamlined into the administrative principles of New Public Management. In the 1990s, Sweden introduced a performance-based funding system for universities at the same time as the Bologna Declaration on a European level announced that one of the three main goals of its reform programme for higher education was to promote employability (see Stausberg 2011). In Sweden the laws regulating PhD education were changed so that it became impossible to be a PhD student for more than four fully funded years. Doctoral candidates now became the employees, rather than merely the students of their universities (Thurfjell 2015). I was one of the very last PhD students who were admitted in the old system at Uppsala university.

For History of Religions – as it was traditionally understood as a language-oriented philological discipline – these changes were potentially fatal. Language studies and the acquiring of philological skills took years. Often, PhD projects in the discipline had previously stretched over decades, ending in the obtaining of specialized competences of little use for the labour market. In the new system, such an academic environment was labelled dysfunctional and considered obsolete. For the History of Religions, as a discipline, the rescue came from another societal development, namely the return of religion as an issue of political and societal relevance. The challenges presented by a more religious multicultural situation in Sweden and the growth of religio-political conflicts in the world suddenly made competence in the History of Religions topical and needed. It is no exaggeration to say that this new situation shaped the generation of scholars to which I belong. For better or worse, the focus of my and younger generations is more oriented towards the contemporary, more concerned with societal and political relevance, more social-scientific in profile and less language-based than that of our teachers. It is also – and this I think is especially relevant for the position of PoR – more engaged with theory. Whether it was critical, sociological, psychological, cognitivist, post-colonial, de-colonial, feminist, constructivist, structuralist, post-structuralist or discourse-oriented, positioning yourself theoretically and learning to master the lingo of the preferred theoretical discourse has become increasingly important. One can speculate about the reasons for this. Claiming to quote his doctor father Geo Widengren, Jan Bergman jokingly used to say that "theory is for those who have no actual knowledge". He used to say this as a witticism and he always amended it by adding that this in no way reflected his actual position. Yet, the joke said something about the shift that was about to take place in the Study of Religions in Sweden and beyond in the 1990s, a situation that seemed to me to provoke a certain nostalgia on the part of Ulf Drobin. Perhaps, there is some truth to the claim that, as Drobin puts it, the theory-driven focus on the overarching concepts is an expression of a general tendency towards shallowness and triviality. But, regardless of what the case may be with that, the newly discovered assessment of theory entailed a massive influx of perspectives, concepts and ideas from other disciplines and scholarly traditions. Hardly surprising, alternative uses of the word phenomenology also found their way into the Study of Religions as a part of this process. Not only continental philosophy, but also anthropology, ethnology, psychology, archaeology and educational studies have their own specific and circuitously intertwined usages of this term, and many of these were now imported into the Study of Religions.

I think that the distancing from PoR that we discuss in the interview was a part of this process. It was a consequence and an expression of the generational shift that happened in the 1990s. PoR was for me, and for many of the other PhD students of my generation, heavily associated with Eliade. It was also, as we saw it, the interpretational paradigm of the a-theoretical generation that had come before us and whose perspectives and styles of scholarship the Study of Religions, more or less voluntarily, was now moving away from.

My conversation with Ulf Drobin has for me given rise to a saddening insight about the ways scholarly knowledge is passed on from one generation to another. It is sometimes said that we stand on the shoulders of giants. Applied to the academic world, this expression entails a certain view of tradition. It suggests a situation where the strenuously acquired knowledge of one generation is passed on, from professor to student, and picked up by the next generation which continues to think and to collect knowledge where the old generation left off. The destiny of PoR in Sweden makes me wonder whether this idealized account is not itself a reflection of a certain historical, social and institutional context. Rather than taking up the task where the previous generations left off, it seems new generations sometimes neglect or discredit the findings of their teachers in order to reinvent their own wheel again and again, all while being tossed hither and thither by political schemes they cannot control. This, at least, seems to have been what happened in Sweden, both in the shift between my generation and our professors, and in the shift between them and the generation before them. It strikes me that, despite the fact that I got my training in Uppsala, the work of Geo Widengren was not particularly present in my education, neither was the work of Stig Wikander (1908–1983), Tor Andre or, for that matter, Nathan Söderblom. All of these were world renowned historians of religion from my university, but – except for one short book by Andrae – none of their work was included in my curriculum. Perhaps, this shows that the same lapsus that took place when my generation took over from our teachers happened when they took over from theirs. Through both these generational shifts, our desire to open ourselves for new perspectives and distance ourselves from previous generations, PoR – at least as defined by Ulf Drobin – became misconstrued, defamed and forgotten.

David Thurfjell is Professor in the Study of Religions at Södertörn University, Stockholm. His research circles around themes pertaining to Shi'ite and Pentecostal revivalism, religion as a means of social mobilisation and the discourse surrounding religion and secularity in northern Europe. Among his publications are the monographs *Living Shi'ism* (Brill, 2006), *Faith and Revivalism in a Nordic Romani Community* (Tauris, 2011) and *Godless People* (Norstedts, 2015).

References

Asad, Talal. 2003. *Formations of the Secular: Christianity, Islam, Modernity*. Stanford, CA: Stanford University Press.

Bowie, Fiona. 2006. *The Anthropology of Religion: An Introduction*, 2nd edn. Oxford: Blackwell.

Cox, James L. 2006. *A Guide to the Phenomenology of Religion: Key Figures, Formative Influences and Subsequent Debates*. London: Continuum.

Drobin, Ulf. 1980. *Indogermanische Religion und Kultur? Eine Analyse des Begriffes indogermanisch*. Stockholm: Religionshistoriska inst., Univ.

Drobin, Ulf. 1982. *Psychology, Philosophy, Theology and Epistemology: Some Reflections*. Stockholm: Stockholm University.

Drobin, Ulf. 1983. *Folklore and Comparative Religion*. Stockholm: Stockholm University.

Drobin, Ulf. 1983. "Om teori och empiri i religionshistorisk forskning." Dissertation, Stockholm University.

Drobin, Ulf. 2016. "Introduction." In *Horizons of Shamanism: A Triangular Approach to the History and Anthropology of Ecstatic Techniques*, edited by Peter Jackson. Stockholm: Stockholm University Press. https://doi.org/10.16993/bag.b

Fitzgerald, Timothy. 2000. *The Ideology of Religious Studies*. New York: Oxford University Press.

Hultkrantz, Åke. 1970. "The Phenomenology of Religion – Aims and Methods." *Temenos* 6: 68–88.

Masuzawa, Tomoko. 2005. *The Invention of World Religions, or, How European Universalism Was Preserved in the Language of Pluralism*. Chicago, IL: University of Chicago Press.

Stausberg, Michael. 2011. "The Bologna Process and the Study of Religion/s in (Western) Europe." *Religion* 41(2): 187–207. https://doi.org/10.1080/0048721x.2011.586259

Thurfjell, David. 2015. "The Dissolution of the History of Religions: Contemporary Challenges of a Humanities Discipline in Sweden." *Temenos* 51(2): 161–175. https://doi.org/10.33356/temenos.53566

Tuckett, Jonathan. 2016. "Clarifying Phenomenologies in the Study of Religion: Separating Kristensen and van der Leeuw from Otto and Eliade." *Religion* 46(1): 75–101. https://doi.org/10.1080/0048721x.2015.1057773

Widengren, Geo. 1969. *Religionsphänomenologie*. Berlin: Walter de Gruyter & Co.

Widengren, Geo. 1972. "La méthode comparative: entre philologie et phenomenologie." In *Problems and Methods of the History of Religions*, edited by Ugo Bianchi, C. J. Bleeker and Alessandro Bausani, 5–14. Leiden: Brill.

2

Universal Parallels, Meaningful Lives and Predisposed Minds

A Conversation (Finland)

VEIKKO ANTTONEN AND TEUVO LAITILA

Veikko Anttonen earned his Ph.D. at the University of Helsinki in 1996. He was the Professor and Chair of Comparative Religion at the School of History, Culture and Arts Studies at the University of Turku between 1997 and 2015. He was the Editor-in-Chief of Temenos, Nordic Journal of Comparative religion between 2005 and 2011. He served as the President of the Finnish Society for the Study of Religion between 2006 and 2011, the Vice-President of the European Association for the Study of Religions between 2008 and 2010, a Vice-President of the International Association for the History of Religions between 2015 and 2020. He is a member of the Finnish Academy of Sciences since 2011. He was awarded Doctor Honoris Causa at the University of Debrecen, Hungary in June 2010. He has authored an intellectual biography on Uno Holmberg-Harva, a pioneer of Comparative Religion in Finland Uno Harva ja suomalainen uskontotiede, 1987), a book Ihmisen ja maan rajat, 'Pyhä' kulttuurisena kategoriana, 1996 [The Making of Corporeal and Territorial Boundaries. The Sacred as a Cultural Category] and Uskontotieteen maastot ja kartat, 2010 [Territories and Maps of Religious Studies]. The three publications above are published by the Finnish Literature Society. Together with Ilkka Pyysiäinen, he edited a book Current Approaches in the Cognitive Science of Religion (Continuum, 2002) and contributed to such international works as The Sacred and its Scholars (Brill, 1996), Guide to the Study of Religion (Cassell, 2000), Perspectives on Method and Theory in the Study of Religion (Brill, 2000) and Religion as a Human Capacity (Brill, 2004).

Keywords: Finland, comparative religion, regional phenomenology, folk religion, comparative method, cognitive science of religion

Teuvo Laitila is University Lecturer, Associate Professor of Comparative Religion and Orthodox Church History at University of Eastern Finland, Joensuu, Finland. His research interests cover religious life in Eastern Europe, including the Balkans and Caucasus, as well as the history of religious studies in Finland. His publications include *Ihmisen jumalat: johdatus uskontotieteeseen* [Gods of the Humans: An Introduction to Comparative Religion]. Joensuu Open University. 2006 (an e-book version in 2015), *Löytöretkiä Georgiaan* [Explorations in the Republic of Georgia]. Edited by Krista Berglund, Susan Ikonen, Teuvo Laitila & Ville Ropponen. University of Eastern Finland Press. 2013, *Uskonto, isänmaa ja antisemitismi: kiistely juutalaisista suomalaisessa julkisuudessa ennen talvisotaa* [Religion, Fatherland and Antisemitism: Disputes on Jews in Finland before the Winter War]. Arator. 2014, *Jumalat, haltiat ja pyhät: elettyä ortodoksisuus karjalassa 1000–1900* [Gods, Spirits and Saints: Lived Orthodoxy in Karelia 1000–1900. Finnish Society of Church History. 2017. He has also written articles about Martti Haavio and, more recently, on religion and politics in Ukraine. A book on the latter, together with a colleague, is in preparation and hopefully will appear in 2022.

Introduction

This chapter was created in the form of a dialogue between Veikko Anttonen and Teuvo Laitila. Both authors participated as interviewers and interviewees. We met and discussed twice at the main building of the University of Helsinki in October 2017 and February 2018. Being both experts by experience, there was no need to carry out an actual, structured or non-structured, interview. Our contribution is a result of two free-floating conversation sessions over the scope and contents of the chapter and an email exchange of Q&A-type comments in a shared file.

Veikko Anttonen retired from his position at the School of History, Culture and Arts Studies at the University of Turku in 2015. Teuvo Laitila has since 2003 taught at the University of Eastern Finland, School of Theology. Anttonen started his academic career at the Department of Comparative Religion at the University of Helsinki in the early 1970s and Laitila in the next decade. Both have been integrated in the Finnish scholarly community of the study of religion for many decades, and also have been active participants in international scholarship. In what follows, Anttonen (in bold type) and Laitila (in regular type) present an overview over what has been called 'regional phenomenology' in Finland: its background and an evaluation of the scholarly work of its most prominent practitioners.

Ethnographic Foundation of Finnish Phenomenology

Veikko Anttonen: Let me raise the first question concerning the starting point of our dialogue: what would count as phenomenology of religion (PoR) in our attempt to map the still unwritten history of this research domain within the academic study of religion in Finland? I would like to suggest that we first consider the work of two scholars, Uno Holmberg-Harva (1882–1949) and Martti Haavio (1899–1973), who had a ground-breaking effect on the shaping of comparative religion in Finland as an autonomous academic field. There is no question that, in addition to Edward Westermarck (1862–1939), the founding father of social anthropology in Finland, Uno Harva[1] was one of the first internationally recognized Finnish scholars of religion who had a phenomenological bent in his research, even though Harva's work cannot be subsumed under the category of "phenomenology" as we have come to know it. Harva was trained first as a Lutheran priest but resigned from his office in 1907 in order to pursue studies in comparative religion. He became a comparativist, empiricist and a positivist adopting methodology closely connected with Westermarck's anthropological school, even though he did not belong to the core group comprising Westermarck's disciples.

Westermarck imported British evolutionary anthropology to the Finnish academic world. He carried out extensive fieldwork in Morocco starting in 1898 and worked closely with such prominent figures in British social anthropology as Charles Seligman and Alfred Cort Haddon. Westermarck's interests ranged from his ethnography in Morocco (*Ritual and Belief in Morocco*, 1926) to the evolutionary study of human marriage and moral ideas (*The History of Human Marriage*, 1891; *The Origin and Development of Moral Ideas*, 1906–1908; *Christianity and Morals*, 1939). Westermarck was appointed Professor of Practical Philosophy at the University of Helsinki in 1906 as well as Professor of Sociology at the University of London in 1907 where – as George W. Stocking has written – fieldwork expeditions had become a symbol of ethnographic enterprise (Stocking 1984). Westermarck was universalist and cosmopolitan by his methodological attitude, representing a study-of-man type research. He strongly opposed narrow, provincial ideological positions as well as the German *geisteswissenschaftliche Metaphysik*, which characterized the academic work of nationalist-minded Fennomans and Protestant theologians in Finland (on the Fennoman movement, see Liikanen 1995).

Unlike his fellow Westermarckians, who belonged to the Swedish-speaking liberal academics, Harva's pursuit of knowledge was in part

---

1.   Uno Harva finnocized his last name from Holmberg to Harva in 1927.

politically motivated. Through his comparative analysis of vernacular culture, Harva's main concern was to explore the ancient religion of peoples belonging to the Uralic and Finno-Ugric language family. Harva held that the religious past of the Finns could still be observed, not only among the Finnic peoples in the Baltic Sea area, but also among "the kinfolk" in European Russia and Siberia. Harva became a field-ethnographer, carrying out religio-anthropological research in seventeen villages among the Mari and Udmurt people, as well as among the Ket and Evenki in Siberia. As a comparative religionist, Harva pioneered a phenomenological comparison reminiscent of that which Mircea Eliade (1907–1986) made famous. Unlike Eliade, however, Harva did not argue for the *sui generis* nature of religion nor did he pursue the study of subjective meanings bestowed on diverse items in oral tradition, but focused on exploring cultural parallels in collectively shared mythical worldviews among premodern indigenous population in Eurasia and the Near East.

The Legacy of Finnish Folklore and Mythology School

In the early 1920s, when a distinct research domain known as PoR did not exist, Uno Harva wrote a book *Elämänpuu* (The Tree of Life), published first in Finnish, and two years later in German translation. When *Der Baum des Lebens* (1922) was published, Uno Harva's wife, Elin Münsterhjelm-Harva, wrote in her family diary that "Uno's new book has caught wide international attention from the specialists in the field. Uno himself says that his discovery in the book is the greatest and wondrous that he has ever been able to make, and the plot is far-reaching and new in the field of the study of religion" (Anttonen 1987, 179). It took only three months to write the Finnish draft of the book. Along with other major publications that followed *Der Baum des Lebens*,[2] Harva's aim was to disclose mythic structures in the ancient cosmology of the palaeo-Siberian hunter–gatherers and cattle-breeding agriculturalists, and the nomadic peoples of Central Asia. *Der Baum des Lebens* was a collection of essays based partly on his own ethnographic field notes, supplemented with diverse data on mythic narratives revolving around *axis mundi* motifs in cosmological conceptions focusing on the world pillar, on the tree of life,

---

2. *Finno-Ugric and Siberian Mythology*, published in Mythology of All Races, Volume 4, 1927, and *Die Religiösen Vorstellungen der altaischen Völker* (1938), the latter also translated and published in French in 1959, *Les Représentations religieuses des peuples altaïques*, and in Japanese by the University of Foreign Languages in 1971 by Professor Katsuhiko Tanaka.

on Babel's Tower, on Paradise imaginations, on Mother Goddesses, on conceptions of lifeline and fate as well as on the shaman's ascent to the heavens along the branches of a shaman's tree, which all represented a mythical link between earth and sky, located in the centre of the world. I find it extremely interesting that Harva's teacher Kaarle Krohn (1863–1933), Professor of Folklore at the University of Helsinki, did not want to recommend the German translation of *Elämänpuu* to the publisher, Finnish Academy of Science and Letters, although he was a member of the board. According to Harva, Krohn was suspicious about the arguments and the organization of data in his study (Anttonen 1987, 120). Krohn was a devout Christian, and it can be assumed that he shunned Harva's methodological choice to set mythic themes and structures in the Bible in comparison with Islamic and Near Eastern popular traditions. Harva argued that the motives of the world pillar and the tree of life date back to ancient Iran and to the Indo-Iranian times. Departing from his rationalist mindset, Harva aimed at overall explanation of "beliefs and dreams" which premodern peoples had stored in their mythical worldview prior to the Copernican revolution in the world of knowledge. It is noteworthy that much of what Eliade wrote on the centre of the world and *axis mundi* symbolism owes to Harva's work.

Teuvo Laitila: Yes, I agree that Krohn's Christian conviction had an influence on his academic work. In his *Suomalaisten runojen uskonto* (The Religion of the Finnish Runes, 1914), Krohn sketched an evolutionary scheme of transitions in Finnish folk religion from shamanism and the worship of the dead to beliefs and rituals revolving around the Virgin Mary and Catholic saints. However, there is also a phenomenological dimension in the patterning of his data, namely, his manner of thematizing it. In addition to shamans, the dead and the saints, Krohn also discusses various kinds of spirits, "worshipping" of the animals, devils, heroes and some other topics as well. That is, his way of grouping Finnish folk religious data into distinct types resembles that of such historians of religions as P. D. Chantepie de la Saussaye (1848–1920) or Gerardus van der Leeuw (1890–1950).

Kaarle Krohn employed typologies developed by his father. He was a son of Julius Krohn, Professor of Finnish Literature at the Imperial Alexander University (University of Helsinki after Finland declared independence in 1917). Julius Krohn created a folklore method based on geographic-historical comparison of epic poetry and other folklore genres. Before Julius Krohn drowned in a sailing boat accident in 1888, he had been in personal communication with Friedrich Max Müller, the founding father of *Vergleichende und allgemeine Religionswissenschaft*, whose Hibbert Lectures were scheduled to be translated into Finnish by him. Kaarle Krohn inherited his father's scholarly contacts and was a key person in creating a community of scholars, who dedicated themselves to the study of folklore and religion. Uno Harva was Krohn's "star disciple", whom he sent to Russia to collect data and write monographs on four Finno-Ugric ethnic groups, the Mari, Udmurt, Komi and Sámi (Lapps). Kaarle Krohn further developed the method that was designed to reconstruct the "Ur-form" of a folklore item – such as a folk poem – and its variants with mythological content by delineating their recurrent forms of representation and stages of development in a particular geographical area.

Kaarle Krohn's legacy becomes visible not only in the work of Uno Harva, but most specifically in studies by Martti Haavio, who was appointed the Chair and Professor of Folklore Studies at the University of Helsinki in 1948, the first holder of which had been Kaarle Krohn from 1898 until 1928. Haavio's theoretical openings aimed at remodelling the geographic-historical method, aka the Finnish method, by influences from comparative religion and sociology. In *Karjalan jumalat* (The Gods of Karelia, 1959), Haavio aimed to solve mythological puzzles hidden in the list of heathen Finnish "gods", published in 1551 by the Lutheran reformer Mikael Agricola in the preface to his translation of the Psalter. Haavio's main concern was the reliability of Agricola's list as a representation of late medieval folk religion.

Various judgments have been passed on the character of the catalogue itself and the principles followed by Agricola in drawing it up (see Anttonen 2012). In *Karjalan jumalat*, Haavio provided a detailed analysis of agents in the Karelian section of the list. He rejected the notion that Agricola's purpose was to follow Homer and reconstruct the Olympus of ancient Finnish gods. In the light of oral tradition collected since the seventeenth century, Haavio proposed a new phenomenological-type interpretation of the cultural background of mythological agents and of the role played by them in Karelian folk life and popular tradition. Behind the obscure names of "gods" in the Karelian section of the list, Haavio claimed, lay Roman Catholic patron saints of agriculture, adopted during the roughly three hundred years during which Finland was Catholic, who the Karelians[3] worshipped (even after Finland had turned to Protestantism during the sixteenth century) at critical times of the year in order to secure a good harvest.

---

3.   A people living on both sides of the present Finno-Russian border.

Phenomenological Turn in Finland

I would say that Haavio adopted an Eliadean phenomenological view – that Karelian "gods" and calendric rituals performed at critical times of the agricultural year were local parallels to universal and eternal mythical themes of decay and revival. According to Eliade these themes were expressions of the unchanging and age-old mindset of illiterate "traditional societies". In other words, a Karelian peasant is a *homo religiosus* who reactivates and reproduces mythical, "eternal" models in his way of behaving and thinking.

Haavio's other book along the same lines, *Kuolemattonten lehdot* (Sacred Groves of the Immortal, 1961), also published in German as *Die Heilige Heine in Ingermanland*, was in *strictu sensu* phenomenological. He focused on a sowing ritual performed in a sacred grove to an enigmatic Ingrian mythological agent of agriculture, *Sämpsöi Pellervoinen*, who in Haavio's view was equivalent to the Greek god Dionysos. As the plural in the work's title indicates, Haavio "found" the meaning of these groves and rituals performed in them by comparing them to sacred groves and rites described in ancient Greek and Egyptian mythologies and the Baltic-Finnic folklore. His comparison, which was not historical but relied on presupposed functional, psychological and other such similarities, is in my opinion a red thread connecting Haavio to Eliade. Moreover, in his preface to *The Gods of Karelia*, Haavio stated that Eliade's "fresh works in comparative religion have given me incomparable delight" (Haavio 1959, vi). Evidently, they were *Le mythe l'éternel retour* (1949) and *Traitè d'histoire des religions* (1949), both in German translations.

In the introduction to his Die Heilige Heine in Ingermanland, Haavio was explicit about his interest in phenomenology. What he had learned from Eliade's "fresh works" was that there does not need to be tension between the synchronic and diachronic approaches to data on folklore and religion. Haavio wrote (1961, 6) that "in principle, for phenomenology, history does not exist". He added, however, that a "phenomenological study sets light on historical connections. A phenomenon, met in two cultures wide apart, does not need to be historic-genetically connected in the sense of being a cultural loan from one tradition to another" (ibid.). Haavio's background may partly explain his "phenomenological turn". As a scholar of folklore, he was a comparativist who posed both diachronic and synchronic questions to his data, as the Finnish folklorist Lotte Tarkka has pointed out (1987). He called his approach a motif-historical method, which was in effect a redefinition of the Krohnian geographic-historical paradigm; both aimed at bracketing the contours of a religious phenomenon to capture its intent or core (*das Ding an sich*). It must be added that Haavio was a very influential academic person in Finland during the late 1950s and throughout the 1960s. He was both an academic scholar and a highly esteemed poet and literary figure in Finland. In 1954 he was appointed as one of the twelve distinguished members of the Academy of Finland.[4]

Lauri Honko's Impact: The Birth of Regional Phenomenology

When comparative religion started to gain ground in Finnish Academia in the late 1950s and early 1960s, the new generation of scholars was educated under the tutelage of Martti Haavio. In the 1950s, a separate chair for comparative religion did not exist. The first one was established at the Swedish-language Åbo Akademi, in Turku, in July 1962.[5] In December of the same year, Lauri Honko (1932–2002), the brilliant disciple of Haavio, was appointed to the Chair of Comparative Religion and Folklore at the University of Turku, where Uno Harva had carried out the study of religion, albeit as a professor of sociology. Honko was an expert in method and theory in the study of religion and folklore, and well versed in the social sciences. It was his academic achievements that created conditions for establishing an internationally oriented community of scholars of religion in Finland.

By the initiative of Haavio and Honko, the Finnish Society for the Study of Comparative Religion was founded on 1 November 1963. They also initiated *Temenos, the Nordic Journal of Comparative Religion*, the first issue of which was published in July 1965. Honko organized and chaired an influential study conference of the IAHR in Turku in 1973 to discuss burning methodological issues within the science of religion (being a literal translation of the Finnish title of the discipline, *uskontotiede*). The future of PoR was one of the key topics in the conference. Honko's aim was to create a fruitful dialogue between phenomenologically oriented historians of religions and social scientific scholars of religion regarding the validity and methodological basis of comparisons in the study of religion. In the introduction to the conference volume *Science of Religion: Studies in Methodology* (1979, xxviii), Honko summed up the outcome of

---

4. The four represented natural sciences, three the humanities, another three arts, and the other two were alternating members.
5. The first professor (1962–1965) was the Swedish scholar of the Old Testament, Helmer Ringgren (1917–2012), who also wrote a Swedish-language introduction *Religions form och function* (1968, a Finnish translation appeared in 1972) to what he called "religionshistoria" (History of Religions). We thank Björn Dahla from the Donner Institute, Åbo, for this information.

discussions as follows: "neither historical nor hermeneutic particularism is adequate for the study of religions; besides these we shall continue to need flexible universal categories ... in order to make the transfer of results from one investigation to another possible." Honko was frustrated with the fact that comparisons by phenomenologists were not empirically grounded and that generalizations remained speculative if the historical context of a phenomenon were deliberately ignored. Armin Geertz and Russell T. McCutcheon have placed the Turku conference in the wider context of methodological considerations within the study of religion in their introduction to the edited volume *Perspectives on Method and Theory in the Study of Religion* (Geertz and McCutcheon 2000).

Honko's concern was shared by Haralds Biezais (1909–1995), a Latvian expatriate to Finland and Professor of Comparative Religion at Åbo Akademi from 1969 to 1978. In arguing against the Italian historian of religion, Ugo Bianchi (1922–1995), Biezais made a distinction between "typology", "morphology", and "phenomenology". The structures that a phenomenologist discloses, for example, "axis of the world" or "centre of the world", do not constitute the meaning of a phenomenon. Biezais pointed out that "if phenomenology wishes to remain in the field of the empirical sciences, then it can only deal with the given, concrete, total phenomenon, or, we would say, with the facts of religious history" (Biezais 1979, 152).

In the manner of Haavio, Biezais also emphasized folk traditions, although focusing almost solely on Latvian religious figures, who he usually called gods. I would say that the Biezais kind of phenomenology focused on territorial comparison aiming at clarifying how a given local figure (god) was understood and ritually worshipped (see his *Die himmlische Götterfamilie der alten Letten* of 1972 and *Lichtgott der alten Letten* of 1976, both published in Sweden). Thus, like Haavio and Eliade (he was familiar with the latter's work), Biezais insisted on comparison, but he disagreed with their ahistorical interpretation of religious meanings; he argued that these can be understood only within their context, historically or otherwise.

When it comes to Honko, in the introduction to his post-doctoral study on Ingrian belief traditions *Geisterglaube in Ingermanland* (1962), he explicitly stated that the work belongs to regional studies; the second sub-chapter was entitled "Eine regionale Untersuchung". However, Honko followed a Haavioan type of phenomenological thinking when speaking of religious experience (*Erlebnis*), and *homo religiosus*. For example, in his *Suomalaiset kodinhaltiat* (Finnish Domestic Guardian Spirits, 1942), Haavio, leaning on Harva, had explained the existence of spirits as figments of human imagination, according to which each place and locality must have an invisible "host" or guardian who controls its use and who disciplines (morally or physically) those who do not behave correctly (transgressing the local society's social rules). Honko discussed this in detail by, first, introducing conceptual frameworks from social psychology (perceptual psychology and role analysis) and cultural anthropology (functionalism) and, second, by arguing that the "mechanism" behind the spirit-experience consists of locally known traditions rendering spirits and their encounters possible and providing each with a "role" that help locals to behave in a proper way and to interpret the event in an appropriate way.

Eliade's phenomenology and terminology did not play any special role in Honko's analysis; rather his occasional reference to Traitè d'histoire des religions (in German translation) was a way to argue that each tradition bearer, who has internalized their culture's notion of the existence of spirits, is a *homo religiosus*, whose behaviour needs to be analysed by using tools developed within the academic (that is, social scientific) study of religion. Concomitantly, Honko focused on demonstrating social functions (in an anthropological sense of the word), not singling out "ahistorical" meanings.

Honko's student and later colleague, Juha Pentikäinen (b. 1940), Professor of Comparative Religion at the University of Helsinki from 1970 to 2008, also began with a Haavioan perspective. In his doctoral dissertation, "The Nordic Dead-child Tradition: Nordic Dead-child Beings: A Study in Comparative Religion" (1968), Pentikäinen organized his archival data in a manner similar to that of Haavio, namely, thematically breaking down folk beliefs on dead children and discussing each theme in its geographical context. Thus the dissertation had little to do with phenomenology, which, as Pentikäinen stated in his introduction, merely formed a part of the study's conceptual background; and his conclusion was that of a folklorist. He did not refer to Eliade or any other scholar who could be identified as a phenomenologist of religion, nor did he discuss his methodological choices in the framework of phenomenological scholarship.

To sum up, both Honko and Pentikäinen carried out a regional study in folk beliefs. They did not compare these with other religious traditions to find out the "essence" or "meaning" of religion, what all these terms may convey. Neither did they, unlike Gerardus van der Leeuw (1956), for example, apply any variant of phenomenological philosophy to construct "ideal types" ("essences" or building-blocks of religion) to understand the logic or world view of *homo religiosus*. Their goal was neither understanding (*Verstehen*), nor a morphology or typology of religion (for example, variety in the manifestations of the sacred), but exploring a belief's social and societal use and function.

The Nordic Alliance and the Common Phenomenological Frame

By now, we have reached the point in this dialogue where we need to stop for a while and think more closely about what constitutes the scholarly domain of PoR and how the research carried out in Finland resonates with its diverse definitions. There is a well-grounded reason why the Swedish Professor of Comparative Religion at the University of Stockholm, Åke Hultkrantz (1920–2006), called the Finnish school of comparative religion "regional phenomenology". In his article "The Phenomenology of Religion. Aims and Methods", which appeared in *Temenos* in 1970, Hultkrantz rightly pointed out that the self-understanding of scholars working in this branch of scholarship differ significantly "at the very root". Nevertheless, in Sweden and Finland, there was no disagreement regarding the direction of research: "our discipline (in Stockholm) has provoked a special alliance (with Turku) ... under the fine leadership of Professor Honko". Scholars in both Nordic institutions "conduct advanced scientific research of a type which I should like to denote as predominantly phenomenological" (Hultkrantz 1970, 69).

Hultkrantz argued that his notion of phenomenology was more empirical than that of Eliade or the Dutch school of phenomenology, both of which tried, through introspection and platonic empathy, to fathom "the essence of religion". Hultkrantz passed a very stern judgment on van der Leeuw, who claimed that his notion of phenomenology was not metaphysical; according to Hultkrantz, it was too speculative, even incomprehensible, to be of much use for a seriously working empirical scholar of religion (Hultkrantz 1970, 72). As for Eliade, Hultkrantz held his interpretation of universal symbols "too weak and figureless to provide us with any meaningful interpretation of religion as such" (ibid., 78). In Hultkrantz's view, a PoR was methodologically justified on the grounds that "it facilitates comparisons between different religious areas" (ibid.).

There are two basic prerequisites that, according to Hultkrantz, are required to make PoR successful: (1) "the seeking of objectiveness and neutrality"; and (2) "the connection with the problems within anthropology (including ethnology) and folklore". The viability of PoR as "the systematic study of the forms of religion" arises from its cross-cultural task in aiming to gain empirically valid knowledge on religion as a global, human phenomenon. PoR constitutes a specific domain in which scholars "make careful inventories of religious categories throughout the world, providing in this way a synthesized complete atlas of the morphology of conceptions, rites and myths" (Hultkrantz 1970, 78).

It is this global PoR that forms the larger picture against which the Finnish regional-studies perspective becomes comprehensible. In Hultkrantz's mapping of the field, regional phenomenology is a stage on the way to a larger goal, the looming universal phenomenology (Hultkrantz 1970, 82). As for Finland, as we have seen, scholars in the field have classified, identified, and compared types, forms, functions and structures of religious representations not so much on a worldwide scale, but rather within the boundaries of a limited geographic area. Genre analysis was a distinct method, developed by folklorists, which enabled the attainment of a deeper level of analysis of ethnographic data on religious representations. It was a primary tool for folklorists to classify data for archival purposes. In the field of religion, the method has played an important role as a tool for source criticism because different genres of religious tradition convey narrative-specific information in local and historical contexts.

As Lauri Honko defined the method, genre analysis is a taxonomical device that is designed by scholars to recognize, classify, name and make distinctions in orally transmitted narrative tradition. These distinctions convey information on the narrators' religion and worldview. In his study on Ingrian spirits mentioned above, Honko discerned the following narrative genres: myths, etiological tales, incantations, prayer charms, memorates, beliefs, belief legends, historical legends, migratory tales, amusing stories, fairy tales, pedagogical fict(ions), laments, metaphors and ritual accounts (Honko 1962). From a genre analytic point of view, religion is a context-dependent and communicative-specific variable that is collectively shared, but that constitutes an individually alternating repertoire of genre-specific discourses that help to analyse and explain its contents (cf. Pentikäinen 1978).

For instance, an ethnographer's recurrent encounter of narratives in which the informant describes ways of dealing with the spirit of fire does not actually testify to the real existence of such a spirit; instead, it points to the behavioural norms, rules, and prohibitions connected with the treating of fire in those contexts in which special social values are at stake. Prohibitions, rules of avoidance, and behavioural norms are markers by which fire is made "sacred", that is, set apart and forbidden. A religion's narrative world may consist of diverse noumenal agents, such as gods, ghosts, spirits of specific sites in a domestic setting or in nature. However, a scholar of religion aiming at analysing these narratives makes a serious mistake by taking narratives at their face value or by insisting on the existence of a specific agent or an item in the religious world under scrutiny.

Regional phenomenology provides an excellent opportunity for the critical analysis of tradition-specific features by which such worlds are construed in specific value-laden settings. Haavio's critical remarks on Pentikäinen's study of Nordic dead-child beings are a case in point. While the author argued for the reckoning of serious religious belief in dead-child beings in his material, Haavio objected by saying that the main question is not religious, but social. Dead-child beings are conceived as social agents, even though they lack social status in the community. Haavio presents a nice analogy by saying that the position of the departed can be compared to a neglected minority group, which begins to disturb the community for the reason that their presence obscures the boundaries by which members make sense of their belonging to the community (Haavio 1969, 240). I think that Haavio's observation is remarkable in light of current immigration issues that scholars struggle to come grips with. Haavio's view can be taken to explain and understand why immigrants face hatred, racism, and discrimination in today's migration situation.

Here we can see that phenomenological comparison explains not only similarities in socio-religious representations, but also in cognitive information-processing regarding ambivalent agents, whether deities, dead beings or immigrants. Haavio was able to come up with a general mechanism that governs human behaviour, whether the context is religious or non-religious.

Helsinki School of Phenomenology Sets the Stage

Haavio, Honko and Pentikäinen all represent a Hultkrantzian type of regional phenomenology, usually bypassed in standard works on PoR (for example, Cox 2006; Sharpe 1998). However, not all Finnish scholars of religion flocked in their wake. Of these, I would like to mention Seppo Syrjänen, Terhi Utriainen, and René Gothóni (see also Laitila 2004, 2007). These scholars were inspired by new versions of old PoR or by continental phenomenological philosophy. The most important event, bringing together them and other Finnish and international scholars of methodological issues, was the 2002 conference in Helsinki. I will have a few words to say about it later, together with Gothóni. I will first turn to Syrjänen and Utriainen.

As a Lutheran theologian, Seppo Syrjänen (1939–1988) was a typical representative of old (North European) PoR. He worked in Pakistan for years as a missionary, and later for the Helsinki-based Finnish Missionary Society. His academic work, terminated by his premature death, was known to the international audience interested in missions among Muslims, but did not have an impact on Finnish religious studies.

As the title of his dissertation indicates, *In Search of Meaning and Identity: Conversion to Christianity in Pakistani Muslim Culture* (1984), Syrjänen focused on questions important for several phenomenologists of religion: what does religion mean for a believer? How can a believer's way of constructing and making sense of religion be understood? Nevertheless, in his discussion of theory and method, Syrjänen merely refers to PoR (understood in a traditional Dutch and German sense) and, following Hultkrantz (1973, 78–101), defines it as a perspective not a method, probably because he was more interested in the theological motives of Muslim converts than, for example, the "essence" of a phenomenon called conversion.

Although his dissertation did not generate methodological discussion, he was instrumental in another way, namely, by introducing Jacques Waardenburg (1930–2015) to the Finnish scholars of religion. Waardenburg's studies on Islam and his emphasis that phenomenology is about the intention of believers had a strong influence on Syrjänen. Waardenburg was also his opponent in the public defence of his dissertation and later visited Finland several times, lecturing on phenomenology. Syrjänen was also one of the two translators of Waardenburg's introduction to comparative religion, entitled *Religionen und Religion: Systematische Einführung in die Religionswisssenschaft*, which appeared in 1986 simultaneously in German and Finnish.

Terhi Utriainen (b. 1962), Professor of Religious Studies at the University of Turku since January 2018, has during her academic career focused on a few topics, such as the human body, particularly female or dead bodies, and post-secular beliefs in angels (see, for example, Utriainen 1999; 2017). In her study of the body, Utriainen has partly applied Julia Kristeva's conception of "abject", human horror in the breakdown of meaning, to understand the identity transformation of the subject in relation to another subjects. She argues that her interest in phenomenology is limited to finding out what is common, or overarching, in such changes (Utriainen 2006, 18). However, her emphasis on the general structures of human experience (for example, Utriainen 1999, 40–43) propels her study toward a kind of PoR as well, even though her philosophical guide, Maurice Merleau-Ponty's famous *Phenomenology of Perception* (originally in French in 1945), is not counted as a standard work in the field.

Why do I think that Utriainen's studies have connections to, and partly belong to, the field of PoR? The connecting link, in my opinion, is Utriainen's leaning on Merleau-Ponty's view that our perception and understanding of reality and being in the world is bodily-mediated; thus, if our being-in-the-world is shaped by social practices related to the body, then comparison and understanding of "religion" have a concrete basis. For example, in her dissertation, Utriainen pointed out how women participating in end-of-life care used their involvement with dying and the dead to give their corporeal co-existence a meaning, which Utriainen called "being authentically present" (Utriainen 1999, 286). In her Finnish-language *Naked and Clothed: Bounds of Body and*

Religion (Utriainen 2006), she proceeded along the same lines. The study was about death-related events and episodes as narrated (in written form) by a large number of informants, in addition to drawing on pertinent Christian data, particularly biblical texts relative to being naked or clothed. In her analysis, Utriainen illustrated how in narratives, including the Bible, bodily experiences of being naked or clothed gave rise to new interpretative practices that led the narrator to a new "reality" that Utriainen called "ontological safety" (Utriainen 2006, 264).

In my view, in her studies, Utriainen transfers the focus of phenomenological analyses from typologizing ancient folklore and religious history to making sense of present praxis, with an emphasis on lived, Christianity-related, religiosity. Here, her research certainly differs from that of Haavio, Honko and Pentikäinen. She does not try to find out the "original" master story or to show the social functions of a given phenomenon. Instead, she is interested in the subject's action in a concrete situation, such as being naked/clothed. In a way reminiscent of early Honko, she also stresses a person's own activity in creating her identity as an existential and social being, and as an individual.

I see this transformation of regional phenomenology like a reversed version of Mary Douglas's idea that ontology (existence), society, and the way in which social rules "educate" an individual's body, are closely connected. However, where Douglas tried to find out the logic by which conceptions of the self, society, and human body are linked socially (Douglas 2000), Utriainen employs the metaphor of being undressed in analysing end-of-life situations in hospice in contexts in which the individuality of a dying person is laid bare. Following the clues provided by Kristeva, she suggests (2006, 13–19) that what is common to being naked or clothed in a particular situation is that people feel somehow anxious because they experience the situation as a collapse of borders between ontology, society and personal identity and that this "feeling anxious" brings about rethinking that changes both mind and body. The study argues that what guides a person's orientation in a given moment is *not* given (although "models" for, and of, it exist in societal and other context), but is rather "called forth" by the situation. Utriainen thus connects the study of experience and phenomena with the study of lived religiosity and humans as conscious agents in steering their life and is, therefore, one example of the possibilities of combining phenomenology and social science, which Honko stressed and which also has been suggested, among others, by Ilkka Pyysiäinen, who we discuss below.

My third choice, Professor Emeritus of Comparative Religion at the University of Helsinki René Gothóni (b. 1950), focused on monasticism and pilgrimage. His doctoral dissertation, *Modes of Life of Theravāda Monks: A Case Study of Buddhist Monasticism in Sri Lanka* (1982), represents rather an anthropological than phenomenological tradition. Since the 1990s, he has been interested in Orthodox Christian monasticism in Athos, Greece (for example, Gothóni 1993). The shift in field – based on his personal religious orientation, which later led to his conversion to Orthodoxy – also brought a shift in methodology. While not abandoning anthropological fieldwork, in his study of Athos, Gothóni posed to his fieldwork data a question reminiscent of that of Syrjänen: How it is possible for a scholar to understand the world and mindset of Orthodox monks and pilgrims?

According to Gothóni, this is possible by using a tripartite model of understanding. It consists of (1) critical inspection of the term "religion", (2) suspense of one's value judgment, and (3) ability to critical analysis (Gothóni 2000, 35–43). He adds that a scholar of religion needs first to become emotionally involved "in our subject and its inherent problems", and then to detach from them (ibid., 44). The three points and the two additions are neither linked together nor explained. Neither does he connect his sketch with previous phenomenological discussions, although it bears similarities, for example, with Husserlian "steps" making up a phenomenological method (see Ryba 2006, 103–104; cf. Gothóni 2004).

In the context of the above-mentioned international workshop in Helsinki in 2002, entitled "Approaches in Comparative Religion Reconsidered", Gothóni reformulated his view. In a response to Donald Wiebe's presentation "Beyond Thick Descriptions and Interpretive Sciences: Explaining Religious Meaning" (Wiebe 2005), where Wiebe argued for re-establishing a cognitive approach to the scientific study of religion, Gothóni aimed at building a counter-argument by referring to an issue of understanding the other (Gothóni 2005). However, there was no common meeting point between Wiebe's naturalistic, evolutionary register and Gothóni's reference to hermeneutics, based on Hans-Georg Gadamer's *Wahrheit und Methode* (first published in 1960). Where Wiebe's methodological position was based on a claim to establish scientific explanation of religious behaviour, thought and experience, Gothóni referred to the inter-subjective potential in language (Gothóni 2005, 122) in understanding and "feeling" the other. Gothóni's position, therefore, was neither a comment on Wiebe's paper nor a novelty. Within traditional PoR, privileging the view of the person under study has been a standard practice.

In principle, I see Gothóni's insistence on phenomenological philosophy as important, although not sufficiently used within PoR (cf. Laitila 2004; Ryba 2006). After all, for example Kant, Hegel, Husserl and Heidegger had a major impact on a certain type of PoR; and Martti Haavio made use of etymologies (for example, Haavio 1959); so why not try to learn something about Gadamer's explorations on the meaning of texts and the scholar's limits in understanding them (cf. Smith 2017).

On the other hand, I regard Gothóni's manner of remaining on the level of assertions and claims (instead of exemplifying his approach in detail), as well as his presupposition that religion has some unchanging "core" which can be reached solely by analysing religious terms (see Gothóni 2004), as methodologically problematic. I fully agree that inter-subjectivity is important if we try to understand religious phenomena – Gavin Flood (whom Gothóni does not refer to) suggested one way to make use of Gadamer in order to go "beyond phenomenology" – but a mere statement of that is of little help in scholarly practice. To understand all aspects of religiosity, we need a theoretical framework which takes into account not only verbal (or rational) expressions of what is considered religion or religious, but also their affective and material aspects (for example, Utriainen's studies, or some elaboration of van der Leeuw's "typologizing method"; van der Leeuw 1956, 672–675). To achieve this kind on "realistic" turn, we also need re-remembering, rereading and rethinking of both the Finnish and international legacies of PoR.

Besides Utriainen, another example of how to combine empirical and phenomenological approaches is Nils G. Holm (b. 1943). Now retired, he was Professor of Comparative Religion at the Åbo Akademi University from 1978 to 2008. His area of expertise is actually psychology of religion, but because phenomenology and psychology cannot, in my opinion, be separated, I see his studies as relevant for phenomenology proper as well, more so because he himself has occasionally spoken of "psychophenomenology" (Holm 2006, 7) and, to use traditional terms, has emphasized the need of "hermeneutical" approach in explaining religious phenomena (see Holm 2005).

By phenomenology, Holm means "description of the most important elements and parts of religion" (Holm 2006, 7), such as myths and rituals. By psychology, he means a role theory, adapted from Hjalmar Sundén (1908–1993), a Swedish Professor of Psychology of Religion in Uppsala. Much simplified, Holm's (and partly also Sundén's) argument is that those "most important elements" offer various roles, which a believer may adopt relative to a religious figure, from gods and heroes to any important being within a given religious tradition. A comparative analysis of the "roles" a person takes may reveal something important about "lived religion", the ways humans construct, by their actions and narratives, and through their bodies, "practices" that we can term "religions". One may also call them "categories", and this brings us to the study of mind in general, or cognitive studies.

Turku Strikes Back: Re-establishing the Science of Religion

What comes to the cognitive turn in the study of religion, its emergence has been especially harsh on conventional methodologies, particularly on phenomenological and hermeneutic approaches to religion (cf. Lawson and McCauley 1993). There are, however, points of contact between phenomenology and cognitive science of religion (CSR) that need to be paid attention to. Ilkka Pyysiäinen (b. 1959), with whom I have worked closely, uses in his analysis an *explanandum* that is closely linked with the interest of knowledge among phenomenologists of religion (cf. Pyysiäinen 2004). Before going to it, let me first explain the emergence of the CSR in Finland, in which Pyysiäinen and I were instrumental.

In 1995, we applied to Rector of the University of Helsinki to invite Professor E. Thomas Lawson from the Western Michigan University in Kalamazoo as a guest of the university to give lectures on CSR. The Rector accepted our proposal. The visit marked a big change, especially in Ilkka Pyysiäinen's and to a certain extent also in my own way of thinking about religion as a conceptual entity. Another big change took place when Lauri Honko retired a year after, in 1996, and I was appointed to become Honko's successor as Professor of Comparative Religion at the University of Turku. At the time of the Donner Institute[6] conference on methodology in Turku in the summer of 1997, Ilkka Pyysiäinen, Tom Lawson, Pascal Boyer and I enjoyed the warmth of the sauna together and took up the issue of organizing a small-scale international workshop on CSR in Finland. The workshop took place two years later, in June 1999, on the island of Seili, a research station of the University of Turku at the Archipelago Sea off Turku. Papers based on talks at the conference were edited by Ilkka and me and published by Continuum in 2002 under the title *Current Approaches in the Cognitive Science of Religion*. Besides that, Pyysiäinen has published several books in the field of CSR (Pyysiäinen 2001, 2004, 2009).

Pyysiäinen has consistently advanced his methodological conviction according to which there exist real phenomena that can be taken to form the basis of what is generally known and meant by the folk-category "religion". The point of departure in his cognitive theorizing is based on the view that it is necessary to distinguish the underlying mechanism of religion. This justifies the value of a separate concept of religion, distinct from worldview, society, nation, sense of belonging, social order, social cohesion, orientation, psychodynamic conflict or whatever is taken as an *explanans* of religion (Pyysiäinen 2001, 143–158; 2002, 112–113, 124–127). Pyysiäinen locates the constraining characteristic of religion in the domain-specificity of the human mind and its evolutionary

---

6. The Donner Institute is a private institute maintained by Åbo Akademi University. Founded in 1958, the institute focuses on supporting religious studies by grants, by organizing conferences and seminars, and by hosting the largest Nordic library on comparative religion.

evolved intuitive ontology. He grounds his theorizing on the concept of counter-intuitiveness, which is a technical term proposed by the French anthropologist and scholar of human cognition Pascal Boyer to refer to a group of phenomena which violate intuitive expectations regarding the properties of ontological categories such as plant, artifact, animal and person (on PoR and CSR, see Pyysiäinen 2004, 211–218). According to Boyer, in religious traditions the world over counter-intuitive representations have an impact on the ways in which cultural information is processed in the human mind in order to produce specific social effects in people (Boyer 2001, 65).

Without going further into Boyer's cognitive theory of religion, I will just say that Pyysiäinen has employed the theory extensively in his studies on the spread of counter-intuitive ideas both in world religions and in folk religions. For Pyysiäinen, counter-intuitiveness is instrumental in identifying real, cross-culturally recurrent phenomena for analysis. On the one hand his approach is a radical critique and an alternative to PoR as practised in Finland, on the other an amicable call for a division of labour in order to overcome limitations of PoR in its attempt to describe mental contents of the subject. He argues that CSR can base a factual science of the mind for phenomenological descriptions with its underlying causal mechanisms (Pyysiäinen 2004, 2009; we return this in our final comments).

As for my own approach to religion, I have theorized the concept of the sacred, also much studied in PoR, from the standpoint of CSR. Toward the end of the 1980s, at the time when I was writing my doctoral dissertation, I was inspired by Mary Douglas's ideas revolving around perceptual schemes, categorization skills and systems of classification in which notions of anomaly and ambiguity in thinking about the human body, space and territoriality played a key role in analysing ethnographic data (Anttonen 1996; Douglas 1989). I started my theorizing on religion from a Durkheimian understanding (as did Douglas), and consequently explained the sacred on the basis of the term's attributions, whether employed in religious or non-religious contexts of discourse. In addition to Mary Douglas, I drew heavily on the works of Jonathan Z. Smith, Dan Sperber, George Lakoff, and Mark Johnson. I came up with a theory of the sacred as a boundary category.

I have argued in my publications (for example, Anttonen 1996, 2000, 2002, 2004) that there exist in human languages and cultures the world over both vernacular and more elaborate theological, that is, doctrinally codified, notions of the sacred, which goes to show that human beings possess an evolutionary evolved capacity to make value-laden distinctions between events, objects, sites, places and times, persons and animals, which leads them, by means of rituals, to set specific, for example, anomalous and ambiguous, members of a category apart from other similarly classified entities, and in this way express the category's symbolic value and content.

In order to understand, for example, the socio-cognitive constraints in dietary rules or in hunting rituals, I traced the logic behind the system of categorization in which pigs among the Jews and Muslims or bears among the peoples of the circumpolar region are assigned a status of a sacred animal, forbidden, taboo and thus sacred for particular persons acting in particular positions and situations. In this, I was very much influenced by the work of Lakoff and Johnson, who suggest a shift from the fictive nature of phenomenological approaches to a more systematic knowledge on the operations of the human mind. I took seriously their criticism regarding the notion of "the phenomenological person", who, according to them, "through phenomenological introspection alone can discover everything there is to know about the mind and nature of experience". Although they gave credit to phenomenological approaches in pointing out valuable structures of human experience, I was convinced of their claim that phenomenological reflection needs to be supplemented by empirical research into the cognitive unconscious (Lakoff and Johnson 1999, 5).

Final Comments

Discussion on PoR in the present-day methodological situation of the academic study of religion in Finland may seem to be out of place. PoR suffers from loss of reputation, sometimes attributed to its (alleged) inherent theological agenda (cf. Fitzgerald 2000, 10; Ryba 2006, 91–92). Our disciplinary landscape has changed dramatically in the twenty-first century and practitioners in the field have a wide array of methodological choices to select for their analytic or descriptive purposes. Traditionally, methodological choices within religious studies have been divided into understanding and explaining religion. The former is considered to aspire to comprehend religions and religious realities emphatically as matrices of life-space, in which people make sense of their experiences both to themselves and to others (cf. Paden 2000). The latter, applying explanatory methodology, is said to approach religion either from the cognitive and/or social scientific standpoint. Present discursive methodology often disregards this kind of division and rather pays attention to, for example, how the category of religion is constructed by public print or digital media, or other textual data, or explores why discourse on religion leaks into diverse secular contexts, and for what reasons (see McCutcheon 2013, 342; Taira 2013).

I agree that traditional PoR is rarely discussed, and even more rarely pursued, in Finland. Scholars in religious studies departments still, of course, investigate what the "founding-fathers" of PoR called phenomena (such as various beliefs and actions related to "gods"), but while for example Eliade and van der Leeuw were in quest of the "origins" or "essence" of religion and often focused on "world religions", aiming to describe systematically what religion actually is, apart from human beings, Finnish scholars of religion have always been more empirically-oriented and, with a few exceptions, have stressed the role of human practice and material context in the making and understanding of religion.

This raises a question: do we still need PoR, traditional or otherwise? Ilkka Pyysiäinen, among others, suggested that PoR is needed "to develop taxonomies, typologies, or catalogues of religious representations and the related behaviours" (Pyysiäinen 2000, 130), while cognitive science, or other empirical/experimental approach, would be responsible for the actual explanation. It is, of course, possible to attribute PoR a descriptive role and leave the analysis for some "real" science. However, in my opinion, for example Ann Taves (2009) has pointed out that PoR can be "ennobled" to cover both description and analysis.

As I suggested above, we may also rethink traditional PoR and, without privileging any ontology, textual approach, or mind (as separated from the body) try to develop a regionally or globally comparative analysis, which takes into account historical contexts, social functions, psychological motivations, cognitive strategies and affects – briefly, behaviours and thoughts which I classify as (religious) phenomena (cf. Ryba 2006, 99–103). The kind of analysis which I have in mind considers phenomena as descriptions of (concrete and abstract) relations, which we re-describe (or re-categorize) as, for example, religious or secular, and thus make "objects" of our academic study to understand, how and why these relations materialized, were described in a certain way and were used in societal, political, economic and other arenas of human life (cf. Holm 2006; Hultkrantz 1973, 97–99; Laitila 2017; Ryba 2006, 95–97, 111–112; Utriainen 2017). This could be one way of developing a "realistic" PoR, a study of human praxis embodying in multiple abstract and concrete forms.

References

Anttonen, Veikko. 1987. *Uno Harva ja suomalainen uskontotiede* [*Uno Harva and the Science of Religion in Finland*]. Helsinki: Suomalaisen Kirjallisuuden Seura.

Anttonen, Veikko. 1996. "Rethinking the Sacred: The Notions of 'Human Body' and 'Territory' in Conceptualizing Religion." In *The Sacred and its Scholars: Comparative Methodologies for the Study of Primary Religious Data*, edited by Thomas A. Idinopulos and Edward A. Yonan, 36–64. Leiden: Brill. https://doi.org/10.1163/9789004378957_005

Anttonen, Veikko. 2000. "The Sacred." In *Guide to the Study of Religion*, edited by Willi Braun and Russell T. McCutcheon, 271–282. London: Cassell.

Anttonen, Veikko. 2002. "Identifying the Generative Mechanisms of Religion. The Issue of Origin Revisited." In *Current Approaches in the Cognitive Science of Religion*, edited by Ilkka Pyysiäinen and Veikko Anttonen, 14–37. London: Continuum.

Anttonen, Veikko. 2004. "Pathways to Knowledge in Comparative Religion." In *Religion as a Human Capacity*. A Festschrift in Honor of E. Thomas Lawson, edited by Timothy Light and Brian C. Wilson, 105–119. Leiden: Brill. https://doi.org/10.1163/9789047401698_008

Anttonen, Veikko. 2012. "Literary Representation of Oral Religion. Organizing Principles in Mikael Agricola's List of Mythological Agents in Late Medieval Finland." In *More Than Mythology. Narratives, Ritual Practices and Regional Distribution in Pre-Christian Scandinavian Religions*, edited by Catharina Raudvere & Jens Peter Schødt, 185–223. Lund: Nordic Academic Press.

Biezais, Harald. 1979. "Typology of Religion and the Phenomenological Method." In *Science of Religion. Studies in Methodology*, Proceedings of the Study Conference of the International Association for the History of Religions, held in Turku, Finland, 27–31 August 1973, edited by Lauri Honko, 143–161. The Hague: Mouton. https://doi.org/10.1515/9783110814507.143

Boyer, Pascal. 1994. *The Naturalness of Religious Ideas: A Cognitive Theory of Religion*. Berkeley, CA: University of California Press.

Boyer, Pascal. 2001. *Religion Explained: The Evolutionary Origins of Religious Thought*. New York: Basic Books.

Cox, James L. 2006. *A Guide to the Phenomenology of Religion*. London: T. & T. Clark International.

Douglas, Mary. 1989 [1966]. *Purity and Danger: An Analysis of the Concepts of Pollution and Taboo*. London: Ark Paperbacks.

Douglas, Mary. 2000 (1970). *Natural Symbols: Explorations in Cosmology*. London: Barrie & Rockliff.

Fitzgerald, Timothy 2000. *The Ideology of Religious Studies*. New York: Oxford University Press.

Geertz, Armin W. and Russell T. McCutcheon. 2000. "The Role of Method and Theory in the IAHR." In *Perspectives on Method and Theory in the Study of Religion*, Adjunct Proceedings of the XVIIth Congress for the History of Religions,

Mexico City, 1995, edited by Armin W. Geertz and Russell T. McCutcheon, 3–37. Leiden: Brill. https://doi.org/10.1163/9789004308466_015

Gothóni, René. 1993. *Paradise within Reach: Monasticism and Pilgrimage on Mt Athos.* Helsinki: Helsinki University Press.

Gothóni, René. 2000. *Attitudes and Interpretations in Comparative Religion.* FF Communications 272. Helsinki: Academia Scientiarum Fennica.

Gothóni, René. 2004. "Ymmärtäminen uskontotieteessä" ["Understanding in Comparative Religion"]. In *Mikä ihmeen uskonto? Suomalaisten tutkijoiden puheenvuoroja uskonnosta [What on Earth is Religion? Finnish Scholars Speak about Religion]*, edited by Tom Sjöblom and Terhi Utriainen, 37–49. Helsinki: Department of Comparative Religion.

Gothóni, René. 2005. "Understanding the Other." In *How to do Comparative Religion? Three Ways, Many Goals*, edited René Gothóni, 99–126. Religion and Reason 44. Berlin: de Gruyter. https://doi.org/10.1515/9783110922608.99

Haavio, Martti. 1959. *Karjalan jumalat: Uskontotieteellinen tutkimus [Gods of Karelia: A Study in Comparative Religion]*. Porvoo: WSOY.

Haavio, Martti. 1961. *Kuolemattonten lehdot: Sämpsöi Pellervoisen arvoitus* [Sacred Groves of the Immortal: The Enigma of Sämpsöi Pellervoinen]. Porvoo: WSOY.

Haavio, Martti. 1969. "Review: The Nordic Dead-Child Tradition." *Temenos* 5: 238–243.

Holm, Nils G. 2005. "The Limits of Explaining in Religious Studies." In *How to do Comparative Religion? Three Ways, Many Goals*, edited René Gothóni, 83–91. Religion and Reason 44. Berlin: de Gruyter. https://doi.org/10.1515/9783110922608.83

Holm, Nils G. 2006. *Människans symboliska verklighetsbygge: En psykofenomenologisk studie [Human Symbolic Construction of Reality: A Psychophenomenological Study]*. Religionsvetenskapliga skrifter 40. Åbo: Åbo Akademi.

Holmberg [Harva], Uno. 1922. *Der Baum des Lebens.* Annales Academiae Scientiarum Fennicae B 16:3. Helsinki: Academia Scientiarum Fennica.

Honko, Lauri. 1962. *Geisterglaube in Ingermanland I.* FF Communications 185. Helsinki: Academia Scientiarum Fennica.

Honko, Lauri. (ed.). 1979. *Science of Religion. Studies in Methodology*, Proceedings of the Study Conference of the International Association for the History of Religions, held in Turku, Finland, 27–31 August 1973. The Hague: Mouton. https://doi.org/10.1515/9783110814507

Hultkrantz, Åke. 1970. "The Phenomenology of Religion: Aims and Methods." *Temenos* 6: 68–88.

Hultkrantz, Åke. 1973. *Metodvägar inom den jämförande religionsforskning* [*Methods in Comparative Religion*]. Stockholm: Esselte Studium.

Laitila, Teuvo. 2004. "Kokemus, merkitys, historia: Uskontofenomenologisia lähtökohtia ihmisen uskonnollisuuden tutkimiseen" ["Experience, Meaning, History: Phenomenological Starting-points for the Study of Human Religiosity"]. *Uskonnon paikka: Kirjoituksia uskontoteorioiden rajoista* [*The Place of Religion: Essays on the Borders of Theories on Religion*], edited by Outi Fingerroos, Minna Opas and Teemu Taira, 71–114. Tietolipas 205. Helsinki: Suomalaisen Kirjallisuuden Seura.

Laitila, Teuvo. 2007. "From Reality to Subject: A Sympathetic, yet Critical Reading of Eliade." *Temenos* 43(1): 99–114. https://doi.org/10.33356/temenos.4626

Laitila, Teuvo. 2017. *Jumalat, haltiat ja pyhät: Eletty ortodoksisuus Karjalassa 1000–1900* [*Gods, Spirits and Saints: Lived Orthodox Christianity in Karelia, 1000-1900*]. Suomen kirkkohistoriallisen seuran toimituksia 234. Helsinki: Suomen kirkkohistoriallinen seura.

Lakoff, George and Mark Johnson. 1999. *Philosophy in the Flesh: The Embodied Mind and its Challenge to Western Thought*. New York: Basic Books.

Lawson, E. Thomas and Robert N. McCauley. 1993. "Crisis of Conscience, Riddle of Identity: Making Space for Cognitive Approach to Religious Phenomena." *Journal of American Academy of Religion* 61: 201–223. https://doi.org/10.1093/jaarel/lxi.2.201

Liikanen, Ilkka. 1995. *Fennomania ja kansa* [*The Fennoman Movement and the People*]. Diss. Helsinki: Suomen historiallinen seura.

McCutcheon, Russell T. 2013. "A Modest Proposal on Method." *Method and Theory in the Study of Religion* 25(4–5): 339–49.

Paden, William E. 2000. "World." In *Guide to the Study of Religion*, edited by Willi Braun and Russell T. McCutcheon, 334–347. London: Cassell.

Pentikäinen, Juha. 1968. *The Nordic Dead-Child Tradition*. FF Communication 202. Helsinki: Academia Scientiarum Fennica.

Pentikäinen, Juha. 1978. *Oral Repertoire and World View: An Anthropological Study of Marina Takalo's Life History*. FF Communications 219. Helsinki: Academia Scientiarum Fennica.

Pyysiäinen, Ilkka. 2000. "Phenomenology of Religion and Cognitive Science: The Case of Religious Experience. Why Phenomenology and Cognitive Science? Categories, Taxonomies and Comparison." *Temenos* 35–36: 125–153. https://doi.org/10.33356/temenos.4865

Pyysiäinen, Ilkka. 2001. *How Religion Works: Towards a New Cognitive Science of Religion*. Leiden: Brill.

Pyysiäinen, Ilkka. 2002. "Religion and the Counter-Intuitive." In *Current Approaches in the Cognitive Science of Religion*, edited by Ilkka Pyysiäinen and Veikko Anttonen, 110–132. London: Continuum.

Pyysiäinen, Ilkka. 2004. *Magic, Miracles, and Religion: A Scientist's Perspective.* Walnut Creek, CA: AltaMira Press.

Pyysiäinen, Ilkka. 2009. *Supernatural Agents: Why We Believe in Souls, Gods and Buddhas.* New York: Oxford University Press.

Ryba, Thomas. 2006. "Phenomenology of Religion." In *The Blackwell Companion to the Study of Religion*, edited by Robert A. Segal, 91–121. Malden, MA: Blackwell. https://doi.org/10.1002/9781405168748.ch5

Sharpe, Eric. 1998. *Comparative Religion: A History*, 2nd edition. London: Duckworth.

Smith, James K. A. 2017. "Staging an Encounter between Anthropology and Philosophy: Hits and Misses in the Work of Michael Jackson." *Review in Anthropology* 46(4): 151–163. https://doi.org/10.1080/00938157.2017.140 8394

Stocking Jr., George W. 1984. The Ethnographer's Magic: Fieldwork in British Anthropology from Tylor to Malinowski. In *Observers Observed: Essays on Ethnographic Fieldwork*, edited by George W. Stocking Jr., 70–120. Madison, WI: University of Wisconsin Press.

Syrjänen, Seppo. 1984. *In Search of Meaning and Identity: Conversion to Christianity in Pakistani Muslim Culture.* Annals of the Finnish Society for Missiology and Ecumenics 45. Helsinki: The Finnish Society for Missiology and Ecumenics.

Taira, Teemu. 2013. "Making Space for Discursive Study in Religious Studies." *Religion* 43(1): 26–45.

Tarkka, Lotte. 1987. "Tutkimuksia 'puiden varjojen muistoista': Martti Haavion *Kuolemattonten lehtojen* metodin arviointia [Studies in the 'Memories of the Shadows of the Trees': An Evaluation of Martti Haavio's Method in His Sacred Groves of the Immortal]." *Suomen Antropologi* 12(2): 60–72.

Taves, Ann. 2009. *Religious Experience Reconsidered: A Building-block Approach to the Study of Religion and Other Special Things.* Princeton, NJ: Princeton University Press.

Utriainen, Terhi. 1999. *Läsnä, riisuttu, puhdas: Uskontoantropologinen tutkimus naisista kuolevan vierellä [Present, Naked, Pure: A Study in the Anthropology of Religion on Women by the Side of the Dying].* Suomalaisen Kirjallisuuden Seuran Toimituksia 751. Helsinki: Suomalaisen Kirjallisuuden Seura.

Utriainen, Terhi. 2006. *Alaston ja puettu: Ruumiin ja uskonnon ääret [Naked and Clothed: Bounds of Body and Religion].* Tampere: Vastapaino.

Utriainen, Terhi. 2017. *Enkeleitä työpöydällä: Arjen ja lumon etnografiaa [Angels on the Study Desk: Ethnography of Everyday and Enchantment].* Tietolipas 257. Helsinki: Suomalaisen Kirjallisuuden Seura.

van der Leeuw, Gerardus. 1956 [1933]. *Phänomenologie der Religion*. Tübingen: Mohr.

Wiebe, Donald. 2005. "Beyond Thick Descriptions and Interpretive Sciences: Explaining Religious Meaning." In *How to do Comparative Religion? Three Ways, Many Goals*, edited by René Gothóni, 65–82. Berlin: de Gruyter. https://doi.org/10.1515/9783110922608.65

3

Phenomenology of Religion Meets Theory of Science - A Lethal Encounter

Interviews with Peter Antes and Hubert Seiwert (Germany)

KATJA TRIPLETT

Peter Antes (b. 1942) is a retired professor for the study of religions at the University of Hannover, Germany. A specialist in Islam within the study of religions, he graduated in 1970 with Master of Arts in Study of Religions having studied Roman Catholic Theology and Islamic Studies at the Universities of Freiburg/Breisgau and Paris. DTheol. (1970) DPhil. (1971). He acquired his postdoctoral qualification (*Habilitation*) in the history and comparative study of religion. In 1973 he became professor for the study of religions in Hannover. He lectured worldwide and from 1995 to 2000 he acted as vice-president of the IAHR. From 2000 to 2005 he was its president. He is an Honorary Life Member of the IAHR.

Hubert Seiwert (b. 1949) is a retired professor at the University of Leipzig. He studied in Bonn, obtaining a doctorate there in the study of religions in 1978. He specializes in the field of Chinese religions, among others. He was a Visiting Scholar at Wolfson College, University of Oxford from 2004 to 2006. Since 2016 he has been Permanent Senior Fellow at the Centre for Advanced Studies in the Humanities and Social Sciences "Multiple Secularities – Beyond the West, Beyond Modernities", University of Leipzig. He is an Honorary Life Member of the IAHR.

Keywords: phenomenology of religion, German academia, Rudolf Otto, Friedrich Heiler, Annemarie Schimmel

Katja Triplett

Introduction

Phenomenology of religion started to disappear during the 1960s and 70s in Germany and has remained marginal as a method in the comparative study of religions, with some notable exceptions mentioned in the interviews with Peter Antes and Hubert Seiwert. The two interviewees also address developments in Germany between 1948/9 and 1990 covering what was happening in two nations during the German division and two quite different academic cultures. German language publications of relevance appeared also in other European countries. Revisiting the history of the phenomenology of religion (PoR) in the memory of scholars in German-language contexts thus includes scholars active in Switzerland and Austria and other countries.[1] The interview texts with the commentaries aim to give an overview of the overall situation and the current state of debate. The two interviewees both clearly emphasize in differing ways that they reject, even strongly disapprove of, PoR because of significant flaws. They point out these flaws and recount the academic and political contexts of past debates.

Antes is one of the witnesses of the demise of PoR in Germany in the 1970s and has remained a strong defender of the academic study of religions.

Seiwert belonged to a group of young students who vehemently criticized PoR in the 1970s. From 1979 to 1994, the year he became professor in Leipzig, he worked at the University of Hannover. An essay with his critique appeared as early as 1977 in the journal *Zeitschrift für Missionswissenschaft und Religionswissenschaft* (Journal for Missionary Studies and Religious Studies). The essay of the then doctoral student is accompanied by a short supportive introduction by a professor in the field: Peter Antes. In his essay, Seiwert shows, following Karl Popper, that Friedrich Heiler's (1892–1967)[2] proposition that the cause for the act of

---

1. A conference held in Zürich in 2000, for example, discussed whether PoR is truly finished or can still be a viable methodology for the study of religions. The contributions to the conference appeared in a substantial 500-page volume (Michaels et al. 2001).

2. The best-known post-war German language scholarship in PoR is a book by the Marburg Protestant theologian Friedrich Heiler (1892–1967) with the title *Erscheinungsformen und Wesen der Religion* (1979 [1961]). One reason for its relatively marginal reception in the English language scholarship is that *Erscheinungsformen und Wesen der Religion* was only partially translated into English (*The Manifestations and Essence of Religion*). One exception is Peter McKenzie's *The Christians: Their Practices and Beliefs* (1988), a faithful adaptation of Heiler's PoR. The excerpt *The Manifestations and Essence of Religion* appeared in Jean Jacques Waardenburg's English

transcending the "belief in immortality" cannot be falsified, and therefore does not qualify as a result of an empirically verifiable methodology. This shows, in a nutshell, Hubert Seiwert's fundamental and critical view of PoR.

The interview with Peter Antes took place on 23 February 2018 at his home in Hannover. It was conducted in German. The interview with Hubert Seiwert took place in a series of short e-mail sessions between March and May 2018 and was conducted in English.

PETER ANTES

Personal Experience and the 1972 Éclat in Berchtesgaden

Katja Triplett: How did you view PoR at the beginning or during your studies, to the extent that you encountered it?

Peter Antes: In classes at Freiburg we did practically no phenomenology. Phenomenology was taught by [Bernhard] Welte (1906–1983) as part of philosophy of religion. His presentation was quite impressive. Otto Stegmüller (1906–1970), my teacher back then, was decidedly oriented towards history. He studied religions via texts, if possible in the original language. I was confronted with PoR when I already worked as an assistant and went to Berchtesgaden to the congress [of the German Association for the History of Religion] in 1972, where [Gustav] Mensching (1901–1978) was voted out of office as Chair. That is where this controversy (*Streit*) came to a head. I experienced this congress in a special way because I was very young compared to the other participants. But somehow I was also very much involved. Even then the critique surfaced that PoR is not verifiable and that it wasn't clear how one in fact proceeds in terms of methods. Now in hindsight I see that

---

language reader of "classical" approaches to the study of religions (1973, 471–479). Waardenburg has also included excerpts from Heiler's English translation of *Das Gebet* (1918), which is based on Heiler's 1917 doctoral dissertation: *Prayer: A Study in the History and Psychology of Religion* (1932). *Prayer* is the only book authored by Heiler that has appeared in full in English. Heiler was professor in Marburg from 1920 until his retirement, with a short interruption in 1934/5 due to political reasons.

there were two different concepts of religion that later played a role in the discussion of comparison.

One of the concepts says that religion is something like music and that, therefore, musicality is required in order to study it. And then perhaps one needs a religious experience. The other concept assumes that it is as with medicine. One cannot demand that the doctor has to have had the disease that he studies and that he publishes about. The representatives of the first position who compare it with music always accuse the others of reductionism. There may be something to it if we were to consider the question what can be experienced in terms of deeper dimensions (*Tiefendimensionen*). These dimensions are not accessible to those who approach the matter from the outside. I don't know what to do with such an extreme version of the insider-outsider position. Because when one carries it to the extent that was done in discussions back then, then we have to assume that a dialogue with believers from another religious tradition is not possible. The study-of-religions scholar (*Religionswissenschaftler*) must have the skill to *simulate* the situation of the believer.

When I give a presentation about Islam, people do not expect that I say what *I* think about Islam. They expect that I present the situation of Muslims in such a way that also Muslims recognize themselves in it. However, the claim that one can simulate the situation from the outside presumes that one can achieve a close approximation, though it does not preclude that some minimal portion of emotional connection (*Gebundenheit*) will perhaps remain inaccessible. In contrast, when one represents the other position – that it is like music and I need to be musical – then there is no dialogue possible. And that is actually what [Rudolf] Otto (1869–1937)[3] says: "Whoever has not had this experience should not continue reading the book."[4] But when one continues reading one will not encounter anything amazing [laughs]. Actually, this was done rather clumsily in his book.

And so this has led to an éclat in Berchtesgaden in 1972. The old squad was voted out of office. Then came [Peter] Weidkuhn (b. 1926) but this didn't work out for very long. And then came [Gunther] Stephenson (b. 1925) as Chair. He convened the congress (of the German Association for

---

3. Rudolf Otto was professor for Protestant theology in Marburg from 1917 to his early retirement due to an illness in 1929. The Marburg "school" of PoR can be traced to him.

4. This passage is found in Otto's *Das Heilige: über das Irrationale in der Idee des Göttlichen und sein Verhältnis zum Rationalen* (1917); in the English translation, the passage reads, "The reader is invited to direct his mind to a moment of deeply-felt religious experience, as little as possible qualified by other forms of consciousness. Whoever cannot do this, whoever knows no such moments in his experience, is requested to read no farther" (Otto 1969 [1923], 8).

the History of Religion) in Darmstadt in 1975. That congress was about religious change in the study of religions. He included four additional papers by young people, namely [Harald] Motzki, [Sigurd] Körber, [Gerhard] Neuf and [Hubert] Seiwert, who expressed criticism of then current academic approaches.

Why Darmstadt as the site of the congress?

Stephenson was director of the Darmstadt Library. He managed to have the congress proceedings published by the Wissenschaftliche Buchgesellschaft[5] in Darmstadt. He mentioned several times to me that Mensching had tried to prevent the Wissenschaftliche Buchgesellschaft from ever publishing these four critical contributions in the volume.[6] This controversy was in my opinion a catastrophe, as it caused a collapse in communication. One could not speak with them. There is also the publication of [Günter] Lanczkowski (1917–1993), the *Einführung in die Religionsphänomenologie* (Introduction to the phenomenology of religion) [1978], which had a weak and ultimately meaningless chapter on method.

Basically they have not contributed anything to defend their positions. They have simply not replied to the criticism. They were not interested because they thought that the critics were somehow unreligious. But by withdrawing into religiosity and insisting on religion as a discipline *sui generis* it is essentially impossible to remain in the academy. Such a position cannot possibly be represented in the university, and the content is utter nonsense. I have never really understood this. I wish they would engage in discussion. But they have not. Interestingly, the remake (*Neuauflage*) (of PoR) by [Wolfgang] Gantke[7] and [Reinhold] Esterbauer,[8] took no note whatsoever of these 30 years of discussion.

Before and After the Anthropological Turn and the Question of Translating Mysticism

Would you say that this is a kind of fossilization, an insistence on a particular position?

---

5.   The WBG, founded in 1949, is a publishing company as well as a book club. It has its seat in Darmstadt.
6.   All four papers have been included in the volume in a separate section titled "Methodologische Versuche" ("methodological experiments"; see Motzki 1976; Körber 1976; Neuf 1976; Seiwert 1976).
7.   See Gantke (1998).
8.   See Esterbauer (2002).

They think somehow they have found enlightenment [laughs]. But this is, of course, not a basis for academic research. The anthropological turn in the 70s meant that it was of no interest anymore whether there *were* any gods or what was happening with the holy, only that human beings believed in them, that they were occupied with this, and that it could be described and explored. But I think that the results were actually not that different [laughs]! What Rudolf Otto wrote, for example, is comprehensible if you are not religious. This is even more true for what Heiler wrote. The totally absurd attempt by [Kurt] Goldammer (1916–1997) – who differentiated between inner and outer forms of piety[9] and so on – is itself no more than cataloguing. None of this has anything to do with deep insight, let alone with enlightenment because of religiosity. However, one should mention that the anthropological turn conceivably reflected generational change.

In Germany or in general?

Worldwide. I should add that, at the IAHR regional conference in Harare in September 1992, the Dutch planned to publish an anniversary volume by the year 2000, 50 years after the (IAHR) Congress in Amsterdam. They circulated the group photo taken at the 1950 Congress with the request to identify anyone we would recognize on the photo. What struck me was that they all looked the same [laughs]!

All were men?

All men and all dressed the same. Phenotypically they looked so much alike that it was indeed difficult to identify them. The homogeneity began to change in the 70s when totally different people started to engage in the study of religions. When you look around nowadays – at the group pictures of the Congresses of the year 2000 or 2005 or recently in Erfurt in 2015 – you do not see the same degree of homogeneity. I think that this homogeneity reflects embedded thought structures that explain why these scholars reached such similar results. Everyone who had a different opinion was ejected from the circle. This would also explain why a particular trend was equipped with such taken-for-grantedness and followed an inner evidence, so that one neither wanted nor could afford such a discussion any longer. I believe that they were actually not able to defend it. They were used to being admired wherever they appeared, and that was how it went.

The only exception at the time perhaps was Annemarie Schimmel.

---

9.   Kurt Goldammer, a doctoral student of Friedrich Heiler, also counts as a phenomenologist of religion. Antes refers to Goldammer's *Die Formenwelt des Religiösen* (1960).

Annemarie Schimmel[10] was not an exception. As I wrote in my contribution to Tim Jensen's festschrift,[11] she uses the Heilerian vocabulary in order to emphasize the insider perspective.

Annemarie Schimmel does not represent liberal Protestantism or liberal theology when she speaks from the Islamic tradition. So, on the one hand, she speaks from the mystical traditions, in connection to Heiler, and, on the other, she doesn't speak from the Islamic tradition as her other contribution shows. She has both approaches.

Yes, she has both.

She used to teach, as we know, in Turkey. Has she talked about this and also whether PoR was practised there?

In Turkey she has a whole range of followers especially in regard to PoR. To my surprise she has recently been strongly criticized in orientalist circles. In Vienna for example you can only quote her with qualifying comments. They claim – as was confirmed to me by [Rüdiger] Lohlker the other day – that "there is too much rose oil", as he put it, in her presentation of Islamic mysticism. And I think that she overindulged her religious feeling, which fits the Heiler lineage. And she is extremely closely connected to it when she says that this deeper level has to be experienced in regard to the *deus absconditus* and so on.[12] I am really not convinced. I would like to add that research on mysticism, including even the serious and respectable study of mysticism, starts from a basic assumption that I am not sure is correct. When someone reads a mystical text in translation he will come to the conclusion that these are thoughts very similar to the thoughts of Meister Eckhart and the German mysticism. But this idea is not a coincidence. Because – as I know well from [Richard] Gramlich[13] (1925–2006) and [Fritz] Meier[14] (1912–1998) and so

---

10. Annemarie Schimmel was President of the IAHR from 1990 to 2000. She received a doctorate in Islamic languages and civilizations of the University of Berlin in 1941. During her time as a professor of Arabic at the University of Marburg, in 1951, she earned a doctorate in the history of religions there. Shortly after, she moved to Turkey and started teaching, in Turkish, as a professor of history of religions at the University of Ankara in Turkey for five years. From 1967 to 1992 Schimmel worked at Harvard University and became professor emeritus of Indo-Muslim culture there after her retirement. She is well known for her open enthusiasm for Islamic mysticism. In *Deciphering the Signs of God* (1994), Schimmel closely follows her former doctoral advisor Heiler's phenomenological model. Her dissertation was *Studien zum Begriff der mystischen Liebe in der frühislamischen Mystik* (1954).

11. See Antes (2016).

12. Antes is referring to Schimmel's *Deciphering the Signs of God*.

13. See for example Gramlich (1992).

14. See for example Meier (1957).

forth – they used the vocabulary of Meister Eckhart as terms for the translation! In their German translation they simply used the mystical stages from Meister Eckhart and the German mysticism as translation terms for the mystical stages in Arabic. One has to question that when they address the highest stage, *fanā'*, and translate this with *Entwerden* (passing away, annihilation) whether this is actually meant in Arabic – I am not so sure! This was never debated by them in any way. I referred to this problem of translation in the festschrift for [Carsten] Colpe.[15] We are persuaded to believe something [by such as a translation technique]. Evidently we must translate terms. You cannot simply use the Arabic terms as they are, because then nobody will understand them either. On the other hand, we must at least express some doubt whether the equation (*Gleichsetzung*) of these terms with our terms in regard to mysticism is legitimate or not.

PoR presupposes that such an equation is possible.

Yes, because the phenomenology champions the following kind of mysticism: the differences between the religions are located on the visible level of dogmatic terminologies and behind it there is a supposedly universal religious experience. Annemarie Schimmel's book *Wie universal ist die Mystik?* (How universal is mysticism?, 1996) starts precisely from the assumption that the Buddhist who has some kind of enlightenment, and the Christian, and the Muslim with his *fanā'* all basically experience something similar. I would like to say two things about this. One is that this is not evident to me. And the second is, do they all actually have the same experience? This kind of thinking has more to do with Hinduism, such as the Hinduism the Hindu Swami Vivekananda (1863–1902) proposed, than with reputable inquiry.

Dangerous Liaisons: Methodological Agnosticism and Departmental Politics

I would be interested in your view on academic debate, the international exchange about methods in general. What is your personal view, which encounters and conversations at IAHR congresses or other conferences are still fresh in your mind?

I see again two different schools of thought. There were those who were very strongly theologically oriented and in principle wanted to consider a certain doctrinal system and proceed, as Heiler actually wrote, in a crypto-theological way. At these conferences (in the 1970s) there was somebody with whom

---

15. See Antes (1994).

I got along very well, because I did not want to participate in this school of thought, and this was Kurt Rudolph. However, Kurt Rudolph also saw this yet from another angle. He said that, considering his academic context, he must do it with Marxism! [laughs] He was in the *DDR* (German Democratic Republic) at the time.[16] He was attracted to my own position when I said: let us leave everything out, it is of no concern to us; all these dogmatic pre-suppositions, may they be Marxist or Catholic or Protestant or Islamic – we do not need them. Of course, this creates yet another problem that we have to deal with increasingly today. We have the problem of demarcation between theology and the study of religions, although theology has long applied study-of-religions methods in broad areas of exegesis and so on. Here, religious commitments do not play any role. Recently we have had the same problem with Islamic and Jewish theology, complicated by the terminological nonsense of insisting that there is no difference between *Islamwissenschaft* (the academic study of Islam) and *Islamische Studien* (Islamic theology). In English the academic study of Islam is called "Islamic Studies". And the same goes for Judaism; even there we cannot keep the disciplines apart termino-logically. And then the question is: what does commitment to the content mean here?

One can imagine that, with this new phase of commitment, something like a PoR could re-enter.

It could, but not necessarily. In this context, I think we must look at what PoR actually does in terms of content. Either PoR catalogues content, and for this one doesn't need to have any belief: everyone can do it. You just have to create categories for the cataloguing. And whoever is just a little bit trained in the humanities can do it. *Or* you can say, "behind it is an experience." But this is methodologically not obtainable. That is why I would say that a PoR that presupposes that it focuses on *that*, well – it may be quite nice but this cannot be advocated in the university.

The university as an institution is very central, but did PoR have any in-fluence on public education, in the public sphere, for example by public presentations in communities?

---

16. Critical engagement for an empiricist approach to studying religions is usually connected to Kurt Rudolph who taught at Karl Marx University in Leipzig from 1961 until he moved to Chicago in 1984. After World War II, the academic research of religion in the German Democratic Republic centred on the department for the study of religions in Leipzig. Rudolph decided to emigrate instead of returning to Leipzig and accepted, after teaching in the United States for two years, a chair for the history of religion at the University of Marburg where he remained until his retirement in 1994.

I personally was never guided by it. Because I am convinced that this cata-loguing does not live up to the religious sentiment of the people about whom I speak. If you use for example the grid developed by Heiler, as Annemarie Schimmel did in her *Deciphering the Signs of God* [1994],[17] then what the peo-ple actually expected to learn only comes at the very end. Most of the book does not fit with it at all. I see a large discrepancy between what a religion teaches, as in a catechism, and popular piety (*Volksfrömmigkeit*). What people actually practice differs from the catechism. When I speak about Islam, the audience usually expects me to prioritize the teaching. So you have to say in places that the teaching does not appear in the practice in pure form. But I would not engage head-on with the holy stones[18] because I think it's not adequate. When you teach at schools then clear educational information (*Aufklärung*) is important. We need to state that not all forms taken for relig-iosity appear in all expressions of Islam, for example honor killing. You could actually do pure phenomenology and say there is also honor killing in Spain or in Sicily. Then most would probably say, yes, but this is *not* Christianity. But when we talk about Islam, then most in the public sphere would say: this is Islamic.

Explaining Miracles in the Study of Religions

The cognitive science of religion is seen by some as a supersession of the old PoR. Some contest this but some say that PoR still has a chance in the form of a cognitive science of religion. What is your view on this?

I don't think it is. I think that cognitive science has taken a divergent path. Basically it is an application of neurobiological evolutionary models. But the question is: what have I actually understood when I know about the brain waves? I don't think that it is actually leading us any further. What one can possibly see is that medicine as it is taught at universities and clinics (*Schulmedizin*) is rather less universal than previously thought. There is an unexploited potential of mental abilities. We have not been able to explain its origin but it constitutes (human) behaviour and can also produce marvels. Explaining miracles is always difficult in the study of religions [laughs]. We quickly tend to deliver rational substantiations but they don't have to be true! In this context I always recount the story of how my contacts with Lancaster have come about. Have I told you the story yet?

---

17. This book is based on the 1992 edition of Schimmel's Gifford Lectures in natural theology.

18. The reference is to Schimmel's *Deciphering the Signs of God*, which begins with a section on holy stones.

No.

When the British Association for the Study of Religions celebrated its 50th anniversary, I was president of the IAHR and those joining in the celebrations were asked to recount how they came initially into contact. Following their request, I said I would present two versions [The first version involves a chance meeting with a friendly lady, a mental patient as it turned out later, on the tube in London and her invitation to a conference on world religions at her hospital; when Peter arrived to join the fictional conference he ended up having a conversation with the hospital vicar who incidentally mentioned a friend, Bob Morgan from the study of religions department in Lancaster. Peter became curious and went to Lancaster to visit Morgan and also met Ninian Smart and Eric Sharpe there; the second version is that Morgan remembered Peter to have been a patient at the hospital himself and that the vicar sent Peter to Lancaster to help him]. I tell the story because it shows that the rational version is not always the correct one. In my case, the *improbable* version was true! With the texts that we deal with, we basically tend to give rational explanations. I want to show with this example that when we radically abridge we often trip ourselves up in regard to the contents. We should be a bit more careful, and when you take such a book as von Hirschhausen's *Wunder wirken Wunder* [2016] (Miracles work miracles) then you see that the range of possible influences is much wider. What comes up in the cognitive sciences is perhaps less crucial than some phenomena for which we do not presently have any explanation. Because I think that [knowledge about the] mental level is — if you compare it with physics — comparable to alchemy. Probably there are equally clear laws (*Regeln*) that we do not yet know.

How do you view the works of Eric Sharpe and James Cox?

James Cox says that this question [of PoR] occupies us constantly and is always present. I would not say this for Germany, because phenomenology played no role, not even in my studies in Freiburg. It simply did not come up. We were working strictly historically, linguistically and philologically. In contrast, as I have heard, first-year students in the US were reading Otto's book, *The Idea of the Holy*. We did not read it at all.

My final question is which books or articles have played a prominent role in the history of PoR, apart from those we have already talked about.

I think that we should continue to read the book by Eric Sharpe, and Cox's book is also important. For the German case, I see things in a rather negative light. The rescue attempts by [Wolfgang] Gantke[19] did not succeed. I have

---

19.   See Gantke (1998).

a strained relationship with him because when he published his work I met him by chance and said to him: I cannot comprehend how you can write a thesis in which you do not take note of 30 years of debate. As if he wrote it in 1972! And [Reinhold] Esterbauer's work[20] is of the same nature. I also cannot comprehend that these two works are postdoctoral qualification theses (*Habilitationen*) [note: PA expresses his bewilderment that the two, in his view poor, theses have been seriously regarded and accepted by an academic committee]. I have frequently squabbled with Gantke after that. This line of thought is haunted by nonsense about "reductionism". I do not want to rule out that there are these deeper levels (*Tiefenebene*) that we cannot get close to, but he didn't articulate it at all. Saying that there are these deeper levels and the others are reductionists requires stating somehow what these deeper levels actually entail. And he doesn't say anything. I suggest that you interview him, too [laughs].

HUBERT SEIWERT

PoR and its Complete Lack of Methodological Reflection

Katja Triplett: How did you define PoR when you began your career?

Hubert Seiwert: When I was an undergraduate, PoR was not defined in any particular way but simply taken for being the same as comparative religion or *Religionswissenschaft*. There were authorities such as Rudolf Otto and [Gerardus] van der Leeuw (1890–1950), and no need was felt to worry about methodologies. At my university, *Religionswissenschaft* was mainly taught as a German-speaking discipline, including scholars from Scandinavia and the Netherlands. All of them had been trained as Protestant theologians. [Mircea] Eliade was read but for some reason not highly regarded. It's hard to imagine today how provincialized the discipline was in the 60s and 70s in Germany.

When I spent my second year in France, I experienced an enormous difference, because there were no comparative, only historical studies of religions based on philology. This seemed to me to provide a much more solid ground than the work of the German-speaking phenomenologists. In these days, I saw phenomenology as rather shallow compendia of religions by

---

20. See Esterbauer (2002).

liberal theologians who ignored historical contexts. I wouldn't have been able to define it because it seemed to lack any methodological foundation except a vague reference to "understanding".

How do you define it now? Do you see yourself as a phenomenologist?

Let me start with the second question. I have never considered myself a phenomenologist. This is partly due to the uneasiness I felt as a student with the apparently complete lack of methodological reflection on the part of the then prevalent form of *Religionswissenschaft*. Consider that I was a student when the student movement of 1968 was in full motion. Part of this movement was not only a political critique of traditional scholarship, but also a strong awareness of methodological issues. In Germany, the disputes were mainly between the Critical Theory of the Frankfurt School and the Critical Rationalism of Popper and his school. Given the theoretical standard of these discussions, religious studies were plainly undertheorized. My teachers simply could not understand these methodological discussions or at least would not respond to the problems discussed.

Against this backdrop, the form of *Religionswissenschaft* that today is called "PoR" seemed to be completely unacceptable as a scientific approach. However, those who voiced critique were like heretics facing an established orthodoxy. This probably explains why I distanced myself from phenomenology.

As to the definition of PoR, I do not think there is any clear one. In common parlance today, the term simply seems to refer to those forms of religious studies that preceded or kept aloof from theoretical discourses originating in other disciplines during the last decades. It is also usually assumed that PoR takes an affirmative stance on religion, which results from confusing hermeneutical understanding with affirmative understanding. Personally, I think that van der Leeuw is the only one who in the epilegomena of his *Phänomenologie der Religion* attempted to formulate something like a theoretical explanation of PoR as a methodology. Although it's difficult to read and more difficult to agree with, it's still worthy of being considered and possibly developed and transformed against the background of more recent methodological discourses. But this is not my business.

Studying Religions in the Germanophone World

I understand from what you say about the situation in Germany in the 60s that PoR was in the hands of (German) Protestant theologians. In France the situation seemed to have been very different at the time. Do you think there is any connection between phenomenologists of religion and

their religious affiliations? I am very interested, in this same context, in hearing more about the political issues discussed during the 60s and the effect that these discussions had on something like PoR.

The germanophone phenomenologists – not all of them were German – were trained as Protestant theologians. This is not to say that what they did was theology, but their understanding of religion was certainly shaped by their theological socialization. We mustn't overlook that the study of religion was poorly institutionalized in German universities up to the 1990s and therefore very few academics had degrees in this discipline. Being interested in religion meant studying theology in the first place. Liberal Protestant faculties probably left more room for theologically unorthodox religious studies than the Catholic ones.

The alternative to being a trained theologian was being trained as a philologist. It is interesting that the two chairs not occupied by theologians – in Leipzig and Tübingen – were not engaged in PoR. Walter Baetke (1884–1978)[21] in Leipzig, who had been trained in Scandinavian studies, sharply criticized PoR early on. His successor Kurt Rudolph continued a critical attitude, although he has a degree in Protestant theology. This shows that there is no direct connection between religious affiliation and PoR. This is also the case with Michael Pye, who in the early 1980s became professor in Marburg.

Of course, it is an intriguing question whether socialization as a Protestant, Catholic, Jew or agnostic has effects on the way the study of religion is approached. However, the sample of German academics is too small to allow for generalizations. Beyond Germany, the religious affiliation of most scholars is not known to me nowadays. I do suppose that personal experiences with religion, including religious socialization but also field research, has effects on one's view on religion, but this has to be studied empirically.

You ask about the possible influence of the political issues of the student movement on the critique of PoR. This critique started in West Germany – Leipzig at that time belonged to East Germany – only in 1975, with four conference papers on methodology presented by graduate students from Bonn. The presentations caused considerable unrest among senior academics. I was then asked by the editor of a journal to write a further article on method and theory.[22] Since nobody took pains to critically and publicly respond to these papers, PoR left the field of methodology to its critics and simply vanished with the next generation of scholars.

In retrospect, I do not think that the critique was politically motivated. It certainly was influenced by the upsurge of methodological debates in the

---

21.   For an assessment of Baetke's work during the periods of National Socialism and Marxist ideology, see Rudoph and Heinrich (2001).
22.   See Seiwert (1977).

1960s, which of course were a political issue. The so-called positivism dispute in Germany was about the political function of the social sciences. PoR in no way reacted to these discussions. The result was that students of religion who wanted to be methodologically informed had to turn to the social sciences. I guess this is one of reasons why the study of religion increasingly became conceived of as a social science. Another reason was the aspiration to be socially relevant, which led to discovering contemporary religions as a field of research in contrast to historical oriented PoR.

Scholars and Their Political and Social Engagement

This issue – that aspirations to social relevance led to changes in the study of religions – is connected to the historical descriptions and evaluations of PoR given by James Cox in *A Guide to the Phenomenology of Religion*. Cox devoted much of his conclusion to views of the scholar's political and social engagement, including his own (for example 2006, 242). I would like to invite you to comment on this.

The question of whether or not scholars can or should be engaged in political discourses and activities does not concern PoR specifically. It applies to all the social sciences and humanities. In Germany, this debate started a hundred years ago with the *Werturteilsstreit* (value judgment dispute), it resurfaced in the 1960s with the positivism dispute, and it has now reappeared in methodological disputes in the study of religion. In this context, PoR is not alone in being criticized for uncritically upholding a concept of religion that is deeply affected by, and so sustains, theological and colonial interests.

This critique, which sometimes is labelled as "critical studies of religion", is obviously inspired by the Critical Theory of the Frankfurt School even if, as far as I know, there is no explicit reference to the latter. They both share the view that it is the obligation of scholars not only to analyse social reality but to do so in order to unveil the structures that produce social injustices and the ideologies that legitimize them, and to deconstruct these structures. This is a legitimate progressive political agenda. I doubt, however, that this or any other political position can ground methodological claims in the study of religion.

From a historical perspective, phenomenologists of religion have been no less politically engaged than today's advocates of the critical studies of religion. Rudolf Otto was founder of the *Religiöser Menschheitsbund* (Religious League of Humanity) and a deputy in the Prussian Parliament, and Gerardus van der Leeuw was a minister in the Dutch government. One cannot accuse phenomenologists of religion of having been unpolitical. They just had other political agendas than their critics today. What is framed as a methodological critique is basically a political critique.

I personally do not think that the study of religion profits from mixing up methodological and political arguments. It is justified where it uncovers the political contexts and implications of PoR and other methodological approaches. However, we cannot reasonably demand that the study of religion should be based on a particular political position. The study of religion is no longer a parochial discipline. It is not the arena for discussing political preferences of Western academics. If methodological claims can legitimately be founded on political agendas, why then not on religious ones, let's say of Hindus or Muslims? I therefore do not think that a political critique invalidates PoR methodologically. Normative arguments could only be countered by other normative arguments, be they political or religious.

The Problem of Decontextualization

What other portions of Cox's book do you find worthy of consideration?

In my view, the most interesting point made by Jim Cox is the contention that "the phenomenology of religion defines the methodology that is uniquely associated with religious studies as a distinct discipline studying 'religion' itself." (2006, 3) He is probably right that religious studies could not be distinguished from other disciplines that study religion by any methodology apart from PoR. The question however is whether disciplines in the humanities and social sciences can be defined by specific methodologies in the first place. It is impossible to discuss this question here in detail. It should be observed, however, that phenomenology did not originate in the study of religion nor is it confined to it. There is, for instance, the phenomenological sociology of Alfred Schütz (1899–1959). While PoR might be peculiar, a phenomenological approach is not specific to a particular discipline but rather to a particular interest in understanding the meanings embedded in life-worlds. This is also a legitimate interest in religious studies, but certainly not the only one.

PoR is one possible methodological approach in the study of religion. As with any other approach, it can be criticized methodologically. Personally, I do not subscribe to Cox's idea that the aim of the discipline can or should be "studying 'religion' itself". As I see it, as scholars of religion we study human beings and the ways they live in, shape and give meaning to the world. Since there cannot be religions without humans, religion "itself" is a decontextualized abstraction. This is my main objection to PoR.

The problem of decontextualization also affects two otherwise productive principles of PoR: comparison and understanding. Comparison is the key to any attempt at generalizations. However, we cannot reasonably compare religious "phenomena" to the study of religion "itself", that is, without considering their contexts, including the non-religious ones. Even if we were interested exclusively in understanding their meaning, we have to take into account the contexts in which they have meaning. To cultivate a feeling for the religious sentiment in humanity (Cox 2006, 153) is clearly not sufficient and may even lead one down the wrong track.

In short, PoR has deeply influenced the way that the study of religion developed in the last century, and it is still an important point of reference for methodological reflections in the discipline. Some of its methodological principles such as comparison, understanding and bracketing value judgments haven't lost their significance. However, its methodological foundation is weak and out-dated. Unfortunately, phenomenologists haven't attempted to keep pace with methodological discourses in the last decades. Cox's book, which traces the twists and turns of PoR and the critiques levelled against it, does not remedy its methodological flaws.

Mind-centred Theories of Religion

You mentioned that phenomenologists haven't attempted to keep pace with methodological discourses in the last decades. Some say that the cognitive science of religion is an advancement of PoR, some say it is a completely different development, still others state that is merely a remake. What is your position on this?

I wouldn't think that the cognitive science of religion consciously builds on PoR. There are obviously fundamental differences between the two with regard to methodology and ontology. The cognitive science of religion is by definition reductionist, because it attempts to reduce religion basically to cognitive processes inside individual brains. For phenomenologists, reducing religion to non-religious things is anathema. Furthermore, while PoR usually takes an affirmative stance on religion, the cognitive science of religion is ambiguous in its evaluation. Some researchers see religion as a by-product of the evolution of the cognitive architecture of the brain: it has no positive function, but rather prompts wrong conceptions of the world. Others believe that religion has evolved as an adaptation to support human cooperation and enhance the survival of groups.

Despite the fundamental differences in methodology and theoretical ambition, the cognitive science of religion shares with PoR some assumptions. They both regard religion as a universal phenomenon that is part of human nature. In addition, they both take religion to originate from mental processes

– religious experiences and cognitive algorithms respectively – although hard-core cognitive scientists would interpret both of these as material processes in the brain. Nevertheless, I would say that both are mind-centred theories of religion, which also implies that they focus on individuals. Because of this individualist approach, they share the tendency to ignore the social and cultural contexts of what they take to be religion.

Since the cognitive science of religion is developing in different directions, it is difficult to generalize as to its compatibility with PoR. However, for the time being I do not see how they could be reconciled methodologically.

Commentary: The Violent Death and Some Afterlives of the German Phenomenology of Religion

In his interview, Peter Antes was adamant that attempts by two German scholars to "remake" or "rescue" PoR both failed. Hubert Seiwert also sees little hope for a fruitful revival. He holds that flaws in the fundamental approach of PoR greatly outweigh his agreement with PoR's basic commitment to comparing religions. In a famous quote Seiwert states that PoR became the victim of the demand for precision and empirical verifiability of theories: PoR "was slaughtered with the knife of the theory of science" (not least wielded by himself) (2014, 22). Seiwert then paints a somewhat hopeful future picture of "a study of religions liberated from the fetters of positivistic science," and that PoR might be "resuscitated" (ibid.). He does not see the resuscitation as his task, as he expressed during a conversation in preparation for this interview.

In a volume that explores intellectual thought cultures across borders, some words on the term theory of science used in the present chapter may be in order to pinpoint specifics of the German-speaking context. While theory, or philosophy, of science as the conventional translation of the German term *Wissenschaftstheorie* – the word used by Seiwert in his 2014 essay to which the title of the present chapter alludes – refers to the natural sciences in the narrower sense, the German term *Wissenschaft* is more inclusive. *Wissenschaft* refers to systems of knowledge (*Wissen*) in both the humanities and the natural sciences. The terms *Religionswissenschaft* for the academic study of religions, and *Islamwissenschaft* for the academic study of Islam – explained by Peter Antes during the interview – are prime examples.

From the viewpoint of developing PoR, or parts of it, into an approach that keeps up with current methodological debates, the writings of Gantke and Esterbauer must appear like failed attempts. Viewed in their own terms, however, both continue what they see as a scholarly legacy.

Indeed, there are some more recent attempts by scholars in the German study of religion to work with Otto's phenomenological approach, such as by Dirk Johannsen in his book on the numinous as a cultural studies category (2008).

At most universities in the German-speaking world, PoR is studied as an historical phenomenon. Students are discouraged by the majority of scholars from faithfully following in the footsteps of Heiler, Otto and others; reasons for this and reviews of critiques that the interviewees outlined above are central lessons in class. Heiler would never have thought of himself as a "phenomenologist of religion."[23] As he has not generated any "Heilerian school" in Marburg, he currently receives little, if any, attention in class or in research in the academic study of religions in Germany. In contrast, Otto is more present, because his *The Idea of the Holy* has had the ability to enchant a wide audience – its instant success on publication surprised Otto himself. As to the reception within the present circle of German scholars in the academic study of religions, most, I included, have kept on reading after reaching the famous passage that requests the reader to feel deep religious feelings, because we had to study the whole book as a class assignment. By the late 1980s the book had become standard reading in *Religionswissenschaft* classes on the history of the comparative study of religions, at least at Marburg University.

Another, perhaps less well-known, part of Otto's legacy is the Marburg university collection of objects he established in 1927 as the *Religionskundliche Sammlung* (Religious Studies Collection – known today as the Marburg Museum of Religion). Otto's interest in religious objects was clearly guided by his inspiration to encounter the holy. He gathered several hundred items not as religious art but as objects that expressed certain categories of religious experience, such as the *mysterium tremendum*. To date, the university collection has grown to over 9,000 items, and its curators and directors, starting with Martin Kraatz, long ago abandoned Otto's approach in order to emphasize the historical, cultural and social contexts of the material objects in the collection. The exploration of religion and religions in the museum has also become an important topic for Kraatz's successors, Michael Pye, Peter Bräunlein and the current director Edith Franke and her team. Still, the idea of studying material and sensual forms of religion such as music is an important and original contribution to the study of religions, though Otto's phenomenological approach is no longer endorsed.

In some German Protestant circles, *The Idea of the Holy* attracts an undiminished interest, culminating in revivalist tendencies of Otto's legacy.

---

23.   Personal communication with Dr Martin Kraatz.

In recent years, theologians in Germany and elsewhere have produced new scholarship on Otto. A conference volume edited by Jörg Lauster et al. and published in 2013 is a prominent example. The volume also includes contributions by study of religions scholars and academics from other fields as well. As is often the case, academics use anniversaries as focal points of scholarly pursuit, and the conference organizers of the Marburg congress dedicated it to the 75th anniversary of Otto's death and to the 95th anniversary of the publication of *The Idea of the Holy*. The book is still in print and has been translated into numerous languages, the earliest translations being in English (1923) and Japanese (1927). The book incited some attention at the annual conference of the German Association for the Study of Religions in Marburg in 2017, marking the 100th anniversary of its publication.[24] The 90th year anniversary of the founding of the *Religionskundliche Sammlung* was duly celebrated during the conference.

A final point is German PoR's impact on non-Christian academic contexts. Peter Antes noted in his interview that PoR is quite popular in Turkey, where Annemarie Schimmel taught for some years, and the impact can be traced to her efforts there. Recalling a conversation with Annemarie Schimmel, Christoph Bochinger, professor for the study of religions in Bayreuth, says that Schimmel told him once with a chuckle that she was a "dinosaur" in German *Religionswissenschaft*.[25] Influenced by her teaching activity at the theology (*ilahiyat*) faculty at the University of Ankara, PoR has had a lasting impact in Turkey where comparative religion is primarily, if not exclusively, studied in *ilahiyat* faculties. Bochinger surmised, at a meeting in Ankara some years ago, that while the non-confessional study of religions may be suspected of being critical towards religion – even of supporting atheism, or, at the other extreme, of favouring "idolatrous" forms of religiosity – PoR remains attractive as a methodology in Turkey because of its fundamentally pro-religious stance.

Katja Triplett graduated in the study of religions, Japanese linguistics and anthropology and obtained her doctorate from the University of Marburg. She held a postdoctoral research fellowship at the Centre for the Study of Japanese Religions, SOAS, University of London (2004–2005). From 2007 to 2012 Triplett was associate professor at the Department of the Study of Religions and curator of the Museum of Religion (Religionskundliche Sammlung) in Marburg. From

---

24. See Gantke and Serikov (2017).
25. This paragraph reflects the interviewer's personal communication with Professor Bochinger on 9 May 2017. For the history of the study of religions in Turkey, see Şenay (2004).

2012 to 2016 she was professor for the study of religions at the University of Göttingen. She is currently affiliated with the Centre for Advanced Studies in the Humanities and Social Sciences "Multiple Secularities – Beyond the West, Beyond Modernities" at the University of Leipzig. Triplett has published widely on topics relating to Japanese Buddhism and medicine.

References

Antes, Peter. 1994. "Mystische Erfahrung als Problem von Übersetzungen." In *Tradition und Translation: zum Problem der interkulturellen Übersetzbarkeit religiöser Phänomene; Festschrift für Carsten Colpe zum 65. Geburtstag*, edited by Christoph Elsas, Renate Haffke, Hans-Michael Haußig, Andreas Löw, Gesine Palmer, Bert Sommer and Marco S. Torini, 1–9. Berlin: de Gruyter. https://doi.org/10.1515/9783110864694.1

Antes, Peter. 2016. "Phenomenology of Religion Revisited." In *Contemporary Views on Comparative Religion in Celebration of Tim Jensen's 65th Birthday*, edited by Peter Antes, Armin W. Geertz and Mikael Rothstein, 141–152. Sheffield: Equinox.

Cox, James L. 2006. *A Guide to the Phenomenology of Religion: Key Figures, Formative Influences and Subsequent Debates*. London: Continuum.

Esterbauer, Reinhold. 2002. *Anspruch und Entscheidung: Zu einer Phänomenologie der Erfahrung des Heiligen*. Münchener philosophische Studien, N.F. Stuttgart: W. Kohlhammer.

Gantke, Wolfgang. 1998. *Der umstrittene Begriff des Heiligen: Eine problemorientierte religionswissenschaftliche Untersuchung*. Marburg: Diagonal-Verlag.

Gantke, Wolfgang and Serikov, Vladislav, eds. 2017. *100 Jahre "Das Heilige": Beiträge zu Rudolf Ottos Grundlagenwerk*. THEION – Studien zur Religionskultur, Frankfurt am Main: Peter Lang.

Goldammer, Kurt. 1960. *Die Formenwelt des Religiösen: Grundriss der systematischen Religionswissenschaft*. Stuttgart: Kröner.

Gramlich, Richard. 1992. *Islamische Mystik: Sufische Texte aus zehn Jahrhunderten*. Stuttgart: Kohlhammer.

Heiler, Friedrich. 1918. *Das Gebet: eine religionsgeschichtliche und religionspsychologische Untersuchung*. Charleston, NC: Nabu Press, 2015 ed. Munich: Reinhardt.

Heiler, Friedrich. 1932. *Prayer: A Study in the History and Psychology of Religion*. New York: Oxford University Press.

Heiler, Friedrich. 1979 [1961]. *Erscheinungsformen und Wesen der Religion*. Die Religionen der Menschheit. Stuttgart: W. Kohlhammer.

Johannsen, Dirk. 2008. *Das Numinose als kulturwissenschaftliche Kategorie: Norwegische Sagenwelt in religionswissenschaftlicher Deutung*. Religionswissenschaft Heute. Diss (Bayreuth).

Körber, Sigurd. 1976. "Bedingtheit und Distanzbemühen. Zur anthropologischen Situation des Religionswissenschaftlers." In *Der Religionswandel unserer Zeit im Spiegel der Religionswissenschaft*, edited by Gunther Stephenson, 293–308. Darmstadt: Wissenschaftliche Buchgesellschaft.

Lanczkowski, Günter. 1978. *Einführung in die Religionsphänomenologie*. Darmstadt: Wissenschaftliche Buchgesellschaft.

Lauster, Jörg, Peter Schüz, Roderich Barth and Christian Danz, eds. 2013. *Rudolf Otto: Theologie, Religionsphilosophie, Religionsgeschichte*. Berlin: de Gruyter. https://doi.org/10.1515/9783110310962

McKenzie, Peter. 1988. *The Christians: Their Practices and Beliefs*. London: SPCK.

Meier, Fritz. 1957. *Die Fawāʾiḥ al-ğamāl wa-fawātiḥ al-ğalāl des Naǧm ad-dīn al-Kubrā. Eine Darstellung mystischer Erfahrungen im Islam aus der Zeit um 1200 n. Chr. Herausgegeben und erläutert von Fritz Meier*. Veröffentlichungen der Orientalischen Kommission. Wiesbaden: Akademie der Wissenschaften und der Literatur (Mainz).

Michaels, Axel, Daria Pezzoli-Olgiati and Erika Stolz, eds. 2001. *Noch eine Chance für die Religionsphänomenologie?*, Studia religiosa Helvetica, vol. 6/7. Bern: Lang.

Motzki, Harald. 1976. "Wissenschaftstheoretische und -praktische Probleme der religionswissenschaftlichen Terminologie." In *Der Religionswandel unserer Zeit im Spiegel der Religionswissenschaft*, edited by Gunther Stephenson, 323–338. Darmstadt: Wissenschaftliche Buchgesellschaft.

Neuf, Gerhard. 1976. "Religionswissenschaft aus der Sicht der Analytischen Philosophie." In *Der Religionswandel unserer Zeit im Spiegel der Religionswissenschaft*, edited by Gunther Stephenson, 339–354. Darmstadt: Wissenschaftliche Buchgesellschaft.

Otto, Rudolf. 1917. *Das Heilige: über das Irrationale in der Idee des Göttlichen und sein Verhältnis zum Rationalen*. Breslau: Trewendt & Granier.

Otto, Rudolf. 1969 [1923]. *The Idea of the Holy: An Inquiry into the Non-Rational Factor in the Idea of the Divine and Its Relation to the Rational, translated by John W. Harvey*. Oxford: Oxford University Press.

Rudolph, Kurt, and Fritz Heinrich. 2001. "Walter Baetke (1884–1978)." *Zeitschrift für Religionswissenschaft* 9(2): 169–184. https://doi.org/10.1515/0033.169

Schimmel, Annemarie. 1954. *Studien zum Begriff der mystischen Liebe in der frühislamischen Mystik*. Marburg: Univ., Diss. 1951.

Schimmel, Annemarie. 1994. *Deciphering the Signs of God: A Phenomenological Approach to Islam*. Albany, NY: University of New York Press.

Schimmel, Annemarie. 1996. *Wie universal ist die Mystik? Die Seelenreise in den großen Religionen der Welt*. Freiburg im Breisgau: Herder.

Seiwert, Hubert. 1976. "Religiöser Wandel: Alternativen religionswissen-schaftlicher Fragestellungen und Erklärungsmodelle." In *Der Religionswandel unserer Zeit im Spiegel der Religionswissenschaft*, edited by Gunther Stephenson, 309–322. Darmstadt: Wissenschaftliche Buchgesellschaft.

Seiwert, Hubert. 1977. "Systematische Religionswissenschaft: Theoriebildung und Empiriebezug." *Zeitschrift für Missionswissenschaft und Religionswissenschaft: ZMR* 61: 1–18.

Seiwert, Hubert. 2014. "Religionswissenschaft zwischen Sozialwissenschaften, Geschichtswissenschaften und Kognitionswissenschaften." In *Religions-wissenschaft zwischen Sozialwissenschaften, Geschichtswissenschaften und Kognitionsforschung: Ein Autoren-Workshop mit Hubert Seiwert*, edited by Edith Franke and Verena Maske. Marburg Online Books, 15–32. Marburg: IVK-Religionswissenschaft.

Şenay, Bülent. 2004. "The Study of Religion, the History of Religions and Islamic Studies in Turkey: Approaches from 'Phenomenological Theology' to Contextualism." In *New Approaches to the Study of Religion, Vol. 1: Regional, Critical, and Historical Approaches*, edited by Peter Antes, Armin W. Geertz and Randi R. Warne. Religion and Reason, 63–100. Berlin: Walter de Gruyter. https://doi.org/10.1515/9783110211702.1.63

Stephenson, Gunther, ed. 1976. *Der Religionswandel unserer Zeit im Spiegel der Religionswissenschaft*. Darmstadt: Wissenschaftliche Buchgesellschaft.

von Hirschhausen, Eckart. 2016. *Wunder wirken Wunder: Wie Medizin und Magie uns heilen*. Berlin: Rowohlt.

Waardenburg, Jacques. 1973. *Classical Approaches to the Study of Religion: Aims, Methods and Theories of Research, vol. 1. Introduction and Anthology*. Religion and Reason. The Hague: Mouton. https://doi.org/10.1515/9783110800722

4

Nec cum te nec sine te

An Interview with Giovanni Casadio (Italy)

ALESSANDRO TESTA

Giovanni Casadio (b. 1950) is Professor of History of Religions at the University of Salerno. MA Bologna, PhD Rome. EASR Vice-President (2013-2019). IAHR Honorary Life Member. Associate editor of the II ed. of the Eliade's *Encyclopedia of Religion* (2005) and co-director of *Symposia Cumana* (2002–2012). Around 160 contributions about ancient Mediterranean religions, Christianity, Gnosticism, Manichaeism, method and theory in the study of religion, history of religious scholarship, with a special focus on R. Pettazzoni and M. Eliade. Books: *Storia del culto di Dioniso in Argolide* (1994), *Vie gnostiche all'immortalità* (1997), *Il vino dell'anima* (1999), *Ugo Bianchi: Una vita per la storia delle religioni* (ed. 2002), *Mystic Cults in Magna Graecia* (co-ed. 2009), *Lo sciamanesimo prima e dopo Mircea Eliade* (2014).

Introduction

I have known Giovanni Casadio and have been familiar with his scholarship for several years now. He is not only a renowned specialist of ancient and comparative religions – among other things – but also a prominent figure in the field of history of religions in Italy and Europe. Casadio has authored a vast number of works on the history of the history of religions and on Italian as well as non-Italian scholars in the realm of *Religionswissenschaft* (Raffaele Pettazzoni, Ugo Bianchi, Ioan Petru

Keywords: "Rome School", Raffaele Pettazzoni, Ernesto de Martino, Ugo Bianchi, History of Religions, Methodology

Culianu, Mircea Eliade). His penchant for establishing lines of intellectual genealogies as well as for historiography and scientific biographies made him the ideal candidate for the writing of this interview.

This interview's themes and general planning sprang from a number of conversations held in person between the interviewer and the interviewee mostly in Rome and Leuven (Belgium; the location of EASR 2017 Conference) during the second half of 2017. However, the text as it is presented here has taken shape mostly through phone calls and e-mail interaction between the second half of 2017 and the beginning of 2018.

Alessandro Testa: How would you define phenomenology of religion (PoR)?

Giovanni Casadio: Within the framework of the (comparative) study of religion as an academic field, PoR has its own status as a scientific discipline or, more appropriately, as a particular perspective, or method, or approach, or paradigm. At one end of the spectrum we find a philosophical-psychological (virtually theological) PoR and, at the other end, a descriptive, systematic, comparative and historical phenomenology, which verges from the pure descriptive style of the first Dutch and British comparative religionists to an approach aiming at comprehensive phenomenology (*phänomenologisches Verstehen*) which is typical of the second generation of the Dutch and German schools. A *tertium genus*, combining the two perspectives outlined above, is the hermeneutical phenomenology (Gilhus 1984, 32–34), whose most productive and characteristic representative is Mircea Eliade (1907–1986).

Classical definitions of phenomenology were given by historians of religions previous or contemporaneous to the generation of my academic grandparent, Raffaele Pettazzoni (1883–1959), perhaps the real founding father of the modern discipline history of religions (Widengren 1983, a fundamental contribution that has gone completely ignored, due to having been published in German in an Italian journal) and a seminal influence in the field of religious studies (admittedly mentor of Mircea Eliade, not to mention his own notable Roman school), with all due respect to Cox (2006, 6), who gives priority to a North European and Afro-centric perspective. In my green years, I had the privilege to be in contact with the two Swedish upholders of historical and typological phenomenology (Widengren and Hultkrantz), whose scholarly vision has been of great relevance for my own formation as a historian of religions. But there are also explicit or, more often, implicit definitions of religious phenomenology in the works of scholars belonging to the generation of my master Ugo Bianchi (1922–1995), or to my own generation, with whom I have shared conference sessions, graduate defences and publications. Thus I intend to extend to this group of scholars who have studied, or still study, religions in a phenomenological perspective the label of "new-style phenomenology" that Jacques Waardenburg (1930–2015) adopted for his own approach. Waardenburg called for due attention to the intentionality of religious actors (2001), and that also holds for the theoretical project of Jeppe Sinding Jensen (b. 1951), which aims at a description of religion as a cultural system (Gilhus 1994; for details cf. Jensen 1994, 279, 282).

In my long career in the field of religious studies, I have had the opportunity to meet scholars who have consciously practised a type of history of religions within a phenomenological perspective. Notably enough, they are all characterized by a religious affiliation (which has somewhat influenced their outlook with no direct bearing on the scholarly quality of their work) and by a hectic international activity crossing through different cultural and academic milieus. The eldest, who has been extremely active during his long life, is the Belgian Catholic priest and eventually cardinal Julien Ries (1920–2013). His formation was obviously Belgian but for many years he had close contacts with the Italian academic and especially (lay) ecclesiastic milieu (Communion and Liberation). The "Père Ries" (as he was confidentially called in Ugo Bianchi's Rome and Milan school) never wrote or said "I am a phenomenologist". In his entire theoretical and historiographical work he was more descriptive than assertive, but the man who founded a series entitled "Homo religiosus", including a trilogy *L'expression du sacré dans les grandes religions* (Louvain-la-Neuve, 1978–1986), and another one entitled *Trattato di antropologia del sacro* (Jaca Book, Milano 1989–2009), had an evidently "substantial" vision of religion and the sacred, conceived in more essentialist terms than that of his inspiration Eliade (Nanini 2008, 2015, 2016).

Raffaele Pettazzoni was one of the founding fathers of modern comparative religion, and the founding father of history of religions in Italy. Has PoR influenced the early Italian history of religions, and Pettazzoni more in particular? If so, how?

In the introduction to a Swedish "IAHR Special conference", Jackson and Thurfjell (2008, 7) include Raffaele Pettazzoni (IAHR co-founder and second president) in a list of scholars (comprising R. Otto, M. Eliade and M. Douglas) that understood the "sacred" as a sphere secluded "from everyday human consumption and interaction". The claim that the sacred (religion) constitutes a unique domain, irreducible to any other dimension within human experience and conceived as isolated by any historical, social, and cultural context looks distinctly phenomenological. In the same vein, another Scandinavian scholar, T. Laitila (2008, 168), mentions Pettazzoni, along with G. Widengren, N. Söderblom and F. Heiler, as a scholar that Cox should have included in the group of top phenomenologists of religion. Paradoxically enough, the standard image we have of Pettazzoni in Italy (esp. among the exponents of the so-called Roman School: exhaustive evidence collected by Nanini 2003, 93–96; 2012b, 82) is that of a stout supporter of historicism and an unyielding adversary of phenomenology and hermeneutics. This representation of Pettazzoni as a full-fledged historicist is shared by Eliade who, as is well-known, positioned himself in the middle ground between the Dutch and German phenomenologists and historical and social reductionists. Pettazzoni's disciple, and my professor, Ugo Bianchi (1922–1995) considered him a positivist: and this was not a compliment! The truth, perhaps, lies in the middle. Clearly, if to be a phenomenologist you have to practise the *epoché* and eidetic vision, seeking the structure and meaning of single religions to show that they all share a common essence, and to exert empathy or sympathetic understanding in your appreciation of a religious tradition or experience, the Italian scholar was not a phenomenologist. On the other hand, he went further than the second Scandinavian school, which advocated a purely descriptive and classificatory approach, aiming to point out categories and conceptions to be used for comparison and eliminating any metaphysical presupposition about the nature of religion. Pettazzoni had, in fact, his own secular faith from his juvenile adhesion to Freemasonry to the civil religion ideals of his older years. And this was not without influence on his scholarly vision.

In an insightful review of Pettazzoni's first important work on the formation of monotheism, philosopher Giovanni Gentile (1875–1944) pointed out that the posited distinction or opposition in religious phenomena between conceptual and natural elements was flawed and, more generally, that it is impossible to do an ethnographic or historical research in the study of religion without a general concept of the subject matter, i.e. religions, and its ideal genesis (Gentile 1922, 985–986). In the letter where he paid due homage to his reviewer (Severino 2002, 115–116), the Bologna professor recognized that a preliminary "concept of religion" is necessary in order to do "history of religions" in a fruitful way – a requirement which is typical of the phenomenological approach. But in the following he declares, with some embarrassment, that at present he is unable to decide whether to adopt an inductive method of inference (based on empirical investigation), or a method of deductive inference (based on theorizing). As underscored by Severino in his comments (2002, 116), Pettazzoni felt this necessity to figure out "the central and vital problem of our discipline" until the end of his life.

After the dialogue with the Sicilian idealist philosopher Gentile, most decisive was, for Pettazzoni, the encounter with the foremost Dutch phenomenologist G. van der Leeuw, whose systematic works (*Einführung in die Phänomenologie der Religion*, 1925; *Phänomenologie der Religion*, 1933) were both enthusiastically – although not without some reservation – reviewed by him, and exerted a great impact on his vision of the study of religion and his own attempt at founding a new epistemology of the study of religion where "religious phenomenology and history are not two sciences but are two complementary aspects of the integral science of religion" (Pettazzoni 1959a,

66; all the materials concerning the relationship between the two scholars are collected and discussed by Nanini 2012b, 84–87).

We find Pettazzoni's official programmatic position in an essay with a very telling title: "History and Phenomenology in the Science of Religion" (1954). In his view, in order to undertake the study of religions, there are two requirements which are evidently inherent to the heritage of phenomenology: (1) the recognition of the peculiar nature of religious facts and of the science of religion which studies them; (2) a deeper understanding of the (religious) meaning of these events. However, he is reluctant to admit "a cleaving of the science of religion into phenomenology and history" (Pettazzoni 1954, 218). Instead, "the studies of comparative religion form a unity. Only in close contact with the history of religion does phenomenology have a meaningful function" (Pettersson in Pettersson and Åkerberg 1981, 47). Pettazzoni returns to the question of the relation between history and phenomenology in his last contribution to NVMEN (1959b). His conclusion is well-known: the two approaches should integrate and somewhat interpenetrate each other, by strengthening religious phenomenology with the historicist concept of development and historicist historiography with the phenomenological requirement of the autonomous value of religion. Consequently, phenomenology remains resolved in history, and religious history acquires the character of a qualified historical science ("una scienza storica qualificata"), in other words, a specific, sui generis, historical science (Pettazzoni 1959b, 14). His middle-way position met immediate approval as well as notable criticism from his two companions in the governance of the IAHR who were at the same time the two upholders of the Dutch and Scandinavian phenomenology: C. J. Bleeker and G. Widengren. (In my view, Pettazzoni's position is somewhat facile: cf. Bleeker 1972, 38, stating that this attitude of reconciliation "does not give the solution of the problem at stake.") For Bleeker, Pettazzoni had not done full justice to the phenomenological method (Bleeker 1959; 1972, 37: "It is questionable whether he fully understood the nature of the phenomenology of religion"). Widengren (in Bianchi, Bleeker and Bausani 1972, 5–14; expanded by Widengren 1983, 34–44), instead, underscored some historico-philological shortcomings in Pettazzoni's last great comparative work and pleaded for a rigorous demarcation between the historical method and the comparative one. Echoes of this methodological debate can be found also in scholars of later generations who were somewhat extraneous to this inner-European discourse. It is a fact that, in private notes of his later years (around 1957), he put phenomenology in the list of the four enemies of the history of religions, in third place, after "psychologism" and before "philology" (cf. Nanini 2012a, 342).

Our impression is that Pettazzoni's "third way", with his continuous plea for history (an hypostatized concept of history which became the specious, somewhat abusive, slogan of the various branches of his Roman school), is certainly a personal utopia, in the sense that it is virtually impossible to "revive" such a scholarly personality, given his own unique talents and experience. But it also seems to me that his project of a new science had inherent, as well as insoluble, contradictions in its attempt to conciliate the irreconcilable – the static with the dynamic, historicism with hermeneutics, *Verstehen* (interpretative understanding) with *Erklären* (causal explanation), and empiricism with intuitionism. How can a cultural or historical reason clarify an "ineffable mystery" (Pettazzoni's own definition of religion: cf. the passage quoted by Nanini 2003, 73, and a further discussion of the evidence by Montanari 2016, 89–103)? The conflict of interpretations that was born immediately after his death gives evidence of this epistemological *cul-de-sac* but at the same time shows the fertility of the theoretical challenge, which led to a series of interventions that spread from the drastic criticism of Franco Bolgiani (in Bianchi, Bleeker and Bausani 1972, 45–51) to the apologetic approach of Pisi (1990) pleading for the view of a fully historicist Pettazzoni triumphing on all sides, passing through the thought-provoking questions raised by Nanini (2012b, 87–95).

Among the disciples of Pettazzoni the only one who has not harboured an utterly negative attitude toward phenomenology has been Ugo Bianchi, a foremost scholar of the history of religions who was an IAHR President (1990–1995) like his mentor Pettazzoni. Bianchi's official position toward (Dutch) PoR is expounded in a chapter of his treatise (Bianchi 1975, 178–181). Van der Leeuw's and Bleeker's efforts in "understanding the faith of believers" are "useful to historico-religious research", even if certain philosophical (van der Leeuw) and theological (Bleeker) inclinations "leave some fundamental perplexities" (for more detail and criticism see Terrin 2002, 372–375). Bianchi's stance is more articulated in a work where he attempted to clarify "the epistemological statute of the discipline we call the History of Religions" (Bianchi 1980, 10) by situating the category of dualism in the frame of the "historical phenomenology of religion", an approach that implies a combination of "historical research and typological categorization" (ibid., 17). He adopts that expression instead of his favourite formula "historical typology" (derived from Pettazzoni and Gustav Mensching) in order to familiarize with his Scandinavian readers, but he insists that any positive religio-historical treatment of the matter religion ("that vast 'concrete universal' we call 'religion'": Bianchi 1980, 23) must exclude the classical tools of philosophical phenomenology and hermeneutics: "No intuition, no 'eidetic reduction', no philosophical 'concept' of religion will be of use under those conditions" (Bianchi 1980, 18–19). Instead, any special research in the field "must always be built on a historical and philological basis" (Åkerberg, in Pettersson and Åkerberg 1981, 77), being susceptible of revision "in view of the progress of historical research". Apparently, like his mentor Pettazzoni, Bianchi adopted a "third way". Religion is a human experience *sui generis* but conditioned by cultural variety and historical circumstances. Comparison can lead to a better understanding of the more or less similar ("analogous" in Bianchi's terminology) formations of a certain phenomenological type, as it appears in various religious worlds. PoR is just an aspect of history of religions and can be absorbed by it, as a precisely comparative history of religions. Bianchi is criticized (as is Widengren, who shared similar rationalistic lines) for his marked "attitude of hesitation against the importance of the psychological view in history of religion and phenomenology" (Åkerberg, in Pettersson and Åkerberg 1981, 85). According to an exponent of the Lund phenomenological school (influenced by Car-Martin Edsman and Erland Ehnmark), Bianchi's stern rejection of the psychological, emotional and somewhat irrational components of religious phenomena implies "a certain rationalistic one-sidedness which definitely limits his field of vision as to science of religion, as well as his ability to understand religion in its invariably integrated historical-psychological contexts" (Åkerberg, in Pettersson and Åkerberg 1981, 85–86).

In my view, in his practical, idiographic work Bianchi was not so rigorous as in his theoretical statements, leaving space for a variety of psychological intuitions, in pure phenomenological style, as has been brilliantly (with some overstatement) stressed by A. N. Terrin. In this light, Bianchi moves toward the goal indicated by Paul Feyerabend: "we need a dreamworld in order to discover the features of the real world we think we inhabit" (Terrin 2002, 390).

Which Italian authors have better represented, in your opinion, the phenomenological study of religion? In other words, is or was there an "Italian PoR"?

Unlike the preceding two questions, the answer to question 3 is very straightforward. In Italy we have in fact had only one eminent scholar of religion that has professed to be a full-fledged phenomenologist of religion, namely Aldo Natale Terrin (b. 1941). Terrin is an ordained Catholic priest but his approach is far from being confessional, in spite of the charges of theological bias frequently levelled against him. He expressly adheres to the positions of classical phenomenology inasmuch as he claims that "our approaches must take better account of the irreducibly religious nature of religious experience by doing justice to the nature of *religious symbolism*; that is, considering it from the 'inside' of culture and not 'outside' of it" (Terrin 1998, 380–381). Even more explicitly he professes that PoR is "the best method with which to study and to understand other religions" (ibid., 383). Along with a host of monographs dedicated to specific forms of religiosity (especially New age and Neo-Hindu religious movements) and thematic issues (ritual, neuroscience, water mythologies and fundamentalism), all studied in close connection to religious experience, Terrin has produced a series of theoretical and histo-riographical textbooks (Terrin 1983, 1991 and especially 2008) where he severely criticizes other scholarly approaches and pleads for a genuinely phe-nomenological, hermeneutical and experiential approach (cf. Nanini 2015, 84–90; 2016, 21–24). Quite recently, Terrin has eloquently described the theory and practice of his phenomenological method (or outlook) in the foreword and the first introductory chapter of a book dedicated to one of the most characteristic (and controversial) among the new religious move-ments of the mid- to late– twentieth century, Scientology, which arose as part of the counterculture response to the growth of American Science (Terrin 2017).

According to Terrin, the phenomenologist who studies a religious group (in this specific case the Church of Scientology) must adopt a sympathetic attitude to grasp the eidos (in other words the original and founding element) of that group through its self-perception, in order to avoid a reductionist approach and instead access the original vision (Terrin 2017, 6–7). Currently the phenomenological approach, by adopting a "participatory" attitude, finds an endorsement in the crisis of objective visions and indisputable perceptions that implies the dissolution of the notion of "hard facts". Terrin (ibid., 29–31) therefore opines that one is able to adequately describe a reality only when in some way he has empathized himself in that given reality. Those who describe a reality that in fact does not touch and does not convince them will not be very effective in their description, let alone have a real capacity for in-vestigation. Only some tuning with the object of inquiry makes the researcher more attentive and more able to grasp all the nuances of a cognized and lived experience. Knowledge itself, as such, is nothing but a kind of identification and leads to an act of assumption, of appropriation of the reality itself that we intend to describe. In the study of a religious experience, one is somehow always involved. In other words, when we study the religious beliefs of oth-ers, we study them as beliefs that have their possible and probable internal coherence, which is valid and acceptable and have a meaning that involves us directly or indirectly. From this perspective, the "hermeneutics of suspicion" must never involve our research area beforehand. Phenomenology, without ever giving a final judgment of truth or non-truth, is only brought to take note and to value the world of such experiences, especially insofar as they are expressions shared by a circle of believers.

In sum, phenomenology moves from two fundamental assumptions that are expressions of "respect" and "recognition" of what is offered to the ob-server's gaze. The first prerequisite is the empathy (Einfühlung) or empathic look. As pointed out by L. Wittgenstein at the linguistic level, it is logically impossible to deny the believer when he claims to believe. The second prerequisite is the bracketing of one's own ideas (*epoché*), of the load of judgments and prejudices of which we are carriers, applying a kind of "suspension of disbelief" (S. T. Coleridge). Inspired in a certain way by the theory of "methodological ludism" recently proposed by K. Knibbe and A. Droogers and by the "participant observation" of the anthropological tradition, Terrin (2017, 32–34) proposes that the investigator of religious reality assumes an attitude similar to that of a player, seeking to interact with the object and, in a way of speaking, to play with alternative ways of conceptualizing the world, without interfering with the concept of truth.

An original application of a phenomenological hermeneutics without any explicit reference to Terrin's neo-phenomenology is that of Massimo Campanini (b. 1954), in regard to the field of Islamic studies, more specifically exploring a possible phenomenological and hermeneutical reading of the Holy Qur'an (Campanini 2017). On the wake of Annemarie Schimmel (1922–2003) and Fazlur Rahman (1919–1988), two scholars of Islam who adopted a phenomenological if not theological approach, Campanini reads the Qur'an as a genuine message of God living in the faith and the daily worship of the believers, and he puts its historical and authorial context in brackets. Moving further from the phenomenology of Husserl to the ontology of Heidegger, he contends that if we want to arrive at an immediate vision of divinity we must reduce it to its pure essence. The profound meaning of the *tawhid* (the uniqueness of God) is grasped by reducing the essence to existence, while other Heidegerrian concepts are applied to a linguistic-symbolic analysis of the holy text. In a phenomenological perspective, the Islamic vision of God and Truth (*haqq*) is presented in a dialectical key: as presence and lack or absence, as immanence and transcendence, as revelation and concealment (Campanini 2017, 316–319).

What are the reasons for the lesser impact that PoR has had in Italy, compared to other theories and methods?

The reasons are mostly to be traced back to the influence of both Catholicism (PoR originated against the background of Protestant liberal theology) and Historicism, two conceptions of the world and man within history that look and are opposite but share some basic elements, including a deep distrust toward the irrational and emotional components of life and history. A Catholic influence (the Thomistic doctrine of analogy and definition) is evident in Bianchi and some of his pupils; historicism – in fact a mixture of elements variously borrowed from the idealism of Benedetto Croce (1866–1952) and dialectic materialism of Marxism (especially in the Italian variant elaborated by Antonio Gramsci [1891–1937]) is the battering ram used against every sort of phenomenology or irrationalism (the two terms being used as quasi synonyms; cf. Terrin 1998, 378; Prandi 2006, 167–169).

Croce himself wrote a painfully dismissive 1934 review of van der Leeuw's masterpiece (cf. Nanini 2000a, 805–806, n. 6). Among the disciples or associates of Pettazzoni, Vittorio Lanternari (1918–2010) and Alfonso Maria Di Nola (1926–1997) made only occasional (disparaging) references to phenomenology. Instead, PoR is a haunting presence in the methodological writings of Ernesto de Martino (1908–1965), Angelo Brelich (1913–1977) and Dario Sabbatucci (1923–2004). For Sabbatucci (1990, esp. 234–246) the only phenomenologies worthy (or unworthy) of being taken in consideration were those of van der Leeuw and Eliade, though both were rapidly dismissed with (supposedly) historical arguments.

De Martino looks theoretically more sophisticated, and it will be worthwhile to briefly present his arguments (carefully examined by Nanini 2000a). Of the two methodological essays (de Martino 1953–1954, and 1957, repr. in de Martino 1995, 47–95), written when the Neapolitan intellectual had not yet obtained the chair of history of religions in Cagliari, the titles themselves are telling: in the first one, phenomenology (the "Other") is drastically opposed to his own "absolute historicism"; in the second one, "irrationalism" is virtually used as a synonym of phenomenology, as noted above. De Martino easily highlights the basic flaw of van der Leeuw's PoR and Rudolf Otto's ontology of the sacred and experience of the numinous, a flaw that can be resumed in the felicitous metaphor of the "mitsingen ist verboten" (de Martino 1995, 77). In other words, the attempt of the phenomenologist to reach a pure intuition, to grasp the deep essence of the phenomenon implies the risk of a confusion of planes between subject and object, of a loss of distinction between religious outlook and scientific outlook (ibid., 54), producing a hybrid product "in which historical science of religious life and real religious life merge" (ibid., 77). Therefore, Otto's concept of the numinous as well as van der Leeuw's meta-historical *Erlebnis* (lived experience) of religious mystery (ibid., 47–55) belong to the manifestations of current religious life rather than to the methodology of religious studies (ibid., 78). The epistemological problem with de Martino arises when he attempts to build up his own hermeneutics of the origin and formation of religious phenomena (the hierogenetic process – ibid., 88–94, 120 – where he attempts a definition of the roots of religious life and sacred which indulges in psychological reductionism). In fact, he introduces a set of categories (loss of presence or risk of not being in history aka religious destorification: ibid., 62, 82, 94) that have evident philosophical roots (Martin Heidegger's metaphysical existentialism, as recognized by M. Massenzio in the introduction to de Martino 1995, 22–26) and are overtly psychologistic in spite of his own denial of this (ibid., 94–96), being reductionistic and deeply embedded in his own psychological drama (cf. Casadio 2013).

Angelo Brelich's attitude toward phenomenology was irreducibly hostile, perhaps even more than that of his senior colleague. In supporting the cause of historicism, he exhibited a zeal that can only be found in a fresh convert to a religion. In fact, before meeting Pettazzoni and the historicist Italian milieu, the Hungarian historian of religions had mentors like Karoly Kerényi (1897–1973) and – in a more subliminal form – Julius Evola (1898–1974), two personages both belonging – in very different ways – to the "ambiguous family of the irrationalists" (to use a notorious derogatory formula coined by de Martino). Brelich was inflexible in refusing and reviling all approaches to the study of religion that were different from his own, labelling them as aridly philological and scientifically inadequate, or definitely theological, or dangerously irrationalist (a label which is, of course, unacceptable according to current academic standards). In his coherent, staunchly partisan vision, all opponents of the good historicist method were irrationalists, a stigma which grouped Catholics like Pater W. Schmidt and U. Bianchi with hermeneuts like Kerényi and Eliade, or phenomenologists like van der Leeuw and F. Heiler, all scholars who – in his view – shared the same ultraconservative, politically regressive if not overtly fascist ideology (for a partial collection of these militant interventions, see Nanini 2004, esp. 18, 28, 32). The importance of Brelich's belligerent advocacy of historicism in the Italian context of religious studies cannot be overstated. With a single notable exception (Enrico Montanari, b. 1942), all his direct disciples that have taken up teaching positions in Italian universities, from Gilberto Mazzoleni (1936–2013) and Ileana Chirassi (b. 1936) to Anna Maria Gloria Capomacchia (b. 1952), have, with various nuances, shared Brelich's uncompromising, monolithic attitude.

Do you integrate theories and methods belonging to – or associated with – PoR in your own methodological endeavour as a historian of religions? If so, why, and how?

This is an intriguing question and difficult to answer simply. As a member of the third generation of the Roman School of History of Religions my education was surrounded by the cult of history and philology. Consequently, I have never been particularly sympathetic to PoR as practised by the Dutch (van der Leeuw, Bleeker) and German schools (Otto, Wach and Heiler) and definitely I feel more at home with the rather empirical, descriptive and taxonomical approaches practised by Scandinavian scholars (Kristensen, Widengren, and Hultkrantz in particular). My encounter with Eliade, in so far as he can be considered a phenomenologist, took place quite late, at the beginning of the century, following an invitation by Larry Sullivan and Bryan Rennie, but I was fascinated by his intellectual acumen in the perception and comparison of human phenomena much more than by his ontological vision of the sacred and the series of hierophanies.

However, having said this, I must confess that I find the stance of phenomenological *epoché* (with its Pyrrhonist more than Husserlian ring) – or "bracketing", a suspension of judgment that blocks our biases and assumptions in order to examine how the phenomenon presents itself in the world of the participant and explain/understand it in terms of its own inherent system of meaning – intellectually fascinating and epistemologically convincing.

Descending from theory to practice, if I examine my own scholarly production spanning through 40 years of activity I can find among my inspirers the names of famous "irrationalists", such as L. Frobenius, W. F. Otto, K. Kerényi, W. B. Kristensen and – of course – M. Eliade, along with mentors belonging to other intellectual milieus like Giambattista Vico or Sigmund Freud. Based on these premises, I think I may be placed at the edges of the Roman School of history of religions in its various declensions and inflections.

Commentary

In these final remarks and comments on Giovanni Casadio's thorough survey, I will complement some of his arguments by focusing mainly on the heritage and the ongoing influence of the greatest Italian tradition in the academic study of religions: the so-called "School of Rome".[1] This is somewhat inevitable, since all discussions concerning the modern study of religions in Italy cannot but centre around said school, its founder Pettazzoni, and his epigones. Moreover, I will take the liberty of offering a few biographic insights centred around the memories of my years as a young student at the department of "Studi storico-religiosi" at "La Sapienza" University in Rome – the locus of the so called "School of Rome".

As should be patent after reading the interview, Italy has never produced a systematic discussion about the theses and methods of PoR, comparable to that of the historical-comparative method. Nor has it ever reached any general conclusion about the phenomenological approach. With the exception of Aldo Natale Terrin, Italy has actually never produced a phenomenologist of religion nor, therefore, a "new-style phenomenology" (Waardenburg 2001).

---

1.   The literature in Italian about this ensemble of scholars, who have navigated the panorama of religious studies in Italy for the last hundred years, is enormous (it is reviewed in the second half of the book Testa 2010). Much poorer is the English one (for a short overview, see Stausberg 2008, 2009). In these final remarks, I am intentionally limiting the bibliographic apparatus to the very essential.

Therefore, the history of PoR in Italy takes a limited and peculiar form. However, its limited appeal as a method for the study of religions does not mean that it has been absent from the Italian intellectual landscape. In fact, apart from Terrin's scholarship, it has been present in two main forms: (1) as an explicit polemical "other" for most Italian historians of religions of the last century, and (2) in the shape of implicit (if not crypto-) phenomenological tendencies that have characterized several Italian historians of religions from Pettazzoni to Casadio himself.

There was, obviously, no "conventional" or normative stance of the entire "Rome School" on phenomenology, but rather a variety of stances, associated with a generally shared mistrust. This state of things lasted from the post-Second World War period until the first decade of the new Millennium. And here is where my personal memories merge with more general considerations on PoR's eminent role as a methodological "other" in Italy – particularly in Rome. As a student during the years 2003–2009 (not continuously), I remember very well the insistence of many teachers on considering their historical-comparative method as not only different, but actually *opposite* to the phenomenological one. The rants were frequent, even repetitive, and at times vehement. What puzzled me at the time, and still puzzles me today, is that most of this critical verve was being exercised against scholars that were then long gone (van der Leeuw, Rudolf Otto, Eliade), and especially, but not exclusively, by former disciples of Angelo Brelich. Although not an orthodox phenomenologist – and certainly not a self-declared one – Eliade (and the Eliadian "variation" of PoR) was the common rhetorical target, with the Romanian scholar actually coming to represent, rather oddly, a veritable symbol of phenomenology and its mistakes. Until a few years ago this polarization, which constituted a veritable "us vs. them" discourse, was still very much alive at the department. (I might mention, for example, my BA thesis mentor, Anna Maria Capomacchia, a historian of ancient religions, who was always eager to challenge – and almost delighted in chastising – the phenomenological approach.)

The narrative of my lecturers and professors back then was that the School of Rome had been, between the twenties and the fifties, a reaction to *Urmonotheismus* and phenomenology, then, between the fifties and the seventies, a reaction to both phenomenology (especially in its Eliadian declension) and structuralism. Things, however, stand rather differently, as Casadio claims in the interview – and as I have claimed elsewhere and claim here.

Today, the former polemical tones and mistrust for PoR have mostly given way to indifference: the new generation of scholars of the "Roman School" (Sergio Botta and Marianna Ferrara) are much more interested in new topics and approaches (materialism, cognitivism, post-modern and post-colonial theories, etc.) than in old ones. Eliade is mentioned seldom, and more in regard to his alleged political stances than anything else.

The second question, of implicit (if not crypto-) phenomenological tendencies of many Italian (and "Roman") historians of religions, is thornier. One preliminary consideration: the assumed "unity" of the "School of Rome", which was accepted until not so long ago, is actually only partial: if we take into consideration the most important Italian historians of religions of the two generations following Pettazzoni and productive until the end of last century (i.e. Ernesto de Martino, Angelo Brelich, Ugo Bianchi, Vittorio Lanternari, Dario Sabbatucci, Cristiano Grottanelli, Giovanni Casadio and others) we discover that the differences in their methodologies and in their conceptions of religion are at least as significant as the similarities.[2]

In his interview, Casadio summarizes and evokes the ambiguities of Pettazzoni's method, especially with regards to PoR; no wonder, then, that we find discrepancies in the methods of his disciples. The most senior and perhaps important was the Italo-Hungarian Angelo Brelich.

While more or less all scholars of religion affiliated with Rome expressed reservations about the phenomenological approach, the most vocal were Brelich and his disciples, up to a few years ago at least. Nevertheless, it is also possible to isolate a few elements of direct influence of phenomenological, or rather Eliadian traits in him; as noted, for the second generation of Italian historians of religions, Eliade represented, along with van der Leeuw, and however odd this judgment will seem to non-Italians, *the* phenomenologist of religion – with Rudolf Otto usually following as the third one in the *trittico* (irrationalist and phenomenological approaches and authors have traditionally been associated in Italian scholarship).

The categories and concepts that Brelich relied upon to exercise his "*storicizzazione*" were often not dissimilar from those used by phenomenologists, even though he never gave any real credit to the empathetic and irrational dimensions that were central for the phenomenologists, and instead always placed central emphasis on the operation of historicizing ("*storicizzare*") religious facts by paying attention to their contexts and to the conditions of their emergence and developments. Several categories presented in Brelich's books, and most crucially in his

---

2.   In my first book (Testa 2010), I tried to expose some of the methodological ambiguities or even inconsistencies of the "Roman" historians of religions.

handbook, *Introduzione alla storia delle religioni*[3] (Brelich 1966), resemble typical phenomenological and/or Eliadian ones: the conception of time in festive ritualism, for example, or his theorization about the nature and functions of myth, which shows a rather interesting fusion of ideas from both Mircea Eliade and Bronisław Malinowski.[4]

Ernesto de Martino comes second, in this ideal genealogy of the now "classical" Italian scholars of religions who had, in one way or another, contacts/contrasts with PoR and with Eliade and his personal variant of it. Although much younger than Pettazzoni, de Martino – a scholar not fully belonging but rather tangential to the Rome School – is the only Italian historian (and anthropologist) of religions, along with Pettazzoni, who in those times engaged in direct intellectual duel with Eliade, mainly by means of mutual-reviews and replies, chiefly about magic and shamanism.[5] Along with Vittorio Lanterari and Dario Sabbatucci, he also remained mostly uninfluenced by Eliade's theories, methods, and historical conclusions. De Martino remained sceptical of Eliade's endeavour throughout his life. He also remained sceptical of another coeval giant in the field, Claude Lévi-Strauss, who himself ignored or disregarded both de Martino and Eliade throughout his career – even though other parallels among these scholars do exist (Testa 2015).[6]

Perhaps more importantly, de Martino wrote what is likely the most important Italian critique of PoR, as theorized and diffused by Gerardus van der Leeuw: de Martino (1953–1954). A dense and rather complex text, this critique has been thoroughly analysed in Nanini (2000a). De Martino's firm theoretical and methodological distancing does not prevent him from recognizing the great importance, and even the historical primacy, of van der Leeuw's approach in the scientific study of religion: *nec cum te nec sine te* (neither with nor without you), as de Martino concluded, a motto that still functions, in part, to describe the entire attitude of many Italian scholars of religion of the twentieth century

---

3. This book has been repeatedly published for decades, in dozens of editions. It has been taught to dozens of cohorts of students, and, in spite of its author's intentions, it is probably the work most influenced by Eliade in the entire production of the "Roman School".

4. Be it noticed here that Brelich's first master, Károly Kerényi, was much prone to archetypical and irrationalist types of explanations for religious matters, and was methodologically much closer – unsurprisingly – to phenomenology and Eliade than Brelich's second master, Pettazzoni.

5. The reviews, critiques, and exchanges between de Martino and Eliade have been the object of a rather rich scholarship, which is mostly reported and discussed in Testa (2015).

6. English translation presented at the 2018 EASR conference.

towards PoR, and also the attitude of the most dissident ones (after all, criticizing and refusing a specific tradition of studies also means taking it into consideration seriously). In addition, the influence of Eliadian PoR, especially his idea of religion as a "rupture of levels" has also been noticed in Ugo Bianchi (Stausberg 2009, 267).

In short, a veritable direct or indirect influence of Eliade is only completely absent, in my opinion, in scholars such as Dario Sabbatucci, Vittorio Lanternari and Cristiano Grottanelli, although of course they discuss his ideas and influence in their works. The latter two developed a distaste for PoR because they considered it too theological (as did others) and for Eliade more because of his alleged political views than for his scholarship (a motivation which is not to be discovered in other Italian scholars until the sixties or even seventies of the last century). In Lanternari, a more prolific author and a more internationally known one than Grottanelli, this also happened, probably, because of his experience as a fieldworker (which Eliade never was) and his interest in more contemporary matters, beyond a genuine methodological distance between his materialistic stance and those that, on the contrary, opted for fideistic/theological, irrationalistic and/or phenomenological ones.

In Sabbatucci, we find another true example of an Italian religionist showing a profound, genuine theoretical incompatibility with Eliade, van der Leeuw and classical phenomenology more generally: if we consider that, as Casadio writes in the interview (and I firmly believe), "the claim that the sacred (religion) constitutes a unique domain, irreducible to any other dimension within human experience" as "distinctly phenomenological", then the least phenomenological of Italian scholars of religions was precisely Dario Sabbatucci, who, in a rather structuralist fashion (and probably precisely on the basis of the direct influence of Lévi-Strauss's speculation, as I claim in Testa 2010), did not credit any ontological autonomy to religion,[2] and remained unimpressed by irrationalistic or phenomenological approaches throughout his career.

It is thus perhaps not by chance that the greatest interest in PoR and in Eliade in more recent scholars has been shown by two disciples of Bianchi, the one Italian professor in the history of religions of his generation who did not stand in fierce stance against PoR: I refer to Paola Pisi,

---

7.   Lévi-Strauss notoriously held Eliade's work and thought in utter disregard. However, Lévi-Strauss's and Sabbatucci's political views were also at odds, not to say completely opposite. Moreover, Sabbatucci remains one of the most parochial scholars of religion Italy produced throughout the twentieth century, even though he strongly influenced certain French historical anthropologists (namely Marcel Detienne and Jean-Pierre Vernant: Testa 2010). Lévi-Strauss probably never heard of Sabbatucci in his life.

who devoted a few book-long articles to Eliade and to the history of the history of religions, and especially Giovanni Casadio, who has devoted numerous books and writings to Italian religionists as well as to Eliade (unlike Casadio, Pisi was an active scholar only for a relatively short span of time).

In the works and thought of Casadio, a tension can be found between different visions of history, religion, and the role religion and particular religions have had in history: for example, in one of his last books, which is dedicated to the historiography of shamanism "before and after Eliade" (Casadio 2014), we see clearly at work a theoretical-methodological – if not epistemological – tension between two different conceptions of history of religions: the former could be defined as historicist and relativistic, the latter historicist and phenomenological. The former theorizes a form of "absolute" historicism, which would lead to a relativistic posture undermining the very idea of shamanism (here read: religion) itself; according to this vision, each cultural fact conventionally defined or definable as shamanic should be investigated according to their own developments, specificities, and contexts, and perhaps associated (but nothing else than that) to others on the basis of analogies, homogeneities, and homologies,[8] just for the sake of saving the comparative method. The latter embraces a historical-phenomenological vision according to which the individuation (or construction) of a religious type, like that of shamanism, cannot but depend on the recognition and the acceptance of an ontological or experiential (and maybe also morphological or historical) "kernel", in other words, a sort of "essence", that would associate all the phenomena that contribute to recognizing/constructing such a type. Perhaps another sort of "crypto-phenomenology" among the Italians?

Last but perhaps not least – considering his prominence in historical sciences – comes the work of Carlo Ginzburg: an Eliadian influence on his conception of shamanism – which in turn informs his most renowned work about the European Sabbath (Ginzburg 1991) – is easily recognizable, in spite of the author's overt dislike of Eliade's methodology.

Alessandro Testa (b. 1983) is Assistant Professor at the Department of Social Sciences, Charles University, Prague. He has a background in Classics, History, Religious Studies, and Anthropology. In the last 15 years he has studied, worked, or undertaken ethnographic fieldwork in Italy, France, Estonia, Czech Republic, Germany, Austria, and Catalonia (Spain). He can write and speak seven languages and has a good understanding or a passive knowledge of another half a

---

8. For a typological distinction between analogy, homogeneity, and homology in comparing similar religious traits or facts, see Testa (2017).

dozen. His publications include some seventy articles in journals and chapters in volumes, four edited volumes, and four books (*Miti antichi e moderne mitologie. Saggi di storia delle religioni e storia degli studi sul mondo antico*, 2010; *Il carnevale dell'uomo-animale*, 2014; *La religiosità dei Sanniti*, 2016; *Rituality and Social (Dis) Order: The Historical Anthropology of Popular Carnival in Europe*, 2020).

References

Bianchi, Ugo. 1975. *The History of Religions*. Leiden: E. J. Brill.

Bianchi, Ugo. 1980. "The Category of Dualism in the Historical Phenomenology of Religion." *Temenos* 16: 10–25. https://doi.org/10.33356/temenos.6251

Bianchi, Ugo, Bleeker, C. J. and Bausani, Alessandro (eds). 1972. *Problems and Methods of the History of Religions*. Leiden: Brill.

Bleeker, C. J. 1959. "The Phenomenological Method." *Numen* 6(2): 96–111.

Bleeker, C. J. 1972. "The Contribution of the Phenomenology of Religion to the Study of the History of Religions." In *Problems and Methods of the History of Religions*, edited by Ugo Bianchi, C. J. Bleeker and Alessandro Bausani, 35–54. Leiden: Brill.

Brelich Angelo. 1966. *Introduzione alla storia delle religioni*. Rome: Edizioni dell'Ateneo.

Campanini, Massimo. 2017. "Filosofia e Corano: un percorso ermeneutico tra ontologia e fenomenologia." In *Appropriation, Interpretation and Criticism: Philosophical and Theological Exchanges between the Arabic, Hebrew and Latin Intellectual Traditions*, edited by A. Fidora and N. Polloni, 303–321. Barcelona: Féderation Internationale des Instituts d'Études Médiévales. https://doi.org/10.1484/m.tema-eb.4.2017182

Casadio, Giovanni. 2010. "Comparative Religion Scholars in Debate: Theology vs History in Letters Addressed to Ugo Bianchi". In *Chasing Down Religion: In the Sights of History and the Cognitive Sciences. Essays in Honor of Luther H. Martin*, edited by P. Pachis and D. Wiebe, 59–80. Thessaloniki: Barbounaki Publications.

Casadio, Giovanni (ed.). 2002. *Ugo Bianchi. Una vita per la storia delle religioni*. Rome: Il Calamo.

Casadio, Giovanni. 2013. "Ernesto de Martino at Home and Abroad: Fortunes and Misfortunes." In *Studium Sapientiae*, edited by A. Cosentino and M. Monaca, 75–86. Soveria Mannelli (CS): Rubbettino.

Casadio, Giovanni. 2014. *Lo sciamanesimo prima e dopo Mircea Eliade*, Rome: Il Calamo.

Cox, James L. 2006. *A Guide to the Phenomenology of Religion: Key Figures, Formative Influences and Subsequent Debates*. London: T. & T. Clark International.

Cox, James L. 2010. *An Introduction to the Phenomenology of Religion*. London: T. & T. Clark International.

De Martino, Ernesto. 1953-1954. "Fenomenologia religiosa e storicismo assoluto." *Studi e materiali di storia delle religioni* 24-25: 1-25.

De Martino, Ernesto. 1957. "Storicismo e irrazionalismo nella storia delle religioni." *Studi e materiali di storia delle religioni* 28(1): 89-107. https://doi.org/10.2307/3269473

De Martino, Ernesto. 1995. *Storia e metastoria. I fondamenti di una teoria del sacro*. Lecce: Argo.

Gentile, Giovanni. 1922. "La formazione del monoteismo." *La critica*: 298-30. Repr. in G. Gentile, *Frammenti di storia della filosofia*, edited by H. A. Cavallera, 983-985. Firenze 1999: Le Lettere.

Gilhus, Ingvild Sælid. 1984. "The Phenomenology of Religion and Theories of Interpretation." *Temenos* 20: 26-39.

Gilhus, Ingvild Sælid. 1994. "Is a Phenomenology of Religion Possible?: A Response to Jeppe Sinding Jensen." *Method and Theory in the Study of Religion* 6(2): 163-171. https://doi.org/10.1163/157006894x00082

Gilhus, Ingvild Sælid. 1999-2000. "Phenomenology of Religion Critically Observed: Introduction." *Temenos* 35-36: 7-23. https://doi.org/10.33356/temenos.4859

Ginzburg, Carlo. 1991. *Ecstasies: Deciphering the Witches' Sabbath*, translated by Raymond Rosenthal. New York: Pantheon (original edition: *Storia notturna: Una decifrazione del sabba*, Torino: Einaudi, 1989).

Hultkrantz, Åke. 1970. "The Phenomenology of Religion: Aims and Methods." *Temenos* 6: 68-88.

Jackson, Peter and Thurfjell, David. 2008. "Introduction: Reflections on the Concept of 'Border' and its Present Status in the Study of Religion." *Temenos* 44(1): 6-11.

Jensen, Jeppe Sinding. 1993. "Is a Phenomenology of Religion Possible? On the Ideas of a Human and Social Science of Religion." *Method and Theory in the Study of Religion* 5(2): 109-133. https://doi.org/10.1163/157006894x00082

Jensen, Jeppe Sinding. 1994. "The Name of the Game is 'Nominalism': A Reply to Ingvild Sælid Gilhus." *Method and Theory in the Study of Religion* 6(3): 277-284. https://doi.org/10.1163/157006894x00145

Jensen, Jeppe Sinding. 2001. "Universals, General Terms and the Comparative Study of Religion." *Numen* 48(3): 238-266. https://doi.org/10.1163/156852701752245550

Laitila, Teuvo. 2008. Review of James L. Cox, *A Guide to the Phenomenology of Religion: Key Figures, Formative Influences and Subsequent Debates*. London: Continuum, 2006. *Temenos* 44(1): 165–167.

Montanari, Enrico. 2016. *Storia e tradizione. Orientamenti storico-religiosi e concezioni del mondo*. Rome: Lithos.

Nanini, Riccardo. 2000a. "Fenomenologia religiosa o storicismo assoluto?: Gerardus van der Leeuw secondo Ernesto de Martino." *Studi urbinati* 70(B): 803–851.

Nanini, Riccardo. 2000b. "Tipi ideali e fenomenologia della religione in Gerardus van der Leeuw." *Studia patavina* 47: 439–459, 679–706.

Nanini, Riccardo. 2003. "Raffaele Pettazzoni e la fenomenologia della religione." *Studia Patavina* 50: 377–413.

Nanini, Riccardo. 2004. "'La storia sta in scelte'. Lo storicismo di Angelo Brelich alla luce della sua critica alla fenomenologia della religione." *Annali dell'Università di Ferrara*, n.s., sez. III, Filosofia, Discussion Paper 71.

Nanini, Riccardo. 2008. "Julien Ries e la 'nuova' fenomenologia della religione." *Communio. Rivista internazionale di teologia e cultura* 27(216): 26–37.

Nanini, Riccardo. 2012a. "'Cette connaissance plus profonde, ce n'est pas à l'histoire des religions que nous pouvons la demander ...'. La fenomenologia della religione di Gerardus van der Leeuw e la 'scienza integrale delle religioni' pettazzoniana". In *Il mistero che rivelato ci divide e sofferto ci unisce. Studi pettazzoniani in onore di Mario Gandini*. Supplemento speciale a *Strada maestra*, edited by G. P. Basello, P. Ognibene, A. Panaino, 341–357. Milan: Mimesis.

Nanini, Riccardo. 2012b. "Law and Freedom. Raffaele Pettazzoni's Attitude Towards Gerardus van der Leeuw's Phenomenology of Religion." *Mythos* 6 (n.s.): 81–97.

Nanini, Riccardo. 2015. "Sacro vissuto e intenzionalità. Osservazioni sull'approccio fenomenologico-religioso di Julien Ries." In *Julien Ries. Le sfide dell'antropologia simbolica*, edited by S. Petrosino, 77–91. Milan: Jaca Book.

Nanini, Riccardo. 2016. "Julien Ries e il sacro in metamorfosi. Il fondamentalismo religioso." In *La religione. Natura, tensioni, prospettive*, edited by S. Petrosino, 13–26.

Pettazzoni, Raffaele. 1954. "History and Phenomenology in the Science of Religion." In Raffaele Pettazzoni, *Essays on the History of Religions*, 215–219. Leiden: Brill. https://doi.org/10.1163/1877-5888_rpp_sim_024498

Pettazzoni, Raffaele. 1959a. "The Supreme Being: Phenomenological Structure and Historical Development." In *The History of Religion: Essays in Methodology*, edited by Mircea Eliade and Joseph. M. Kitagawa, 59–66. Chicago, IL: University of Chicago Press.

Pettazzoni, Raffaele. 1959b. "Il metodo comparativo." *Numen* 6(1): 1–14.

Pettersson, Olof and Åkerberg, Hans. 1981. *Interpreting Religious Phenomena: Studies with Reference to the Phenomenology of Religion.* Stockholm: Almqvist & Wiksell International.

Pisi, Paola. 1990. "Storicismo e fenomenologia nel pensiero di Raffaele Pettazzoni." *Studi e materiali di Storia delle Religioni* 56: 245–277.

Prandi, Carlo. 2006. "Note in margine al convegno per gli 80 anni di 'SMSR'." *Studi e materiali di storia delle religioni* 72(1): 165–179.

Ries, Julien. 1994. "Un regard sur la méthode historico-comparative en histoire des religions." In Agathè elpis. *Studi storico-religiosi in onore di Ugo Bianchi,* edited by G. Sfameni Gasparro, 121–148. Rome: L'«Erma» di Bretschneider.

Sabbatucci, Dario. 1990. *La prospettiva storico-religiosa: Fede, religione e cultura.* Milan: Il Saggiatore

Severino, Valerio Salvatore. 2002. "Giovanni Gentile e Raffaele Pettazzoni (1922–1924). Un carteggio sulla storia delle religioni e l'università in Italia." *Storiografia* 6: 107–126.

Stausberg, Michael. 2008. "Western Europe." In *Religious Studies: A Global View,* edited by Gregory D. Alles, 16–39. New York: Routledge.

Stausberg, Michael. 2009. "The Study of Religion(s) in Western Europe III: Further Developments After World War II." *Religion* 39: 261–282. https://doi.org/10.1016/j.religion.2009.06.001

Terrin, Aldo Natale. 1983. *Spiegare o comprendere la religione? Le scienze della religione a confronto.* Padova: Edizioni Messaggero/Abbazia di Santa Giustina.

Terrin, Aldo Natale. 1991. *Introduzione allo studio comparato delle religioni.* Brescia: Morcelliana.

Terrin, Aldo Natale. 1998. "The Study of Religions in Italy: Some Data and Reflections." *Method and Theory in the Study of Religion* 10(4): 373–387. https://doi.org/10.1163/157006898x00169

Terrin, Aldo Natale. 2002. "Fenomenologia 'criptica' della religione in Ugo Bianchi? Interpretazione critica del metodo di studio delle religioni del maestro romano." In *Ugo Bianchi: Una vita per la storia delle religioni,* edited by G. Casadio, 353–391. Rome: Il Calamo.

Terrin, Aldo Natale. 2008. *La religione: temi e problemi.* Brescia: Morcelliana.

Terrin, Aldo Natale. 2017. *Scientology. Libertà e immortalità.* Brescia: Morcelliana.

Testa, Alessandro. 2010. *Miti antichi e moderne mitologie. Saggi di storia delle religioni e storia degli studi sul mondo antico.* Rome: Aracne.

Alessandro Testa

Testa, Alessandro. 2015. "Estasi e crisi: Note su sciamanismo e pessimismo storico in Eliade, de Martino e Lévi-Strauss." In *Sciamanesimo e sciamanesimi: un problema storiografico*, edited by L. Arcari and A. Saggioro, 101–114. Rome: Edizioni Nuova Cultura.

Testa, Alessandro. 2017. "Ritual Zoomorphism in Medieval and Modern European Folklore: Some Skeptical Remarks on a Possible Connection with Shamanism." *Religio: Revue pro religionistiku* 25(1): 3–24.

Waardenburg, Jacques. 2001. "Foreword." In Sharma, Arvind. 2001. *To the Things Themselves: Essays on the Discourse and Practice of the Phenomenology of Religion*, IX–XXI. Berlin: Walter de Gruyter. https://doi.org/10.1515/9783110888447

Widengren, Geo. 1972. "La méthode comparative: entre philologie et phenomenologie." In *Problems and Methods of the History of Religions; Proceedings of the Study Conference organized by the Italian Society for the History of Religions on the Occasion of the Tenth Anniversary of the Death of Raffaele Pettazzoni, Rome, 6th to 8th December 1969.* edited by Ugo Bianchi, C. J. Bleeker, and Alessandro Bausani, 5–14. Leiden: Brill. https://doi.org/10.1163/9789004378100_003

Widengren, Geo. 1983. "Pettazzoni's Untersuchungen zum Problem des Hochgottglaubens: Erinnerungen und Betrachtungen." *Studi e materiali di storia delle religioni* 7(1): 29–53.

5

"What's Wrong with Philosophy?"

Interviews with Toshimaro Hanazono and Yoshiko Oda (Japan)

SATOKO FUJIWARA

Toshimaro Hanazono was born in Yamagata Prefecture, located in the Tohoku (Northeast) region of Japan, in 1936. He was awarded his BA from the Department of Religious Studies at Tohoku University in 1959, followed by an MA in 1961, and taught as an associate/full professor at the department from 1983 to 2000. He is now Professor Emeritus at Tohoku University. He is the author of *Shūkyō genshōgaku nyūmon: Ningengaku eno sisen kara* (*Introduction to the Phenomenology of Religion: From an Anthropological Perspective*; Heibonsha, 2016). As explained in the interview, Hanazono's "anthropology" is a synthetic, largely philosophical, understanding of the human, as opposed to cultural/social anthropology in the line of E. B. Tylor and J. Frazer. The book consists of one introductory chapter and four chapters, respectively on R. Otto, G. van der Leeuw, M. Eliade and G. Mensching. Hanazono has also translated Rudolf Otto's *Das Heilige* and *West-Östliche Mystik* into Japanese.

Yoshiko Oda was born in Kobe in 1948. She achieved her BA from the Department of Persian Language at Osaka University of Foreign Studies in 1971, and an MA from the Department of Religious Studies at Kyoto University in 1974. She pursued a PhD in the History of Religions of the Divinity School of the University of Chicago from 1978 to 1984. Oda taught from 1997 to 2018 in the Comparative Religion programme at Kansai

---

Keywords: Teruji Ishizu, Tohoku University, Kyoto School, Chicago School of the history of religions, anthropology

University, which is a secular, private university in Osaka. She specializes in Islamic law and theories on religious community and is also a series editor of ten volumes of *Iwanami kōza shūkyo* (*Iwanami Series: Religion*; Iwanami Shoten, 2003–2004). Her English articles include "Muhammad as the Judge: An examination of the specific quality of Muhammad's charismatic authority" in *Orient* (Society for Near Eastern Studies in Japan), vol. 20, 1987.

Introduction

This chapter consists of two interviews. The first is with Toshimaro Hanazono, a retired professor from the Department of Religious Studies at Tohoku University, which is known among Japanese scholars as a central institution for the study of the phenomenology of religion (PoR). While Hanazono encountered PoR through engagement with European scholarship, German philosophy in particular, the second interviewee, Yoshiko Oda, has taken a radically different route to PoR. She started her graduate study at the Department of Religious Studies at Kyoto University, where scholars focused on German philosophy. However, she then went to the University of Chicago and enrolled in the Divinity School's area of the History of Religions, which has often been considered to be a North American equivalent to PoR. Having experienced two very different disciplines, she was completely "converted" from the Kyoto School[1] to the Chicago School and has been trying to revalorize J. M. Kitagawa's history of religions. Tohoku and Kyoto University make two of the seven national universities established before the Second World War.

Both interviews were conducted separately in Fall 2016, with Hanazono at Tohoku University and with Oda at the University of Tokyo.[2]

---

1. The Kyoto School is a name for a group of philosophers from Kyoto University, headed by Kitaro Nishida (1870–1945). There is no strict consensus as to who are its members. Our interviewee, Oda, argues that both some in the Department of Philosophy, such as Nishida and Hajime Tanabe, and some in the Department of Religious Studies, such as Keiji Nishitani, Yoshinori Takeuchi and Shizuteru Ueda, belong to the school.

2. Although the interviewer is indicated as singular for the sake of simplification, the interview was conducted as a part of a group research, and five members were present: Toshiaki Kimura (Tohoku University), Hiroshi Kubota (Rikkyo University), Shunichi Miyajima (Hokkaido University), Junichi Egawa (University of Tokyo), and Fumiaki Okuyama (Hokkaido University of Science Junior College).

TOSHIMARO HANAZONO

Defining the Phenomenology of Religion

Satoko Fujiwara: Upon launching this research project on the reception history of PoR in Japan, I decided to ask you to be my first interviewee, assuming that Tohoku University is *the* centre of PoR in Japan. Among other things, you have written much on PoR and also translated R. Otto's *Das Heilige* (*The Idea of the Holy*). When I first contacted you, though, you made it very clear that you are not a phenomenologist of religion. You were also negative about my assumption that Tohoku University represents Japanese PoR. Therefore, I would like to start by asking how you define the "phenomenology of religion".

Toshimaro Hanazono: This can be answered three different ways. First, it is possible to define PoR as a comparative study of various religions in the tradition of Comparative Religion. It seems to me that in Western countries, especially in Europe, this has been the most common understanding of the term. That is, PoR as typology or morphology.

Second, some scholars take PoR to be a kind of methodology, a method for understanding the meanings of religious phenomena. Some even go so far as to include more or less descriptive approaches to religion in PoR. In this case, the term "phenomenological" can be applied to anthropological or psychological studies as well. I myself am interested in this view of PoR.

Third, another view draws PoR closer to philosophical phenomenology. This view was affected by Max Scheler, who appreciated Otto's description of the holy and called it "phenomenological". There are many who regard PoR as an area of study that explores the essence or *eidos* of religion. However, some scholars have uncritically appropriated the Ottoian idea of the holy in order to provide an easy foundation for their comparative study of religion, thereby justifying their typology. I think such an uncritical attitude has undermined the academic credibility of PoR.

Your understanding of PoR is not much different from mine or my fellow researchers'. Would it be more accurate to say, then, that PoR is what you study, but not what you are?

Yes, it is. [Pointing to a book.] To be honest, this book of mine just came out. It is called *Introduction to the Phenomenology of Religion*, and it is a collection of my previous lectures and research. However, as its subtitle ("From an

125

Anthropological Perspective") suggests, I feel much more comfortable calling my approach "anthropological". I tried to interpret van der Leeuw and Eliade from an anthropological viewpoint. I did not mean to wave the banner of "PoR".

Dawn of the Phenomenology of Religion in Japan

Do you know who introduced PoR, under whichever definition, from Europe to Japan?

Not exactly, but I guess it was Prof. Teruji Ishizu.[3] He published an article on PoR in 1934,[4] in which he introduced van der Leeuw's PoR, calling it a "morphology (*keitaigaku*)". He referred to van der Leeuw's *Einführung in die Phänomenologie der Religion* and his RGG article, "Phänomenologie der Religion", in a footnote.

When did you come to know PoR?

When I was a junior at Tohoku University. Prof. Ishizu offered a seminar for both undergraduate and graduate students in which we read van der Leeuw's *Phänomenologie der Religion* in German. The class started with the chapter of "Die Macht" from the first section of the book. I assume senior students had read "Epilegomena" with Prof. Ishizu the year before. Well, to be honest, I could not understand what it was all about at that time. In retrospect, Prof. Ishizu probably expected his students to learn about various religious phenomena from the book, rather than for them to have a discussion over PoR.

Was there any scholar who proclaimed him/herself a phenomenologist of religion back then?

I think Prof. Kiyoshi Ohata[5] at the University of Tokyo used to say that he was "doing" PoR rather than just studying it. He came to Tohoku University every year to give an intensive course on the history of Christianity. I remember he said he always read van der Leeuw's *Phänomenologie der Religion* with students in his seminar at the University of Tokyo. I guess he had been

---

3. Teruji Ishizu (1903-1972) – a graduate of the Department of Religious Studies at the University of Tokyo – was a professor of the Department of Religious Studies at Tohoku University from 1943 to 1966. He was Vice-President of the IAHR from 1960 to 1965.
4. Ishizu (1934, 18–19).
5. Kiyoshi Ohata (1904–1983) was a graduate and also a professor of the Department of Religious Studies at the University of Tokyo from 1936 to 1965. He specialized in ancient Judaism.

influenced by Prof. Ishizu. Or maybe they had discussed which book to use as a textbook in their seminars. Also, of course, Prof. Ohata wrote a book titled *The Phenomenology of Religion*.[6] Prof. Masahiro Kusunoki[7] at Tohoku University also attempted to apply a phenomenological method to the study of religion.

Blessing, as a Philosophical Enterprise

Looking at the back issues of *Shūkyō kenyū* (*Journal of Religious Studies*) [the journal of Japanese Association for Religious Studies], articles on PoR increased in the mid-1960s. Why did Japanese scholars take interest in PoR at that time?

PoR became popular as a form of typology or morphology in Europe and in North America, but not in Japan. Japanese scholars expected PoR to be, above all, a study of the essence or essential features of religion. Accordingly, many works on PoR became theoretical.

To name scholars who worked a significant amount on PoR, among the older generation, there was Prof. Masanao Katayama (1903–1994), who was influenced by the Kyoto School, and in the subsequent generation, there were Prof. Sojun Moroto and Prof. Tomomi Horikoshi. Max Scheler was also quite popular. That said, even in the heyday of PoR, there was no significant collaboration among the Japanese scholars of religion who preferred studying PoR.

In Europe, scholars of religion, if they ever expected anything from PoR, viewed it as a means to detach the study of religion from theology and to secure its objectivity as a science.[8] Where scholars of religion were in

---

6. This book was published in 1982. According to Ohata, it was only when he was ready to publish the book that he realized that he was "doing" PoR. In its preface he says, "Upon publishing this book, I showed my publisher and old friend, Shichihei Yamamoto [a Christian publisher/writer], a few possible titles I thought of, such as 'On the Foundation of Religious Phenomena'. Then he said, 'The shorter the better', and suggested 'Phenomenology of Religion'. Hearing his advice, I suddenly realized that what I had been doing was the phenomenology of religion!" (Ohata 1982, 2).

7. Masahiro Kusunoki (1921-2009) was a professor of the Research Institute for Japanese Culture at Tohoku University until 1985. He co-translated Mircea Eliade, *Occultism, Witchcraft, and Cultural Fashions*.

8. This observation by Hanazono may be different from the prevalent view among European scholars of religion. To take a typical example, Eric Sharpe argues that it was problematic that van der Leeuw's PoR was not differentiated from metaphysics or theology, quoting Hultkrantz's criticism of van der Leeuw (Sharpe 1986 [1975], 232–235). It is noteworthy that Hanazono is, nonetheless, sufficiently familiar with Sharpe's *Comparative Religion: A History* to quote Sharpe's account of the history of

tension with theologians, they seemed to believe that phenomenology, which required "*epoché*", was effective in establishing the study of religion. However, in Japan, where the rivalry between the study of religion and theology was not as strong as it was in Europe, PoR played a different role.

Why did PoR in Japan become a philosophical study of the essence of religion rather than a typology?

It was difficult in the academic environment of Japan to conduct a comparative study of religions in the way European scholars did. Europeans obtained a large amount of materials from their colonial countries. It was also due to the lack of linguistic ability among Japanese scholars as compared with European scholars.

In addition, I think that many historians of religions[9] in Japan were educated in history departments in those days. Therefore, they were not familiar with the idea of the *sui generis* development of religion. For example, Prof. Ichiro Hori[10] explored and presented a unique view of the history of religions that he called "the history of Japanese religions". It was not a mere chronology of religions in Japan. He attempted to apprehend the uniform characters of Japanese religions in the past and present. Encountering Eliade, he came to regard shamanism as the *basso continuo* of the history of Japanese religions. He would not like me calling it transhistorical, but I believe it was.

If we can call Eliade a phenomenologist of religion, we can also say that Hori was a phenomenologist. However, I never heard him calling himself such. He always identified himself as a historian.

Was there no Japanese scholar who sought to write an "*allgemeine Geschichte der Religionen*" (general/universal history of religions)"?[11]

There are some Japanese textbooks on the general history of religions in the world. However, there has been no Japanese scholar bold enough to write

---

PoR in his own book, *Shūkyō genshōgaku nyūmon* (*Introduction to the Phenomenology of Religion*) without criticism. In my commentary following this interview, I will argue that it is safer to say that at least Hanazono and his fellow Japanese scholars expected the philosophical method of PoR to firmly ground their study of religion.

9. In Japanese there is no plural form for nouns. It is impossible to tell in many contexts whether a speaker is saying "study/history of religion" or "study/history of religions".

10. Ichiro Hori (1910–1974) was a graduate from the Department of Indian Philosophy (meaning Buddhist studies) of the University of Tokyo who taught at the Department of Religious Studies at Tohoku University and the University of Tokyo. He was a son-in-law of Kunio Yanagita, the most famous Japanese folklorist. He introduced the work of Mircea Eliade to Japan, most notably by translating a number of his books into Japanese.

11. A classic, nineteenth-century term to describe the history of world religions.

an "*allegmeine Geschichte*" or even an outline of religious studies after early scholars such as Masaharu Anesaki[12] or Enku Uno.[13] At least not anything comparable to those masterpieces written by European scholars. Even for Anesaki and Uno's generation, it was difficult to write an outline drawing on a massive number of primary sources.

However, the situation has greatly improved these days in terms of the availability of primary sources as well as in terms of international collaborations. Prof. Michio Araki,[14] whose death was a great loss to the study of religion, attempted to compare and summarize folk religions of the world. If that kind of research can be conducted as a large project, we may be able to write "*allegemeine Geschichte der Religionen*" in the future.

Shaping the Tohoku Tradition of the Study of Religion

I have an impression that your department at Tohoku University is the keenest on PoR among Japanese universities.

I have no idea why our department gives that impression. I have never thought of us that way. But it might be the case that some have called Profs. Ishizu and Kusunoki's respective works phenomenological.

Prof. Ishizu discussed van der Leeuw's PoR and also mentioned Bleeker in his lectures. He was rather critical of van der Leeuw, though, saying that he had ended up creating a typology and failed to exercise phenomenological reduction to reach the eidetic vision of religion, which is the ultimate goal of PoR. When Prof. Ishizu met Joachim Wach in America, he heard Wach's plan to move from typology to eidetic reduction and came to think that van der

<hr>

12. Masaharu Anesaki (1873–1949) is a scholar of religion who established the chair of religious studies at the (Imperial) University of Tokyo in 1905. He published *An Outline of the Study of Religion* in 1900 (Anesaki 1900).

13. Enku Uno (1885–1949), scholar of religion and ethnologist, was a professor at the Institute for Advanced Studies on Asia at the (Imperial) University of Tokyo till 1946. He published *An Outline of the Study of Religion* in 1927 (Uno 1927).

14. Michio Araki (1938–2008) is known as a wholehearted Eliadean. Just like the second interviewee, he first studied at the graduate school of Kyoto University and majored in German philosophers, including Kant. He then went to the University of Chicago and became fascinated by Eliade. He taught at Tsukuba University from 1985. Opinions are divided on his scholarship, as is the case with Eliade. The second interviewee has been trying to revalorize some parts of Eliade while being rather critical of Araki. She suggests that Araki only worshipped Eliade without trying to go beyond him by overcoming his shortcomings. Being an Executive Committee member of the IAHR from 1990 to 2000 (later an Honorary Life Member), Araki also gave an impression to Japanese scholars that the IAHR was a pro-Eliadean organization.

Leeuw should go in the same direction. This is my guess. Nevertheless, Prof. Ishizu never said that he himself was a phenomenologist of religion.

Prof. Kusunoki advocated "the phenomenology of dynamic belief". I never asked him directly if he had gotten a hint from P. Tillich's idea of "the dynamics of faith", but I think the two ideas are similar to each other. Prof. Kusunoki reached the idea from the assumption that people's faiths acquire a dynamic character in Japan where religious plurality is prevalent. He called the faiths "common people's belief (*shomin shinkō*)" and employed a phenomenological method in order to describe, understand and interpret the structure of the faiths.

Scheler's phenomenology, which achieves eidetic reduction through concrete phenomena, had influenced Prof. Kusunoki's understanding of phenomenology. His idea of "common people's belief" is not a sociological or an ethnological concept. Rather, it indicates the nature of "common people-ness" of popular beliefs. He explained "common people-ness" by referring to the binary yet coexistent aspects of the dynamics of faith, such as "magical–religious", "secular–nonsecular", "scriptural–non-scriptural" and "functional–non-functional". He drew out these aspects through eidetic reduction from empirical religious phenomena, such as pilgrimage to Mt. Osore and the worship of the silkworm deity *oshirasan* in the Tohoku region.[15] His idea of "common people's belief" was meant to be a criticism of the folklorist idea of "folk belief (*minkan shinkō*)". According to him, folklorists explained away folk belief with the notion of syncretism and the like, and they failed to clarify the nature or structure of religious belief among common people.

May we say that one of the characteristics of the study of religion at Tohoku University is a constant endeavour to combine PoR with a fieldwork-based method similar to the one used in folklore studies?

Yes, the two methods share a core based on "the interpretation of meaning". I have also written empirical, scientific articles where I employed a quantitative method and gathered various data. Regardless, as I have never learned statistics on a professional level, I cannot produce anything purely scientific in the sense of positivism. Moreover, I do not feel satisfied unless I understand or interpret the meaning(s) of the cases I investigate.

My generation used to say that, whereas the study of religion at the University of Tokyo is largely empirical and at Kyoto University it is philosophical, at Tohoku University, it is a mishmash!

---

15. Tohoku is the northeast region of Japan. Fieldwork was conducted among agricultural communities in the region.

Did all the professors in your department share the idea that the study of religion should have both components?

I do not know how Prof. Kusunoki reached the idea, but I personally owe my style to the influence of Prof. Ishizu. He told me that we could not do without learning the history of theories. And that to learn the history of theories enables us to acquire concepts and further methods. At the same time, he also stressed that we should not be "monsters of methodologies". He said we needed materials, not just theories.

Therefore, whenever I read Japanese historical materials or did fieldwork, I was preoccupied with how to connect the data with concepts and methods. As a result, if you read my work on Japanese religions, you will abruptly encounter phenomenological terms such as "understanding (*Verstehen*)" or "intentionality". In these terms, I have kept my interest in PoR.

"Anthropology", Not Phenomenology

What do you mean when you identify your research as "anthropological" instead of phenomenological?

I got a hint from Prof. Kusunoki for the concept. I think the study of religion can be included in what David Hume called the "science of man". Hume said that any study, be it mathematics or astronomy, is a science of man because it is based on human perception. As a student, I read Hume's *A Treatise of Human Nature* in a seminar offered by Prof. Kusunoki. I remember he said that he had been studying British empiricism, from which the idea of the science of man had emerged. He also said that the idea was different from the German concept of *Anthropologie*. He preferred the Humean idea. It is true that he does not often refer to Hume in his works, and from some point he started mentioning Scheler more often. But that is only because Hume did not present any methodology. I took over Prof. Kusunoki's understanding of the Humean science of man.

Therefore, my "anthropology" is a bit different from the German philosophical anthropology of Helmuth Plessner or Arnold Gehlen. The Germans begin by defining the human but do not reach the examination of religion. In contrast, my approach is an anthropology based on the study of religion. I have been exploring the nature and traits of human beings from the perspective of a scholar of religions who tries to understand religion. Whether reading Max Müller or Rudolf Otto, I always focused on their understandings of human beings. But it was probably van der Leeuw who most influenced my approach. I found his works interesting from a methodological viewpoint as well.

Recent cognitive scientists have an interest in discussing religion. The premise of their interest is that human beings all share some fundamental traits. That is what the classic scholars of religion such as E. Troeltsch and Otto argued using the term "religious *apriori*". I believe it is more logical to assume that a human being has a receptor of religious matters in his/her mind. Otherwise, he/she will not come to have a faith. Neither will he/she be inspired by religious discourses. Otto made a significant contribution to the study of religion in relation to these aspects of human experience by reflecting on religious *apriori* and presenting the idea of *sensus numinis*.

The Decline and the Legacy of the Phenomenology of Religion

While the cognitive science of religion came to the fore, PoR disappeared after the mid-1990s. Jacques Waardenburg's proposal of "new phenomenology" failed to become a movement. What do you think are the causes of PoR's decline?

I had some expectations for Waardenburg, but, to be honest, I have not followed his works since then. He did come to the Tokyo World Congress of the IAHR in 2005, but I did not talk to him because he did not present a paper on PoR.

It is true that PoR or comparative study of religion has declined. It was inevitable. No single scholar can work on a global scale equipped with just his/her ideas and methods. At least not these days. You could also say that phenomenologists were unable to develop their works collaboratively because it was hard to build up any common understanding of the van der Leeuwean PoR.

Nevertheless, some kind of collaborative research is not impossible if scholars can at least share a sympathetic attitude to others' religions and the methods of description and understanding. As I mentioned earlier, *Sekaino minshū shūkyō* (*Folk Religions in the World*),[16] edited by Prof. Araki, was a promising attempt. Innovations in information technologies have made it much easier to work with international scholars. What is needed is the critical and creative mind that can identify good questions to explore.

---

16. A festschrift for Araki, which includes twenty-two chapters, of which six are on folk religions in the Americas, seven on those in Japan, three on those in Africa and Oceania, three on those in Europe and three on "Contemporary States and Religion", written by nine international and thirteen Japanese scholars and published in 2004 in Kyoto (Araki 2004).

If we properly recognize similarities and differences between religions and share our knowledge, our common understanding of religions will spread globally. From an anthropological perspective, religion is inseparably tied with the deepest dimension of the human mind, for example, with self-awareness, worldview, sense of wellbeing and view of life and death. Therefore, religion can unite different people and groups together even if it sometimes works in the opposite direction. If historical conditions had been better, Otto's project of *Religiöser Menschheitsbund*[17] could have yielded real benefit to society. He was convinced that scholars of religion and representatives of religious groups could work together for world peace and also that such a work was a duty for scholars. As you know, F. Heiler shared Otto's ideal. I believe we should not forget that tradition.

In your opinion, what did PoR in the twentieth century accomplish in the context of the study of religion?

The typology or morphology of religions attempted by many phenomenologists of religion enabled holistic understandings of religion and, in so doing, presented frameworks for the interpretation of individual religions and particular religious phenomena. Such frameworks are necessary for interfaith understandings. If, for example, Islamic society comes to accommodate a free study of religion with a comparative approach, it will probably affect actual problem-solving processes in that society.

In my understanding, the Tokyo World Congress of the IAHR in 2005 delivered the clear message that scholars of religion have a practical role and need to be engaged in the globalized world. I have heard that Heiler's lecture for the 1958 Tokyo Congress, which mentioned the role of scholars of religion in promoting interfaith understanding and cooperation, was criticized during the following IAHR meeting. Scholars who criticized Heiler insisted that scholars should stay isolated from actual problem-solving. However, we have to admit that times have changed. In addition, we also have to remember that Eliade's vision of "new humanism" was meant to be a criticism of modern civilization. That was also an accomplishment of comparative religion, or PoR, that we should not forget. But that is my opinion, and I guess you have entirely different views on these issues.

---

17.   An international league to work for right, justice and peace, founded in 1920.

YOSHIKO ODA

Before Enrolling at the University of Chicago

Satoko Fujiwara: Before you went to Chicago, you were a graduate student of the Department of Religious Studies at Kyoto University, known for its centrality in the area of the philosophy of religion in Japan. It must be unusual for a Kyoto student of religion to specialize in Islamic studies. When did you choose your major?

Yoshiko Oda: For my undergraduate study, I went to Osaka University of Foreign (Language) Studies and entered the Persian language department. Students could choose any theme for their graduation theses, not just in linguistics or literature, but also in economy, society, politics or history. I chose Sufism, having been a bit disillusioned by the student movement at that time. I could not get anything significant from the movement. Although I was interested in politics, I ended up being exhausted from arguments with other students. I found a volume of Rumi's poems edited by R. A. Nicholson in Prof. Eiichi Imoto's[18] office around that time, and I thought it would not be bad to study a mystic who secluded himself from society and politics.

When I brought my application form to the Department of Religious Studies at the Graduate School of Kyoto University, I was told, "We have no class on Islam. Are you sure you want to enter our department?" I wanted to study religion, though, so I took an entrance exam anyway and passed (in 1971). I soon found out, however, that classes offered at the department were mostly on Western philosophy. Prof. Yoshinori Takeuchi[19]taught classes on Hegel, Kant, Heidegger, Nietzsche and other modern Western philosophers. He also taught some on Christian thinkers such as Luther, Kierkegaard and Tillich. Out of all his classes, the one that was most interesting to me was a lecture on the outline of the study of religion for undergraduate students. The lecture covered everything from Otto, van der Leeuw, Wach, and Eliade to Durkheim, Lévi-Strauss, W. James and even a bit on Widengren of the Uppsala School. He went into details regarding van der Leeuw, using the Torchbooks version of the English translation of his book. Prof. Takeuchi

---

18. Eiichi Imoto (1930–2014) was a Japanese Iranologist who studied at the University of Tehran.
19. Yoshinori Takeuchi (1913–2002) was a professor of the Department of Religious Studies at Kyoto University. As an undergraduate student, he worked with Hajime Tanabe, a prominent scholar of the Kyoto School.

actually planned to publish a book on PoR and asked me to record his lecture, though it wound up never being published, unfortunately.

I worked on Sufism all by myself and wrote a master's thesis on it. Upon finishing my doctoral coursework in 1977, I started thinking about going abroad to study Islam more professionally. Prof. Kojiro Nakamura[20] recommended that I go directly to Iran instead of imitating Western scholarship, but I gave up on the idea because it was the dawn of the Revolution. Instead, I decided to go to the University of Chicago. Prof. Nakamura then recommended the Department of Near Eastern Languages and Civilizations rather than the Divinity School, but I eventually chose the latter because I was strongly interested in religious studies and also because Prof. Kitagawa[21] had taken care of various things for my study aboard.

The "History of Religions" and the "Phenomenology of Religion"

Did you often hear the word "PoR" while you were a University of Chicago student from 1978 to 1984?

The "history of religions" was the term commonly used in Chicago. Nevertheless, I can say that the History of Religions faculty thought highly of PoR because I remember one of the questions on the certifying exam I took in September of 1978 was on "epoché".

The faculty members were confident of being the Chicago School and had a strong feeling of rivalry with Harvard over, for example, whether to add "s" to the "religion" of the "history of religion(s)", as you know. Chicago people preferred "history of religions" because they dealt with concrete religions. On the other hand, W. C. Smith favoured "history of religion", arguing that religion, being internal, was not countable. Kitagawa did not hide his feeling of rivalry with W. C. Smith and his followers. He once said to me, "When you write an article on Islam, be sure to defeat Charles Adams's arguments. He

---

20. Kojiro Nakamura (1936–) was the first chair of Islamic studies at the University of Tokyo. His wife, Kyoko Nakamura (1932–2001), was a graduate student of the History of Religions area of the University of Chicago's Divinity School from 1959 to 1962 and later translated some of Eliade's books into Japanese.

21. Joseph Mitsuo Kitagawa (1915–1992) was a scholar of religion who was born in Japan and later became Dean of the Divinity School at the University of Chicago, forming the so-called Chicago School of the history of religions with Eliade and Charles Long. Being an Episcopalian, he obtained a bachelor's degree from Rikkyo University, an Anglican university in Tokyo, and later became a minister. He went to the University of Chicago initially with the intention of studying theology.

knows historical details but lacks a good understanding of what religion is."[22] Kitagawa never forced his students to follow the Chicago way, though. He was never as pushy as Araki [laughter].[23]

As his disciple, Kitagawa was heavily influenced by Wach. Wach wrote *Sociology of Religion*, having found that van der Leeuw's PoR was comprehensive, yet weak in sociological issues. Following Wach, Kitagawa gave lectures on religious community, loyalty and charisma. At the same time, he was critical of sociologists and social/cultural anthropologists. For example, he even criticized Clifford Geertz, who is usually viewed as pro-religion, for missing the transcendent in his discussions on religion. In his defence of the *sui generis* nature of religion, Kitagawa teamed up with Eliade.

When I was in Chicago, Eliade did not give lectures and just offered one three-hour-long seminar from 7 p.m. once a week, which Gary L. Ebersole, Lawrence E. Sullivan and Richard Gardner attended with me. When Eliade became interested in a student's presentation, his comments tended to become so long that it was almost like a lecture. The paper I wrote for him was about the symbolism of Sufi poetry. He gave me comments such as "This symbol also appears in the Vedas".

Eliade was influential at that time. Here is a story I heard from Araki. There were many students in the Divinity School who were going to be missionaries to proselytize Christianity among indigenous peoples around the world. However, not a few of them had an identity crisis after listening to Eliade's lectures and being impressed by the rich spirituality of indigenous cultures. I was touched by this story.

Welcome to Chicago and Farewell to Kyoto

How about you yourself? Were you influenced by Eliade?

What was, and still is, attractive about Eliade is his ability to disclose the profoundness of the religious world of "archaic" and indigenous people. It took me two years to understand his thought, as it was completely new to

---

22. Hearing such a hostile remark, Oda believed that Adams was a Harvard graduate. However, after this interview, I found out that he had actually obtained his PhD in the History of Religions from the University of Chicago, having worked with Wach. He later became close to W. C. Smith and taught at McGill University. Kitagawa may have thought that he and the Chicago School had been betrayed by Adams, but the truth is unknown.

23. As noted, Michio Araki was an ardent Eliadean and advocated the Chicago School's HR throughout his teaching career in Japan. He was Oda's fellow student in Chicago.

someone who had been trained at Kyoto University. In Kyoto we learned almost nothing about indigenous religions.

On the other front, in Chicago I increasingly realized how narrow the philosophy of religion at Kyoto University was. Whenever I said "In Buddhism, it is ...", Frank Reynolds[24] said, "Yoshiko! That is Mahayana Buddhism and not Buddhism in general!" I noticed what I learned about Buddhism in Kyoto was nothing but early Indian philosophy and Kamakura Buddhist[25] thought, and, as for Christianity, only Pauline and Protestant theology.

In Kyoto, I did not learn the sociology of religion, either. As mentioned, Prof. Takeuchi lectured on Durkheim, but I could not understand why he was important. In Chicago, I was shocked to hear Kitagawa say, "Religion establishes itself only when a community is formed" or "Buddha alone was not enough. For a religion to be grounded in history, it needs a community of adherents". It took me quite a long time to understand what he meant because Kyoto professors had told me that religion was primarily a matter of subjectivity and of inner life and that religious orders or communities were unimportant.

This also had to do with the Japanese context in those days. For a Japanese woman in her twenties, a community[26] was one of the most oppressive and depressive things back then. I was guarded against communities, trying not to yield to their value systems. So, had I stayed in Japan, I would never have studied anything about community. However, living in the United States I soon found out that Americans often talked about communities on various occasions in their daily lives. I wondered why. Then I figured out that Americans consider it important to think about communities all the time, as their society is an assembly of different and independent individuals. Knowing that background and also enjoying freedom from Japanese society, I no longer felt annoyed by the idea of community. On the contrary, I chose it as my research topic. Needless to say, there was no way to understand Islamic law without understanding the nature of religious communities. And Kitagawa stressed the importance of the sociology of religion. As a result, I finally studied the sociology of religion and planned to write my dissertation on "The soteriological meanings of *shari'a* as expressed in the Quran".

---

24. Frank E. Reynolds (1930–2019) was a scholar of Theravada Buddhism, who taught at the University of Chicago from 1967 to 2001.

25. Kamakura Buddhism is a generic name for Japanese Buddhist sects that were founded in the twelfth and thirteenth centuries. Often called "new Buddhism", Kamakura Buddhism has been likened to Protestantism by modern Japanese scholars.

26. A community in the sense of a traditional, patriarchal village community in general.

When I came back to Japan and paid a visit to Prof. Takeuchi, I dared to say to his face, "I am not going back to Kyoto University's philosophy of religion. But I would like to integrate it with the history of religions, including Islam, that I have learned from Chicago". I still am trying to do it. Takeuchi taught me as a student about the problem of evil from a philosophical perspective, centring it on the ideas of original sin and of karma, referring to Kant and Ricœur. That was very important, but with that interpretation of evil and its emphasis on sin, it is impossible to understand why Islamic law is significant for Muslims.[27]

It seems your view on religion as well as on society has radically changed from when you did your earlier studies in Japan. Did your subsequent research on Islam go well?

To tell the truth, there was little on Islamic studies at the Chicago Divinity School, either. I was lucky to be able to work with Prof. Fazlur Rahman, who was a very liberal scholar of Islam from Pakistan. He did not teach traditional Islamic studies but interpreted the Quran by himself, referring to *tafsir* occasionally. He supported my research plan to explore the religious meanings of *shari'a*. He gave some classes on Islam for the Divinity School. Kitagawa had a high opinion of his ample knowledge of Islam and his unapologetic, academic approach to Islam. Nonetheless, he also clearly stated that Rahman was not a historian of religions. Rather, he intended to create and present a liberal type of Islam adjusted to modernity, and he also tried to justify the relevancy of his interpretation by referring to verses in the Quran. Kitagawa told me that Rahman interpreted the Quran in the same way as believers, and that I should approach Islam as a historian of religions.

Kitagawa then gave me an overwhelming requirement. He said, "If you are going to write your thesis on *shari'a*, start by overviewing religious laws in the world. Also ancient Roman law, ancient Chinese legalism and the like". He told me to write an overview on religious laws or on religion and law for my introduction, and to examine *shari'a* in the main part of my thesis. That was the way of the Chicago history of religions. But it was just too much for me.

Bringing the Chicago Way Back to Japan

You often talk about Japanese religions in addition to Islam. Is that also an influence from Chicago?

---

27. By this sentence, Oda does not mean she thinks that Muslims believe in Original Sin. On the contrary, she is criticizing Takeuchi's narrow view on evil.

After I returned to Japan, I came to a question, "Why have Japanese religious traditions been functioning without shari'a-like religious laws?" In *Religions of the East*, Kitagawa argued that Japanese people belong to two heterogeneous religious traditions at the same time, Buddhism and Shinto, and that they use them for different purposes in different situations without feeling that the two contradict each other. He called it division of religions (religious division of labour). Japanese religious traditions cannot be explained solely in terms of syncretism between Buddhism and Shinto. I believe Kitagawa's idea of the division of religions is better than syncretism as an explanation for the study of religion. *Religions of the East* was translated into Japanese by Fujio Ikado in the 1960s, but Kitagawa's idea has never become popular in Japan. Neither Buddhist nor Shinto scholars welcomed the idea because they did not want to meddle in each other's territory. Japanese scholars of religion have also rarely employed Kitagawa's theories. I have been trying to revalorize Kitagawa. Compared with Islam, Japanese Buddhism has never developed its own social norms; instead, it let Shinto and Confucianism control communities. In this manner, a division of labour between Buddhism and Shinto underlies Japanese religious communities.

Rehabilitating the Phenomenology of Religion

Then, how do you identify yourself academically, if you do not call yourself a phenomenologist of religion?

I regard my work as the study of religion, called "an integrative understanding of religions"[28] by Eliade. It does embrace the tradition of PoR, centred as it was on the search for the meanings and structures of religions. However, as with many others, I no longer use the term.

In my introductory course on the study of religion, I describe PoR as "a department store of religious studies". PoR was a new trend when I was a student, and it gave my generation the impression that it was a rising star or an advanced stage of religious studies. Van der Leeuw's works integrated the wide range of myth and ritual studies of anthropologists and philological studies of Orientalists. Both Wach and Eliade presented a macro perspective and theories of religion. For my generation, department stores used to be the best places to buy a wide-selection of high-quality products. In this sense, PoR was a department store of religious studies. However, just as young people no longer shop at department stores, preferring smaller fast fashion stores like UNIQLO or internet stores, PoR has become unpopular and

---

28.   See Eliade's idea of "total hermeneutics" (Eliade 1984 [1969], 58).

declined. A star that was expected to be the queen of religious studies is now almost completely forgotten.

I am aware that the main cause of its decline is post-colonial and Orientalist criticism, or, rather, all-out attack against Western scholarship until around the mid-twentieth century. However, the critics, who came to the fore around the 1980s, threw out the baby with the bath-water. They denied valuable parts of PoR and of Eliade all together. Yet they have not created an alternative that makes the study of religion attractive, resulting in loss of interest in macro-theories or perspectives. The study of religion has become increasingly specialized and fractionalized. It remains our task to study religion synthetically, as Eliade attempted. Scholars of religion do not necessarily deal with first-hand materials, but they can grasp the structures and meanings of religions, both their diversities and common features, in a unique way not shared by philologists or cultural anthropologists. In order to do so, students of religion need a type of training that is different from the mastery of languages required of philologists.

Another challenge is to explain Islam, Buddhism and Christianity from the perspective of the study of religion. Buddhist studies in Japan have been divided into dogmatics and historical studies. As a result, scholars of religion have not successfully described and analysed the religious situation[29] of Japanese people in its richness at all. I believe there is a lot to do for the Japanese scholars of religion.

Commentary

Why do the two interviewees have nearly opposite attitudes towards philosophy? Their reactions reflect the history of the Japanese study of religion, which used to be closely tied to philosophy. Some Japanese scholars of religion approached PoR because of their interest in philosophy. Clearly being aware of the differences between "phenomenology" in the context of PoR and Husserlian philosophical phenomenology, those scholars nonetheless studied PoR along with various strands of Continental philosophy. At the same time, however, other scholars found that the philosophical approach to religion was too narrow. They attempted to widen the scope of their research and conceptual frames,

---

29. Scholars now use the word "practice" to express what the interviewee wants to say here. The word "(religious) practice (shūkyōteki jissen)" was rarely used by Japanese scholars of religion in the twentieth century. This is reflected in the first interviewee's consistent use of the word "faith/belief", where scholars would now normally use the word "practice".

especially after encountering American History of Religions, particularly as practised at the University of Chicago, which aimed to be a more comparative and holistic approach to studying religion.

My research partners and I interviewed several more scholars of religion, who could not be included in this chapter. We interviewed Yoshitsugu Sawai (1951–), Shoto Hase (1937–), Masakazu Tanatsugu (1949–), Hiroshi Tsuchiya (1938–), Teruhisa Tajima (1947–) and Shinji Kanai (1942–). The selection was based on our understanding that key figures in the history of PoR in Japan come primarily from three national universities,[30] Tohoku, Kyoto, and Tokyo, and a secular private university, Waseda.[31] Though these scholars each belong to departments of religious studies, they have all eagerly studied and used philosophy, particularly its German tradition, throughout their respective careers.

Why Philosophy?

Then why is it that the study of religion in Japan has been close to philosophy? Comparing the study of religion in Japan with its European counterpart, the largest factor is an institutional one. In modern Japan, major research universities have been either national or secular-private. The secular universities have had neither faculties of theology nor divinity schools. Therefore, departments of religious studies at such universities were initially established within those universities' respective faculties of letters (or the humanities), which comprised three areas-at-large (larger units than departments), philosophy, history and literature. Out of these, it was the area of philosophy-at-large that embraced the study of religion. The reason for this was that the study of religion in Japan, unlike in some parts of Europe, did not arise as an anti-theological movement and, as a result, was not opposed to speculation. Neither did it arise

---

30. All national universities in both pre- and post-Second World War Japan are constitutionally secular.
31. Sawai, along with Hanazono, is a graduate from Tohoku. Hase and Tanatsugu are from Kyoto. Tajima and Kanai are from Waseda. After graduation, Kanai went to Tokyo Union Theological Seminary and then entered the graduate school of the University of Tokyo. He later became a faculty member of its department of religious studies succeeding Noriyoshi Tamaru (1931–2014), who translated van der Leeuw's *Einführung in die Phänomenologie der Religion* into Japanese. Tamaru himself is a graduate from Tokyo. Tsuchiya is from another national university, Hokkaido, which is secular, but its department of religious studies has a closer connection with Christian theology. Tsuchiya is thus similar to Kanai in this respect. In Tajima's case, his predecessors at Waseda such as Tomomi Horikoshi (1928–) were deeply engaged with PoR.

from textual-historical studies in the line of Biblical studies, nor from myth studies in the line of Greco-Roman classical studies, and hence, it did not find its place in the areas of history or literature.

A more substantial reason for the close link between philosophy and the study of religion in Japan lies in the modernist inclination of academics at that time. As represented by Tetsujiro Inoue (1856–1944), the head of the philosophy area of the National (then Imperial) University of Tokyo, academics favoured philosophy as a rational, intellectual enterprise propelling modernization. They opposed that rational pursuit to religion, which was seen as irrational convention. Accordingly, those academics took it for granted that only the philosophical components of religion were worthy of academic investigation. Such an assumption is also evident in the naming of the department for Buddhist studies, a sister-department of religious studies at national universities, as "Indian philosophy". "Philosophy" was a prominent tag of academic authority that granted legitimacy to the study of religion.

In such an institutional environment, adopting a philosophical approach did not undermine the validity of religious studies. Scholars did not see anything wrong with being speculative or using the method of "intuition (*Wesensanschauung*)". Rather, philosophy was considered to be a firm foundation for producing scholarship on religion. Japanese scholars looking for theories to employ also turned to sociology, psychology and anthropology, but philosophy remained a fundamental frame of reference. Even later critical reflection on foundationalism was accepted, by way of philosophers like Richard Rorty.

As a result, PoR in Japan has developed along with the philosophy of religion rather than as a typological attempt, which was dominant in European PoR, with the exception of a few scholars under the influence of the Chicago School, like the second interviewee Oda. It is true that, in his interview, Hanazono started by defining PoR and identified himself as standing between typology and philosophy. However, European scholars of religion would find him to be quite philosophical, as evidenced by the rest of the interview. Furthermore, as Hanazono mentioned in his interview, the lack of linguistic abilities and of self-owned historical materials from various corners of the world could be additional, negative reasons why Japanese PoR did not become an expansive, typological project.

Characteristics of the Japanese Phenomenology of Religion

Interestingly, while my research partners and I, who are all in our forties and fifties, regard the interviewees as largely "phenomenological", the interviewees did not call themselves "phenomenologists of religion"[32] even though both sides shared the basic understanding of what PoR was (see Hanazono's interview on p. 125). This was probably because few scholars are willing to be subsumed under the fixed categories of "-isms", "schools", "movements", etc., especially when the category has been exposed to ambivalent evaluations, as has been the case with PoR. Therefore, after the interviews, my research partners and I reflected on why the interviewees looked phenomenological to us. We found that they commonly had two characteristics. First, they ardently read and translated Western PoR works and regarded them as presenting an important, even central, approach to religion. Second, they attempted to deeply understand what religion truly is, or alternatively, what human beings are or what "existence" (Heideggerian *Sein*) is. Concomitantly, they argued that the merely empirical approaches of social sciences or historical/textual studies would not suffice.

That said, it is also remarkable that these scholars are not necessarily "religionists" or apologists for the *sui generis* nature of religion, even though they generally sympathize with religions. The interview with Hanazono reveals that he and his fellow scholars were primarily interested in what human beings are; as a result, they could be called "human essentialists" rather than "religious essentialists". The academic context of Hanazono's interest can be traced to the influence of philosophical anthropology. Although he says his anthropology is slightly different from typical German anthropology, the latter's representatives – such as Gehlen, Plessner, Max Scheler and more broadly Karl Jaspers and Heidegger – were quite popular among philosophy-lovers of Hanazono's generation.

It is also possible to relate Hanazono's "human essentialism" to the post-Second World War ideological context of Japanese society. The liberal academics of Hanazono's generation, who were born before or around the end of the Second World War, started with a full-blown criticism of pre-war and wartime totalitarianism and ultra-nationalism. They attempted to reconstruct democracy by advocating for the importance of human rights and equality as well as the autonomy of individuals. Philosophical anthropology was consonant with the political liberalism of the time, as both focused on the fundamental core of human beings. While liberal academics today emphasize the diversity of human beings in order to respect the individual, liberals of Hanazono's generation, during the period following the war, emphasized similarities between

---

32. Except for one interviewee, Kanai, whose interview included too much of his personal background to be added to this chapter.

people around the world for the same purpose. Likewise, while "community" as *Gemeinschaft* as opposed to *Gesellschaft* was a reactionary, patriarchal concept for young Oda and other modernists, "community" is currently being revalorized among Japanese liberal academics.

In a similar vein, it is also noteworthy that Hanazono and other scholars of religion at Tohoku University combined philosophical PoR with fieldwork-based folklore studies. In doing so they shed the ethnocentric tones of Japanese folklore, established by Kunino Yanagita (1875–1962) during the pre-war period. Whereas Japanese folklorists tended to emphasize the uniqueness of Japanese cultural and religious traditions, Hanazono and others attempted to synthetize universality and locality.

In addition, it is not coincidental that all of the interviewees – as well as the scholars they mentioned as key figures in the history of PoR in Japan – were from either national or secular-private universities established before the Second World War. None of them were from religious-private universities. As Oda implies when referring to Kitagawa's unpopularity in Japan, religious studies at religious-private universities were inclined to be sectarian. In part opposed to that inclination, scholars of religion at national or secular-private universities were more concerned with religion as such, which made PoR attractive to them. Yet such scholars' impact was limited. After the Second World War new national/secular-private universities of different types were founded. At those universities, which did not necessarily adopt the aforementioned classical trichotomy of philosophy, history and literature, the study of religion was usually merged with area studies, social sciences and other new fields of study. PoR did not appeal to scholars from such backgrounds as those scholars did not view the study of religion as an integrated discipline.

Thus, it should be remembered that the "universalist" and "essentialist" PoR played a politically/academically critical role in Japan in those days. At the same time, however, it cannot be overlooked that PoR scholars' critical consciousness was somehow insular, directed mostly towards Japan's own imperialist past. Such self-criticism was an ethical attitude, but, remarkably, none of our interviewees mentioned that they had ever regarded the Nazi connections of van der Leeuw and Gustav Mensching as problematic. Instead, both of these scholars were popular among post-war Japanese scholars who took interest in PoR, as is the case with other, also politically liberal, post-war Japanese scholars who admired Heidegger.

Satoko Fujiwara is Professor of the Department of Religious Studies, Faculty of Letters/Graduate School of the Humanities and Sociology, at the University of Tokyo. She received a PhD in the History of Religions from the Divinity School of the University of Chicago. She is Secretary General of the International Association for the History of Religions (2020–). Her publications include "The Reception of Otto and *Das Heilige* in Japan: In and Outside the Phenomenology of Religion" *Religion*, 47(4), 2017 and "Japan" in *Religious Studies: A Global View*, edited by Gregory D. Alles (Routledge, 2008).

References

Anesaki, Masaharu. 1900. *Shūkyo gaku gairon* [*An Outline of the Study of Religion*]. Tokyo: Tokyo Senmon Gakkō Shuppanbu.

Araki, Michio (ed.). 2004. *Sekaino minshū shūkyō* [*Folk Religions in the World*]. Kyoto: Mineruba Shobō.

Eliade, Mircea. 1984 [1969]. *The Quest: History and Meaning in Religion*. Chicago, IL: University of Chicago Press.

Ishizu, Teruji. 1934. "Bukkyō tetsgaku: zoku." In *Shūkyo tetsugaku* (Bukkyō daigaku kōza 8), edited by T. Ishizu. Tokyo: Bukkyō Nenkansha.

Ohata, Kiyoshi. 1982. *Shūkyo genshō gaku* [*The Phenomenology of Religion*]. Tokyo: Yamamoto shoten.

Sharpe, Eric. 1986 [1975]. *Comparative Religion: A History*, 2nd edition. London: Duckworth.

Uno, Enku. 1935. *Shūkyo gaku gairon* [*An Outline of the Study of Religion*]. Bukkyō daigaku kōza 12. Tokyo: Bukkyō Nenkansha.

6

The Grammar to Read "Religion in Culture"

An Interview with Chin-Hong Chung (South Korea)

SUKMAN JANG

Translated by Hwasun Choe

Chin-Hong Chung was born in 1937 in Gongju, South Chungcheong Province. He received his BA from Seoul National University in 1960, followed by an MA (1965), STM from United Theological Seminary (1971) and DMin from San Francisco Theological Seminary (1981). He was Professor of Religious Studies at Seoul National University from 1982 to 2003, and Chair of the Korean Association for Religious Studies from 1992 to 1994. He has been a Member of the Republic of Korea's National Academy of Science since 1999, and was Chairman of Korea Institute for Religion and Culture from 2000 to 2017. He is currently Professor Emeritus at Seoul National University. His 13 books include *Jonggyohak Seoseol* (*Introduction to the Study of Religion*, 1980), *Jonggyomunhwaui Insikgwa Haeseok: Jonggyohyeonsanghakui Jeongye* (*Understanding and Interpretation of Religion in Culture: the Development of Phenomenology of Religion*, 1996), *Jeongjikhan Insikgwa Yeolin Sangsangryeok: Jonggyo Damronui Jiseongjeok Gongganeul Wihayeo* (*Cognition and Imagination: For a Discourse of Religion in the Intellectual Domain*, 2010), and three translations into Korean, including Eliade's *Cosmos and History* (1976).

Keywords: category of religion, pre-religion religion and post-religion religion, cultural hermeneutics, imagination, religion-in-culture, studies of religious phenomena

Introduction

Chin-Hong Chung has consistently emphasized the importance of phenomenology of religion (PoR) and introduced the works of Mircea Eliade to Korea. He has called for scholars of religion to expand beyond the limits of single religious traditions, such as Christianity, Buddhism and Confucianism, long before criticisms about the paradigm of world religions were raised. Also, he identified problems with the concept of religion and emphasized that the study of religion should not be confined to that concept. His research has focused primarily on the themes of intellectual honesty and free imagination.[1]

The interview was conducted in three sessions, at Prof. Chung's office in Yongsan District, Seoul, on 21 March, 18 April and 5 June 2018.

Sukman Jang: Some people call you a scholar of the study of religion, but others refer to you as a scholar of phenomenology of religion (PoR). Which do you prefer?

Chin-Hong Chung: People usually start their inquiries about religion from their own religious traditions. However, my concern has always been about the more general understanding of the phenomenon called "religion". When I was in college in the late 1950s in Korea, religion was considered a subsidiary phenomenon, and there were very few academic discussions about it. I think the study of religion started to emerge in Korean academia when theories of primitive religions and early study-of-religion scholars such as Max Müller were introduced to the curriculum of the Department of Religious Studies at Seoul National University (SNU). However, I don't think my concept of religion was formed through the academic curriculum of the study of religion back then. Two arguments account for this.

First, the academic identity of the study of religion in those days was not clearly distinguished. The history of the study of religion was relatively short compared to that of philosophy, sociology, psychology, anthropology, or ethnography. Also, critical incorporation of earlier studies and theories about religion was not an easy job.

Second, I was not satisfied with certain premises of the study of religion. For example, the descriptive category of "world religions" was very confusing to me. It seemed not to include all religions of humankind, and I thought that if we only considered what belongs to that category as "religion", we were

---

1.   The romanization of Korean words in this article follows the Revised Romanization of Korean (RR) maintained by the National Institute of the Korean Language (NIKL), South Korea.

being dishonest. I still think "world religions" is a political category based on Western standards. Sometimes I try to fathom the extent to which the history of religion has been distorted since people started adopting that category. I could not help but question the appropriateness of the category, because concepts within it such as "primitive" religions, theism/atheism, and the use of scripture or doctrine as a standard for defining religion were incapable of describing what I had experienced as religion in my life.

Yet, the study of religion was still the only area where I could pursue my questions and concerns since these were not permitted in the study of religious traditions.[2] There I was supposed to simply accept the answers offered by the religious traditions. I saw this as forcing me to abandon my own questions. Also, I could not stand the tendency to reduce religion to something subsidiary to other academic disciplines. I felt I was losing the point of my own concerns. As such, I did not mind being called a scholar of the study of religion since the study of religion was a place where I could pursue my questions and concerns.

However, the atmosphere of the study of religion that I experienced was not entirely free. In the late 1950s, when courses on the study of religion began to be taught in Korea, most were dominated by Christian theology. Only gradually did courses on other traditions such as Buddhism and Confucianism start to be included. Since then, the mainstream of the curriculum of Religious Studies at SNU has continued to be the study of religious traditions. The rationale is still that we have to start our academic research about religion from the specific materials of the "great" traditions of "world religions". Although the course title of PoR appeared in the curriculum in the early 1970s at SNU, it was only almost ten years later that the course was actually taught. The dominant thought was that a historical approach to the traditions of world religions was essential to the study of religion, and scholars of PoR were considered as not belonging to a proper academic discipline. Under such circumstances, I, who claimed to be a scholar of PoR, could not find a niche.

Whenever I suggested a specific phenomenon as the main subject of my research, I was uncertain as to whether my chosen subject would be recognized as a legitimate topic in the study of religion. For example, concern about Dangun mythology was considered to belong to Korean religion, so it could not be discussed in PoR. Likewise, the names of God were considered

---

2. Here, what Prof. Chung means by the study of religious traditions is to study religions within the frame of faith of each religion, acknowledging its doctrine and justifying it, such as in Christian theology or emic Buddhist studies. On the other hand, religious studies, or the study of religion, is meant to study religion regardless of personal faith or acceptance of specific religious doctrines.

to belong to Christian Theology, Mandala to Buddhism, the Book on the Five Rites of State (Gukjooryeui國朝五禮儀) to Confucianism, and the Yoido Full Gospel Church to the Sociology of Religion. In this situation, all I could do was to clarify that PoR was not about specific themes but methods for approaching themes. I tried to explain that in PoR, you pursued meanings through an encounter with the phenomenon itself, while other fields in the study of religion pursued understandings through historical approaches. I did not come to have an identity as a scholar of PoR through the study of religion. However, I sympathized with the ideas of PoR and explored problems, methods, and hermeneutics that were tested and developed in PoR. I think it would be more suitable to say that I "encountered" PoR than "learned" it. Learning is mainly about having knowledge of something. An encounter is an event for the subject who experiences it.

If you consider PoR only as a Western tradition and a specific field or methodology developed in the study of religion, then I am not a scholar of PoR in that sense. However, if you recognize that my concerns about religion could be most freely expressed through the encounter with PoR, I have no problem being called a scholar of PoR. I am a scholar of PoR in that it freed me to ask any question about religion in general.

There are two particularly interesting points in your statement. One is why your concerns about religion developed into "what is it that we call religion?", instead of "how can we become good believers?"

Academic pursuit is not derived solely from intellectual curiosity, especially in the study of religion. If there is no existential motivation making you ask about religion, it is very difficult to pursue the study of religion. My father came from a traditional Confucian family, and my mother from a Christian family. But there was no religious conflict in our home. However, I came to realize that people who were very devoted to their own religion tended to assume that conflicts between two different religions were inevitable. Even now, I see that some attempts at, or theological discourses for, interreligious dialogue do not aim to solve the conflicts among religions but to win a victory for one's own religion. I could not turn a blind eye to religious conflicts, to the violence and murders. The reality of religion was extremely violent, which was quite the opposite of the general understanding of religion.

But that was not the only reality that made me question religion. I witnessed war when I was young. I can't forget the battlefields. Battlefields are different from war. War can be explained; there are winners, losers, heroes, and sometimes justice is even mentioned. However, in battlefields there are only massacres and destruction; there are no explanations. Religion was powerless to stop the tragedy, but still – most of the time – both the people who were dying and the people who survived the battlefields called for religion.

Faced by this reality, as a person who survived the battlefields, I could not help but ask what religion is. However, the "theology" of each religious tradition rejected my question.

Accordingly, the study of religion was the only way for me, since it was the only place where I could ask my questions without "substantive premises" (as opposed to methodological ones) or interruption. In the study of religion, I did not have to evaluate or modify my questions to make them sound more sophisticated. I expect to hear the author's autobiographical voice even in academic articles and books. It can be a little dangerous to show yourself in academic works. However, I think scholars should reflect on the tendency of academic research to sacrifice its humanity while pursuing universality and truth. At least I think PoR is willing to reveal that aspect a lot more than other academic disciplines; it tries to avoid the academic tendency of losing humanity on the pretext of intellectual exploration of human beings.

If we cannot deny that our modernization was achieved under the influence of the West, it seems we have to emphasize the meaning of "learning" more than "encountering". But you think "encounter" is more important. Can you explain?

Our modernization was achieved by accepting Western culture. This kind of change is generally explained through cultural superiority; we became "enlightened" and modernized through "superior" Western culture and eventually shed our lagging development in the course of world history. However, we have to think about this. The framework for superiority is a comparison. The important thing in any comparison is "the orientation of the question" of the subject, that is to say, whom, why, and for what we compare.

Thus, we have to ask first what measures became criteria for determining superiority. In the West, of course, they regarded their place as superior and compared other cultures to themselves. We, who were regarded as inferior in this context, accepted this standard of comparison. Although Western academic disciplines have undergone considerable change since the "discovery" of the East, colonial rule, and the development of anthropology, it is still doubtful whether there has been sufficient self-reflective questioning or epistemological reflection among Western scholars regarding their own position. It is also questionable whether we have carried out such epistemological reflection sufficiently. Although postmodernism and postcolonial studies have criticized a Western-centrist point of view, the criticisms also came from such Western perspectives; it is probably unavoidable for them. Therefore, we need more non-Western outlooks.

Diffusion, expansion, exchange of cultures and the resultant acculturation are very common. The problem is why such phenomena were interpreted as signs of superiority. When we only focus on the standard of superiority, we miss a critical point; our states before and after our encounter with the West are qualitatively different. I think now it is time for us to treat seriously the encounter with the West as a cultural phenomenon beyond the standards of superiority or inferiority.

"Religion (jongkyo, 종교)" was a new term that appeared after our encounter with the West. It is a Western term. Since modernization, all the descriptive terms of our cultural discourse became dominated by Western terminology. "Culture", "politics", "economics" and even "arts" are translated terms, as is "religion". All terms have their own cultural contexts when they first appear. It is like an accumulation of memory. All conceptual terms are abstractions of experiences that have long taken place in the context of each language; they contain categories of classification and built-in logic. Words also reflect the world in which they were born. Therefore, translation and acceptance of a term are not fundamentally different from transplantation of the culture in which that term was born. Also, using these terms to discuss our experience is no different from judging our culture by criteria other than our own. This leads to two phenomena: first, our memories before this new language, and the reality contained in those memories, are erased by the terminology; and second, our reality here and now does not connect well with those terms from the past.

This can be summarized as the loss of old traditions and the grafting of new ones. This also happened in regard to religion. I think we cannot help but distinguish between "pre-religion religion (religion before encounter)" and "post-religion religion (religion after encounter)" when we discuss our religious culture. Religion before the encounter with the West is still vividly present in our experience and memories, but when we use the concept of religion, it becomes invisible. Therefore, we should bear in mind that so many "religious" experiences in our history and culture, that is to say, "pre-religion religion" have been discarded by the standard of "post-religion religion". Of course, what I said above is not "mechanically" fixed. The translated language, which already deviates from the original context, undergoes a morphological and semantic transformation by the users of the language in a newly established context. However, such a transformation does not happen naturally; it is a result of describing the facts that new language users have experienced and of giving them novel meanings and recognition.

Accepting the current unstable connection to the new tradition as the matrix of our culture without discussing the loss of old traditions can lead to distorted perception. This can be the result of "learning", but it shows the cost of overlooking the reality of the "encounter". So, I think we should develop a hermeneutics of encounter as an event. Future tasks of PoR will be cultural hermeneutics, which includes problems like this.

Can you explain a little bit more about "hermeneutics of encounter as an event", or "cultural hermeneutics"?

We often take into account Western culture's formulations of history and ideas when we seek to recognize and try to describe our current problems and issues. For example, sometimes we equate the Renaissance to our own past. I think there is a very unstable connection here.

The merging of Asian or Korean culture and Western culture may be described as participation in the universal human community brought about by modernization. However, we must not allow our perception of the world to be distorted by such an unstable connection. We must not be obsessed by the idea that "we must learn to follow the West". We must look inward to our own experience of encounter as a phenomenon and see it representing or embodying its own unique and equally legitimate symbolic system.

Therefore, I think we should first develop the hermeneutics of encounter as an event, rather than simply describing it as "the result of learning". I think one of the future tasks of PoR would be to analyse and recognize what I would call "cultural hermeneutics", since I am worried that the insistence on Western interpretation may be insufficient and cause us to insufficiently reflect on what might be another legitimate interpretation through our own eyes. I am not saying that this work has never been done before, but perhaps, we must be more rigorous in considering our own or another approach. I think your works on the modernization of Korea and the concept of "religion" in modern Korea[3] can be a good example of this kind of "cultural hermeneutics" or "hermeneutics of encounter as an event".

I would like to hear more about your "encounter" with PoR.

Well, it is true that I "learned" PoR, which was started and developed in the West. But I think there is a difference between when you come to know something you didn't know before by learning and when some recognition already inside you comes to be revealed by learning. In the case of the former, what you learn constructs reality, but in the case of the latter, reality constructs what you learn. It was in the early 1960s that I began to construct my concerns about religion in the ways of PoR. I was teaching religion at a high school at that time, and I found that the terminologies of various religious traditions were difficult jargon for students who were new to those traditions. As a result, most of my students struggled to engage with what I said about religion. However, when I talked about symbol and myth after reading *Patterns in Comparative Religion* by Mircea Eliade, their responses were entirely different; surprisingly, they were quite enthusiastic.

---

3.   See Jang (2017).

Patterns in Comparative Religion opened my eyes to the fact that I could talk about religion even though I didn't follow each religious tradition of the category of "world religions". That book was not a book of theology, philosophy, or history. It was different from any other books of sociology, psychology, or even anthropology, and ethnography. It was even different from other books on the study of religion. It didn't insist on seeking the origin of religion, the function of religion, nor the similarities and differences between religions as in the comparative study of religion. However, it did not exclude any of those subjects discussed in the study of religion. Instead, it took a view of subjects in a totally new way. To me, it seemed like such a peculiar view. Instead of pursuing the essence, this book questioned the background experiences behind the phenomena that are encountered, and tried to understand the humans who were the subjects of those experiences. In this book, all phenomena of different times and spaces became materials for the study of religion, and it was almost like listening to an orchestral work comprised of all phenomena. There, anything could serve as material for discussions of religion, and the realities that were typically overlooked, forgotten, or concealed while discussing religion were scrupulously examined. I wanted to probe religious phenomena in that particular way. In other words, I wanted to ask, "what is it that people call 'religion'" rather than "what is religion?" This kind of concern had developed in discussions of PoR, and I wanted to participate in them too.

People have asked so many questions about religion, and there have been so many answers. Therefore, when you find some question that has not been asked yet, your intellectual curiosity is piqued. However, more urgent than unasked questions are questions about the validity of current assumptions. These questions entail the tension of existence itself. I felt such tension in the flow of PoR. I think perception of things is not that different from having a grammar for reading things. Grammar does not bear language; language bears grammar. So, grammar is made out of language, not outside of language. Regarding that, when we intend to perceive things, we are participating in the process of making a grammar. I think the same is true with the epistemology of religion in its questioning and answering about religion. PoR embodies such participation.

Of course, we should not forget that language is also a historical phenomenon. Changes of grammar are inevitable. The language also changes; it is born, grows, ages and goes extinct. The same is true with religions. Religions are living phenomena. So, the language for describing it – i.e. the grammar for reading it – should also change throughout the life of the religion. Therefore, the frame with which I sympathize and the manner in which I explore religion do not have to always be those of PoR. I can imagine why Eliade called his subject the "history of religions" while avoiding other conventional expressions such as "comparative religion", or "PoR". However, even that position cannot be permanent. Even though I admit the change of the position and I also have to intend to change myself, I still think the position where I ask my questions and get answers is the place of PoR.

In PoR, I was particularly interested in three scholars: Max Müller, Gerardus van der Leeuw and Mircea Eliade. The origins of their problems, their processes of solving them, and their conclusions all differ. Nevertheless, they have something in common that differs from other scholars – I call it "imagination of culture", or "imagination of human beings". I want to say that imagination is a trigger for the emergence of something new which allows us to see beyond the visible, to hear beyond the audible. However, imagination could lead to deviation from contexts, sometimes even destroying the existing academic system. That is why academics fear and avoid using imagination. However, I think, these three scholars have a commonality in expressing their imagination without hesitation and carrying out their epistemological tasks. They did not modify or complement the previous understanding of religion but changed the place and frame of the question, discarding previous terms in order to change the questions themselves. Naturally, the object of recognition – that is to say, religion – had to be re-established. I understood their "attitudes" of learning in this way.

I also thought that what they imagined and what the focus of that imagination implied was not a particular religion or religion in general but the whole life in which religion is included along with all the phenomena that religion explores. I think we can call it the "culture" that people share. What they intended was not to understand religion as separate from other things but to discover the place of religion in life as a whole. If I attempt to articulate what I found and sympathized with in these three scholars, it would be like this: they understood religion as a phenomenon of transcendental reality in culture, not above it. In other words, they saw religion as a practical phenomenon of transcendental reality in the mundane, not as a transcendental phenomenon of the super-mundane. Therefore, the study of religion is the study of that culture which is called "religion". I agreed with these scholars about that. I also felt uncomfortable with people who separated religion from everyday life by establishing it as a totally different concept from culture. After my encounter with these scholars, it felt easier to say "religion in culture" instead of "religion".

How did your research about religion develop since your encounter with PoR? Also, how do you describe your methodology of PoR?

I summarized PoR as an exploration of the grammar needed to read "religion in culture". I also emphasized that questions about religion start from "what is religion", and shift towards "why is it called religion", then finally end with "who had experiences from which this kind of question cannot help but emerge?" I also claimed that what has been called "religion" and questions about it become "materials" for us to encounter here and now, and they materialize as stories or discourses of religion. Then, it becomes the material or text of the subject of the question, and is finally interpreted by that subject. I wanted to clarify that this is the task of PoR.

I did not develop my own methodology of PoR. I thought methodology appears by itself at the moment when the subject and object of the question encounter each other, and I myself have such experiences all the time. When I did my own research about certain religious phenomena such as marriage in the Unification Church or Yoido Full Gospel Church, I did not start from a certain methodology. Usually, I felt that the field itself made me focus on a certain phenomenon whenever I entered the field, and I tried to use every measure possible to analyse and conceptualize the phenomenon and to understand tentatively what the phenomenon represents. To use the terms of PoR, I "bracketed" my intention to define the essence of the phenomenon. I think that "the interest in essence" leads to the "declaration" of an argument, not an "understanding" of phenomena, while impelling metaphysical thinking. Surprisingly, I sometimes find this kind of tendency in historical positivism: the need of the historical research to declare an argument surpasses the need to read the present through the inquiry about the past. On the other hand, the result of bracketing is to listen to the manifestation of the phenomenon itself, to encounter "the fact" revealed in listening, and to consider it as the essence of the phenomenon. To use the terms of PoR again, this is the "eidetic vision".

The logical process for answering the question about essence always has a gap at the end. When that gap is filled with imagination, even though it declares that this is the essence, the question about essence remains open. However, when that gap is filled with faith, the question about essence closes and the essence becomes unchangeable reality. Then one is not allowed to ask questions about essence. In this way, historical consciousness or religion itself become instruments for justifying certain ideologies.

PoR is often viewed as the "art" of creating phenomena called "religion" – as an enterprise that contributes to the construction of religion rather than just describing it scientifically, which means that it is not a scientific study. I view this criticism rather positively; I believe that if PoR intentionally tries to exclude the practical effects of art, it would cause a critical defect in descriptions of phenomena. For example, scholars who do philological commentaries on texts of religious traditions always claim that their texts are recreated and rectified by their linguistic research and cultural discoveries. So, they say there is no way for the imagination to intervene. However, commentaries are not always the result of logical positivism. If the quest for meaning is the final expectation of commentary work, it inevitably ends with imagination. There is no other way to explain various traditions of interpretations unless we admit that works of commentary have filled the gap between logical proof and the essence they seek with imagination. However, this does not mean that I disregard positivism or history. It has been said about scholars of PoR, especially Eliade, that "there are only stories, not histories". This is a very insightful comment, but I would like to emphasize that if there is no story, there is no history.

I think you are the first to have taught a college course titled "PoR" in Korea. Could you explain a bit about the situation when you started teaching it and how your interest in PoR developed during that period?

I had already been teaching my own version of PoR in courses like "Introduction to the Study of Religion", and "The Study of Religion" at SNU and Ewha Womans University[4] since the 1970s. In the early 1980s, when I got the position of professor at SNU, I started to teach "Phenomenology of Religion". As far as I remember, PoR was a required course, as were "Introduction to the Study of Religion", "History of the Study of Religion" and "History of World Religions". However, even in the beginning, there were opinions that PoR could be addressed in "Introduction of the Study of Religion", or "History of the Study of Religion", and some were questioning whether it was necessary to offer a separate course for PoR. Also, PoR was neglected because it was alleged that PoR did not start from "world religions" or was not a study of religion proper. Another thing that should be noted is that the scholars of religion generally identified PoR with Eliade. Therefore, criticisms of Eliade became critiques of PoR; both were criticized as failing to empirically examine historical facts, spreading ahistorical ideas by discussing ancient existentialism or archetypes, and making the study of religion another form of religion by claiming a new humanism. In the Korea of the early 1970s, PoR was regarded as a new trend in the study of religion; but in the 1980s, opinions of PoR at SNU changed dramatically.

However, responses from students about PoR were always enthusiastic. During my 20 years at SNU, many were interested in my courses, "Introduction to the Study of Religion" and "PoR". "Introduction to the Study of Religion" was filled with over 200 students every semester. I still remember some of the topics in which my students were especially interested: religion as a phenomenon of religious history; reading modern myth as hidden, made, and transmitted; myth as a poetry of history; and transcendence as a concept made out of the body. In the early 1990s, I started teaching "Religion and Literature", "Religion and the Arts", and "Myth and History", and I approached

---

4. The use of "womans" carries special meaning. The early founders of the college thought that every woman is to be respected; to promote this idea, they chose the word "woman" to avoid lumping students together under the word "women".

these subjects from the perspective of PoR. Rather than exploring the essence of religion, literature, arts, history, myth, and symbol, I asked myself what is called religion, literature, arts, history, myth, symbol in our experience and explored why these things had emerged as these kinds of phenomena and what their meaning is. I also lectured on this subject in "Religion and the Study of Religion" in the last semester before my retirement. In this course, compiling my thoughts on religion and PoR, I emphasized the study of religion as an exploration of human life. This lecture was surprisingly well received. I still cannot figure out why my stories about religion in the style of PoR were disregarded by my academic colleagues but so well accepted by students and general audiences. I wonder if maybe it was because PoR's structure of question and answer made it semantically relevant to our lives.

Your last comment – that your lectures were more welcomed by students and general audiences than by your colleagues – is very interesting. Could you explain why?

First of all, I was so impressed by students' responses. They might have experienced and understood in my class on PoR that discourses about religion could be more than discussions about religious texts and doctrines, questions about the origin and functions of religion. That is to say, through the discourses of PoR, they might have become attuned to some questions and answers of their own that they could not express. For example, the expectation of relying on religion despite hesitation about devoting oneself wholly to it, or the persistence of religions for thousands of years despite the disappointment and betrayal constantly experienced in the reality of religion. They probably wanted to ask these kinds of questions but could not, because such questions were considered arrogant, blasphemous, or insincere and forbidden. However, these questions were freely discussed in PoR, so they felt that they could participate in the discussion too.

Also, I think it had something to do with the Korean situation in the 1970s and 1980s – that is to say, some aspects of the political, economic and cultural upheavals. After the Korean War, during the 30 years of democratization under military dictatorship and achievement of economic growth, individuals from each class of society faced fierce challenges, conflicts, and confusion regarding their identity. It was more urgent in the case of college students than in any other group. Their every day was a series of instances of resistance, suppression, imprisonment, and escape. This was a time that called for new rather than old stories. Put differently, it was a time when the imagination of "myth and symbol" was more needed than the analytical and systematic logics of knowledge. I think the category of myth and symbol in life was rediscovered regardless of existing religions' institutions and authorities at that time.

You've been actively engaged in domestic and international academic circles, spreading the view of PoR. Can you say more on that?

Let me briefly review the situation of the academic society of Religious Studies in Korea. The Korean Association for Religious Studies (KARS) was launched by Prof. Byeong-Gil Jang at SNU in the early 1970s. Professors from Dongguk University, which is affiliated to Buddhism, Methodist Theological University, and Sungkyunkwan University, which is affiliated with Confucianism, participated. But after one issue of the journal, KARS had no actual academic activity until the early 1980s. All the members had concerns about religion, but since it was an assembly of scholars from each religious tradition, it was limited in its ability to establish itself as an academic society for religious studies. Also, it lacked a sufficient financial base to run an academic society. When KARS resumed its academic activity, it emphasized that it should include all different religious traditions, so it was more like the Korean Association of Religions rather than the Korean Association for Religious Studies. KARS included religious history, phenomenology of religion, sociology of religion, psychology of religion, philosophy of religion, and Korean religions, as well as Buddhism, Confucianism, and Christianity. In the name of "Religious Studies", all the areas related to religion were incorporated and the organization was based on the idea that there would be no Religious Studies without religions, or "great" religious traditions. It was noteworthy that the Korean religion section was very active.

Meanwhile, the PoR section of KARS was inert. Most papers read in the section were not about a certain religious phenomenon but theories of PoR.

Studies about actual religious phenomena from a PoR perspective were pursued more freely outside the academic society or institutions. The Korea Institute for Religion and Culture (KIRC), which became a foundation in 2001, is one such example. This institute had originally been founded as the Korea Institute for Study of Religion in 1988 by some young scholars of the study of religion who had PhDs in SNU but could not find a tenured position in the university system. The KIRC is the only official institute of the study of religion outside of academic institutions in Korea, holds two symposiums annually, and publishes a journal called *Critical Review of Religion and Culture* twice yearly.

I think we can trace the development of the study of religion or PoR through the achievements of the KIRC. Most of the studies done by members of the Institute focused on religious phenomena rather than the essence of religion, and explored what human experiences link to the phenomena. Any phenomenon which makes us question the existing category of religion could be a topic of research. Methods can be chosen freely according to the place of the researcher and the context of the research object. Naturally, they have attempted contacts and exchanges with other disciplines and the re-establishment of new perceptions and methods through these.

Exchange with foreign scholars was also active. For example, we can think of the academic exchanges and mutual-visit conferences between the department of Religious Studies at the University of Tokyo and the KIRC, which had been going on for a while. These were meaningful opportunities for conversations and exchanges between scholars from the two countries. Also, I want to include translations of important foreign books on religion in the category of academic exchange. Many classics of the study of religion have been translated into Korean. Many contemporary books and articles are being read and translated too.

Both inside and outside of Korean academia, PoR is being re-examined these days. What do you think about this trend, and what are its implications?

Regarding this question, I want to consider the general character of the study of religion first. I think all the discussions in the study of religion have centred on the relationship between the study of religion and theology. To put it roughly, even though the study of religion views itself as freed from theology, it is still under the influence of the category of theology. This is not very different from how atheism loses its foundation outside of the category of theism. More specifically, the study of religion has always been based on the logic of negation, no matter how it defines itself. That is to say, the study of religion has tried to establish its identity in contrast to what it is not.

We can see this tendency in the works of Van der Leeuw, who is referred to as a scholar who constructed the methodology of PoR. He said that PoR is not religious poetry, not religious history, not psychology of religion, not philosophy of religion, and not theology. These descriptions covered all the negative critiques of PoR, and also arguments to defend itself against these criticisms.

However, in this situation, we can focus on two things. First, theology, which was "the object of denial" for the study of religion, has changed a lot since then. Whether defending or attacking, theology was impacted by its encounter with the study of religion, and it could not maintain the position of exclusively claiming self-absoluteness anymore. Likewise, the study of religion or PoR cannot stay on the same spot where it first started. It needs to keep changing and making itself more persuasive.

The other thing I want to point out is that PoR describes and explains the meanings of religious phenomena while encountering them in the field. PoR constructs itself in the field. In this context, a symposium titled "What and how can we teach about religion?" held by the KIRC in November, 2015 provides an example of PoR's exploration of what can be done and how, in the fields of religious phenomena. This is an effort to establish PoR's stance while empirically verifying the practical applicability of the research premises and methods to our reality.

In this context, I think the two major streams of the study of religion – that is to say, an approach to the "great traditions" of "world religions" and an approach to explore phenomena in the field of encountering religion, such as PoR's – have become increasingly separate. The former usually focuses on "textual studies". Texts are the objects – the materials – of understanding. However, most often, textual studies are not distinguished from the religion's own explanations of the text, since textual studies tend not to be studies "about texts" but studies "of texts".

In my view, PoR is illuminated again by the disappointment with the studies focusing on textual annotations and also by the search for alternatives. In the changing climate of academia nowadays, it is certain that PoR is beyond the stage of identifying itself as "not something". It is showing what it is through practical and empirical studies. As I already insinuated, I think it is time for the study of religion to move beyond the shadow of philosophical phenomenology and to be "studies of religious phenomena", not "phenomenology of religion".

You pointed out that the two major streams of the study of religion – the historical and the phenomenological – stagnate if they don't find a way to surpass traditional ways of thinking when they encounter new tasks. What are the new tasks that they cannot avoid nowadays?

I can think of subjects like language, memories, imagination, violence, gender, nuclear weapons, environment, etc., but what I want to point out are the discourses of cognitive science. Even if scholars of the study of religion cannot participate in experiments of scientists such as brain science, and must rely on scientists' results, if they fail to reflect on new discussions in these areas, I think that only shows how lazy they are. Fortunately, we have already had a lot of discussions about this in academia, and papers and books have been published.

I want to talk about two things in this regard. One is that the discourses of cognitive science show that there is still room for new questions. Asking something that was never asked before changes our place in life. Therefore, the discourse of cognitive science made us realize that it is possible to ask about religion from such a perspective. The other is about the focus of that question, or its foundation. As people say, it might be biological evolutionism or brain science. However, I would like to conceptualize it tentatively as "material" or "materialism". The root of cognitive science is the body. Not the body which is the counterpart of the soul, just the body itself. The body discussed in cognitive science is not the body from the dualism of body and soul, everything is caused by the body and resulted in the body. So, it can be concluded that religion is a phenomenon of the body. Therefore, the discourse of cognitive science challenges us to explore our discourses about religion so far.

PoR is facing these new challenges. Even the study of religion that focuses on textual studies cannot avoid these challenges. Whether you do text-centred studies or research based upon PoR, I think you should confront these challenges seriously and honestly, and reconstruct the methods and contents of your studies beyond what people have been doing so far. The discourse of cognitive science reminds me of the days when *religionswissenschaft* made a new era in history. Like Max Müller's remarks that *religionswissenschaft* would change the world, I think, the shock from cognitive science has made all academic disciplines more alert, including the study of religion. I think the anxiety that the discourse of cognitive science might cause the extinction of religion is ungrounded, just as the study of religion did not cause the end of religion; rather, the study of religion has coexisted with religion. As long as it claims that religion is a phenomenon of the body, religion is going to continue with the body. Now, studies about religious traditions and PoR should respond seriously to this shock. It will expand our horizon of perception and contribute toward refining our identity.

If there is anything that needs to be done for the development of PoR, what would it be?

Maybe I am repeating myself, but I think if PoR wants to construct appropriate epistemology and hermeneutics, it should be "studies of religious phenomena", not "phenomenology of religion". If I dare say, we have to re-establish the concept of a phenomenon and PoR outside the shadow of philosophical phenomenology. In this way, I think, we can resolve the tension between the study of religion and other academic disciplines, such as philosophy, theology, and sociology, and even share problems and methods with other disciplines.

Commentary

The discussion about the origins of the academic study of religion in Korea is surprisingly complicated, for there are different opinions as to when modern concepts of "religion" began to be used, and how to define "academic interest or attitude". In general, the differences reveal either the authors' religious tendencies or the perspectives of their schools.[5]

---

5. See the following books and articles about this: Jang Byeonggil gyosu Euntoe Ginyeom Nonchong Ganhaengwiweonhoe (1985), Hanguk Jonggyohakhoe (1997), Hanguk Jonggyomunhwa Yeonguso (2003) and Kim (2017).

However, it is noticeable that most of the authors considered academic interest in religion to be a matter of comparing different religions (i.e. comparative studies of religion). Whether from apologetic or cultural-historical concerns, they understood "the schematization of the sameness and differences" of religions as "an academic attitude". The establishment of the Korean Association for the Studies of Religion (KASR) in 1970[6] was also done from this point of view, as scholars from Buddhism, Confucianism, Christianity and Won Buddhism participated. In 1969, another association of religious studies scholars was organized, the Korean Association for the History of Religions (KAHR). Scholars of Christian theology and shamanism were the main members of this group. In 1970 the KASR paused its activity for 14 years, after publishing one issue of its journal, and in 1969 the KAHR paused its activity for 23 years, after publishing three issues of its journal.[7]

Even given in this atmosphere of the 1970s, the ground for Western *Religionswissenscahft* was gradually established. Prof. Chung wrote as follows in "The Tasks of the Study of Religion: Some Reflections on its Methodology" (published in 1972 in the first issue of the journal of KASR, *Journal of the Studies of Religion* [한국종교학]):

> The study of religion is neither ideographic nor nomothetic ... The method of the study of religion is empirical. However, the study of religion not only describes, narrates, and organizes religious data but also classifies religious representations and structures in the data and seeks to discern the essential meaning of their patterns and structures ... The study of religion is the study of the meaning of the manifestations of religious phenomena in human history. These manifestations are open to a wide variety of interpretations.
>
> (Chung 1980, 65–74)

---

6. The English name of the association was originally the Korean Association for the Studies of Religion (KASR). In 1986, when it relaunched, it changed its English name to the Korean Association for the History of Religions (KAHR), and in 2010, the association changed its English name from KAHR to the Korean Association for Religious Studies (KARS). The association's second English name, KAHR, should not be confused with another group organized in 1969, which also had the same English name.

7. See note 2. The KAHR in 1969 was launched by Sanghee Moon at Yonsei University, College of Theology, and Taegon Kim, who was a researcher of shamanism in 1969. Moon studied at the University of Chicago and translated excerpts from Eliade's *Shamanism*. Kim collected many vivid data about shamanism through his widely ranging fieldwork. However, there were problems with securing members and with Moon's and Kim's different research perspectives. Their journal, *Journal of the History of Korean Religions* (한국종교사연구) was launched in 1972, with two issues in 1973. This journal restarted in 1996 publishing volumes 4–13 between 1996 and 2005, and it has stopped since then.

In the context of the time when other scholars attempted to define the study of religion in relation to comparing "great" or "world" religions, Chung's remarks like this were entirely different from others'. When your questions become new, the objects of questions change. Then, the concept of religion expands, the method of research opens, and new understandings emerge.

Before the resumption of the KASR as the KAHR in 1986, Prof. Chung launched the Association for Religious Studies in Korea in 1977 with several scholars. In the first volume of its journal, *Journal of Religious Studies*, Vol. 1, 1978, he stated the purpose of the association:

> The history of the study of religion is still not that long ... However, we are in a situation when a theory of religion and an epistemological hermeneutics of religion may be needed. In this situation, we can assume two facts. First, the identity of the study of religion should be established and rooted in the field of academic disciplines – indeed, I think this is happening. It means that the field of the study of religion in Korea has been grafted onto a hundred years of Western religious studies tradition. ... Second, it is necessary to begin a journey of reflecting on the limit of previous studies of religion. However, I feel quite sceptical when I reflect on how meaningful the study of religion has been so far as a science, as a field of understanding, as a study of human beings, and as a source of theories and methods for religious studies. Therefore, we are confronted with the fact that now we should make another gesture to reclaim our existing academic body of the study of religion and existing research on religion.
>
> (Reprinted in Hanguk Jonggyomunhwa Yeonguso 2002, 205–209)[8]

Chung's comments such as these could not be understood in the Korean academy back in those days. However, he has led the study of religion in Korea, more specifically PoR in Korea.

Chung repeatedly emphasizes that his motivation for the study of religion was not derived from intellectual curiosity but from existential questions. He said that he cannot forget his elementary school days under Japanese colonization when he was severely punished when he spoke Korean in school, and that he cannot forget his experiences of the Korean war where he witnessed the slaughter and the ruin carried out in the name of a grand ideology. He made it clear that these experiences could not be separated from his academic pursuits. He witnessed that the reality of religion was an infinite consolation, and at the same time, it was an often-unrecognized violence. Perhaps such experiences may

---

8. When the KASR was restarted as the KAHR in 1986, the Association for Religious Studies in Korea was disassembled and joined it. The *Journal of Religious Studies* is still being published as a journal of the Department of Religious Studies at SNU.

be the reasons why he chose to study religion rather than commit to religion.

In the preface of his 1996 work, which focused on Western PoR, he wrote:

> If you feel really uncomfortable with the word, "religion", while you are studying "religion", you may say it is a disease. And I am in that situation. I feel pressured with the word, "religion", and sometimes I believe that this is the word that the study of religion should discard first and last. It is the word that is so old that it causes a lot of trouble now – so parochial, so normative, even authoritarian. Sometimes this word blocks or rejects our understanding. If I were more courageous, I would use "ordinary structure and history experiencing the extraordinary" instead of that word.
>
> (Chung 1996, 7)

He described his academic attitudes in the final chapter titled "nonacademic postscript". Here, he admitted that his academic attitude was considered as a metaphysical rebellion:

> It seems now I finally entered the place of the study of religion. I would like to say that. It seems I finally managed to ask freely all the questions I have wanted to ask. I want to talk about life with the language of the study of religion to which I have now only barely arrived. I promise to do so.
>
> (Chung 1996, 349)

Chung's academic works are occasionally criticized as being too abstruse or romantic. However, critics often overlook what he considered most important. It is that the reality of life cannot be separated from academic theories. Chung argues that PoR confirms that the two are the same, and he has shown it with his works, including research on the wedding ceremony of the Unification Church (Chung 1980, 161–187) and the structure and phenomenon of Yoido Full Gospel Church (Chung 1986, 211–267). He also appreciates new academic discussions and the achievements of other disciplines. Recently he has been very interested in the discourse of cognitive science of religion. His article, "Where is the Hometown of God?" is the result of this kind of interest (Chung 2010, 637–665).

In the collected essays recently published in honour of Chung, each of the twelve scholars gave a keen criticism of his works on the subject of perception, experience and imagination (Hanguk Jonggyomunhwa Yeonguso 2013). In this book, there are critical discussions on various of Chung's topics such as "religion-in-culture", humanism, concepts and reality, phenomenology of gesture, cultural criticism, phenomenology, imagination, myth and history, and death. Contributors sharply interrogated the theoretical foundation of Chung's methodology, problems in his choice and use of materials, the suitability of imagination in a poetic application, the limits of understanding the Western tradition of PoR, and the paradox of normative oughtness under the name of cultural criticism. In fact, these criticisms were directed at both him and other scholars of the study of religion in Korea.

It is not easy to clarify the nature of Prof. Chung Chin-Hong's PoR. He does not assume that there is some defined way of "PoR" that can be followed, and, furthermore, the themes and methodologies of his research always demonstrate the dynamics of change. It is clear that he has a critical attitude to the existing "traditional, thus, orthodox" religious studies when he prefers to be called a scholar of PoR, rather than a scholar of religious studies. Such a perspective is apparent in his recent book (Chung 2015).

He made the following remarks in the preface of his book: "The (academic) interest in religion should not take a "religious" attitude" (Chung 2015, p. 6). His comment shows his judgement on the fact that at least now in the study of religion in general in Korea is showing some "religious" aspects and affirms that his PoR is embodied in his effort not to be "religious".

What is clear is that Chung has developed new questions of the study of religion in the Korean academy, and has developed them under the name of PoR. He has prepared a stepping stone for us to use, as is confirmed by this interview.

Sukman Jang is Researcher at The Korea Institute for Religion and Culture. Jang's research interests include Modern Korean religions, Death Studies, and Anthropological theory. His dissertation "The Conceptual Formation of "Religion" in Modern Korea" (1992) focused on the emergence of the new concept of "Jonggyo" in Korea. His book *What is the Modern Korean Religion?* (2017) concerns the changing contexts of Korean religions in the first half of the twentieth century. He is presently working on the project "Changing Attitudes towards the Elderly in Modern Korea".

References

Chung, Chin-Hong. 1980. *Jonggyohak Seoseol* [*Introduction to the Study of Religion*]. Seoul: Jeonmangsa.

Chung, Chin-Hong. 1986. *Hangukjonggyomunhwaui Jeongye* [*Unfolding Korean Religious Culture*]. Seoul: Jipmundang.

Chung, Chin-Hong. 1996. *Jonggyomunhwaui Insikgwa Haeseok: Jonggyohyeon-sanghakui Jeongye* [*Understanding and Interpretation of Religion in Culture: The Development of Phenomenology of Religion*]. Seoul: Seoul National University Press.

Chung, Chin-Hong. 2010. *Jeongjikhan Insikgwa Yeolin Sangsangryeok: Jonggyo Damronui Jiseongjeok Gongganeul Wihayeo* [*Cognition and Imagination: For a Discourse of Religion in the Intellectual Domain*]. Paju: Cheongnyeonsa.

Chung, Chin-Hong. 2015. *Jiseongjeok Gonggananeseoui Jonggyo: Jonggyomunhwae daehan Bipanjeok Insikeul wihayeo* [*Religion in Intellectual Space: For the Critical Recognition of Religious Culture*]. Seoul: Sechang chulpansa.

Hanguk Jonggyohakhoe (ed.). 1997. *Haebanghu 50nyeon, Hanguk Jonggyo Yeongusa* [*The Half-century History of Research in Korean Religions after 1945*]. Seoul: Doseochulpan Chang.

Hanguk Jonggyomunhwa Yeonguso [Korea Institute for Religion and Culture]. 2002. *Jonggyomunhwa Bipyeong* [*The Critical Review of Religion and Culture*], vol. 1.

Hanguk Jonggyomunhwa Yeonguso (ed.). 2003. *Hanguk Jonggyowa Jonggyohak* [*Korean Religions and the Study of Religion*]. Seoul: Cheongnyeonsa.

Hanguk Jonggyomunhwa Yeonguso (ed.). 2013. *Jeongjikhan Isakjupgi: Sojeon Jeong Jinhong gyosu Jonggyo Yeonguui Jipyeong* [*The Honest Gleaning: The Study of Religion from Prof. Chung, Chin-Hong's Perspective*]. Seoul: Mosineun saramdeul.

Jang, Sukman. 2017. *Hanguk Geundaejonggyoran Mueotinga?* [*What is the Modern Korean Religion?*]. Seoul: Mosineun saramdeul.

Jang Byeonggil gyosu Euntoe Ginyeom Nonchong Ganhaengwiweonhoe (ed.). 1985. *Hanguk Jonggyoui Ihae* [*Understanding Korean Religion*]. Seoul: Jipmundang.

Kim, Chae Young. 2017. "Religious Studies as a Modern Academic Discipline in Korea." *Religion* 46(2).

7

Religiologie and Existential/Therapeutic Phenomenologies of Religion

Interviews with Louis Rousseau and Earle H. Waugh (Canada)

STEVEN ENGLER

Louis Rousseau is Professeur émérite in the Département de sciences des religions at the Université du Québec à Montréal (UQAM). He was a founding member, in 1969, of the programme in *religiologie* at that public university, an approach that explicitly draws on phenomenology of religion (PoR). Rousseau is well known for his religiologic approach to relations between religion and *québécoise* culture (e.g. Rousseau 1976, 1994, 1998, 2006, 2007). For a series of interviews with Rousseau, addressing his research, see Baillargeon (1994).

Earle H. Waugh is Emeritus Professor of Religious Studies and Emeritus Director of the Centre for Health and Culture, Department of Family Medicine, at the University of Alberta, Edmonton. He is one of few Canadian scholars who explicitly identifies himself as practising phenomenology of religion (PoR). Rejecting philosophical phenomenology, he pursued what he calls "existential phenomenology" during his fieldwork on Sufi traditions in North Africa (Waugh 1989, 2005, 2008), supplemented by work on Islam in North America (Waugh et al. 1983, 1991, 1998; Waugh 1999, 2018). He has a long-standing interest in Canada's First Nations (Waugh 1996; LeClaire et al. 1998). He is rounding out his career working on cross-cultural aspects of health care, informed by "therapeutic phenomenology" (Waugh et al. 2011, 2014, 2016, forthcoming).

Keywords – phenomenology of religion, Canada, Québec, Louis Rousseau, Earle H. Waugh, *religiologie*, religious studies, *sciences religieuses*

Introduction

PoR has been largely neglected or it is almost universally dominant in Canada, depending on how you define it. In either case, there is little or nothing distinctively Canadian about PoR in Canada. Canadian-born scholars of religion are often trained in and/or work in the USA, and many scholars working in Canadian SoR departments were born and trained in the USA. There is perhaps something distinctive about the ambivalent way that "PoR" is used in Canadian meta-theoretical debates, a point developed in the Commentary, after the interviews below.

The interview with Louis Rousseau that follows consists of written responses provided by Rousseau, translated and with footnotes added by Engler. The second interview, with Earle H. Waugh, is a transcribed and edited version of an 80-minute phone interview that took place on 2 March 2018, intercalated with additional written responses, with footnotes by Engler.

LOUIS ROUSSEAU

Québec: Religiology

Steven Engler: How do you see the situation in Québec, and your own work, fitting into the project represented by this book?

Louis Rousseau: This collective project, which aims to take stock of the evolution of practices of phenomenology of religion (PoR) over the past half-century, responds to a variety of needs. One of these in particular concerns the Québec university scene. The tradition of non-denominational religious studies – based on the epistemological intuitions of phenomenology (Husserl, Dilthey, etc.), and renewing the already secular tradition of *la Science de la religion* (Burnouf), Science of Religion (Müller) and *Religionswissenchaft* – received a significant boost during the 1960s. PoR's basic intuition energized a large disciplinary space. No assessment of this aspect of Québec's university history has been written to date. I can only offer my personal reflection, as a committed actor in a particular academic environment. My particular arguments would need to be confronted with other documents and other perspectives.

How did you define PoR when you began your career? How do you define it now? Do you see yourself as a phenomenologist?

My career as a university teacher began in September 1969. I was part of the small team that founded a *département de sciences religieuses* at Québec's first state university, the Université du Québec à Montréal (UQAM). As one would expect of a public institution in a rapidly changing society, the department was not theological.[1] It was positioned not as part of the humanities but of the human sciences. The new state Université du Québec cut all organic ties with the Catholic Church. They applied principles of faculty and student autonomy, born of the student protests of 1968. Like most new instructors hired at the time, I was just starting my doctoral studies, with a certificate in Philosophy and a BA in Theology from a Dominican college, and an M.A. from the Institut supérieur de sciences religieuses of the Université de Montréal (a Catholic university).

I did not have a precise definition of the nature of PoR in 1969. I began to discover it then. I was looking for a method for studying religion as a specific reality, observable in an empirical field, with a historical dimension that I could master. I had already delineated the broad contours of my specialized area of focus: the three centuries of history of my home society, Québec.

At that time, I knew a little of Husserl's phenomenology. I was sensitive to the epistemological project that aims to study human reality on its own terms (Dilthey), avoiding (as did Merleau-Ponty and Ricoeur) the mathematical reduction of the natural sciences. The discovery of American cultural anthropology (Benedict, Meade) shattered a certain idea of universality that had been inherited from Greek and medieval classics. My reading of Mircea Eliade, during an M.A. course with Yvon Desrosiers, provided me a first example of PoR: the distinction between the categories of sacred and profane, symbolic structures of hierophanies, etc. Here I found initial elements for theorizing the religious field in general terms, taking into account both "religious" forms, as recognized by history, and meaningful structures hidden in cultural facts that were not recognized as religious. Religion could be expressed in terms of specific forms of meaningful relationships to the world. The project of PoR would be to analyse and decode these relationships, which are present everywhere in specific recurrent forms. I saw here a hermeneutical problem that needed elaborating (Gadamer), but I did not yet have a sense of rigorous methods for pursuing this research.

---

1. Québec experienced a rapid period of secularization, the "Quiet Revolution", in the 1960s: beyond significant decline in religious participation, the provincial governmental replaced the Catholic church in running the education and health care systems; the education system was secularized and university education was made more freely available.

I have never identified myself as doing PoR. though I see my interpretations as rooted in the basic phenomenological intuition (a certain definition of the concept of religion, epoché, eidetic variation). I borrowed from other models while developing a personal hybrid: systemic (Bertalanffy 1973), hermeneutical (Ricoeur 1965), symbolic (Rousseau 1969), all drawing on the social history of *mentalités* (Le Goff and Nora 1974). I define myself as a religious historian (given the specificity of the religious object) who practices a nomothetic and diachronic approach to the religious. I seek general rules of the transformations of religious sign systems over time (Foucault).

PoR in Québec

When was PoR born/introduced in Québec? Who introduced it and in which departments? When was PoR most popular and with whom?

If we consider Mircea Eliade's work as an indicator of a certain popularity of PoR, then its distribution in the form of French paperback books from the late 1960s onwards resulted in a major breakthrough in Québec. For a Professor specifically interested in religion, Eliade had a great deal of influence. As early as 1969, his theory of religion played a role in UQAM's undergraduate introductory courses, presenting the religious dimension as a universal fact, and his work remains useful to this day. In particular, Eliade helped make it possible to problematize certain cultural objects (novels, films, visual art) that are not identified as religious according to popular opinion. It allowed them to be studied as embodying typically religious symbolic structures. In this light, Yvon Desrosiers (1977), Guy Ménard (1988) and Jacques Pierre (1990a) developed their research on "the displacement of the sacred".

We must talk about a deeper institutional impact of PoR on UQAM's origins. The initial core of professors of *sciences religieuses* was shaped by an earlier decision at St Mary's Jesuit College, which had decided to move from theology to history of religions, in response to negative student reactions. The intellectual driving force behind this decision was Father Raymond Bourgault, a linguist by training whose conceptual creativity allowed him to paint this transformation with the allure of philosophy of history. He came up with the idea of naming our discipline "religiology". This seemed an excellent strategy for distinguishing our discipline from theology and signalling its membership in the human sciences (Rousseau 2013). But who were our "disciplinary ancestors"?

During the first decades, our department sought its ancestors in a double lineage. The first was the Netherlands and Northern Europe, where a historical and phenomenological approach to the scholarly study of religions had long been institutionalized, sheltered in liberal Protestant theological faculties. The second was France, where various contemporary approaches had been the subject of a symposium in 1970 (Desroche and Séguy 1970). One chapter, by François Isambert, reviewed PoR and pointed out Van der Leeuw's importance. Already a reference for the founder of our department, Yvon Desrosiers, Van der Leeuw's work now became so for several colleagues. PoR allowed us to avoid identifying ourselves with any of the pre-existing disciplines of the human sciences, all of which were seen as ignoring or rejecting the formal object that constitutes the specificity of the religious. At the same time, a new epistemological model of interdisciplinarity was taking root around us, and this made it possible to integrate perspectives from these other disciplines while inventing a disciplinary field that was new in our society. This was religiology, not PoR. At the same time, teams belonging to the Université de Sherbrooke and Université Laval were developing a *sciences humaines des religions* that was closer to the configuration of the fifth section of the École Pratique des Hautes Études in Paris.[2]

Were there academic exchanges with PoR scholars in other countries (or anglophone Canada) and/or in other disciplines?

UQAM's religiologic project, related as it was to PoR, quickly became an issue of debate in Québec (Campbell 1972), in Canada (Pumer 1972) and in France (Séguy 1972). The most extensive discussions took place later with our colleagues from Sherbrooke who rejected the most distinctive aspect that we had inherited from PoR, namely the construction of a formal definition of religion. We held firm to this, and they chose to stick to a common-sense definition (Martel 1985). Our work and our programme were influenced by phenomenological and existential currents (Merleau-Ponty, Ricœur, Sartre, Heidegger), by PoR in the manner of Van der Leeuw, Eliade, Otto, Caillois, by the Freudian movement, and by the functionalist and structuralist movements. This network was made up of French-speaking scholars from Québec, France, Belgium and Switzerland. Guy Ménard's review of the department's history is the best place to explore further this network of intellectual exchanges that originally nourished the UQAM team (1994).

Exchanges with English-speaking colleagues from Canada and the United States took place within the framework of learned societies, including the Canadian Society for the Study of Religion/Société canadienne pour l'étude de la religion (CSSR/SCÉR) and its journal *Studies in Religion/Sciences religieuses*.

---

2. The ÉPHÉ section for the study of *Sciences religieuses* "studies religious facts from a secular perspective ... [as] defined by the object that unites them: practices, discourses and attitudes that imply a relationship with authorities or powers conceived as transcendent or supernatural" (see https://tinyurl.com/y4rmoy6y).

I regret today that I chose not to enter into debate with Willard Oxtoby, who was leading the charge against an impressionistic and uncompromising PoR. (I must add here the important influence that Robert Bellah's "civil religion" framework had on my work, on Québec history.)

The political context of the 1970s and 1980s in Canada is important here. In the face of Québec's nationalist movement, the national project for a bilingual Canada led to a policy of French-English bilingualism at scholarly meetings. Francophones took the opportunity to express themselves in their language, using the conceptual resources specific to their learned traditions. Despite good intentions on the part of English-speaking colleagues, inter-action was minimal. French papers, panels and discussions were attended almost exclusively by Francophone scholars. The latter drew the obvious conclusion, and the Société québécoise pour l'étude de la religion (SQÉR) was founded in 1989, effectively splitting from the CSSR/SCÉR. Both organi-zations continue to represent Canada as part of the International Association for the History of Religions (IAHR).

Do you think there is any connection/correlation between phenomenol-ogists of religion (in Québec or in general) and their religious affiliations?

This hypothesis is suggestive, but not demonstrable. The UQAM team has the same Catholic denominational heritage as that of Sherbrooke and Laval, but it diverges in its view of the formal purpose of the discipline. Raymond Bourgault, who gave religiology its initial intellectual impetus, practised a very creative hermeneutics of biblical texts. Yet Sherbrooke's and Laval's pro-grammes were born in theology faculties, while UQAM was born in the human sciences, where sociology, philosophy, psychology, history and linguis-tics were already present. We didn't want to just combine these disciplines. We had to create another, distinctive one. However, the "liberal" religious commitment of a majority of the UQAM founders was likely a significant factor in their conviction regarding the specificity of the religious. This seems comparable to the case with PoR in the Netherlands and Scandinavia.

The Impact of PoR in Québec

Did PoR decline/fall out of favour in Québec?

I have previously noted my department's explicit affiliation with PoR (Rousseau 1980). At UQAM, we have maintained a continuous link with the PoR approach, but without really insisting on the exclusivity of this connec-tion. No one was ever hired as a scholar of PoR. This epistemology remained an important conceptual reference until recently, a part of the fundamental "toolbox" provided to students.

What did PoR bring to the study of religion (SoR)? What did it accomplish?

PoR provided a fundamental epistemological conception for SoR, linking subject and object in a unique manner. It fueled the development of essential categories, capable of universal application, resulting from comparative study (of "types"). The development and critique of such categories is central to our approach, leading to our discerning the religious in cultural productions not generally identified as such (broadly within a cultural studies framework).

Has PoR exerted any influence upon public education? Or upon any other system of society?

The creation of a non-denominational and mandatory programme of Ethics and Religious Culture in Québec schools was influenced by PoR.[3] It is based on both the epistemological position of suspending ontological judgment (epoché) and on sympathy for the object being interpreted. This epistemic posture was introduced into university culture in the 1960s by phenomenology. In addition to its aim of knowledge based on the criticism of facts, this programme recognizes a humanist horizon, evoked in this case by the aim of civic initiation to the complex heritage inherited from *québécoise* historical experience. In a society currently hostile to confessionality, the term "religious phenomenon" has been one of the conceptual tools that have led to political acceptance of "secular" education concerning religious reality (Rousseau 2011). However, the PoR label itself was not part of these discussions.

Assessing PoR

Do you think Cognitive Science of Religion has any similarities to PoR?

I must admit that I have a poor knowledge of current "cognitive sciences" perspectives. To the extent that they contribute to the unified model of the natural sciences by reducing knowledge to neural operations, I see an impassable epistemological difference. The fundamental question concerns

---

3. In 2008, co-chairs sociologist and historian Gérard Bouchard and philosopher Charles Taylor released their 300-page final report from the Consultation Commission on Accommodation Practices Related to Cultural Differences (see https://is.gd/q8p8xj). The Québec government established the commission in response to public outcry regarding "reasonable accommodation" of religious and cultural practices. Bouchard and Taylor advocated a context-sensitive "open secularism" and developed a normative conception of "interculturalism", meant as an alternative to the federal emphasis on "multiculturalism". Since then, all Québec primary and secondary students have been required to take courses in Éthique et culture religieuse (ÉCR).

cognitive sciences' ability to cope seriously with the existential nature of symbolic functions. I have few expectations of this new field – though it is no doubt very fruitful in attracting funding.

Is there a reason to re-evaluate PoR now, or a path to doing so? What is the future of PoR in the SoR? What would SoR lack if it failed to continue with or to reclaim PoR?

The project of reassessing PoR's contribution to SoR seems very important to me. Hence, my participation in this book. There is a need for detailed archaeological research (in Foucault's sense), for doctoral theses and for collaborative research projects. This project of mapping national epistemological fields could serve as a starting point for more rigorous work. It is quite possible that PoR has been assimilated into redefinitions of knowledge in SoR, becoming lost to sight in that process. Discussions of the specificity of SoR's object(s) should always integrate the fundamental choice that gave rise to PoR.

How far do you agree/disagree with the historical descriptions and evaluations of PoR given by Eric Sharpe (*Comparative Religion: A History*)?

I find myself in broad agreement with Sharpe's diagnosis, as I note the aporias linked to the implementation of PoR that were identifiable in the 1960s. The question of SoR's specificity remains relevant and vital. PoR's fundamental contribution deserves to remain at the heart of epistemological debates. As evidence of this, witness the continued, if fragile, recognition of our specific field of scholarly expertise, in an institutional setting where disciplinary status is subject to competition before Research Grants Tribunals.

EARLE H. WAUGH

English Canada: Philosophical, Existential and Therapeutic Phenomenologies of Religion

Steven Engler: How do you define PoR?

Earle H. Waugh: PoR is the analysis of what constitutes the consciousness of religious positioning in the world in which we live. PoR regards religion as a fundamental component of being in the world, of living in the world. Religion and spiritual insights are basic to the way that we orient ourselves in reality.

In methodological terms, as a kind of scientist, one goes in to observe and to try to comprehend and not to pre-judge what anything is or means. The initial intuition is to try to experience what your subjects are experiencing, not to pre-judge any aspect of the situation, but to say "This is real to them. I should not make assumptions based on my own judgments."

In my view, philosophical phenomenology arose out of antagonism with theology, as an attempt to depart from the kind of dogmatic perspective that is exemplified in theological discourse. They tried to get a much broader kind of perspective on the world than theological dictums allowed. The early phenomenologists were building ultimately on Greek ideas of an independent stance, apart from the religious nexus in which they lived. What they tried to do was to develop first principles and basic structures of thinking, as a way of circumventing dogmatic theological doctrine. The development of an independent philosophical tradition had to cut itself away from the theological system that underlay medieval European thought. That has played into European PoR, where I see religious phenomenology as an attempt to construct a viable world around religion that was not based on theological perceptions.

Did that conception inform your own work? Do you see yourself as a phenomenologist?

It certainly informed my fieldwork, yes. Early in my career, when I went to Chicago, I encountered the whole philosophical thing, from Eliade and Kitagawa and Jonathan Smith and others who raised fundamental issues, in part critiquing the phenomenological approach. I did not consciously apply the type of articulation that I gave you until I went to Egypt and began working on trying to understand the chanter tradition in Sufism, and trying to understand the religious reality that Muslims lived in at that time. Many of the people that I read and the work that I did in Islamic studies confirmed to me that religion, as an entity in and of itself, was not only worth studying but probably had been central to the way in which most humans had reacted to the world from the beginning of human time. That notion became a conviction of mine.

I also found problematic Max Weber's comparative religious standpoint. I agreed with the notion that you had to have some kind of intellectual linkage across religions, in order to be able to know them and to understand them. But I was leery of imposing categories in order to achieve that. My first fieldwork on Sufism and the Mujahedeen tradition in Egypt was really a test case in which I tried to let the data be and to accept that data as a religious expression in and of itself.

PoR in Canada

When and where was PoR introduced in Canada?

In my view, PoR came about in Canada through the work of Wilfred Cantwell Smith and George Grant, who were active in the early days at Harvard/ Dalhousie and McMaster, though they were more comparativists than phenomenologists.[4] Though my own approach was more influenced by Chicago than by Canadian scholars, my early career in religious studies began under Grant's tutelage at McMaster, when Religious Studies was just establishing itself as a discipline in North America.

Smith affirmed the validity of religion as a field of study within the academy. When I went into SoR (the study of religion), most universities across the country housed anthropologists and social scientists who said that there was no validity to religion at all; religion is not something worth studying. This attitude was caught up mainly with logical positivism. Canadian universities had fairly strong secularist bias built into them. After the Second World War, religion was not considered something worth studying. I revolted against that. Maybe that is what drove me toward what I call existential phenomenology [see below] in which I tried to encounter the religious world as it presented itself.

There were a number of elements that allowed Smith and Grant to develop their ideas. One was the supposed duality of religions in Canada, that is, Anglicanism, Methodism and Presbyterianism on the English side and Catholicism on the French side. Such a duality ignored the resilient Indigenous religious traditions completely (among other things), but that dual religious reality could not be ignored by theoreticians. Then the presence of groups like the Jews and Baha'is argued against any kind of religious monopoly. This was signalled by the post-war expansion of Canada's immigration and by [Pierre Elliott] Trudeau's embrace of multiculturalism as a way to bridge Canada's cultural divide. Programmes then developed throughout Canada in universities and colleges utilizing PoR as an operative concept.

When was PoR most popular, and why did it become popular?

---

4. Smith (1916–2000) was a Canadian Islamicist, founder of McGill University's Institute of Islamic Studies in 1952. He taught at Harvard Divinity School from 1960 until 1973, when he became the first appointment at the new department of Religion at Dalhousie University, in Halifax (returning to Harvard in 1978). Grant (1918–1988) was a Canadian philosopher, influential for his centre-right political thought. He was the founder and Chair of Canada's first Religious Studies department, at McMaster University in 1961. See Commentary below.

PoR was most popular in the 1960s and 1970s, when departments of religious studies grew at most major universities in Canada. It was manned by people trained in various other academic areas like philosophy, theology, anthropology and psychology, until programmes like Chicago's and Harvard's began to produce scholars who looked for independent models to investigate religion apart from its confessional aspects.

I think we are now in a completely different place, academically and intellectually. Certainly I am. I see different emphases in each of the labels that we study under now: Religious Studies as a kind of generic mantle resistant to theological concerns; PoR urging the validity of a religious phenomenon quite apart from other ways of seeing the human situation; and SoR as a philosophical meditation on the various elements seen in religion, like its history, morality, ethics and theology.

Who else has done PoR in Canada?

Most scholars of religion – W. C. Smith, and George Grant and, say, Harold Coward – are world religions-type scholars who see common concerns across various religions and see certain kinds of structure in them. My work is much more compatible with Bill [William Closson] James's because of my experiential phenomenology. Bill is interested in the way in which ritual and ritual acts define or shape religious consciousness. I look at the experience of how people perceive their encounter with religion. To my mind, Bill is also interested in the kind of consciousness that people have with their religious tradition.

The Impact of PoR in Canada

Did PoR decline or fall out of favour in Canada? If so, why?

I'm not sure PoR ever "fell". As with many theories, new events and data called for other approaches. There is no doubt that universities have slowly dissolved departments of religious studies, so one would have to say the discipline as a whole has shifted considerably. There was originally a kind of naiveté about the discipline and what it could do: i.e. could it develop a "science of religion"! It has, for example, continued to struggle with the advent of secularism and whether a "secular scholar" can fairly judge religious topics. Individual religions, such as Hinduism or Islam that have never had an inherent and active secular standpoint find PoR strange, if for no other reason than that scholars within those traditions have never had to "stand outside" their religion in order to speak authoritatively about what constitutes human existence. A "value-free" analytic tradition has never been demanded within these cultures, as Western science assumes. Whether it is true or not is another matter.

PoR also has a financial problem in the University.[5] It overlaps with various other disciplines, like anthropology, sociology, political science and philosophy, and this has meant that it is challenged for funding in today's world, where Humanities and Arts programmes are constantly under pressure.

What did PoR accomplish? What has it contributed to the discipline?

PoR argued persuasively for the originality of the religious sentiment, that it was not and could not be reduced to either social analysis, philosophical reasoning or humanist discourse. As I have aged, I have become more and more convinced about the way religion creates a lifestyle and a culture: we damage religion if we don't accept its uniqueness. PoR also underlined the viability of different approaches to religious experience and the validity of allowing religious data to speak on their own terms through various analytic media. On the other hand, I argue against those who say that a religious specialist can determine what the meaning of a phenomenon can ultimately be. I do not think we have the right or the ability to reduce a rite to some psychological theory or to apply our philosophical insights to all religions and determine what they mean. There is an arrogance about such a view that I find disturbing. I also think confessional religionists should openly express their views, even if they disagree with PoR viewpoints. We are not arbiters of "the true"; we are observers and commentators, subject to the categories that we apply in an organized and hopefully scientific manner.

Has PoR in Canada exerted any influence on public education or other institutions?

I suspect it has had subtle impacts on all fields of study, from feminism to so-cial philosophy to scientific definitions. More distantly, new aspects of cultural studies (diversity, sexual variations, critiques of nationalism, etc.) all draw in some way from assumptions built into PoR. It provides a way of addressing multiple cultural viewpoints within society.

To give a specific example, Charles Taylor and Gérard Bouchard utilized forms of PoR in their 2008 report in Québec: their formula was undergirded by a search for commonalities across cultural divides. The report argues con-vincingly that the institutions of Québec can shape the kind of people that *québecois* are and can become. They see religion as one of those components

---

5. Waugh's comments here reflect in part the institutional history of the department of Religious Studies at the University of Alberta, which he chaired for many years. That history is discussed in Neumaier-Dargyay (1995) and Braun and Landy (2011).

that provide citizenry with focus and compassion as humans; it one of the elements that form a society's self.

Assessing PoR

Do you see similarities between PoR and Cognitive Science of Religion (CSR)?

The mind analysing the mind's products is another way of proceeding in the study of religion, but it will bring us no closer to the "thing-in-itself" than any of the other approaches. There is something about religion that affirms a separate place in human culture irrespective of mind constructions, and this is PoR's principle legacy. CSR is different from PoR since it is ultimately looking at putative structures of the mind and "religious" functions or, for example, functions that have bearing on cultural transmission and concept formation in the context of religions. However, neuroplasticity indicates that certain features that appear permanent in the mind can change and even restructure their meanings.

How far do you agree/disagree with the historical descriptions and evaluations of PoR given by Eric Sharpe and by James Cox?

Sharpe's critique arose from his foregrounding the limitations of the comparative perspective. In my view, Islam cannot be across-the-board "compared" to Christianity or to Buddhism; they each have shaped historical civilizations that, in consort with the growth of the religion, are seen to have become one kind of religious culture expressed as a civilization. Each is formed by a unique history, not by any common religious quality that can be compared. Religion takes different configurations in various contexts. In a way, the notion that Comparative Religion is a western creation is correct. I have never found that approach to be at all helpful in understanding traditional Indigenous religion. So some of his ideas I agree with, others I do not.

As for Cox, he is rooted in a continental philosophical tradition and draws strength from the structural assumptions of European philosophical phenomenology. These place his studies of religion within a solid philosophical environment, providing a sense of stability and credibility. Religion in North America is very fluid. Not only do we have vigorous Indigenous traditions, but we have a wide variety of religious experience that is front and centre every day. Here I am thinking of the rise of atheism and other forms of non-religion which could have a marked effect on the study of religion. Handling such diversity without a philosophical framework makes our perception of the phenomena more culture-bound. PoR allows us to operate in a territory less formalized by a structured tradition, and that seems to fit our work better.

Is there a reason to re-evaluate PoR now, or a path to doing so?

I think it has been evolving for the last three decades, but there seems to be a lull in development. I can't conceive that the religious sentiment will be eliminated from human experience. New criteria of analysis are necessary, quite beyond the major world religions. If the world grows any smaller, the melding and modification of all religions will spawn new forms. They will likely come and go, as we saw in the cults of the 1960s and 70s, but the creative influence of religion will continue. It is quite possible that humans will develop quite different forms of religious awareness once robots become part of conscious reality. PoR needs to develop new categories to handle the social and technological developments now under way. PoR doesn't seem to be very creative in engaging with new forms of religion. What is important is for PoR to continually develop its ability to see and translate the religious dimensions of life for people today.

Do you think there is any connection/correlation between phenomenologists of religion and their religious affiliations?

In Canada we were saturated with Christian theological assumptions, and most of the major schools in Canada were begun or stocked by people who had deep theological concerns. George Grant was a very solid Christian theological type guy. Wilfred Cantwell Smith was one of the founders of religious studies in Canada, and it's pretty clear to me that he had a conservative Christian viewpoint on what religion is. He would look at Islam from the standpoint of a way of living one's life, as a lifeworld or a life story. Smith represents one aspect of the study of religion in Canada that was endemic at the time that I was developing my own sense of what I was doing. That theological tradition was very strong in Canada.

More generally, some phenomenologists resonate more with theologians and ethicists than with historians or sociologists. This may be because they perceive permanent structures within the realities they study. Or it may be because they have certain structural models in mind when they do their studies, rather than finding models arising from the data. PoR argues only that one can study human experience, convinced that the religious is present there in some discernible form, but that the scholar cannot pre-determine what that form will be. I think academics with some kind of commitment system feel more at home in general analyses that are compatible with their own value systems. Bringing one's commitment system to the study of religion may distort what is present in an observed culture. The phenomenologist is an engaged observer whose chore is to translate the reality that is seen into understandable terms, to allow others to understand how and what the culture being studied is experiencing. PoR provides a sensitivity stance upon which that translation can take place.

Did your own religious affiliation shape your academic trajectory?

I've wrestled with this throughout my career. I was raised in the very liberal United Church of Canada and then joined a Pentecostal church. I studied philosophical idealism because I came out of that kind of evangelical, fundamentalist tradition. The United Church is quite theological in its approach. Pentecostalism seemed a much more open move toward an existential involvement with God, with reality. This certainly bears some relation to my phenomenological work, which I see as more existential than philosophical or theological. Theology seemed like cutting up the pie in a kind a cookie-cutter way. You had to take each of the slices for what they were. I thought that was too rigid in its approach to religion. The reality of religion seemed much more fluid and existential than philosophical.

Existential PoR

How is your approach to PoR "more existential than philosophical or theological"?

Philosophical phenomenology is a rigid kind of activity, where you focus on the structures of consciousness and you emphasize what fits into those structures. That approach to phenomenology restricted the field. It shut down discussion. It was not adapted to the multi-dimensional aspects of religiosity.

Where the philosophers talked of identifiable structures within human life, I regarded these as better represented by models or tools that they happened to prefer in their analysis, not as ever-present structures. I came to see religion as far more creative and shifting than philosophical phenomenology seemed able to express.

In the field, when I went into a Sufi group, my attitude towards them was, "you are a novel and important expression of religion, so tell me how you understand your world, how do you understand the reality of this world to be coming to you, and how do you inter-relate with it?" So it was a very existential kind of study, if you will. I accepted that, however they wanted to define their experience, I accepted that as real, as the data that I should try to convey in my study.

Has your sense of what it means to do PoR continued to evolve?

It has developed quite a lot. As I aged, I became convinced that what you perceive and what you encounter is much more a social phenomenon. I gave much more credence to tradition. You encounter religious experience within a tradition and people within that tradition represent different dimensions of it. That shift happened when I was doing my research in Morocco. As soon as I started encountering the chant in Morocco, it had all kinds of connections and nuances and organization and structures that I hadn't found in the Egyptian case. So I had to completely revise my whole project as I tried to understand the religious world of the chanter in Morocco. The theme of memory, linked to that of tradition, came to play a central role in my Morocco book (Waugh 2005).

What did you find in your work with the Cree[6]?

In my work among the Cree it was pretty obvious that people encountered a reality that was articulated by the elders. The elders didn't say, "What you're experiencing is this that or the other thing". The elders would just say, "Here's the pathway, and here's what I know about the pathway. Now you walk down it and encounter the spirits. Then you will find your way." In a way, I ended up studying a form of religion that resonates with the way I study religions.

Therapeutic PoR

Have you moved beyond the study of religion to the study of experience more generally?

What this has done for me is to destroy the old meaning of "religion" as an absolute structure or framework. Aboriginal people have taught me that the kind of structures that European religion has bequeathed to us do not encapsulate all that religion means. In other words, there are many different ways of experiencing religious truth than have arisen from European philosophical structures.

It seems that PoR is helping doctors to do a better job of healing. Does PoR itself, like medicine, go beyond describing phenomena to changing people? Should the phenomenological study of experience aim to change experience?

Yes, PoR has a therapeutic value, absolutely. My work has gone beyond an existential phenomenology to what I call a therapeutic phenomenology. SoR more generally is therapeutic in some ways. Maybe fundamentally this is because it helps place, ground and orient people in a world of experience that is chaotic and dissonant and troubling. That's where I stand now. If I were starting my career now, that's the direction I would take it.

---

6.   The Cree are one of the largest First Nations in North America, numbering over 200,000, with traditional lands stretching across most of Canada, from Labrador to British Columbia.

Commentary

"PoR" refers to a range of approaches in Canadian SoR.[7] Canadian philosophers of religion have done important work on European PoR (on Emmanuel Levinas, Jean Luc Marion, Michel Henry etc.): for example, Michelle Rebidoux (2012, 2013, 2014), Morny Joy (2004) and Garth Green (Grondin and Green 2017). (Joy considers herself a hermeneutic, not a philosophical, phenomenologist: "That moves me away from Husserlian idealism to a critical, reflexive approach" [email].) McGill University's School of Religious Studies has been a key centre for this work. Phenomenology, independent of religion, has been pursued by some Canadian philosophers: for example, Gary Brent Madison, James Mensch and Graeme Nicholson. Philosophical phenomenology has had some impact on the psychology of religion (e.g. Fortin et al. 1997). Classic PoR appears in theory courses (Kristensen, Otto, van der Leeuw, etc., granted their differences; see Tuckett 2016) and it sometimes appears in specific works, for example, the study of myth (e.g. Samonà 1996). Social phenomenology (e.g. Alfred Schütz, Peter L. Berger, Thomas Luckmann, and James Spickard) and typological phenomenology (most closely associated with Ninian Smart) have had a broad but loose and varying impacts. Harold Coward underlines the importance of American scholar Frederick J. Streng, whose "view was very influential and often used in ... [SoR] Intro classes in Canada [from 1965 to 1985]" (email; see Coward 2014). For Streng, "phenomenologists of religion ... [set] aside their own cultural biases and religious conditioning, entering the consciousness of the devotee as much as possible, feeling what the devotee feels, then looking at the information that their emphatic nets have collected" (1985 [1969], 226). Philosopher George Grant – founder of Canada's first Religious Studies department at McMaster University in 1961 – drew on European phenomenology (Martin Heidegger and Simone Weil, adding Leo Strauss to that mix) in his writing on religion. Coward echoes Waugh

---

7.   All scholars mentioned in this Commentary (excepting those listed, not cited, in parentheses in the second paragraph) are Canadian, either born and educated in and/or spending most of their careers in Canada. The first stand-alone Canadian department of Religion/Religious Studies was founded in 1961. At present, 34 departments offer a BA and 10 a PhD in SoR. I emailed a number of Canadian scholars of religion in June and July 2018, asking if they might be able to comment on the trajectory of PoR in Canada. Where cited, those conversations are referenced as "email". Michelle Rebidoux and Morny Joy were especially helpful on the philosophical material. Though not cited, Ira Robinson, Marc Lalonde and Jim Linville also provided valuable comments. Thanks to Michael Stausberg for comments on previous drafts. The buck – for errors and miscomprehensions – stops here on my laptop.

in underlining Grant's importance: "PoR was introduced/born in Canada during the 1965–1985 period with the McMaster graduate department playing a leading role ... In those days at McMaster, PoR ... was very influential on all of us, chiefly from Eliade and the Chicago school of thought" (email; see Coward 2014, ch. 4). Islamicist Wilfred Cantwell Smith influentially proposed that SoR should rest on a distinction between "cumulative tradition" ("the entire mass of overt objective data that constitute the historical deposit ... of the past religious life of the community") and "faith" ("an inner religious experience or involvement of a particular person; the impingement on him of the transcendent, putative or real") (Smith 1964, 141). He proposed "tradition-faith analysis", which combines non-phenomenological and phenomenological modes (ibid., 176).

As noted by Louis Rousseau in his interview, PoR in Québec has been important and distinctive, especially in the PoR-related approach of *religiologie*. Jacques Pierre worked with and extended Eliade's approach, seeking "a phenomenological theory intended to capture ... the *eidos* of the encounter between the human subject and the sacred" (Pierre 1990b, 1; see also Pierre 1990a). Yvon Desrosiers, Guy Ménard and Rousseau worked along comparable lines. The journal *Religiologiques* (www.religiologiques.uqam.ca) is a treasure trove of material relevant to the history and current status of these and related issues.

William Closson James is often likened to Waugh in his approach: "Waugh and James certainly are ... among the most well-known and influential [Canadian] phenomenologists" (Willi Braun, email; echoed by Aaron Hughes, email); and Waugh himself highlights similarities (above). James exemplifies a common ambivalence in Canadian views of PoR. He himself rejects the PoR label, because he sees PoR in narrow, philosophical terms: "at the U of Chicago in the late 60s, phenomenology was what a few of my fellow grad students in philosophy of religion were studying when they read Husserl or Merleau-Ponty" (email). At the same time, in his rich study of the variety of religious communities in Kingston, Ontario, he frames his work using a broader understanding of PoR: "assembling an account as experienced by participants is a 'phenomenological' enterprise that describes rather than explains" (James 2011, intro).

The Afterword of this book distinguishes between robust and selective PoR. Robust views of PoR portray it as a highly complex theory, combining most or all of a long list of characteristics. Selective views emphasize only a small number of features from this list (and are sometimes used to create a straw-doll version of PoR for purposes of critique). This distinction is useful for describing divergent uses of "phenomenology" in the meta-theoretical literature in Canada.

The category of selective PoR helps us understand why some Canadian scholars argue that most SoR in Canada – and much outside – is PoR. According to Willi Braun, "the general orientation of Religious Studies in Canada is toward some form of phenomenology" (email). Russell McCutcheon highlights two principles – description and suspension of judgment:

> [PoR] names a broad method in the field meant to suspect judgment ... [in order to] understand, in the classic Verstehen sense of re-experiencing participant worlds/situations/experiences, doing so in a way that presumes one can simply and dispassionately describe "what presents itself to our senses" ... So I'd argue that the field was and still is largely phenomenological ... It's basically the method driving every world religions textbook and class.
>
> (Russell McCutcheon, email)

By contrast, where McCutcheon sees PoR as characterized by a suspension of judgment that undermines critique, Irving Hexham sees critique as essential:

> My own understanding of ... [PoR] is in the broad sense that was popularized by Ninian Smart. His version was really an adaption of British Social Anthropology as pioneered by E. E. Evans-Pritchard that takes empathy seriously. Empathy involves putting oneself into another person's shoes and seeing the world, or religion, as they do. But, then the scholar steps back and makes critical judgments on themselves, on their interaction with their topic, and on the topic itself.
>
> (Irving Hexham, email)

This illustrates the selectivity of selective PoR: different features associated with the archives of robust PoR come to the fore in different contexts. So, for example, when we read a claim like following – "the phenomenology of religion is in fact a phenomenology of the Modern state" – we can ask what part of the archive of robust PoR is being foregrounded (Arnal and McCutcheon 2013, 30; Arnal 2000, 32). In this case, it seems to be a focus on "the lone individual's interior faith ... the pristine, individual person" (Arnal and McCutcheon 2013, 13).

Robust PoR has had little impact in the study of religion in Canada. (It is arguably little used in SoR outside Canada despite its potential contribution; see Tuckett 2018.) One reason was the influence of logical positivism in Canada, followed by the predominance of analytic, as opposed to continental, philosophy in mid- to late-twentieth-century North American philosophy departments. Something similar was felt in SoR as well: "because the discipline of religion in Canada is the product of relatively small departments, and because even in the larger departments the discipline is shaped in particular ways, 'continental philosophy' and [robust] phenomenology have not thrived" (Dawne McCance, email). Michelle Rebidoux offers a related explanation:

> Canada's (at least theoretical) identity as a deeply multicultural nation has cast suspicion on any approach that smacks of structuralism [with its presumption of universality] ... [M]any Canadian religious studies departments today value anthropological and sociological approaches which have been reshaped under the influence of post-structuralism.
>
> (Michelle Rebidoux, email; see also Rebidoux 2013)

The selectivity of selective PoR lies at the heart of PoR's reception in Canadian SoR. Asked to address the issue of PoR's fate in Canada, Lee Rainey suggests:

> Most, if not all, departments ... were founded by those who were primarily interested in Christian theology and history and/or Bible as text. ... The phenomenology of religion was not an issue that excited them because they thought they knew the answers to any questions it might be asking. When it was also clear that those questions could, and should, be extended to other traditions, many found it unacceptable. Even though most of those academics are long gone, their assumptions and attitudes live on in their students and permeate ... Religious Studies departments to this day.[8]
>
> (Lee Rainey, email)

On this view, theology rejected phenomenology as irrelevant or threatening, given its focus on essences and its comparative approach. Yet, McCutcheon suggests almost the opposite, that theologians championed PoR: PoR became popular because it "allowed liberal theological commitments into the public university" (email).

This divergence between Canadian scholars in 2018 reflects competing modes of selective PoR; and it is remarkably similar to formative Canadian debates in the 1960s and 1970s about the relation between religious studies and theology. Foreshadowing Rainey's point – though taking the other, theological side – Joseph McLelland argued that PoR is "an inappropriate discipline for the study of religion" because "our neophyte departments of religion are often self-consciously intoning the creed of no-creed, denying the academic relevance of personal commitment, and attempting a phenomenological approach which is supposed to assure 'objectivity' and to avoid 'theology'" (McLelland 1972, 232, 226; see Wiebe 2006, 480). Coming from the other direction, and foreshadowing McCutcheon's point, Willard Oxtoby argued:

---

8. A view echoed by Irving Hexham and by Michelle Rebidoux, emails.

many ... scholars who associate themselves with phenomenology come from the circles of theological concern rather than from an academic background in the social sciences. ... [P]henomenologists, in conferring approval in principle on the faith of others, preserve it for their own tradition as well. Scholarship is kept from contradicting evangelism. Phenomenology's chief potential clientele is among religiously committed persons as an appreciation of religious commitment. ... The individual scholar enters into a reverent extension of knowledge which strengthens his own private or shared attitudes toward a transcendent reality. In phenomenology, the science of religions has in effect become a religious exercise itself.

(Oxtoby 1968, 598–599; see also Klostermaier 1977)

The perceived relationship between theology and PoR has institutional dimensions that vary by context. For example, the University of Toronto (UofT) has a distinctive college system: all undergraduate Arts & Science students are members of one of seven colleges, though they are free to take courses elsewhere. Two of the colleges are religiously affiliated and offer theology programmes: St. Michael's (Roman Catholic/Basilian, where Jacques Maritain and Étienne Gilson taught) and Trinity (Anglican, where Donald Wiebe swims against the current in the Theological Department, as a critical advocate for a "scientific"/ cognitive study of religion). These two colleges form part of The Toronto School of Theology, a federation that includes five other colleges, all but one on the UofT campus: Emmanuel (United Church of Canada), Knox (Presbyterian), Regis (Roman Catholic/Jesuit), St. Augustine's (Roman Catholic/Archdiocesan), and Wycliffe (Anglican and Evangelical). UofT's Department for the Study of Religion was founded and remains independent of the college system, and PoR has almost no presence there. It is hard not to draw the conclusion that the UofT Department has seen PoR as tarred by the brush of theology, not least in light of the contrast offered by McGill University's School of Religious Studies (SRS). The SRS is the one English-language programme in Canada with a prominent focus on PoR. It arose from a 1912 affiliation between seminaries to form a joint board for the study of theology, and it maintains its close historical affiliation with the Montreal Diocesan Theological College (Anglican/ Episcopal), the Presbyterian College, and the United [Church of Canada] Theological College, under the auspices of the ecumenical Montreal School of Theology.

In sum, divergent views of PoR's allegiances shaped the early years of SoR in Canada and are still present today. Given little presence of robust PoR, selective PoR has long served as an inflection point in Canadian SoR: not in the sense that there was some historical sea-change; but in the sense that views of PoR constitute an on-going discursive moment, a symptomatic fold in the discipline's meta-theoretical debates. Meta-theoretical debates *about* PoR tend to be similarly selective. How could PoR be both anathema to theology and theology's trojan horse? Because "PoR" is a flexible label for a family of theoretical and methodological characteristics that are selected from in different ways. This underlines the value of this book's project of critically assessing the complex range of uses of "phenomenology of religion" in different national contexts.

Steven Engler is Professor of Religious Studies at Mount Royal University in Calgary. He studies religions in Brazil, as well as theories and methodology in the study of religion/s. See http://stevenengler.ca

References

Arnal, William. 2000. "Definition." In *Guide to the Study of Religion*, edited by Willi Braun and Russell T. McCutcheon, 21–34. London: Cassell.

Arnal, William, and Russell T. McCutcheon. 2013. *The Sacred Is the Profane: The Political Nature of Religion*. Oxford: Oxford University Press.

Baillargeon, Stéphane. 1994. *Entretiens avec Louis Rousseau: Religion et modernité au Québec*. Montréal: Liber.

Bertalanffy, Ludwig von. 1973 [1968]. *Théorie générale des systèmes: physique, biologie, psychologie, sociologie, philosophie*. Paris: Dunod.

Braun, Willi and Francis Landy. 2011. "Wither or Whither: The Study of Religion at the University of Alberta." *Religion* 41(2): 145–148. https://doi.org/10.1080/0048721x.2011.579788

Campbell, Michel. 1972. "Notes sur la conjoncture des sciences religieuses au Canada français depuis 1967." In *Guide to Religious Studies in Canada/Guide des sciences religieuses au Canada*, edited by C. P. Anderson, 21–40. Toronto: Corporation for the Publication of Academic Studies in Religion in Canada. https://doi.org/10.1177/000842987200200325

Coward, Harold. 2014. *Fifty Years of Religious Studies in Canada: A Personal Retrospective* (Kindle edition). Waterloo, ON: Wilfrid Laurier University Press.

Desroche, Henri and Jean Séguy (eds). 1970. *Introduction aux sciences humaines des religions*. Paris: Cujas.

Desrosiers, Yvon. 1977. "La dimension religieuse dans l'œuvre d'Émile Nelligan." In *Religion and Culture in Canada*, edited by Peter Slater, 333–349. Montréal: Corporation canadienne des sciences religieuses.

Fortin, Gilles, Jozef Denys, Maurice Carignan and Christiane Gagnon. 1997. "La quête de sens et de transcendance en counselling: importance et discernement à l'aide de la phénoménologie." *Studies in Religion/Sciences Religieuses* 26(3): 337–353. https://doi.org/10.1177/000842989702600304

Grondin, Jean and Garth Green (eds). 2017. *Religion et Vérité: La philosophie de la religion à l'âge séculier*. Strasbourg: Presses universitaires de Strasbourg.

James, William Closson. 2011. *God's Plenty: Religious Diversity in Kingston* (Kindle edition). Montréal: McGill-Queens University Press.

Joy, Morny. 2004. "Philosophy and Religion." In *New Approaches to the Study of Religion. Volume 1: Regional, Critical and Historical Approaches*, edited by Peter Antes, Armin W. Geertz and Randi R. Warne, 185–217. Berlin: Walter de Gruyter.

Klostermaier, Klaus. 1977. "From Phenomenology to Metascience: Reflections on the Study of Religions." *Studies in Religion/Sciences Religieuses* 6(5): 551–564. https://doi.org/10.1177/000842987700600510

LeClaire, Nancy, George Cardinal, Emily Hunter and Earle H. Waugh. 1998. *Alberta Elders' Cree Dictionary - Alperta ohci kehtehayak nehiyaw otwestamâke-wasinahikan*. Edmonton, AB: University of Alberta Press.

Le Goff, Jacques and Pierre Nora (eds). 1974. *Faire de l'histoire: Nouvelles approches*. Paris: Gallimard.

Martel, Gilles. 1985. "Statut épistémologique de la religiologie et des sciences humaines des religions." In *Religion, sciences humaines et théologie: Perspectives pluridisciplinaires*, edited by Claude Lizotte and Yvon R. Théroux, 117–150. Montréal: Polycopié.

McLelland, Joseph C. 1972 "The Teacher of Religion: Professor or Guru?" *Studies in Religion/Sciences Religieuses* 2(3): 226–234. https://doi.org/10.1177/000842987200200305

Ménard, Guy (ed.). 1988. *Aspects du sacré, formes de l'imaginaire*. Montréal: RIER/ICSR.

Ménard, Guy. 1994. "Le noeud de paille et la statue équestre: Considérations sur l'obscur objet du regard religiologique." *Religiologique* 9. Retrieved from https://is.gd/6HxZy3

Neumaier-Dargyay, Eva. 1995. "The Department of Religious Studies at the University of Alberta: An Account of a Restructuring Process 1993–1994." *Method & Theory in the Study of Religion* 7(4): 341–349. https://doi.org/10.1163/157006895x00531

Oxtoby, Willard G. 1968. "Religionswissenschaft Revisited." In *Religions in Antiquity: Essays in Memory of Erwin Ramsdell Goodenough*, edited by Jacob Neusner, 590–608. Leiden, E. J. Brill. https://doi.org/10.1163/9789004378056_034

Pierre, Jacques. 1990a. *Mircea Eliade, Le jour et la nuit. Entre la littérature et la science.* Montréal: Hurtubise HMH.

Pierre, Jacques. 1990b. "L'herméneutique et sa matrice langagière: L'exemple de Mircea Eliade." *Religiologiques* 2. Retrieved from https://is.gd/8gap82

Pummer, Reinhard. 1972. "Religionswissenschaft or Religiology?" *Numen* 19(2/3): 91–127. https://doi.org/10.2307/3269740

Rebidoux, Michelle. 2012. *Philosophy of Michel Henry (1922-2002): A French Christian Phenomenology of Life.* Lewiston, NY: Edwin Mellen.

Rebidoux. Michelle. 2013. "The Phenomenological Method in the Study of Religion." Text and Context Symposium, Memorial University, St. John's, Newfoundland.

Rebidoux, Michelle. 2014. "'Deeper Than the Entrails Is That Great Love!': A Phenomenological Approach to 'Spiritual Sensuality' in Teresa of Ávila." *Heythrop Journal* 55(2): 216–229. https://doi.org/10.1111/j.1468-2265.2011.00703.x

Ricœur, Paul. 1965. *De l'interprétation, Essai sur Freud.* Paris: Seuil.

Rousseau, Louis. 1969 "Le Symbole, la religiologie et la dialectique des interprétations." In *Le symbole, carrefour interdisciplinaire*, edited by Renée Legris and Pierre Pagé, 29–54. Montréal: Les éditions Sainte-Marie.

Rousseau, Louis. 1973. "La naissance du récit mythique des origines québécoises." *Studies in Religion/Sciences religieuses* 3(2): 152–165. https://doi.org/10.1177/000842987300300205

Rousseau, Louis. 1976. *La prédication à Montréal, 1800-1830. Approche religiologique.* Montréal: Fides.

Rousseau, Louis. 1980. "La religiologie à l'UQAM: genèse sociale et direction épistémologique." In *Sciences sociales et églises: Questions sur l'évolution religieuse du Québec*, edited by Paul Strycman et Jean-Paul Rouleau, 73–96. Montréal: Bellarmin.

Rousseau, Louis. 1994. "Silence, bruits, liens, citoyenneté: l'espace de la transcendance québécoise." In *La condition québécoise. Enjeux et horizons d'une société en devenir*, edited by Jean-Marie Fecteau, Gilles Breton and Jocelyn Létourneau, 223–251. Montréal: VLB.

Rousseau, Louis, with Frank W. Remiggi. 1998. *Atlas historique des pratiques religieuses: le sud-ouest du Québec au XIXe siècle.* Ottawa: Ottawa University Press.

Rousseau, Louis. 2006. "Le Canada français comme programme d'Église." In *Le Canada français: son temps, sa nature, son héritage*, edited by Gilles Gagné, 17–28. Québec: Nota Bene.

Rousseau, Louis. 2007. "Pastorale et prédication." In *Les Sulpiciens de Montréal: une histoire de pouvoir et de discrétion, 1657-2007*, edited by Dominique Deslandres, John A. Dickinson and Olivier Hubert, 215–240. Montréal: Fides.

Rousseau, Louis. 2011. "Le cours Éthique et culture religieuse: de sa pertinence dans un État laïque." In *Le Québec en quête de laïcité*, edited by Normand Baillargeon and Jean-Marc Piotte, 99–108. Montréal, Les éditions Écosociété.

Rousseau, Louis. 2013. "La religiologie: une connaissance interdisciplinaire du religieux." *Histoire, monde et cultures religieuses* 26(2): 109–120. https://doi.org/10.3917/hmc.026.0109

Rousseau, Louis. 2016. "Le travail obscur de la mémoire identitaire dans les débats nés d'une nouvelle diversité religieuse au Québec." *Recherches sociographiques* 57(2–3): 289–310. https://doi.org/10.7202/1038429ar

Samonà, Giuseppe A. 1996. "Histoire des religions et analyse des mythes." *Studies in Religion/Sciences Religieuses* 25(3): 287–305. https://doi.org/10.1177/000842989602500304

Séguy, Jean. 1972. "Histoire, sociologie, théologie." *Archives de sociologie des religions* 34: 133–151. https://doi.org/10.3406/assr.1972.1895

Smith, Wilfred Cantwell. 1964 [1962]. *The Meaning and End of Religion*. New York: Mentor Books.

Streng, Frederick J. 1985 [1969]. *Understanding Religious Life* (3rd edition). Belmont, CA: Wadsworth.

Tuckett, Jonathan. 2016. "Clarifying Phenomenologies in the Study of Religion: Separating Kristensen and van der Leeuw from Otto and Eliade." *Religion* 46(1): 75–101. https://doi.org/10.1080/0048721x.2015.1057773

Tuckett, Jonathan. 2018. "Prolegomena to a Philosophical Phenomenology of Religion: A Critique of Sociological Phenomenology." *Method & Theory in the Study of Religion* 30(2): 97–136. https://doi.org/10.1163/15700682-12341420

Waugh, Earle H. 1989. *The Munshidīn of Egypt: Their World and their Song*. Columbia, SC: University of South Carolina Press.

Waugh, Earle H. 1996. *Dissonant Worlds: Roger Vandersteene among the Cree*. Waterloo, ON: Wilfrid Laurier University Press.

Waugh, Earle H. 1999. *The Islamic Tradition: Religious Beliefs and Healthcare Decisions*. Chicago, IL: Park Ridge Center for the Study of Health, Faith, and Ethics.

Waugh, Earle H. 2005. *Memory, Music, and Religion: Morocco's Mystical Chanters*. Columbia, SC: University of South Carolina Press.

Waugh, Earle H. 2008. *Visionaries of Silence: The Reformist Sufi Order of the Demirdashiya al-Khalwatiya in Cairo*. Cairo: American University in Cairo Press. https://doi.org/10.5743/cairo/9789774160899.003.0005

Waugh, Earle H. 2018. *Al Rashid Mosque: Building Canadian Muslim Communities.* Edmonton, AB: University of Alberta Press.

Waugh, Earle H., Baha Abu-Laban, and Regula B. Qureshi. 1983. *The Muslim Community in North America.* Edmonton, AB: University of Alberta Press.

Waugh, Earle H., Sharon McIrvin Abu-Laban, and Regula Qureshi. 1991. *Muslim Families in North America.* Edmonton, AB: University of Alberta Press.

Waugh, Earle H., Frederick Mathewson Denny, and Fazlur Rahman. 1998. *The Shaping of an American Islamic Discourse: A Memorial to Fazlur Rahman.* Atlanta, GA: Scholars Press.

Waugh, Earle H., Olga Szafran, and Rodney A. Crutcher. 2011. *At the Interface of Culture and Medicine.* Edmonton, AB: University of Alberta Press.

Waugh, Earle H., Roger Parent, Olga Szafran, and Jean A. C. Triscott. 2014. *Cultural Competency Skills for Health Professionals: A Workbook for Caring across Cultures.* Edmonton, AB: Brush Education.

Waugh, Earle H., Olga Szafran, Jean A. C. Triscott, and Roger Parent. 2016. *Cultural Competency Skills for Psychologists, Psychotherapists, and Counselling Professionals.* Edmonton, AB: Brush Education.

Waugh, Earle H., S. Ross, and S. Schipper (eds). Forthcoming. *Female Doctors in Canada: Experience and Culture.* Toronto: University of Toronto Press.

Wiebe, Donald. 2006. "The Learned Practice of Religion: A Review of the History of Religious Studies in Canada and Its Portent for the Future." *Studies in Religion/Sciences Religieuses* 35 (3/4): 475–501. https://doi.org/10.1177/000842980603500307

8

"Why ... So Complicated?", "a Term with No Subscribers"

Interviews with Charles H. Long and Ivan Strenski (United States)

ERIC ZIOLKOWSKI

Charles H. Long, who has been called "a living classic" in the study of religion (Carrasco 1995, ix), was born in 1926 in Little Rock, Arkansas, where he was raised and received his primary and secondary education. He then served in the United States Army Air Forces (1944–1946), attaining the rank of Sergeant, before receiving his higher education at Dunbar Jr. College in Little Rock, and then at the University of Chicago Divinity School, where he studied with Joachim Wach. It was at Chicago, alongside such colleagues as Mircea Eliade and Joseph Mitsuo Kitagawa, that Long began his 40-year teaching career. While a student at the Divinity School, he taught there as an instructor in the history of religions (1956–1959), then as an assistant professor (1960–1962), and, after receiving his doctorate, he ascended through the ranks from associate to full professor (1963–1973). Subsequently he taught as professor of the history of religions at Duke University (1974–1987); William Rand Kenan Jr. Professor of the History of Religions at the University of North Carolina, Chapel Hill (1974–1987); Jeannette K. Watson Professor of History of Religions at Syracuse University (1988–1991); and professor and director of the History of Religions programme, and also the Research Center for Black Studies, at the University of California, Santa Barbara (1992–1996), which named him professor emeritus. Over the years, he also taught as visiting professor at a host of institutions in the US and abroad, including: Princeton

Keywords: Émile Durkheim; Mircea Eliade; Gerardus van der Leeuw; phenomenology; Cornelis P. Tiele

University (1960); St Xavier's College, Chicago (1969); Carleton College (1970); University of Tennessee (1980); University of Pittsburgh (1983–1987); University of Queensland, Brisbane, Australia (1983); Tsukuba University, Tsukuba, Japan (1985); and Capetown University, South Africa (1994). Charles H. Long died at the age of 93 in 2020 in Chapel Hill, North Carolina.

Ivan Strenski, who retired in 2015 as the Holstein Family and Community Professor of Religious Studies at the University of California, Riverside, was born in 1943 in Philadelphia, Pennsylvania. Although raised in the US, he took his BA in philosophy and sociology at the University of Toronto in 1966 and his PhD in religious studies three years later at the University of Birmingham University in the UK, where he worked under the direction of Ninian Smart. The year after his completion of his PhD, Strenski returned to the US to obtain a Post-PhD in South Asian and Buddhist Studies at Yale University. Extending 45 years, Strenski's career as a teacher of religious studies began at Connecticut College, where he also taught in the Asian Studies programme (1970–1986); continued in the Departments of Religious Studies and Sociology at the University of California, Santa Barbara (1987–1995); before finishing up at the University of California, Riverside (1995–2015). Also while at UC Riverside, from 1996 on, Strenski taught an annual interactive, inter-campus video conference course with the University of California, Los Angeles on theories of religion. Strenski identifies Émile Durkheim and the Durkheimian school of sociology of religion as the central foci of his scholarship since the mid-1980s. His scholarship represents an effort to present the Durkheimian tradition – Durkheim himself, Marcel Mauss, Henri Hubert, among others – as the "foundation" and "mother school" for the modern study of religion, which he construes as academic, non-theological, non-confessional, humanistic, cross-cultural, comparative, and imaginative.

Introduction

This chapter consists of select portions from two separate interviews I conducted by phone and recorded in late 2017 regarding the history, development, and significance of Phenomenology of Religion (PoR), with a special focus on the United States. The first interview, on 8 December, was with Charles H. Long, who spoke from his home in Chapel Hill, North Carolina. The recording of the interview was transcribed by Jamie Gallagher of Veritext Legal Solutions, Mid-Atlantic Region, Philadelphia, PA. The second interview, on 10 November, was with Ivan Strenski, who spoke from his home in Los Angeles, California. The recording of that interview was transcribed by Laura McKee, administrative assistant of the Department of Religious Studies, Lafayette College. The transcripts of both interviews were redacted, arranged and annotated by myself.

PoR is but one of any number of the approaches to religious studies that Long and Strenski have critically appraised, including also the historical and comparative approaches, as well as theology.

CHARLES H. LONG

"What Appears, What *Appears*"

Eric Ziolkowski: Can you please talk a little bit about your understanding of phenomenology *per se*, then religion, and then PoR? And then we can move on to other more specific topics.

Charles H. Long: Well, these are not questions I would ask myself, because I've never singled out phenomenology or PoR as some kind of distinct area of study. So if you asked me, "where did you learn about phenomenology or whatever", well, to tell the truth, I've never had a course in PoR. And I seldom make use of the term.

But that doesn't mean that I don't use phenomenology. It's just that I didn't come at it that way. It didn't come into the meaning of what I do or of what I thought I was about as a phenomenologist of religion. As a matter of fact, I think if somebody had told me at the time I was a graduate student that you could major in PoR, I wouldn't have touched it. I encountered phenomenology as a dimension within the broader meaning of interpretation as hermeneutics.

Phenomenology came up in my study of religion, so that it's another way in which I got it, you know. And it centred around the issue of reductionism. Let me put it into terms in which it was coming to me. Since we live in a modern period with scientific epistemology, all of these things that have been placed in the taxonomy and category of religion and extra-natural phenomena must be explained in a way other than that in which those people or cultures live through that kind of meaning.

Therefore, these meanings had to be reduced to one of our more scientific disciplines where human agency or the laws of nature as we understood it through science could make sense of them. Therefore, in religion it was either ignorance if people didn't understand or it was illusion or psychology or some sophisticated theory regarding the sociology of collectives.

So the problem was, how does one establish the authenticity of that which religious groups or persons experience and gave expression to? You see? That is, how does one make sense of what appeared to those people or what appeared to that person? In other words, it was a part of a more radical epistemological issue that we were confronting.

The problematic of what goes on in phenomenology came to me through the epistemological problem of what is it that religion is about or what is this thing called religion. And is it — can it stand as a given of experience?

Now, that placed me, given the fact that my teacher was Joachim Wach[1] — in that whole south German school of epistemology, out of which you have names like Wach and Rudolf Otto and Ernst Cassirer. One of the major problems confronted by them was that of the relationship between experience and expression: how does one establish the efficacy of experience? Now, of course, if you know Kant and you know what Kant did, and if you read Kant's *Prolegomena*, you understand it was Hume — he said, "Hume woke me from my dogmatic slumber".

Yes.

So that he's got to figure out how do you establish the fact that there came be some causal connection between this, that, and another thing. All right.

Now, I think Otto and Wach and Cassirer and others were raising that issue in the same vein, but in another manner, and here, they played a great deal with what Kant would call schematization: that is, that which lies between the actuality of experience and its expression. And schematization is behind a great deal of what goes on in the discussion of symbolism. What is the religious symbol? If you take that from the side of either — say someone like Ernst Cassirer or Paul Ricoeur,[2] this is what they are probing: what appears, what *appears*.[3]

---

1. Joachim Wach (1898–1957) was a German-born historian of religions. Dismissed by the Nazis in 1935 from his professorship at the University of Leipzig, he came in 1946 from Brown University to the University of Chicago, where he taught for the remainder of his life as Professor of the History of Religions (*Religionswissenschaft*). As Long elsewhere notes, "Wach's appearance at Chicago marks the beginnings of systematic approaches to the study of religion", encompassing "various disciplines: phenomenology, history, psychology, and sociology" (Long 2018, 78).

2. Paul Ricoeur (1913–2005), French philosopher; colleague of Long's at the University of Chicago Divinity School from Ricoeur's arrival there in 1970 as the newly named John Nuveen Professor of Philosophical Theology (with appointments also in both the Philosophy Department and the Committee on Social Thought in that university), to Long's departure from Chicago.

3. In his repeated use of the phrase, "what appears", hereinafter in this interview, Long is alluding to the ancient Greek etymology of the term, phenomenology:

Now, I see this in several ways. In one sense, Joachim Wach is like William James, because James was concerned with religious experience. Well, I was not as impressed with William James as Joachim Wach, you know. Because William James still had his hidden reductionism there, because he started with biology or psychology.

I wouldn't give him all of that. Wach gave him a little too much. On that side, I would go with Charles Sanders Peirce, who I felt was really still the most important. I think he and Du Bois, in another way, were the most important American philosophers. And then following after them, the late Dewey.

But with Peirce, you have Peirce's logic, where he has "firstness". And firstness has to do with what appears, what manifests itself. He called it the *phaneron*, which is the word from which phenomenology comes.[4]

Phenomenology versus Ratiocination

The *phaneron* is what appears, you see. And it is specifically that which appears which is the phenomenon. And whatever else you're talking about is that appearance. And you have to try to explain what appears. And those people who want to do the reduction want to give you the sense that what appears is a category or a concept. Concepts do not appear, you see.

Concepts are a product of ratiocination. They don't appear.

What *appears*: it's precisely that level in which phenomenology comes in for me. It comes in because if you're going to have a disciplined way of trying to make sense of anything, you have to ask yourself, well, what makes me want to do this? What appeared to be such that I want to study medicine? What appeared to me that makes me want to study trees? Or what *appears*, you see.

Now, that which appears is not a concept. For example, Gaston Bachelard, who was this funny guy who did history of science and a lot of other little things, but in his study of history of science, he said: in the history of science,

---

phainomenon (φαινόμενον), used most often in the plural, *ta phainomena* (τὰ φαινόμενα), denoting "things that appear" or "appearances". As van der Leeuw states in a passage Long quotes elsewhere, "Phenomenology, therefore, is not a method that has been reflectively elaborated, but is man's true vital activity, consisting ... in doing what is given to neither god nor animal, standing aside and understanding *what appears* in view" (cited by Long 1995, 46, emphasis added; Long cites a different edition of *Religion in Essence and Manifestation* from the one I cited earlier).

4. *Phaneron* (neuter nominative of φανερός), the Greek adjective for something open to sight, visible, manifest, evident.

what scientists will do is to give you the sense that once they find something out, they want to tie it up with what came before them in this same area, as if it's a continuity.

He said, but when you really go back and read, and study what happened, for example, in all of those studies that have to do with the elements of water, fire, air, water – he said, what you find is that even though they knew about what they did before in studying water, and studying fire, or whatever – he said that in every major scientific discovery about these things, you will find they went back to the old symbolism of fire and water and air. See?

In other words, it appeared to them new. And out of that appearance, they recreated or created new conceptual structures. So a great deal of science is tied up with the ideology of progress. And therefore, the ideology of progress overwhelms the actuality of the epistemological issue of how did it appear. It's in that way that the phenomenology comes in. Now, it comes in in another way because I was supposed to be writing a dissertation for Wach on the old English anthropology—on the last of the armchair anthropologists at Oxford, Robert Marett. And therefore, I took a lot of courses in anthropology. (Redfield[5] thought that I should go on and take an MA degree in anthropology.) But there was a whole issue of animism, which was Tylor's term, a belief in spiritual beings.[6]

And it's a funny kind of thing because if he said it was the *experience of* spiritual beings, that's one thing. But *belief in* – that gave the notion that it was some erroneous, ignorant whatever. You *believed* that the world is made out of green cheese, you see. So that whole notion of *belief in*, that is not the way he found the data. None of these people Tylor discusses would ever say they *believed in* these things. They would tell you these things *appear* or they *exist*.

But once the investigator from outside comes in, they have to put in these terms like *believe in* because they are forcing their conception of the world on the data which they are receiving. And they do it in a very unseen and seemingly innocent manner.

---

5.   Robert Redfield (1897–1958), American cultural anthropologist and ethnographer; obtained his bachelor's degree (1920), law degree (1921), and doctorate (1928) at the University of Chicago, where he taught from 1927 to his death.

6.   E. B. (Edward Burnett) Tylor (1832–1917), British anthropologist; pioneered cultural anthropology. In his *Primitive Culture: Researches into the Development of Mythology, Philosophy, Religion, Language, Art, and Custom*, Tylor defines animism as "the deep-lying doctrine of Spiritual Beings, which embodies the very essence of Spiritualistic as opposed to Materialistic philosophy" (1903, 425); and "the groundwork of the Philosophy of Religion, from that of savages up to that of civilized men" (ibid., 426). Animism hence furnishes Tylor "a minimum definition of Religion, the belief in Spiritual Beings" (ibid., 424).

Now, if you read an anthropologist of that period, and then read Eliade, you'll find that Eliade hardly ever talks about anybody believing in anything. He would talk about a hierophany,[7] that which appears. And that which appears, appears with other attributes. It appears because it has the power to. It's a kratophany[8] – and so it is about that that I was concerned and not so much something called PoR.

"How I Got Involved with PoR"

Now, I know the genealogy of PoR. I read Husserl. I didn't have any problem understanding this. It wasn't some kind of thing like: "Well, phenomenology, let's see what that means." And for example, when I read Husserl, and he's talking about the eidetic[9] and whatever else, I said, "Why does he have to make it so complicated?" I said, "I could have explained it much better than he did."

And in that sense, I always thought that Ricoeur was a better phenomenologist than Husserl.

I also read Heidegger. And there was a whole series of books on phenomenology that came out Northwestern University Press from the 1960s on.[10]

And then there was another whole series of books on phenomenology out of Wisconsin.[11] So I kept up with phenomenological philosophy. But I was

---

7. Eliade's term for "manifestation of the sacred", formed from the Greek roots ἱερός/ *heiros* (sacred or holy) and φαίνειν/*phainein* (to bring to light, cause to appear, show).

8. Eliade's term for "manifestation of power", formed from the terms κράτος/kratos (power or might, personified in the god or spirit who bears that term as his name) and the verb φαίνειν/*phainein* (to bring to light, cause to appear, show).

9. Eidetic reduction is the technique Husserl introduced by which the philosopher seeks to discern the essential, unchanging, necessary structure, i.e., the εἶδος/ *eidos* (form, shape, figure, of a manifest object). In other words, as Long puts it, this method aims "to transcend the problem raised by the historical existence of the subject through the eidetic translation which changes the historical subject into a transcendental ego – a moment of consciousness which permits the perception of the essence of the phenomenon" (Long 1995, 46).

10. Studies in Phenomenology and Existential Philosophy, book series published by Northwestern University Press from 1964, under the founding editorship of James M. Edie, through the present. The series's website is: http://nupress.northwestern. edu/content/studies-phenomenology-and-existential-philosophy (accessed 21 January 2019).

11. New Studies in Phenomenology and Hermeneutics, book series, was published first by the University of Wisconsin Press, Madison from 2006 to 2007, and then, from 2007 onward, by the University of Toronto Press, where the current series editor is Kenneth Maly, a retired member of Wisconsin's philosophy department.

never concerned to ever write a paper or teach a course on phenomenology, because for me, it was just a part of the apparatus of making sense that this was something to study when you study religion.

A great deal of what went on in the study of religion is that most people who stopped doing theology and said "we're going to do religious studies" didn't have anything to study, because they had no way of saying what their subject matter was, once religious studies took the place of theology in the American academy. Before that, their subject matter was relatively easy. They had the Bible and the Christian tradition.

And now they're going to study "religion". And so they said, that's easy. We're going to do the Max Müller thing. We're going to do the five great world religions.[12] And we add that to the list and that showed that we're liberal, and nice. But they still didn't come to terms with what the hell is religion. And obviously, they didn't read Max Müller.

So it became a funny thing. And this is the reason you have this big mess of things called the American Academy of Religion, and nobody knows what they're talking about but everybody's talking. Because there's — they don't know what the subject matter is.

So that's the way I come at the problem of phenomenology. I don't come at it as a philosopher, as putting forth a philosophical position which I call phenomenology. Now, all of that's well and good. I've learned a lot from those scholars, but my own interest, and what came to be PoR, was a part of the establishment of a datum which was something to study.

It was the *about* that I was *about*, you see. It wasn't *about* sociology. It wasn't *about* history of mind. It wasn't *about* — it was *about* the appearances that human beings have in the normality of their lives. And it moves one away from the notion that every form of datum in the world is the result of human agency, that the appearances occur because there is something other than human agency.

No Tension at Chicago Between the Historical and Phenomenological Approaches to Religion

For a long time, there was a perceived tension between the historical approach to the study of religion and PoR. You wrote about this (e.g. Long 1967, rep. in 1995; see also Long 2018, 80), and Eliade also wrote about it (Eliade 1969, esp. 35–36). The criticism was always that PoR is ahistorical. Could you speak about that alleged tension?

---

12. Hinduism, Buddhism, Judaism, Christianity, Islam.

Yes. Well, let me put it this way: not for us at Chicago, because people will read Eliade's *Patterns* (1958 [1949]), and they would say the problem with it is that it is ahistorical, it doesn't have a context, or whatever. Well, that's because it's that kind of book. But if you look at, let's say, *Yoga* (1958 [1954]), you can't say that's non-historical. Or you look at *Shamanism* (1964 [1951]). What I'm trying to say is that you could have a work where you say I'm going to do a study of chairs, of things people sat on. So I'm going to look at chairs in India, chairs in Japan, chairs in England, and see all of those structures. It's like a comparative anatomy or whatever, and that's okay.

But now if you want to talk about chairs in the Victorian period, that's another kind of study. Now, you can't say that – if you're going to talk about chairs, you always have to talk about chairs in the Victorian period. No. You can talk about chairs any way you want to talk about chairs. All you've got to do is to be clear about why you're talking about chairs in this way.

I don't know why people get all messed up and confused about stuff like that. It's like saying I'm getting a glass of water. Well, you didn't drink the water. No, I got the water because I was cooking. I mean, I didn't want to drink the water now. You know, they think there is just one way of doing something or something. And I don't know why people get messed up like that. And they tend to do that mainly in religion. Mainly when they're talking about religion. Religion always has the heavy burden to go through; then let's say sociology or psychology or whatever. I don't know why, but they do that.

My own feeling is that you're historical when it's necessary to be historical. You're not historical when the element of temporality is not basic to an understanding of what you're trying to understand. Let me put it this way, if I'm doing a problem of double quadratic equations, I don't know where history enters. At some point it may, but that is not at the forefront of me dealing with this issue.

"Much More Ordinary than Abstract"

Well, the history of religions as you practised it, with PoR as a part of it – where is that now?

Well, it's static now. That little group that you were a part of still sustains some of it.[13] Davíd Carrasco and I had a little book series going at the University

---

13. The reference is to a group that originated with a "Symposium on the Work and Legacy of Joachim Wach", held in conjunction with the national AAR meeting, Orlando, 21 November 1998. The group, in which Long was a leading participant, subsequently met each November at the national AAR meetings to discuss issues concerning hermeneutics and the study of religion.

of New Mexico,[14] and about five or six volumes came out and maybe some more. But the editor has left, so we don't know where that stands now.

And what would the prognosis of PoR be? Is it just dissipating?

I must admit that very few scholars in the History of Religions seem interested in hermeneutics, much less phenomenology.

I guess one reason I don't like to use the term PoR in this kind of bare bone way is because it gives a sense that it's some big, abstract theory. And for me, it comes when things appear, even a notion can appear. That it's much more ordinary than the big deal, see. It's much more ordinary than abstract. I'll put it that way.

IVAN STRENSKI

A "Two-Headed Creature"

Eric Ziolkowski: I'd like to start by asking you to talk about your understanding of phenomenology and of religion, and then to put them together, giving a picture of your own understanding of PoR.

Ivan Strenski: I actually have not used the word phenomenology to talk about what I do — even if much of the constructive work I do can be called PoR. I became acquainted with the term in graduate school, like almost everyone else in my cohort. Here is where you got introduced to the supposed "classic" religious studies thinkers, here in particular, people like van der Leeuw and Kristensen, although less frequently, Cornelis P. Tiele. He may be the most interesting, and the most important of the entire group, even though his method leaves out the part that *Verstehen*[15] plays in PoR as I understand it. Tiele brings out the classificatory and structural side of PoR. But we need to wait for the likes of van der Leeuw to assert the method of *Verstehen*

---

14. Religions of the Americas Series, University of New Mexico Press.
15. Jacques Waardenburg: "There was ... in Germany a stress on 'understanding' (*Verstehen*) in the humanities and social sciences and an acceptance of 'religion' as a value category in itself. In the field of cultural history, partly because of the nature of the discipline and partly also as a delimitation of it against the sciences, much stress was laid on the fact that the aim of the cultural historian is not so much to explain, but rather to understand the materials on which he is working" (1999, 53).

and interpretive understanding as an essential part of PoR. In the middle of the nineteenth century, when Tiele initiated an early form of PoR, he and others were really thinking about "science" of religion in the strict sense of the term: putting religion, like a patient, on a table – that kind of thing. And so they imagined that there were actual, natural kinds in religion the same way there were actual kinds of species in the natural world. So, using biological sciences, especially the taxonomical part of that enterprise, they tried to lay out and identify the things that composed religion, just as you would take apart the body and do an anatomy ... Religion was a composite, made up of beliefs, magic, superstitions, cults, rituals, and the like. And, so, like exploring human anatomy, they believed that one could objectively identify a liver, and distinguish it from, say, the spleen.

What does one assume when one deals with a notion like saviour or God? There is some kind of objectivity to these notions, but there's a tremendous amount of play in exactly what those terms will mean. The error of the early phenomenologists of religion was to imagine, wrongly, that one could do a natural science of religion. But that's why their taxonomical work, especially in van der Leeuw, is so tedious and dry.

I didn't understand that strategy fully, or really its impetus, until much later when I got into the history and study of religion. And the other side, the *Verstehen*, and the *Einleben*,[16] and all of the understanding and the empathy, that kind of stuff. That's what I've understood phenomenology to be, this two-sided, this two-headed creature, so to speak. One side was hard and dry, the other softer and engaging the imagination.

The Need that Gave Rise to PoR

What would you say was the defining need, to speak in functional terms, out of which PoR grew? What was it that you think the founders of this trend, or of this movement, thought was missing from the study of religion that would lead them to develop PoR?

The Netherlands is the place you have to look. The Dutch and the French Protestants – leaving out the Catholics for the moment – were always in a very close relationship with one and other, partly because they shared a common – kind of Unitarian, Arminian – theological orientation. You may recall a great tradition of French dissidents, like Descartes, fleeing to the Netherlands to publish their work free of the heavy hand of the Catholic theocratic state

---

16. In contrast to the more intellectual process of *Verstehen, Einleben* (empathy) connotes the sense of feeling one's way intuitively into the subject of study.

of the Bourbons. So, to understand the rise of a non-confessional study of religion, we need to keep the Netherlands and France in focus. So, when they talked about religion as a natural phenomenon, they cast around for what an academic study of it would look like. They immediately lighted upon the natural sciences.

And so, the first thing they did – this was Tiele – was to imagine that you could talk about religion in terms of its evolution. Evolution, a story of growth and development, was fundamental to the way human affairs were imagined in the nineteenth century. It wasn't Darwinian evolution so much. Darwin was never mentioned by Tiele, and so it's hard to track any kind of relationship. But, the idea of evolution was in the air, the notion that you could call the story of growth (and the historical sciences were just coming into their own in that part of the nineteenth century), the idea that you could tell the story of development and growth. They first applied that model to religion. Tiele's first book (1877 [1876]) spoke about how religion grew and what the teleology of religion was. Of course, it handily came down to some form of liberal Christianity. That's where religion was headed. That was the most advanced progeny of religion. So, that is the first form or model, of "evolution" adopted by the early, nineteenth-century PoR. I'm not exactly sure why they dropped evolution and moved to the classificatory one later in the century.

And that's where they lose sight, in some critics' minds, of phenomenology as development with historical shifts.

They ditched that pretty quickly. Yes. Again, they're dependent upon a reputation for fairness and neutrality, and so they are always looking over their shoulders, to defend themselves against claims of confessional biases. No, no, no, we are not theology; we are a hard science. And, when asked what they meant by "science", they said, in effect, "Well, look around you. You have historical *sciences*, biological *sciences*: we're like that, and given the intellectual fashion of the time, we talk about a *growth* science – evolution". To get at this level of understanding of PoR's origins, we have to look more at the history of sciences of the nineteenth century where the prestige of botanical classification became quite high.

As scientific practice changed, the early phenomenologists of religion (or "science of religion" types) were able to find *scientific* justification for a shift to the classificatory mode, themselves. The French as well as the Dutch were doing exactly the same thing. There was a father-and-son team in the École Normale Supérieure section, in Paris – the Réville family – Albert Réville[17]

---

17. Albert Réville (1826–1906), French Protestant minister and historian of religions; considered one of the "founders" of comparative religion, comparable to, albeit not as influential as, Max Müller (see below) and Tiele.

and his son, Jean Réville.[18] They were excited to do classificatory work at the same time as the Dutch, yet, perhaps, not with as much intensity as the Dutch. Like the Dutch, the French wanted to establish the study of religion on a scientific basis. But, unlike the Dutch, they were partly competing with the Germans. Here, history is the measure of scientific practice in the humanities. It all began with the study of texts in a deliberately *scientific* way – the higher criticism of the Bible, pioneered in Germany from the end of the eighteenth century. Following the German example of, say, Strauss,[19] this is where you get French biblical critics, like Ernest Renan, and his *Life of Jesus*.[20] Competition with the Germans spurred the French to get serious about the study of languages and literatures of the ancient world. By the mid-1800s, this scholarly enterprise went far beyond just the study of biblical materials, but extended to cover all the world's religions.

The Stillbirth of van der Leeuw's *Phänomenologie der Religion*

Would you say, because of the influence of van der Leeuw, or as a reflection of his influence, that theology, or at least a theological dimension, is inherent in the whole project of PoR?

I think that there is something there. Although, I'm not sure that van der Leeuw influenced anybody. His great book[21] has fallen dead from the womb. Maybe I'm wrong, maybe I'm missing something. I never really thought it had great impact. Certainly, it has a lot less impact than Eliade's work. And Eliade's kind of lazy, meandering stuff – which he passed off as phenomenology – is far more influential. There is a kind of malady, I think, and there is a way in which I think religious people, who are trying to save or protect or defend their transcendental beliefs in a world that doesn't respect them, might use something like phenomenology to forestall further criticism of belief of transcendence. [They say:] "No, no, no, no … you can't attack religion because

---

18. Jean Réville (1854–1908), son of Albert Réville, was a French Protestant pastor; professor at the École des Hautes Études (beginning in 1885) and on the faculty of theology at the Sorbonne, Paris; and editor of *Revue de l'Histoire des Religions*.

19. David Friedrich Strauss (1808–1874), German Protestant theologian; author of *Das Leben Jesu, kritisch bearbeitet*, 2 vols, 1835–1836 (*The Life of Jesus, Critically Examined*, 3 vols, 1846) – a controversial, seminal contribution to what Albert Schweitzer later called the Quest for the Historical Jesus.

20. Ernest Renan (1823–1892), French Orientalist, historian, and writer; best known for his widely popular *Vie de Jésus*, 1863 (*The Life of Jesus*, 1864).

21. Gerardus van der Leeuw, *Phänomenologie der Religion*, 1933 (*Religion in Essence and Manifestation*, 1938).

you haven't understood it yet. Here's your homework – van der Leeuw's book. Work through that, and when you finish, then come back to me with your critique of religion." [Laughter] You know, that is one thing that he probably wanted to do. He wanted to forestall the hyper-critical attacks on religious faith and belief and a God and so forth. So, that's confessional theologizing. I think using PoR that way is unworthy of the scholar.

The Durkheimians' "Very Superior Kind of PoR"

After getting established in a tenured teaching post at Connecticut College, I went full bore into the French intellectual world in order to try to track down what it was about the French and their study of religion that produced somebody like Lévi-Strauss, Louis Dumont, and others. To that short list, one might add Granet and a host of other people … Conclusion: it all led back to Durkheim, Hubert, and Mauss. So that accounts for my work in Durkheimian studies – really, trying to reconstruct what the Durkheimian programme and study of religion was, and what its place was in the overall study of religion and in the context of the Dutch phenomenologists of religion, of all people, and the French science of religion people.

So, there's Durkheim and his guys doing the study of religion, but there's also this "other crowd" doing the study of religion – the ones all the US religious studies types know as phenomenologists of religion … And it turned out to be that Durkheim and Durkheimians really caught on to the crypto-theological agenda of the *science de la religion* people in the Fifth Section. And the Dutch were no better. So, the study of religion, as I thought we should be doing it, the non-theological one, should see the Durkheim school as its basis, as its foundation, as the mother school of the study of religion. … My work on Durkheim, on sacrifice and Durkheim, and the Jews of France (Strenski 1997, 2009). There's a trilogy there. To make a long story short, the Durkheimians actually wound up doing a very superior kind of PoR – of a rigorous and thoroughgoing sort. The Hubert and Mauss classic on sacrifice (1964 [1899]) is nothing short of a conceptual exercise in defining a use of the term, worth *owning*.

The Arrival of PoR in America

Earlier you mentioned Tiele and the two Révilles. From my own work (Ziolkowski 1993) some years ago on the 1893 World's Parliament of Religions, it's interesting that Tiele and both Révilles spoke there, in the scientific study of religion section of the Parliament. Inasmuch as you placed Tiele and both Révilles in the early stages of the emergence of PoR, would you say that the Parliament in 1893 marks the arrival of PoR in the United States? From what point in time would you chart the awareness of this particular approach to the study of religion in North America?

You're probably right, you're probably right with that. I have to admit, my knowledge of the US and of the transfer is not good, and I can't really say. But that wouldn't be surprising if it were. And also there were earlier links. There was a journal called *The New World* published out of Harvard.[22] It was the kind of the Unitarian-Universalist link between the Americans and the study of religion. Philosophers like Josiah Royce and John Fisk were involved at Harvard.[23] They saw themselves as fellow travelers with the French. So, they imported a lot of French stuff. And Emerson, you know, corresponded extensively with Max Müller. They were aware of each other. So, *The New World* did reviews of classics like Robertson Smith's *Lectures on the Religion of the Semites*. But these links were both fragile and fleeting, based for the most part in the vulnerable situation of progressive, cosmopolitan Unitarian-Universalist liberalism and/or Comtean "religion de l'humanité".

Ninian Smart as Phenomenologist of Religion

In *Understanding Theories of Religion*, the chapter that you devote to the PoR ends with Smart (Strenski 2015).[24]

Oh, yes. And, as it should!

So, you would classify him as a phenomenologist?

Yes, absolutely and self-identified at that. Ninian exhibited such a tendency already back in 1959 when he published *Reasons and Faiths*. That's where he really made his mark with the first book to really try to do philosophy

---

22. *The New World: A Quarterly Review of Religion, Ethics and Theology*, a Unitarian journal, was published in Boston by Houghton, Mifflin, and Company, running from 1892 to 1900. It was edited by Professors Charles Carroll Everett and Crawford Howell Toy of Harvard University; President Orello Cone of Buchtel College; and the Rev. Nicholas Paine Gilman.
23. Josiah Royce (1855–1916), American philosopher, proponent of absolute idealism; taught at Harvard University from 1882 to his death.
24. Ninian Smart (1927–2001), Scottish scholar of religious studies, promoted the field as a professor at, successively, the universities of Birmingham (1961–1966), Lancaster (1967–1982), and California, Santa Barbara (1976–1998), and intermittently as a visiting professor at Yale, Wisconsin, Princeton, Banaras, Queensland, Otago, Cape Town, Bangalore, and Hong Kong.

of religion in a comparative way. Anyway, the title is indicative. It's plural: *Reasons*, plural, and *Faiths*, plural. But Ninian had a very artistic temperament, of a keenly visual sort, and was given to describing the religions as being like tapestries where you had different threads emerging and interwoven, and so forth. If there's a powerful insight to phenomenology, it's this. In brief, it is that religions do form a kind of unity in some sense, in that they may be seen as composed of parts, and that these parts interact in all kinds of ways.

To take the phenomenological perspective on religion is to chart the interacting parts that, taken together as a universe of rules, may explain what happens in other parts of a religious territory. Understanding is about seeing how things hang together. It isn't explanation in every sense of the word. It doesn't explain religion's existence as such. It doesn't explain why people want to get into the "religion game". It doesn't explain why certain players are more motivated than others. It just constitutes the entry level way to make sense of religion. Notice how artistic and gentle the mood of this kind of phenomenological inquiry is. Compare it, for instance, to the starchy pseudo-scientific style of PoR of a van der Leeuw, for instance. I think this kind of PoR has much to recommend itself. Students begin by seeing that religions are organic in their having interrelated parts that can be seen to hang together as do the moves and rules of a game, like baseball. This approach is something that does have perennial value and should be a permanent part of the curriculum.

Smuggling Confessional Positions in Academic Garb

Some people associate the PoR with particular institutions such as Groningen when van der Leeuw was there, the University of Chicago in the US, especially when Eliade was there, and Tohoku University in Japan. Could you share your thoughts on whether or not this has been an approach that's been based institutionally in particular places and with particular institutional centres of gravity? To what extent do you think it is a movement that was associated with particular charismatic figures based at certain places?

I think that's right. But, here's the trick. The critical thing would be to see if and how those programmes were carried on, whether and where they survived, and so on. The way people got appointed at European universities was always a little bit of a mystery to me. There's all these royal appointments, often involving their importance to the national church, you know ... France was a little more secularized, a little more state-based – although appointments in the study of religion were often made with one eye on resisting the

Roman Catholic Church. What I could not abide, however, was the possibility that some of these religiously-informed appointments involved people trying to masquerade, trying to smuggle in religious, confessional positions inside their academic ones. That seemed to me unfairly to take advantage of the reputation of science as *value-free* in order to be anything but value-free.

The Impossibility of Epoché

What do you think about *epoché*, the "bracketing", the vaunted centre-piece to the whole PoR method?

Well, you know it's mixed up again with their attempt to be scientists. They think that you can turn a switch so that you can then take some notion and bracket it in such a way that it has no subjective or contextual complications to it. *Epoché* means, basically: you take it out, and isolate it, and see it for itself, right?

Yes.

But there's a subjective element in selecting or in framing that notion. *Epoché* doesn't happen, it can't happen in the way they thought it would happen. Again, so what you do is you do away with the scientific pretence and *epoché* becomes kind of useful, in a looser form. That is to say, let's try to consider something like myth and let's not try to confuse it with ritual, or things of that sort. It's a way of clarifying your thinking to make an initial approach to things. But there is no switch you can flip that will make sure that you're being objective and that you can pull out something from the mass that is separable and has boundaries that you could identify. It just doesn't happen. It can't happen.

"I Don't Know of Anyone Who Subscribes to that Name"

In sum, what is your assessment of the current status, legacy, and future of the PoR? Is it moribund, dead, transmogrified, resurgent?

I don't know of anyone who subscribes to that name. I mean to say that my knowledge is limited. It's not on any of the programmes of the AAR, I don't think. Is there a PoR section? I don't think so.

Not that I'm aware of.

You might say that it's either been absorbed in some sense, taking it to a broader study of religion, or it's been discredited or misunderstood. I still think what Ninian has done bears consideration, and I think the way he has revived PoR so that it's free of these objectivist pretensions, and that it's a much more fluid kind of operation, is a good thing. It's something we should do, definitely. But, again, I'm one of the few people who have even made a case for that.

It would seem that theories and methods in any field will emerge and have an active life, but that they'll gradually recede in the degree to which they're used and then become objects of historical interest. The overall gist of what you've said would seem to support that that's the case with PoR. And I'm thinking about 1963. Eliade published that essay, "History of Religions in Retrospect" (repr. in Eliade 1969, 12–36), and he closed it by observing that PoR was something that was of _growing_ interest at that time. He spoke about the tension between phenomenologists and historicists. My question is whether, looking back at PoR, inasmuch as it _was_ an active theory in the mid-twentieth century – we could say that that was its "heyday", if it had a "heyday"? What would you say PoR was symptomatic of in the intellectual culture of the West?

If you go back to the early people, the Tieles and such, a new order of authority ruled – epistemologically, "science" ruled; and it was no longer sectarian, religious authority that mattered, if it ever did. It was the nation state, and the nation state's commitment to science, and its subsequent control over education that mattered. So, if you wanted a place in the university, if you wanted a place in that institution, which the nation states were setting up to be the training grounds for their leadership, then you had to "get into that" secular, statist world, characterized by loyalty to science, in some way. And, so, the phenomenologists of religion had to play the science game. For PoR, let's say van der Leeuw, if he wanted to participate in this new regime of knowledge, you had to do PoR as a scientific activity, or otherwise be ignored.

Anyway, when Eliade jumped to the American university scene,[25] he was met with quite a different context than that which I have described for the Netherlands. In the United States, we meet institutional pluralism, with many powerful centres, such as the big seminaries, universities. So, you have Harvard, and you have Chicago, and, you know, minor areas, like Penn, Columbia, and so on ... Berkeley hadn't emerged yet, California hadn't

---

25. In 1956, at the age of forty-nine, while based in Paris, Eliade accepted an appointment as visiting professor at the University of Chicago and was invited to give the Haskell Lectures on the history of religions there. The next year, he joined the faculty of the University of Chicago Divinity School, succeeding the recently, suddenly deceased Joachim Wach, who had taught there since 1946. Eliade later was appointed to the Sewell L. Avery Distinguished Service Professor in the Divinity School and Professor in the Committee on Social Thought, and he remained at Chicago until his death in 1986.

emerged yet when Eliade arrived in the US. It took a while to conceive of the proper institutional setting for religious studies in the largest and most prestigious public university in the nation. Given the state's religious diversity, the East Coast seminary model would not do, for instance. So, for a long while Chicago and Harvard were the only options. It was Wilfred Cantwell Smith at Harvard Divinity and Eliade at Chicago.

Wilfred Cantwell Smith doesn't refer to PoR, as far as I know. He's a self-identified historian. Religion is for him, as for Talal Asad, a kind of contextual construct, shaped by Western culture and history. In this sense, to call the "religions" of India, "Hinduism", is to impose our Western construct upon an alien culture in a way that may well distort its reality. But when Eliade refers to "phenomenology", he is talking about an approach unique to his own theoretical position, even if it shares features of classic Dutch PoR. He's talking about *Patterns in Comparative Religion*. And so, when he's talking about PoR he's talking about doing things in an Eliadean way. Eliade was very good at disguising his theoretical aims by using classic terminology, such as PoR, to hide the full extent of what he was really attempting. No one should really confuse Eliade's radical "creative hermeneutics" with dry-as-dust Dutch PoR. Much of the language used in both coincide with each other, but, as I argued in *Four Theories of Myth in Twentieth-Century History* (Strenski 1987), Eliade has far more radical ambitions than the old, classic scientific PoR. Remember: Eliade claims that his approach to religion should *change* people. It had active, existential ambitions, quite at odds with the putatively "scientific" aims[26] of the Tieles, van der Leeuws, and other Dutch phenomenologists of religion.

Commentary

Consistent with their discussions of it in their prolific published writings, what Charles H. Long and Ivan Strenski said in my interviews with them would bear out two general claims regarding PoR in the US. First, PoR, as an originally Dutch and then generally Western European tradition, never really took root in US soil as a widely, consciously, and explicitly embraced approach to the study of religion. Yet, second, PoR nonetheless exerted a considerable influence as one among the panoply of methodologies that developed and became available in religious studies in

---

26. Indeed, Eliade famously construed his scholarly project in the history of religions as "a new humanism" – though he did so while also referring to it as "the science of religions" (Eliade 1961, 8); see Mircea Eliade, "History of Religions and a New Humanism" (1961). A revised and expanded version of this article appears under the simplified title "A New Humanism" in Eliade's *The Quest* (1969).

the course of the last century in the US. In the interviews, both scholars affirm that it was as graduate students that they first encountered the term PoR, and each of them attests that he "seldom make[s] use of the term" (Long) or "actually [has] not used the word phenomenology to talk about what I do" (Strenski) – though each hastens to add that his seldom or not using the term "doesn't mean that I don't use phenomenology" (Long) or that "much of the constructive work I do can be called PoR" (Strenski).

Long elaborates that he "never singled out phenomenology or PoR as some kind of distinct area of study": he never took a course in PoR as a student, nor, he adds, would he have "touched" a major in PoR if there had been one. However, PoR was hardly irrelevant to him as a historian of religions; rather, phenomenology is for him "just a part of the apparatus of making sense that this was something to study when you study religion". Somewhat similarly, Strenski recalls that, while researching his dissertation on theories of myth, his teacher Ninian Smart guided him to become, as Strenski put it in our conversation, "a kind of phenomenologist without knowing it, in the classificatory sense".

There is, we might add, an unmistakably inverse or antithetical relationship between PoR, with its focus on – as Long puts it, referring to the term's etymology – "what *appears*",[27] and the *non*-phenomenon of "opacity" or "opaqueness" that is central to the conceptual frameworks Long has so powerfully formulated for the study of the religions of Africa, African Americans, and other oppressed peoples (e.g., Long 1995, 117–118, 123n. 14, and 191–211 intermittently throughout).[28] Although the term "opacity" does not explicitly occur in our interview, this category lies in the background of what Long has said elsewhere, adopting Foucault's term, about slavery as the "unthought", the unthought marked by "silence" (Long 1969, 1995). In a sense, it might be inferred that a prime methodological deficiency of PoR for Long is that in professedly dwelling upon *what appears*, PoR *ipso facto* misses what in his view are some of the most important albeit traditionally overlooked and neglected data of religious studies – those that various tragic, oppressive, and often brutal historical-cultural factors have consigned to opacity.

---

27.   See note 3 above for my explanation of Long's use of this expression.
28.   In one of his most seminal discussions of the "symbol" and "structure" of opacity, Long pauses to instruct his reader "to recall the words of Gerardus van der Leeuw", that pioneering Dutch phenomenologist of religion, about the concern religious experience has "with a 'Somewhat'. ... From the point of view of religious history, one could say that [the African American] community in its own self-interpretation has moved from a vague 'Somewhat' to the religious experience of a highly exceptional and *extremely impressive* 'Other'" (Long 1995, 192–193, emphasis original).

Long and Strenski, though they agree that PoR originated largely in reaction to the evolutionism of such nineteenth-century scholars as Tylor, Frazer, and Max Müller (Long 1995, 43–44; Strenski 2015, 77–78), differ somewhat in the *loci classici* by which they chart the early genealogy of PoR. Long, in his article "Archaism and Hermeneutics" (1995, 43–44), originally published in 1967, singles out the work of the Dutch theologian and historian of religions P. D. Chantepie de la Saussaye as one of the earliest exemplars of the sort of systematizations of religious phenomena characteristic of PoR, and traces the development of PoR thenceforth up through Husserl himself, Heidegger, Otto, van der Leeuw, and Pettazzoni, ending with Eliade. Strenski in his chapter on PoR in *Understanding Theories of Religion* (2006; 2nd edition, 2015) concurs with the arguments of Arie L. Molendijk of the University of Groningen (Molendijk 2005, cited by Strenski 2015, 79), looking likewise to the Netherlands as PoR's "true home" (Strenski 2015, 82). Strenski points to Cornelis P. Tiele (rather than Chantepie de la Saussaye), with his "morphologies" of religion, as PoR's chief Dutch precursor, followed by the Norwegian William Brede Kristensen (PoR's "first undisputed" and "first real exponent", in Strenski's view; see Strenski 2015, 81–82), and then Otto, van der Leeuw, Eliade, and – someone Long omits – Strenski's own mentor, Ninian Smart. In their interviews with me, Long and Strenski each rounded out these PoR lineages with evocations of additional figures whose work they find to bear upon PoR – figures such as, in Long's view, Wach and Cassirer in their concern with "schematization", Peirce with his interest in "the *phaneron*", and Ricoeur and Bachalard; and, in Strenski's view, Albert and Jean Réville as "early phenomenologists of religion", and also Durkheim, Hubert, Mauss, and other Durkheimians who "actually wound up doing a very superior kind of PoR".

To be noted is that all the figures Long and Strenski evoke in relation to PoR, excepting Peirce, were Europeans, with the chief "carrier" (my word) of phenomenological tendencies from Europe to the US being Eliade, about whom Long and Strenski evince markedly different attitudes: Long's, favourable; Strenski's, disfavourable.

Practically speaking, as the Long-and-Strenski interviews exemplify, PoR never gained much traction in the US as a method of study that was actively, avowedly pursued. Nothing like a phenomenological "school" ever emerged among US scholars in religious studies. This point is further illustrated by the fact that PoR never established any sort of ongoing, significant "presence" in the American Academy of Religion (AAR), of which Long was president in 1973. Closely associated with the Society of Biblical Literature (SBL), the AAR traces its roots to the Association of Biblical Instructors in American Colleges and Secondary Schools, founded in 1909, which changed its name to the National Association of Biblical Instructors (NABI, or "prophet" in Hebrew), which in turn became in 1963 the AAR (see American Academy of Religion 2019a). Of the almost 200 "units" and nineteen "seminars" currently listed on the "Program Units" website of the American Academy of Religion (www.aarweb. org), none includes the term "phenomenology" or "phenomenological" in its title. From 1985 to 1991, the AAR included an ongoing "seminar" entitled "Theology and the Phenomenological Movement", whose chair in the year of its termination (1991) was the theologian Walter J. Lowe (American Academy of Religion 2019b). That seminar, however, proved a short-lived exception. In fact, PoR demonstrably elicited a strong resistance or, in some instances, outright opposition among US scholars, as illustrated by a job description Thomas Ryba recalls coming across in the mid-1980s. The ad read something like this: "A small college in the Eastern United States is looking for a candidate to teach introductory courses in Western religions and courses in his/her religion of specialization at the upper undergraduate level. Phenomenologists of religion need not apply" (Ryba 2006, 91). Ryba adds that no explanation was offered for this proscription.

As a concluding, personal addendum, I must respond with a qualified "no" to the question posed by this volume's editors as to whether I myself now think, or used to think (as a graduate student at the University of Chicago Divinity School in the early and mid-1980s), that Eliade, Long, and their Chicago colleague J. Z. Smith were "PoR-ish". Some words of explanation are in order on this point.

My acquaintance with PoR is inextricable from my Chicago experience. I first read van der Leeuw as an undergraduate at another institution, studying under the Chicago-trained historian of religions Hans H. Penner, who had compiled the additions to the second German edition of van der Leeuw's *Phänomenologie der Religion* that were incorporated in J. E. Turner's 1963 translation of it. At Chicago, Otto and van der Leeuw figured respectively as a representative anticipator and exemplar of PoR in Eliade's course, "Classics in the Study of Religion", which I audited, and van der Leeuw's PoR came under scrutiny in a seminar I took with Joseph Kitagawa, "Types of Religious Leadership". Additionally, the vexing, timeworn "dichotomy" in the history of religions (*Religionswissenschaft*) between strictly *historical* study on the one hand, and atemporal, classificatory, *phenomenological* study on other, emerged as the dominant overriding concern discussed and debated at the international symposium on the current state of the field that I attended at the Divinity School in 1983, whose speakers included none other than Charles H. Long – then at North Carolina – and Strenski's mentor Ninian Smart of Lancaster,

England, and Santa Barbara, California; as well as Eliade, Kitagawa, and Paul Ricoeur of Chicago; Michel Meslin of the Sorbonne, Paris; and Ugo Bianchi of Rome; to all of whom a host of up-and-coming younger US scholars served as respondents: Davíd Carrasco, Bruce Lincoln, Diana Eck, Lawrence Sullivan, among numerous others.[29]

I can only speak for myself, of course, but in my reading and contemplation of their works over the decades I have never pigeonholed Eliade, Long, or Smith as a "phenomenologist of religion". To be sure, there are saliently "phenomenological" dimensions to their works – most especially in Eliade's case, and least of all in Smith's. Yet, in my view, the common misperception and, often, dismissal of Eliade as simply – and reductively! – a phenomenologist stems from limited reading, or *misreading*, of his voluminous works. In essays of the early 1960s he emphatically voices his conviction, for better or worse, that the study of religions must not confine itself to any one methodology, but "must become a total discipline in the sense that it must use, integrate, and articulate the results obtained *by the various methods of approaching a religious phenomenon*", including the sociological, ethnological, psychological, historical, and phenomenological, and he specifically warns against naively supposing "that the tension between those who try to understand [phenomenologically] the *essence* and the *structures* and those whose only concern is the *history* of religious phenomena will one day be completely done away with" (Eliade 1961, 8–9; see also ibid., 35–36). The effort to balance these two methodological orientations in his own work is evident, for example, not only when his phenomenological (or what he preferred to call "morphological") *Traité d'histoire des religions* (a.k.a. *Patterns in Comparative Religion*) is considered in juxtaposition with his three-volume *History of Religious Ideas* (Eliade 1978–1985), but also when one considers the combining of articles of both phenomenological and historical orientations in the sixteen-volume *Encyclopedia of Religion* (1987) that he edited.

Long, who will now have the last word, makes a similar point in the interview when I ask him about the perceived tension between history and phenomenology in the study of religion: "let me put it this way," he says, "not for us at Chicago". He proceeds to contrast, among Eliade's works,

---

29. The conference papers by these speakers, including also one by Kurt Rudolf of the Karl Marx University, Leipzig (who had missed the conference because his government did not permit him to travel), are gathered in *The History of Religions: Retrospect and Prospect*, including an "Afterword" by Joseph M. Kitagawa and his student Gregory D. Alles which summarizes the papers and the respondents' comments. On the history/phenomenology divide, see esp. Kitagawa (1985, 53, 56–57, 94, 97, 149–150, 156, 171–172, 176).

the allegedly "ahistorical" *Patterns* with *Yoga* and *Shamanism*, which "you can't say [are] non-historical". Then he suggests that it would be equally fine to do either a general, comparative, phenomenological anatomy of chairs in India, China, and England, or a historical investigation of chairs in Victorian England in particular. When it comes to the study of religion, "I don't know why people get all messed up and confused about stuff like that ... My own feeling is that you're historical when it's necessary to be historical" – and, by extension, you're phenomenological when it's necessary to be phenomenological.

Eric Ziolkowski is H. P. Manson Professor of Bible, Head of the Department of Religious Studies, and Co-coordinator of the Medieval, Renaissance, and Early Modern Studies Program at Lafayette College in Pennsylvania. He is the author numerous books, articles, and essays in the comparative study of religion and literature. He has lectured widely in North America, Great Britain, and Western Europe, as well as Poland, Australia, and China (Beijing, Suzhou, Shanghai, Hong Kong). Recent scholarly books include his monographic essay, *Religion and Literature: History and Method* (forthcoming; Leiden: Brill, 2019); *Kierkegaard, Literature, and the Arts* (Evanston, IL: Northwestern University Press, 2018), *The Bible in Folklore Worldwide*, vol. 1: *A Handbook of Biblical Reception in Jewish, European Christian, and Islamic Folklores* (Berlin: De Gruyter, 2017). Formerly the North American Senior Editor of the journal *Literature and Theology* (2004–2012), he is a main editor of the prospective thirty-volume *Encyclopedia of the Bible and Its Reception* (2009–; nineteen volumes published to date), and co-edits two book series: Studies in Religion and the Arts (Brill), and Studies of the Bible and Its Reception (De Gruyter).

References

American Academy of Religion. 2019a. "History of the American Academy of Religion." Retrieved from https://aarweb.org/AARMBR/Who-We-Are-/ History.aspx (accessed 21 January 2019).

American Academy of Religion. 2019b. "Program Units from Past Annual Meetings." Retrieved from www.aarweb.org/node/155 (accessed 21 January 2019).

Carrasco, Davíd. 1995. "Proem" to Charles H. Long, *Significations: Signs, Symbols, and Images in the Interpretation of Religion*, 2nd edition. Aurora, CO: Davies Group.

Eliade, Mircea. 1958 [1949]. *Patterns in Comparative Religion*. Translated by Rosemary Sheed. London: Sheed and Ward. (Original edition: *Traité d'histoire des religions*, Paris: Payot.)

Eliade, Mircea. 1958 [1954]. *Yoga: Immortality and Freedom*. Translated by Willard R. Trask. New York: Pantheon. (Original edition: *Le yoga: immortalité et liberté*, Paris: Payot.)

Eliade, Mircea. 1961. "History of Religions and a New Humanism." *History of Religions* 1(1), 1–8. https://doi.org/10.1086/462437

Eliade, Mircea. 1963. "The History of Religions in Retrospect: 1912–1962." *Journal of Bible and Religion* 31(2), 98–109. https://doi.org/10.1017/s00419 77x00076515

Eliade, Mircea. 1964 [1951]. *Shamanism: Archaic Techniques of Ecstasy* (revised and enlarged edition). Translated by Willard R. Trask. New York: Bollingen Foundation, Pantheon. (Original edition: *Le chamanisme et les techniques archaïques de l'extase*, Paris: Payot.)

Eliade, Mircea. 1969. *The Quest: History and Meaning in Religion*. Chicago, IL: University of Chicago Press.

Eliade, Mircea. 1978–1985. *A History of Religious Ideas*, 3 vols. Translated by Willard R. Trask *et al.* Chicago, IL: University of Chicago Press.

Eliade, Mircea, ed. 1987. *The Encyclopedia of Religion*, 16 vols., New York: Macmillan.

Hubert, Henri, and Marcel Mauss. 1964 [1899]. *Sacrifice: Its Nature and Function*. Translated by W. D. Halls. Chicago, IL: University of Chicago Press. (Original edition: *Essai sur la nature et la fonction du sacrifice*, Paris: Félix Alcan.)

Kitagawa, Joseph M. (ed.). 1985. *The History of Religions: Retrospect and Prospect*. New York: Macmillan.

Long, Charles H. 1967. "Prolegomenon to a Religious Hermeneutic." *History of Religions* 6(3), 254–264. https://doi.org/10.1086/462545

Long, Charles H. 1969. "Silence and Signification." In *Myths and Symbols: Studies in Honor of Mircea Eliade*, edited by Joseph M. Kitagawa and Charles H. Long. Chicago, IL: University of Chicago Press.

Long, Charles H. 1995. *Significations: Signs, Symbols, and Images in the Interpretation of Religion*, 2nd edition. Aurora, CO: Davies Group.

Long, Charles H. 2018. *Ellipsis: The Collected Writings of Charles Long*. London: Bloomsbury.

Molendijk, Arie L. 2005. *The Emergence of the Science of Religion in the Netherlands*. Leiden: Brill.

Renan, Ernest. 1864 [1863]. *The Life of Jesus*. Translated by Charles Edwin Wilbour. New York: Carleton. (Original edition: *Vie de Jésus*, Paris: Calmann-Lévy.)

Ryba, Thomas. 2006. "Phenomenology of Religion." In *The Blackwell Companion to the Study of Religion*, edited by Robert A. Segal. Chichester: Wiley-Blackwell.

Smart, Ninian. 1959. *Reasons and Faiths: An Investigation of Religious Discourse, Christian and Non-Christian*. New York: Humanities Press.

Smith, Robertson. 1894. *Lectures on the Religion of the Semites*, 2nd edition. Edinburgh: A. & C. Black.

Strauss, David Friedrich. 1846 [1835–1836]. *The Life of Jesus, Critically Examined*, 3 vols. Translated by George Eliot. London: Chapman. (Original edition: *Das Leben Jesu, kritisch bearbeitet*, 2 vols, Tübingen: C. F. Osiander.)

Strenski, Ivan. 1987. *Four Theories of Myth in Twentieth-Century History: Cassirer, Eliade, Lévi-Strauss and Malinowski*. Basingstoke: Macmillan.

Strenski, Ivan. 1997. *Durkheim and the Jews of France*. Chicago, IL: University of Chicago Press.

Strenski, Ivan. 2002. *Contesting Sacrifice: Religion, Nation and Social Thought in France*. Chicago, IL: University of Chicago Press.

Strenski, Ivan. 2009. *Émile Durkheim*. Farnham: Ashgate.

Strenski, Ivan. 2015. *Understanding Theories of Religion: An Introduction*, 2nd edition. Chichester: John Wiley. (Originally published in 2006 under the title *Thinking About Religion*.)

Tiele, C. P. 1877 [1876]. *Outlines of the History of Religion, to the Spread of the Universal Religions*. Translated by J. Estlin Carpenter. Boston, MA: James R. Osgood. (Original edition: *Geschiedenis van den Godsdienst, tot aan de heerschappij der Wereldgodsdiensten*. Amsterdam: P. N. van Kampen & Zoon.)

Tylor, Edward Burnett. 1903. *Primitive Culture: Researches into the Development of Mythology, Philosophy, Religion, Language, Art, and Custom*, 2 vols., 4th edition, revised. London: J. Murray.

van der Leeuw, Gerardus. 1938 [1933]. *Religion in Essence and Manifestation*, 2 vols. Translated by J. E. Turner. London: G. Allen and Unwin. (2nd edition, with appendices from the 2nd German edition incorporated by Hans H. Penner: New York: Harper & Row, 1963; 3rd edition: Princeton, NJ: Princeton University Press, 1986; original edition: *Phänomenologie der Religion*, Tübingen: J. C. B. Mohr [Paul Siebeck].) https://doi.org/10.1515/9781400858026.xx

Waardenburg, Jacques. 1999. *Classical Approaches to the Study of Religion: Aims, Methods and Theories of Research. Introduction and Anthology*. Berlin: De Gruyter.

Ziolkowski, Eric (ed.). 1993. *A Museum of Faiths: Histories and Legacies of the 1893 World's Parliament of Religions*, American Academy of Religion Classics in Religious Studies, no. 9. Atlanta, GA: Scholars Press.

9

A Proposal for an Epistemologically Humble Phenomenology

An Interview with Denise Cush (United Kingdom)

SUZANNE OWEN

Denise Cush was Professor of Religion and Education and Head of Department of Study of Religions at Bath Spa University, having earlier taught in a sixth form college (upper level secondary school) and trained teachers in both primary and secondary school religious education. She became the first female professor of religion and education in the UK in 2003. Her publications include *Buddhism: A Student's Approach to World Religions* (Hodder Education, 1994). She was a member of the national commission exploring the future of religious education in England in 2016–2018.

Introduction

Denise Cush was at Lancaster University while Ninian Smart (1927–2001) and Eric Sharpe (1933–2000) were there, both major scholars in the Phenomenology of Religion who also changed the way Religious Education was taught in schools in England. Cush had also switched from Theology to Religious Studies and, taking on board many of Ninian Smart's ideas, went on to become influential in Religious Education.

Keywords: Ninian Smart, methodology, empathy, religious education, theology, critical religion

The following interview was conducted at King's College London on 8 December 2017. We were both in London for the annual general meeting of TRS-UK (representatives of academic departments and scholarly societies for Theology and Religious Studies).

Discovering Phenomenology of Religion

Suzanne Owen: Having pretty much seen the rise and fall of Phenomenology of Religion (PoR) as a methodology for studying religion in various educational contexts, how were you first introduced to it?

Denise Cush: I first became aware of phenomenology as an approach, not in religious studies at University level, but when I first started to think about religious education in schools (RE). My first degree was Theology and I think phenomenology might have been mentioned as a philosophy in passing, but it wasn't a methodology that was *employed*, so I first came across phenomenology through Ninian Smart because he was interested in both religious studies at university, setting up the ground-breaking department at Lancaster, and in what was happening in schools. I came in through a back doorway, if you like, because I came in when phenomenology was starting to be used as a method in education for studying religion in schools. That was in 1975/6 and certainly since that time, in the intervening 42 years, I've noticed that phenomenology means very different things to different people. So, when you hear something like "do away with phenomenology" in the meeting earlier in the day [discussing the Interim Report of the Commission on RE which suggested a range of approaches appropriate for RE in schools, including phenomenology], you need to ask "but what do you mean by phenomenology?" because it's meant different things to different people. You could argue that it has been misunderstood by some people or that it is itself diverse – there are *phenomenologies*.

And you were at Lancaster University?

I did end up at Lancaster. After I did a Theology degree at Oxford I went on to do a PGCE (Postgraduate Certificate in Education) course to train to become a secondary school teacher, and I realized that the Theology degree was not really sufficient for teaching RE in school. It was really a kind of road to Damascus moment for me. It was a relief to come across a new method for looking at religions, and so for me, rather than being a philosophy, it meant a non-confessional approach to studying religion and that the role of a teacher was not to persuade children that they ought to believe in God or that they ought to follow a particular faith. It was that approach, the methodologically agnostic approach, that I found very attractive for use in school.

Also, phenomenology became a kind of proxy for multi-faith religious education, or pluralism, exploring many different religions, as opposed to studying one religion in depth, which is still argued for in many places. So, for me it meant a methodologically agnostic approach, it meant an attitude of *epoché* and empathy as found in the phenomenology of Ninian Smart, trying to put your prejudices to one side and trying to see it from the believers' point of view. This opened up a world for me, that you could look at many different faiths and not just one, and the idea that there were various tools that you could use *across* religions. The comparative element of phenomenology was very attractive. So that's how I came into it.

As a result of encountering his work, I actually wrote to Ninian Smart and said, this is great, what can I do? And then I ended up doing an MA at Lancaster and studied with Eric Sharpe, and Ninian Smart sometimes, who at that time spent half the time in California, and knew about their work, and then through them came across the Dutch phenomenologists, van der Leeuw and Kristensen, who were more influential at that point in British phenomenology.

So, the Sharpe book, *Comparative Religion: A History* (1975), was where I came in. I appreciated phenomenology as a general approach rather than as a specific philosophy.

You were interested in it as a method rather than as a theory?

Yes, in a way. Not even as a method, but as a general approach when starting to study a religion with which you are unfamiliar, or a new group of people, trying to have this "warm detachment" that Ninian Smart taught about: an open mind, bearing in mind that nobody is coming from nowhere or can be completely "objective", but one can try to be as impartial as possible, as fair as possible, and to try and see it from their point of view before rushing in and with a critical evaluation. And I still appreciate that. I've kind of stayed a phenomenologist.

Did you become a member of the Shap Working Party?[1]

I wasn't a member because it wasn't something you could join. It was a working party; they elected themselves, but I used to go to the conferences they put on and they produced various resources. I was a Shap follower, if you like. I think for lots of younger colleagues, in RE and Religious Studies, I don't think they realize how much of a revolution it was to do lots of religions and not

---

1. The Shap Working Party on World Religions in Education was formed during a conference on "Comparative Religion and Education" held in Shap, Cumbria, in 1969. Speakers included Ninian Smart, Eric Sharpe, Geoffrey Parrinder (1910–2005) and John Hinnells (1941–2018).

just one, and that you don't have to teach from a theological point of view. It may seem obvious all these decades later for everyone, but it was new and exciting, and I really enjoyed going off to Lancaster to do this. Buddhism, Hinduism – it was hard at first because it was a completely new world. With perseverance, these new worldviews began to make sense. I used to say to students it may seem completely alien at first but plod away, do more reading, build up your own knowledge of a new tradition. Almost literally, I felt something clicked in my brain. I began to see the world in different ways. That's what phenomenology did for me personally.

I would still call myself a phenomenologist. I know that sounds old fashioned, but it is true in the sense that I still believe in methodological agnosticism and empathy, and trying to understand, and I think I do like the balance of subjectivity and objectivity. Reading James Cox's book (*A Guide to the Phenomenology of Religion*, 2006) in preparation for this interview, reminded me of some of the authors who had influenced me. Ninian Smart's phrase is that it's "a science … that requires a sensitive and artistic heart" (1971, 13). It was a kind of holistic approach about feeling, and your own consciousness, as well as trying to be as clear as possible scientifically about the people you were studying. The idea that you didn't have to be either reductionist or confessional was very attractive.

It is a kind of reduction, though.

Yes, but there are levels to this, subtleties, it depends how you do it, or how far you follow particular forms of phenomenology. That's why it became popular in the 1970s in Britain because it was a refreshing thing for people. We were noticing, even in remote parts of Britain, it was obvious to young people, that the world was wider than the Christian world. Youth culture was looking to the Beatles going to India, Hinduism and Buddhism were coming into the culture and we wanted to know about them – even when I was at school in the late sixties. Eastern traditions were becoming part of the youth culture. We wanted to know about them and no one was teaching us.

That kind of curiosity from the late sixties, came at a time when RE was moving away from church instruction toward an agenda for living in the modern world.

So, it all kind of came together.

Phenomenology of Religion in the UK

The question of who introduced PoR to the UK is debatable because many of us would argue that Ninian Smart's approach was really what laid the foundations for it throughout the country. Another who might have engaged with phenomenology was Geoffrey Parrinder.

When I was rereading James Cox's book I picked that up about Parrinder, because his book was the first book I used to try and teach myself about traditions other than Christianity, without taking a theological approach. I took Cox's point because I think Parrinder is a kind of pre-phenomenologist because he was looking at a wide range of religions without taking a theological approach to it. There is the minimal definition of phenomenology and then you get into all the technicalities of all the different sorts of phenomenologies, but I took Cox's point that there were people like Parrinder who paved the way. It wasn't Ninian Smart putting forward something nobody had ever heard of before. It's just that he successfully popularized it and started that department at Lancaster [the first department of Religious Studies in the UK], and also cared about schools.

Geoffrey Parrinder appeared on early reading lists when you were learning about PoR and approaches to different religions. Probably less so the other scholars mentioned by Cox as forerunners.

Geoffrey Parrinder was so interesting that I remember his importance to me. I learned about Andrew Walls's work later when I was looking at Christianity in Africa, but he wasn't somebody I'd come across in the 1970s because I wasn't thinking about Africa. Perhaps James Cox because of his own African interests has more knowledge of those scholars.[2]

Walls helped promote the study of so-called Primal Religions, which weren't adequately studied outside of anthropology, at least as religious traditions. And that was important for James Cox and then myself who followed Cox into the study of Indigenous Religions.

And that's an important point, and I would defend the view that including the study of indigenous traditions is a very important part of what we try to do in the study of religion.

Going beyond the World Religions? In some ways Walls helped to start that movement but many people contributed to expanding the study of religions beyond the so-called World Religions. This includes those studying New Religious Movements and other areas. Religious Studies in the UK was dominated to begin with by Lancaster, but I think it soon spread to other universities such as the University of Leeds, partly via students of Ninian Smart.

---

2. James Cox was at the University of Aberdeen while Andrew Walls was there, having founded the first Religious Studies Department in Scotland (1970).

Brian Bocking was a student at both Lancaster and Leeds and joined Bath Spa in 1986, and under Brian's leadership (until 1999) the department at Bath Spa definitely took a phenomenological approach. I think the "Lancaster approach" gradually spread but there was also "comparative religion", which had a longer history, for example at Manchester – it wasn't that nobody except Lancaster was studying any other religions apart from Christian Theology. There were things other than Theology happening.

How would you characterize what Manchester was doing?

It was very similar to what became Study of Religions. It may have been considered Oriental Studies in an earlier era.

Yes, because there was an emphasis on South Asian traditions, I think.

Ninian Smart and Lancaster popularized study of religions, it wasn't that nothing was happening before, but it was seen as a new start with new universities [Lancaster was established in 1964], and a new approach. It was the department that was self-consciously Religious Studies, and not Theology.

One of the things that attracted me and still attracts me, and I rather regret that it is not important anymore, or less important, is that phenomenology gave the study of religions a method of its own. As Ninian Smart always said, religious studies is poly-methodic, and we use history and literature, sociology and psychology, and philosophy, but phenomenology we kind of owned. It was part of arguing that Religious Studies was a distinct subject, as that's always a difficult argument to make. That was important. Our own *ology*. Not that it wasn't elsewhere, but it seemed to be our own.

Criticisms of the Phenomenology of Religion

Would you say that's a little eroded now?

Yes, it's been eroded, definitely. I think the heyday was 1970s-1990s, and in the 90s there were critiques from a number of directions. For example, Timothy Fitzgerald (*Ideology of Religious Studies*, 2000) argued that it was "covert theology". He has a point because most of the phenomenologists were liberal Christians. It sprang from northern European liberal Protestantism. It didn't come from nowhere. It didn't come from a secular non-religious background; it came from a liberal Protestant background. And Gavin Flood (*Beyond Phenomenology*, 1999) criticized phenomenology for placing too much stress upon the individual experience.

I think for me, although I would still call myself to some extent a phenomenologist, unlike my younger colleagues who'd say they definitely weren't, the critique that was most powerful was the critique of essentialism. My version of phenomenology was perhaps the somewhat watered-down version of it that went into schools. Little emphasis was placed on the Husserlian eidetic vision – it was there, but it was interpreted more as how you "get it" rather than in its full philosophical meaning of "grasping essences". There is some interesting stuff there about how our consciousness and knowledge works, but the idea that you could grasp the essence of something was downplayed in religious education [in schools]. Given that I studied Buddhism – "no self" and "no essence" – once the essentialism of phenomenology was pointed out to me, I thought, well, yes, but I was never a fan of Mircea Eliade particularly. I have this endless argument with my colleague Catherine Robinson because she thinks Ninian Smart is an essentialist and I think he's not. You can argue that because he does have a concept of "the invisible world", he does consider that there is an essence to religion, but I read him differently, as being much more vague – indefinite about it. I am certainly not an essentialist. I think the Feminist critique of essentialism, including in phenomenology, was strong in all sorts of ways. This had an impact on Religious Studies from the 1990s.

Rosalind Shaw?

For example. There were a lot of things that Feminism queried, such as the idea of objectivity.

Everyone is situated.

You can't put everything in the brackets; you can't stop being yourself when you are looking at things. I suppose I never thought you could. My idea of the *epoché* was not that you were going to end up being totally objective, but I needed to think more about this a bit further down the line.

I saw the reflexive side of *epoché* when I was learning about it, that *epoché* is a chance to examine your own biases.

Yes, if you see it as that, it works. If you think, I can put all my prejudices away, and be totally unbiased, that is impossible, but if you understand that before I study I need to examine my preconceptions – so I'm going to meet this group – what are my existing pictures of this group and where did I get those from and why, so yes, it requires reflexivity. It depends how you inflect these things. Feminism has only just started to overturn the study of religions. There are more women scholars and people study "women *in*" religious traditions – the content has changed a bit. If you go back, Ninian Smart's book was called *The Religious Experience of Mankind* but in its reissued modern version it's just *The Religious Experience*. We have changed. It was all from a male point of view, male scholars, and not only male, but elite and white – it was their view. And all the scholars in this list, just about everybody in this book [Cox's] is male.

I looked at the bibliography and there's only Ursula King and a brief mention of Gerrie ter Haar.

And a brief mention of Danièle Hervieu-Léger. It's tiny. You would expect not to find many women in the early days, but there aren't many later either.

As Cox was writing this book, we spoke about this. Cox did want to include more women. This was a problem with the history of PoR.

There just weren't any women there, for all sorts of reasons. So, they were all men though they weren't explicitly excluding women, but that's how it was because you never notice when you're in an unequal power situation, you just think it's just normal. As an argument against the concept of objectivity – what's said to be objective is just the people in power's view of things.

There is also this question within theoretical and methodological studies generally, even putting aside the specificity of PoR, that any kind of methodological or theoretical focus is not well populated by female scholars generally.

Yes, certainly for whatever reason it appealed more to men than women. Regarding PoR, for me, I wasn't much interested in the philosophy heritage at the time, but it's interesting now.

When I was doing my Masters, I really loved reading Husserl and his Paris lectures. We had a reading group reading it. But the idea of making that your object of study …

As opposed to the actual religions in practice out there …

It was not as appealing.

My interests were wide-ranging – that's the other thing that phenomenology allows, because it's comparative, and you're looking at dynamics and patterns and you can be wide-ranging. I've been interested in contemporary Paganism as well as a wide range of more familiar religious traditions. This can be criticized as leading to a superficial understanding, rather than studying one tradition in depth, but I enjoyed being able to study a variety of traditions, and consider, in the words of a teacher I interviewed recently, that "depth of learning is not achieved by narrowness of content, but by a 'synoptic' view across traditions".

Another criticism of some phenomenologists was that it was a bit of an armchair exercise – to sit and theorize based on other people's materials and fieldwork from various places. Even though I say I am still a phenomenologist

I am also an ethnographer, in a small way. That was just obvious from being a school teacher that you would have a kind of textbook version of a religion and then you would have a child from that tradition in the classroom, and the book would say "Sikhs do this, this, this", and the child would say, "well, we don't". You could be threatened by that, but I thought this was interesting. The child's view, and the practices of their family and community are as important as the textbook. This was a kind of human reaction rather than a theoretical reaction. Robert Jackson popularized ethnography in RE, as opposed to phenomenology, and as well as being supported by theory it springs out of your experience of just meeting people and trying to teach these things and realizing that a textbook version isn't the same as how it is for real people living their lives within traditions.

There's a disconnect there, and it makes me wonder what was the object of PoR, and that it does not really represent what's now called "lived religions", or at least it didn't in the way certain schemas were applied.

It didn't really exclude it, and thinking back to Ninian Smart's TV programmes, he did go and talk to people, but perhaps not in an organized theoretically and methodologically ethnographic way. Phenomenology can be done theoretically, looking for patterns and dimensions.

The exclusion of diversity was one of the criticisms, particularly in the way that it played out in RE.

I think PoR was much misunderstood in RE, because it was first of all a kind of proxy for a multi-faith content – all that "we are going to take a phenomenological approach" to many people meant "we are going to do more than Christianity".

The other misunderstanding was that the idea of the *epoché* and empathy was taken to mean being merely descriptive and never using critical evaluation, and so that became quite boring. If you read Ninian Smart, he's a philosopher, and he says time and time again that you don't do this description stuff for its own sake. You do it to clarify it, because you are going to engage with the truth-claims at a later stage. What should be avoided is making a premature evaluation. People don't read Smart very carefully, or people who were teachers didn't read Smart at all and they saw it as "you just tell them the facts". It is alleged that they describe these so-called facts and you don't make any sort of judgments or engage in discussions, but that never happened in my classrooms or people who'd had some sort of background in this. Smart's view was that you were trying to get people *not* to jump in with an evaluation before they knew anything about something, which often they do on so many topics – we're living in a culture where nowadays everybody is supposed to have an instant opinion on everything.

The World Religions Paradigm

So, PoR was misunderstood in schools and some people saw it as merely descriptive and uncritical, leading to reifying traditions, and associated with a "World Religions" model where there were a series of boxes: "that was Sikhism, and that was Hinduism, and that was Buddhism".

And it didn't have to be – that's the thing, it didn't have to be bound to a World Religions model.

No, it didn't have to be, but it often was. Partly because you do have to simplify things to teach them to children. You can't do academic degree level versions of everything, but there are ways of doing this – and you don't have to distort things in the process of selection. I think it was misunderstood, and I think a lot of criticisms [of RE] in school are not often of PoR *per se* but of phenomenology done badly and not really understood.

You know I wrote a critique of the field? [See Owen 2011.]

Yes.

James Cox in his book *From Primitive to Indigenous* proposed that departments take indigenous religions seriously. I was just finishing my PhD and I thought, great, there was going to be a welcome ... and there wasn't. It was the frustration of applying for jobs that wanted a World Religions specialist rather than a Religion specialist.

Yes, that it had to be the "Big Six" [Buddhism, Christianity, Hinduism, Islam, Judaism, Sikhism]. Whether it meant to or not, the religious studies tradition did contribute to this World Religions Paradigm that's caused us a lot of trouble really. The Big Six emerged in school RE [from "Big Five", before Buddhism was added[3]] in the 1980s – and at various times in my career I've fought against this – trying to include a wider range, whether it's indigenous traditions, or Neo-Paganism, contemporary and new forms of religion, new religious movements, that sort of thing.

It's still categorizing them the same kind of way.

Exactly. I'm with you on that one. I'm not sure that's what PoR set out to do.

---

3.   In the 1980s in England the list of religions in Religious Education included Sikhism rather than Buddhism, which was added later, as seen in two editions of W. Owen Cole's book on religions (Cole 1981, 1984). Then, in the Education Reform Act of 1988, the "principle" religions were presumed to be, in order of adherents in the census: Christianity, Islam, Hinduism, Sikhism, Judaism and Buddhism (Cush 2016).

Considering when you look at the Dutch scholars, they were looking at Ancient Egyptian cultures and all sorts of things. So, PoR grew out of Ancient Near East studies, and theology as well, but they weren't imagining this kind of World Religions Paradigm.

No, it didn't have to be there. I wonder how it came about? Possibly population statistics saying, "X number of people are Christian and the next biggest is Islam". It may be that PoR and identifying certain traditions as "World Religions" came about at the same time rather than a causal connection.

Yeah, through census data and Ninian Smart's work opening it out to studying beyond Christianity.

From Text to Ethnography

So, there are some criticisms of phenomenology *per se* and then there are criticisms of misunderstood or misapplied phenomenology, I would argue. But, certainly over the 40 years or whatever it is since the 1970s when I started, the approaches that I have needed to supplement phenomenology are ethnography as the study of real people and also feminism and feminist critique, those two really. And just sheer experience – I know that people don't fit into those boxes we spoke about. And this privileging of experience is part of a feminist approach.

Methodologically, it doesn't have to be those boxes.

Exactly. I kind of instinctively felt the need to supplement phenomenology with ethnography, because before I started teaching I went off to Lancaster and did my MA dissertation on Tibetan Buddhism in the West. Even at Lancaster, the course I took did not include fieldwork or visits to religious communities.

It was still text-based.

I don't think I was even familiar with the term "ethnography".

So, it wasn't the study of contemporary religion really.

No, it wasn't, not even at Lancaster. People idealized Lancaster, but it was more "studying religions", that was the exciting thing, but I thought, well, I'm going to go off and go to Manjushri [Tibetan Buddhist centre in Cumbria]. I wanted to know what was happening now. There were some Tibetan lamas just up the road in the Lake District, so I took myself off and around and that was quite unusual, and I had no training in anthropology or sociological methods or anything at all, but I just thought well I'm going to talk to these people as well as read books about them. So that ethnographic side, if you want to use the label of ethnography for it, was always there, even before I read about it, because of experience, because of just wanting to make it real. And it's the same with talking to children in the classroom.

Had you had much interaction with scholars in other countries?

Only that we read the Dutch phenomenologists. I didn't attend any conferences abroad until 1997. Communications technology has made international interactions much more possible than when I started my career. Coinciding with the critique of phenomenology was the fact that we had more opportunities to meet with people from all over the world. It was very hard before – you would have to write them a letter when I was young. We did, but it took a long time to get the data back and you just couldn't email somebody on the other side of the world, and nor was the travel so easy if you thought to go to Africa or India.

The first IAHR conference I went to was the one in Japan in 2005. I think prior to that it was in Durban, in South Africa.

That was when I first went, in 2000. Improved travel and technology has made it more possible.

Liberal Protestant Theology

Most phenomenologists seemed to come out of theology. I don't know of one who didn't.

I came out of theology. Well, Ninian Smart came out of philosophy. So, from theology or philosophy. I don't think many anthropologists became phenomenologists.

Although there is part of anthropology, a stage of fieldwork, that is phenomenological, but it was quite a different development, I think.

There are different ways in which phenomenology is a philosophy.

Otherwise it did come out of a liberal theological background.

And it's interesting when you do the comparison with schools, that the countries that pioneered multi-faith non-confessional RE were Sweden and Britain, in other words liberal Protestant countries, and then Norway and Denmark. It wasn't a communist country, nor a secular or anti-religious state that started it, or a Catholic country.

I would even say it was England rather than Britain and Sweden because I was in Scotland and it was different, more about individual experience [in the 1990s when I was planning to do teacher training].

And Northern Ireland was even more different. So, England and Sweden pioneered RE at the end of the 1960s, early 1970s. I don't think it's an accident, because liberal Protestant theology underpinned it, that part of that view of Christianity that you ought to look for the divine in these other traditions. But it didn't mean that everybody bought into that, or that every phenomenologist was a liberal Protestant because it grew out of that. It didn't mean you had to be a liberal Protestant, but I can see why Tim Fitzgerald thought so because so many phenomenologists were or had come from that background.

Particularly influential people. We talked about the study of religions in the RE context. But in terms of academic study, at least when I was studying religions at the University of Edinburgh it was still very much area studies. So Hinduism and Buddhism were taught by people who were in the South Asian department, Islam was taught by somebody from the Middle Eastern Studies department, so it was very much area studies people feeding into the study of religions degree. And I'm wondering if that type of approach – did it really help the discipline develop in its own right as a subject area? Or, are we still talking about one or two staff members in RS (Religious Studies) and then area studies specialists or theologians providing the rest?

It depended where you were. The study of religions probably didn't sweep the nation. And there weren't many – there were never many RS scholars, but it did help establish in people's minds that there was a discipline called Religious Studies or, as Brian Bocking when he was at Bath Spa called it, the Study of Religions, to make it plural, that is something that was not Theology and it's not Social Sciences, and it's not Area Studies. Actually, there were not many such departments.

And not many that actually had staff that were not Theology.

Because the RS staff did not exist. They weren't there to draw upon, but gradually it did happen between the 1970s and the 1990s. There were people who were appointed, and I think that phenomenology did help establish that, because that was something they were, and it was not Theology. So, there were either people who had converted, changing from being a theologian to being a phenomenologist, or there were people a bit younger than me who started off as phenomenologists. But in most places, it was added on – we call the subject now at University level in the UK, "Theology and Religious

Studies". So, in many places it was added on around the edges, with one or two staff members. So, you had a core of theologians and one or two people who were [RS] and it was still sort of "us and them", it was still what John Hull (1935–2015) calls "the fundamental distinction": there are theologians studying Christianity and then there's a phenomenologist studying everybody else. In a way now it's become sociologists of religion studying everybody else, I think.

It never really totally swept the nation and it was always added on to Theology, I think. You probably got more of it in the non-university sector before places like Bath Spa became universities, in these colleges of higher education where they were more linked to what was happening in schools. I think [in those places] you had more phenomenologists and studies of religions that wasn't Theology. It was a bit of an academic class system with less prestigious places doing Religious Studies, and more prestigious places doing Theology.

Well, I chose to do the PGCE in RE at Bath Spa because I looked specifically for "multicultural" approaches to RE. I was there in 1997–1998 when it was still a university college.

It didn't gain full university status until 2005.

I think I met you in passing when you came to welcome the students, but it was mainly with Jo Backus.

I started that course and taught it for the first two years alongside Jo. At that time I was doing a lot of work with Primary School RE, and I had to decide which to do. I thought Primary was a bit more flexible, so I focused more on that. Jo was appointed to do the Secondary.

It was such a wonderful, refreshing relief to me that she was a practising Buddhist because most of my lecturers at Edinburgh were Christian. Some were Quaker, but they were all one or another Christian denomination, and the main lecturer for Religious Studies was ordained.

That's where it's come from. It has taken a long time to shake that off, in a way. Jo's own background was at King's College London. She did Theology and Philosophy before she decided to study religions and before she became a Buddhist. These journeys of individuals and the journey of the subject is interesting.

It informs the way RS developed.

Re-evaluating Phenomenology of Religion

So, PoR cannot be underestimated in its influence on RE in England. This document called *Working Paper 36* (Schools Council 1971) was very influential. It was a Lancaster project under the direction of Ninian Smart. I still agree with most of what it says. That's where I came in and my training, my PGCE, and I thought "this is great". It was a massive sea-change in a way I don't think people nowadays can appreciate. A multi-faith and non-confessional approach. It was such a breath of fresh air. It did change religious education for the better. When I was a young teacher in the late 1970s, or more in the 1980s, I used to go to the Shap conferences on for example Buddhism and Hinduism — they were just fabulous. People don't do that sort of thing anymore and I think we're coming back to the need for it. People want to know something about religions, even if we don't want to put them in boxes.

There's been a move away from that in education perhaps. I don't know if that coincided with the rise of Philosophy and Ethics in schools…

Yes, it has.

Particularly Ethics has been so dominating.

I was never particularly keen on teaching Ethics.

I preferred empirical research. I enjoyed finding out about something.

So did I, which was probably why we've done what we did.

I never studied Ethics at school or university, but from what I've seen since — you get a lot of students' opinions, which are ill-informed.

That is why we were so keen on reforming the examinations in Religious Studies for school students at age 16 and age 18. It's not gone quite as we hoped, but we wanted some empirical information in there and not just "I think abortion is a good idea", because that's easy.

And easy for teachers. In terms of bringing back PoR, I've read criticisms that "lived religion" and "material religion" are PoR in disguise, repackaged.

I've not kept up with those. Where would I find this argument?

I read it most recently in a book edited by Aaron Hughes: *Theory in a Time of Excess* (2017). Russell McCutcheon mentioned it. As I was reading about it, I came to the same conclusion that this looks a lot like PoR.

You've got something there, about the "lived religion" being phenomenology in disguise, I can see it now you say it, because PoR never was *not* "lived religion". It wasn't just theory.

I guess that depends on what type of PoR it is.

One scholar said, "oh, cross out phenomenology" [at the meeting earlier]. I put it back in, because I think we need to admit that it was very influential. There's a paper going around from the Church of England that says religious studies/religious education is a mixture of theology, sociology and philosophy. And my response was, no, it's not. It really isn't. It is religious studies, which has its own identity as a discipline, although it is poly-methodic and draws upon methods from theology, sociology and philosophy as well as many others. Who should you ask about religion? One answer could be theologians, sociologists and philosophers. I would prefer to ask experts in Religious Studies. One problem is that theology, sociology and philosophy tend to be very "Western" in both content and methods.

Perhaps for sociologists it stems from this love of surveys. It's harder to do the ethnographic research. In surveys you can get their opinions and beliefs and such.

Ah, this is interesting. If you do it through quantitative questionnaire and survey models, it does focus on that, you're right, as opposed to lived experiences.

Not all sociologists of religion do this, of course, and others employ more qualitative and ethnographic approaches.

So, can we re-evaluate PoR now? Yes, with hindsight of the intervening decades we can see certain weaknesses, of things that need supplementing. I would always argue with my younger colleagues that it doesn't need to be thrown out: it needs to be supplemented. You could supplement it with feminist and postcolonial and ethnographic materials. But I would be afraid to lose from our study of religions the things that I appreciated about PoR. I would like to hang on to the *epoché* – trying to be fair and impartial, although nobody can be completely impartial, and no-one can be completely objective and we all come from somewhere, etc., but the attempt to be as fair as possible and the attempt to see it from a believer's point-of-view in so far as you can, relatively. You can't be absolutely objective.

Also, there are many believers, with many points of view.

Exactly. The many believers and not the one, one version. One dominant version. And the other thing that I've found that I haven't talked much about, which is the patterns – the typologies and dimensions – I've also found those useful in that from using those it stops you from thinking only about beliefs, because that's only one dimension. I liked Ninian Smart's stress on experience, though that seems to make it about individual autonomy but it's about an individual's experience as well as about – James Cox's "identifiable communities" with "postulated realities" — I like that, but I would want to put against it a more individual experience, about individuals dealing with "the significant limits of experience", I think from Philip Goodchild [philosopher of religion at Nottingham, cited in Bunt 2004]. So, there are individuals asking themselves what their life is all about as well as the traditions and communities. And an interaction between them.

Yes, otherwise it's just about the institutions. You would always then just get that authoritative dominant view of a very limited top-down point of view.

So, I want to put those two in a kind of creative tension with each other. The other good thing about PoR was what my students called "Smart's parts". I've often found those six (or eight) categories (the dimensions) are not categories of the same sort when I've been working with them — you can come up with your own categories. If you don't understand these concepts you're not going to get religion. I like the idea that it's not just beliefs, it's also about ritual, it's about things people do, it's about emotions, it's about art and music, and all the rest of it. And it's about scriptures, and social things, it's about identity and power — so this holistic thing with many different dimensions to it. Yes, you can pick out one of those and study it — "I'm a sociologist and I'm going to study the social dimension" — but then don't say "and that is it". I have loved phenomenology, I've loved the study of religion as a poly-methodic enterprise. Back when I was at school, I used to like all of the subjects. I enjoyed the sciences and the arts and the humanities. Studying religion in the way I have has allowed me to do a bit of everything.

It's been the same for me because I did consider studying other subjects at university, but I was interested in so many things, particularly in different cultures. I thought Religious Studies had everything.

So, it has the best bits of lots of different subjects.

You can study anything within religious studies. That's what I like about it.

And also through many different methods. So, you can focus on the bits that interest you.

You can see even among some colleagues how they meander through traditions, playing with different methods.

It's been interesting. And we're all still fascinated by it. And I'm now officially retired, but still very much involved.

If I get excited by a method, I can use it.

And if you get bored with it you can stop.

Looking at Cox's book, are there aspects you disagree with, particularly in the British chapter? I don't think he said enough about Ninian Smart.

No, possibly not. Again, it might be me. James Cox is writing from James Cox's experience and I was much more influenced by Ninian Smart. So, maybe I would have said more about Ninian Smart, because he is my big hero, really, and it was reading his book *The Religious Experience of Mankind* as well as *Working Paper 36*, that started me on both my RE and my Religious Studies pathways.

Is there a Smart book you would recommend today?

I like all his books on education, perhaps *Secular Education and the Logic of Religion*.

I suppose if I had written a chapter on PoR, there wouldn't have been so much on African studies, but then that was because I didn't study it at university, but I have enjoyed reading about it since. I had a colleague at Bath Spa who was a specialist in African Religion – it coincided with that IAHR in Durban, so I enjoyed reading Andrew Walls, but I wasn't reading that when I first started. I liked Cox's argument that the study of religion is a subject in its own right distinct from either theology or the social sciences.

Cox thought that what linked Walls and Smart and others was that they all advocated "sympathetic bracketing" as characterizing PoR in Britain.

And possibly that led into RE, where although you weren't promoting a particular belief system, there was a kind of "pro-religion" attitude. You would advocate for religion in general. That was rightly criticized by people like Andrew Wright – it could be rather anodyne "isn't it all nice", "we're all fairly similar" and "we don't need to fight each other". It's no more the job of a teacher to promote religion in general than it is to promote Christianity. There's been a lot of writing in RE about "critical realism" and religion being about "truth claims", to which I would always say, if you read Smart properly, it never wasn't about "truth claims". You can engage with the "truth claims", but a) one doesn't know the answer, and b) that's not the point of the study. You can evaluate it, but only later when you know something. There's a premature presentation to people of two sides of A4 of so-and-so thinks this and so-an-so thinks that, who's right?

Do you think there is any correlation between phenomenologists of religion and their religious affiliations?

Well, we said that with the liberal Protestants – there is a "natural affinity" between liberal Protestantism and phenomenology, though it's not a necessary connection. My own personal background, though I don't identify as such now, was Catholic. And there is a kind of Catholic openness to a variety of traditions which has a different feel about it. I started teaching in a Catholic School. They were fine about me teaching Hinduism and Buddhism. But there is a slightly different feel about it from the liberal Protestant context. I may have to go away and analyse what that is.

So, people tend to focus on the people they know. I would say I still find PoR useful – the reaction against PoR can go too far – and I still think it's got something to say that other ways of studying religion are not doing, and especially at the school level. I think sometimes the critique of phenomenology can be reactionary, which goes like this: from "nobody can be objective" to "you cannot possibly understand someone else", so therefore you might as well say, "this is what I'm saying and I'm right". At least a phenomenologist is trying to understand the "other" even if she may not completely succeed.

We should say "phenomenology-plus".

Can I say it's a "humble phenomenology"? An epistemologically humble phenomenology in that it recognizes that, but of course, I'll never totally understand this, of course, I can't be completely objective, and of course, I can't escape from my presumptions altogether, but I can to some extent at least try. A humble version of phenomenology, when it doesn't claim to have found the essence of anything. So that's what I would say.

I've noticed that when I am reading things written in English by people from other countries they use the word "scientifically" very much more widely than we do in Britain, and I think that a value in phenomenology is that you can study religions scientifically *and* sensitively. You can look at things empirically, which require evidence, but also with a kind of subjective sensitivity.

Certainly, that is one of the arguments for choosing religious studies at university and RE in schools is to develop sensitivity, whether or not we agree that it works.

There is some evidence that it works a bit – Leslie Francis, who researches RE at Warwick, for example, has provided quantitative evidence that students who study it academically, e.g. for GCSEs (examinations for 16-year-olds) in religious studies, have more positive attitudes to diversity (Francis et al. 2017). There is an effect. It does work a bit. Obviously, it doesn't turn everybody into love and peace overnight – who would expect it to?

Or even if it should.

Exactly – even if it should. That question is being discussed at school level and at academic level. Or is it a side effect? Could it be the aim of the subject to affect people's attitudes, or is it a kind of useful side effect? But we certainly use it as a selling point.

Problematizing "Religion"

Lastly, one of the problems of course is what we identify as "religion" came out of a modern European enlightenment perception and it doesn't really correlate well...

...with anything out there. That's what I'm finding very interesting as well. Perhaps that's become more sophisticated, so the critique of the notion of religion has become much more sophisticated, since the 1970s, since the birth of PoR. So, if you were doing phenomenology now, you would have to have a much more sophisticated understanding of the whole concept.

You'll have to take that into account.

And I think it's partly the growth of postcolonialism, as well as feminism, etc. It certainly doesn't work, if you define religion in one way it doesn't really work for anything except Christianity, because that's where they got the model from. So, this thing, the very concept of religion, I feel very strongly that we should start problematizing it from Day One with the youngest of children, saying "people call that religion", but why and what, and what does it mean?

So, even in RE it needs to be problematized?

Yes, right from Primary School. I feel very strongly that this... I did a paper at a conference recently at Brunel University and I was asked to come and address the issue of the concept of religion from a Dharmic perspective. I also added Pagan and other perspectives. It had a great title this conference: "The Forgotten Dimensions of Religious Education: Religion and Education". It sounds crazy, but you need to stop and ask, what is religion anyway? What's education anyway? Once you start that, it was really quite an exciting conference. So, we need to problematize it from the start. Sometimes I'm not even sure we can use the word.

We shouldn't dumb it down and then cause the damage that we can't undo.

Because once you set it up, and try to unpick it later, it doesn't work because the ideas had become fixed. "Religion" needs to be problematized right from the start.

Commentary

In the UK, and England in particular, the influence of Ninian Smart on Religious Studies at University and Religious Education in school should not be underestimated. In 1969, he was appointed Director of the Schools Council Secondary Project on Religious Education and in the same year, when he and others formed the Shap Working Party, they directed Religious Education away from a Christian-based confessional approach toward the inclusion of other religious perspectives in a religiously neutral setting. Smart also established the first independent Religious Studies department at Lancaster in 1967, as most universities taught it within a Theology or Divinity department. Later in his career, Smart spent part of his time in Santa Barbara and was elected president of the American Academy of Religion in 2000, the year before his death.

Smart's favoured approach to studying religions, or "worldviews" as he preferred, is by looking at their "dimensions", such as the ritual, experiential, mythic/narrative, doctrinal/philosophical, ethical, social and, added later, the material – all mutually dependent on one another. Human experience is at the centre of his broadly phenomenological model, following Gerardus van der Leeuw's comparative analysis in studying manifestations of religion (Smart 1997, 1). Smart acknowledges that the approach is different from philosophical phenomenology in that it combines the bracketing (*epoché*) with empathy, which he describes as "entering into the experiences and intentions of religious participants" (ibid., 2). His empathic phenomenological approach can be summarized in one of his most famous quotes from his book *The World's Religions*:

> To understand religious and secular worldviews and their practical meaning we have to use imagination. We have to enter into the lives of those for whom such ideas and actions are important. As the Native American proverb says, "Never judge a person until you have walked a mile in his moccasins."
>
> (Smart 1989, 10)

Smart's influence on Religious Studies at university level was more modest, mainly because there were very few Religious Studies positions and often only in departments dominated by theology and biblical studies. In addition, Religious Studies at university had more often followed an Area Studies model where scholars from other departments taught their own areas of expertise alongside each other, usually employing a historical and/or philological approach to a specific religion (or group of religions in particular contexts) where categorial assumptions were not always made explicit. More recently, philosophy of religion has been gaining ground in universities, partly as a result of the shift in focus toward philosophy and ethics in schools. Universities have responded by offering courses on philosophy, ethics and religion (with religion barely present except where it serves philosophy), often at the expense of both theology and the study of religion. This may have contributed to the study of religion diminishing as a subject at universities, though there may be other factors, such as the growth in Christian denominational colleges (which impacts theology as an academic subject), and the squeeze on Humanities subjects in general (which impacts religious studies).

In contrast, academic associations for the study of religion are still thriving. The British Association for the Study of Religions (BASR) regularly sees about an average of 70 delegates, with no significant drop in numbers, and the European Association for the Study of Religions (EASR) has seen a marked increase in recent years. Like the EASR, the BASR has moved to emphasize in its constitution non-confessional approaches to the study of religion. Certainly, the BASR has in more recent years taken on-board Fitzgerald's critique of the subject and seeks papers that avoid "ecumenical theology", with discourse analysis, critical religion (along the lines of Fitzgerald) and anthropological approaches now more common. Few academics participating at BASR conferences have developed PoR after Smart, though in the past Frank Whaling (Emeritus Professor of the Study of Religion at Edinburgh University), for example, had expanded upon Smart's work (Whaling 1995). In recent years, PoR, if not explicitly stated as an approach, is mostly found within anthropological studies of religion.

The BASR's main "competitor", however, is the Sociology of Religion Study Group (SocRel) of the British Sociological Association (BSA). Scholars involved in the latter have been more visible, especially as its focus is often religion in the "public sphere" in the UK, including the activities of Christian churches. There is some crossover of membership and a joint conference was held at St Mary's Twickenham in 1992.[4] More recently there was a joint panel with SocRel at the BASR conference in Winchester in 2012.

The academic study of religion, while less concerned with languages and texts, continues to diverge in its aims from religious education in schools where it can be influenced by changing government agendas toward multiculturalism, citizenship, engendering empathy, values, and so on. Yet, RE varies widely in the UK. Schools with a religious character often, though not exclusively, focus on religious education in a particular religion or denomination. RE in Secondary Schools without a religious character includes teaching about several religions as specified by their local Agreed Syllabus, though philosophy and ethics has been prevalent at examination level with older pupils. However, the recently revised A Level in Religious Education (for pupils aged 16–18) has sought to

---

4.   Thanks to Chris Cotter for information about BASR's joint conferences with SocRel.

re-introduce an in-depth hermeneutical dimension, in the drive to increase "religious literacy", including the study of at least one "religion" and/or biblical texts. It is too early to say whether this will lead to improved recruitment to theology and religious studies.

It is clear that more support for teachers of RE is needed and several RS scholars have responded to that need by providing CPD (Continuing Professional Development) and conferences, such as the one mentioned above by Denise Cush, for improving RE. An adaptation of PoR, with greater critical and ethnographic components, that also interrogates the categories it employs, may provide an engaging method that can raise the status of RE in schools and, by extension, RS in universities.

Suzanne Owen is a Reader at Leeds Trinity University, having gained her PhD in Religious Studies at the University of Edinburgh in 2007, and researches indigeneity in Newfoundland, British Druidry and the critical study of religion. Her monograph, *The Appropriation of Native American Spirituality*, was published by Continuum (now Bloomsbury Academic) in 2008.

References

Bunt, Gary R. 2004. "'Religious Studies – What's the Point' Conference." *Discourse* 3(2), 161–172.

Cole, W. Owen. 1981. *Five Religions in the Twentieth Century*. Cheltenham: Stanley Thornes.

Cole, W. Owen, with P. Morgan. 1984. *Six Religions in the Twentieth Century*. Cheltenham: Stanley Thornes.

Cox, James. 2006. *A Guide to the Phenomenology of Religion: Key Figures, Formative Influences and Subsequent Debates*. London: Continuum.

Cush, Denise. 1994. *Buddhism: A Student's Approach to World Religions*. London: Hodder Education.

Cush, Denise. 2016. "Without Fear or Favour: Equality and Diversity in the Treatment of Religions and Beliefs in Religious Education in England." In *Religion, Equalities and Inequalities*, edited by Dawn Llewellyn and Sonya Sharma, 102–112. Abingdon: Routledge.

Fitzgerald, Timothy. 2000. *Ideology of Religious Studies*. Oxford: Oxford University Press.

Flood, Gavin. 1999. *Beyond Phenomenology: Rethinking the Study of Religion*. London: Continuum.

Francis, Leslie J., Tania ap Siôn, Ursula McKenna and Gemma Penny. 2017. "Does Religious Education as an Examination Subject Work to Promote

Community Cohesion? An Empirical Enquiry among 14- to 15-Year-Old Adolescents in England and Wales." *British Journal of Religious Education* 39(3), 303–316. https://doi.org/10.1080/01416200.2015.1128392

Hughes, Aaron W. (ed.). 2017. *Theory in a Time of Excess: Beyond Reflection and Explanation in Religious Studies Scholarship*. London: Equinox.

Owen, Suzanne. 2011. "The World Religions Paradigm: Time for a Change." *Arts and Humanities in Higher Education* 10(3), 253–268. https://doi.org/10.1177/1474022211408038

Schools Council. 1971. *Working Paper 36: Religious Education in the Secondary School*. London: Evans/Methuen Educational.

Sharpe, Eric J. 1975. *Comparative Religion: A History*. London: Duckworth.

Smart, Ninian. 1968. *Secular Education and the Logic of Religion*. London: Faber & Faber.

Smart, Ninian. 1971. *The Religious Experience of Mankind*. London: Fontana

Smart, Ninian. 1989. *The World's Religions: Old Traditions and Modern Transformations*. Cambridge: Cambridge University Press.

Smart, Ninian. 1997. *Dimensions of the Sacred: An Anatomy of the World's Beliefs*. London: Fontana.

Whaling, Frank (ed.). 1995. *Theory and Method in Religious Studies. Contemporary Approaches to the Study of Religions*. Berlin: Mouton de Gruyter.

Wright, Andrew. 2007. *Critical Religious Education, Multiculturalism and the Pursuit of Truth*. Cardiff: University of Wales Press.

10

"There Was No Dutch School of Phenomenology of Religion"

Academic Implacability and Historical Accidents – An Interview with Jan G. Platvoet (The Netherlands)

MARKUS ALTENA DAVIDSEN

Jan G. Platvoet was born in Oldenzaal, in the Dutch province of Overijssel, in 1935. Platvoet initially trained in Roman Catholic (Philosophy and) Theology at the Major Seminary of the Society for African Missions (*Societas Missionum ad Afros*, SMA) from 1954 to 1961, after which he was ordained to the priesthood. From 1961 to 1966 he worked as a missionary in Ghana, and then returned to the Netherlands to study missiology and anthropology of religion at the Roman Catholic University at Nijmegen. In 1969, he was granted dispensation from celibacy and married An Mercx, a midwife and nurse whom he had met in Ghana. The same year, Platvoet was offered the post of Assistant Professor in the Science of Religion at the Roman Catholic University College of Theology at Utrecht where he worked closely together with the staff of the Section for the Science of Religion at (the public) Utrecht University. He defended his PhD thesis, "Comparing Religions: A Limitative Approach: An Analysis of Akan, Para-Creole, and Ifo-Sananda Rites and Prayers", in 1982 at Utrecht University, and was appointed Associate Professor at Leiden University in 1991 where he taught until his retirement in 2000. Platvoet was instrumental in the foundation of the African Association for the Study of Religions (AASR). He was appointed IAHR Life Honorary Member in 2013.

Keywords: phenomenology of religion, history of the study of religion, comparison, Gerardus van der Leeuw, Theo van Baaren, the Netherlands

Introduction

This chapter contains an interview with Jan G. Platvoet, a retired Associate Professor from Leiden University, about the rise and fall of the phenomenology of religion (PoR) in the Netherlands (c.1877–1973). Reviewing the complex history from Tiele and Chantepie de la Saussaye through Van der Leeuw to Bleeker and Waardenburg, Platvoet points out several overlooked facts of crucial importance for the history of the study of religion. As a corrective to Anglophone scholarship Platvoet stresses that Dutch PoR developed independently of and prior to Husserl's philosophical phenomenology, and he points out that Van der Leeuw only reluctantly accepted the title *Phänomenologie der Religion* for the German translation of his first introduction to the history of religion. More surprising, perhaps, is the fact that there was very little interaction among the Dutch phenomenologists of religion, and that both Van der Leeuw and Waardenburg, despite their international fame, were academically isolated figures in the Netherlands where they had little influence and no academic heirs. The absence of a "Dutch school" made possible the rapid collapse of Dutch PoR during the 1970s. Platvoet never practised PoR himself, but joined the anthropologically inspired assault on this approach that was launched by Theo van Baaren and others in the 1950s, 1960s and 1970s. Within his own generation, Platvoet has been the one to most passionately promote a new, strictly secular and methodologically agnostic comparative science of religion(s) in the Netherlands.

The interview took place in English in Jan Platvoet's home in Bunnik on 20 June 2018.

Platvoet at Utrecht: A Young Scholar Witnesses the Demise of Dutch Phenomenology of Religion

Markus Altena Davidsen: Perhaps it would be good to start this interview by clarifying your own position as a scholar of religion in relation to PoR. Are you a phenomenologist of religion yourself? And if not, how does your own approach compare to PoR?

Jan G. Platvoet: I never considered myself a phenomenologist of religion. I regard PoR a part of the history of the Dutch study of religions – an important and remarkable part – but I have never practised it myself, nor taught it to students other than as a part of the history of Dutch science of religions.[1] Rather, I played, belatedly, a small part in its demise and dissuaded students actively from practising it. The type of science of religion that I have practised myself and which I have trained my students to practise, is of the anthropological and methodologically agnostic kind that was introduced in the Netherlands by Theo van Baaren (1912–1989), among others, in direct opposition to PoR.[2]

So you are an anti-phenomenologist! Did you revolt against phenomeno-logical teachers of your own, just as Van Baaren revolted against Gerardus van der Leeuw, or were you trained in what had already become a post-phenomenological climate?

Neither. It might surprise those who cherish the Dutch contribution to the international PoR, but I myself was not introduced at all to PoR during my studies at Nijmegen in the late 1960s. This was not, however, because PoR had disappeared in the Netherlands by then. The towering figure of Dutch PoR, Gerardus van der Leeuw, had died in 1950, but phenomenologists of re-ligion continued to hold professorships, most importantly C. Jouco Bleeker in Amsterdam.[3] The fact that I remained ignorant about PoR had everything to do with the "pillarized" (i.e. segregated) past of the Dutch university system.[4] Right from the time of Cornelis Petrus Tiele (1830–1902; Leiden), Pierre Daniël Chantepie de la Saussaye (1848–1920; Amsterdam, later Leiden) and William Brede Kristensen (1867–1953; Leiden), via Gerardus van der Leeuw (1890–1950; Groningen) and until its fizzling out in the 1960s and 1970s, PoR was practised only at the four public universities in the Netherlands (Leiden, Groningen, Utrecht and Amsterdam) which were neutral in name but Protestant in practice.[5] PoR taught at these universities was a science of

---

1. Platvoet prefers the term "science of religion(s)", the direct translation of Dutch *godsdienstwetenschap* (cf. German *Religionswissenschaft*) which signals disciplinary coherence and explanatory ambition, to the vaguer "study of religion(s)". Throughout the interview, however, both terms were used interchangeably by both interviewer and interviewee.
2. Van Baaren was Van der Leeuw's successor in Groningen, where he was Professor of Science of Religion from 1952 to 1980. He was also one of Platvoet's two PhD supervisors and the one who most strongly influenced Platvoet's own methodological position.
3. Bleeker (1898–1983) was Professor of History of Religion and PoR at the University of Amsterdam from 1946 to 1969. He served as general secretary of the IAHR from 1950 to 1970 and as editor of *Numen* from 1960 to 1975.
4. On the pillarized nature of the early Dutch science of religion, see Platvoet (2002).
5. From 1876 to 2007, theology at the state universities in Leiden, Groningen and Utrecht and at the municipal University of Amsterdam was organized according to the so-called *duplex ordo* system. This system entailed that the state-appointed professors of theology responsible for teaching such subjects as exegesis, church

religions seen through a Protestant lens that recognized the other religions as fellow religions but insisted on the superiority of the Christian faith.

But I did not study at one of these universities. I had been trained and ordained as a Roman Catholic priest and had worked in Ghana where I had fallen in love with a Dutch nurse, An, whom I would later marry. When we returned from Ghana in mid-1966, my superiors requested that I enrol in the graduate programme in missiology at the Roman Catholic University at Nijmegen. There, as well as at the Free University at Amsterdam – the other Dutch church-affiliated confessional university – the Faculty of Theology was organized after the *simplex ordo*, dogmatic and pastoral theology being its heart and not removed to its margin, as they were in the *duplex ordo* faculties of theology. Until the 1950s, Christianity had in the two confessional universities been regarded as the one true faith – and all other religions as superstitions – following the orthodox *vera/falsa religio* dichotomy. Missiology, therefore, held a central place in these universities, with science of religions, and especially anthropology of religion, as its handmaids. By the mid-1960s, however, the traditional view of other religions as ways of perdition had been replaced at Nijmegen, with full formal approval of Vatican II (1962–1965), by a liberal *theologia religionum* that accepted other religions as co-religions and aimed at developing a "dialogue" with them.

Rather than to PoR, I was introduced, during my two-and-a-half-year graduate study in missiology, to social anthropology, particularly to the study of the preliterate indigenous religions of pre-colonial and colonial sub-Saharan Africa. It was for that reason that I was offered the post as Junior Lecturer in the Science of Religions in 1969 here at Utrecht[6] at the newly founded Katholieke Theologische Hogeschool (at) Utrecht (KThU; Roman Catholic University College of Theology at Utrecht), because the KThU was entering into a close alliance with the (Protestant) Faculty of Theology of Utrecht University (UU), the two planning to merge all teaching and research other than in dogmatic and pastoral theology. The KThU therefore needed research and teaching complementing that of the Section for the Science of Religion

---

history and history of religions were situated in the universities' faculties of theology, whereas the professors appointed by the Dutch Reformed Church to teach dogmatic and pastoral theology were located in an adjunct department outside the theological faculties, and so were teaching *at,* but not *in* them. In practice, however, until the 1950s the state-appointed professors were themselves members of, and loyal to, the Dutch Reformed Church (C. P. Tiele, an Arminian, was an exception). On the *duplex ordo* system, see Platvoet (1998a).

6.   Jan Platvoet's home in Bunnik, where the interview took place, is situated just on the outskirts of Utrecht. The Uithof, the out-of-town campus of Utrecht University, where the KThU and the Utrecht Faculty of Theology were relocated in 1969, was visible from his garden, beyond cornfields and a line of tall trees.

(*vakgroep godsdienstwetenschap*) of the UU Faculty of Theology, to which I was seconded with the task of developing research and teaching in preliterate religions, particularly those of sub-Saharan Africa. The section at the UU consisted of two full professors: the Indologist Prof. Dirk Jan Hoens (1920–2003; Prof. 1964–1982) and the Egyptologist Prof. Jan Zandee (1914–1991; Prof. 1968–1982), and a Senior Lecturer, the Islamologist with a special interest in PoR, Dr Jacques Waardenburg (1930–2015; Senior Lecturer 1968–1975; Lector 1975–1980; Prof. of Islam and PoR 1980–1987).

Koos Waardenburg[7] had just come back from the United States a year before and wanted to propagate a new form of PoR.[8] To this end, and to prepare a series of publications on the history of Dutch PoR (Waardenburg 1972, 1973–1974), Waardenburg organized a graduate seminar, together with Hoens, and I was invited to participate. Throughout the years 1969 and 1970 we had papers on all major Dutch phenomenologists. There were five papers on Van der Leeuw, and one each on P. D. Chantepie de la Saussaye, W. Brede Kristensen, K. A. H. Hidding,[9] C. Jouco Bleeker and Theo van Baaren. The latter three were invited to come and to comment on the paper on their work and to discuss it with us. By then, Van Baaren already had the reputation as the one who was destroying Van der Leeuw's work and position. He had just published, a year before, an article in German on *systematische Religionswissenschaft* (systematic science of religion) which he proposed as the replacement for PoR (Van Baaren 1969).[10]

You say that Van Baaren was a crucial figure for the demise of PoR in the Netherlands. But you also just said that he was one of the living phenomenologists attending Waardenburg's graduate seminar. So was he a phenomenologist or not?

Van Baaren went through a long process of emancipating himself from the PoR that he had been trained in by H. W. Obbink at Utrecht University.[11] Like many other Dutch scholars of religion specializing in ancient religions,

---

7. In Dutch, Waardenburg's first name, Jacobus, can be colloquially abbreviated to Koos.

8. We return to Waardenburg's neo-phenomenology later in the interview.

9. Hidding (1902–1986) was Professor of History of Religion and PoR at Leiden University between 1948 and 1972.

10. A few years later, Van Baaren laid out his position in more detail in Van Baaren (1973). We discuss Van Baaren's programme later in the interview.

11. Hendrik Willem Obbink (1898–1979) was Professor of General History of Religion and Egyptian Language and Literature at the Utrecht Faculty of Theology from 1939 to 1968. Van Baaren enrolled in the Utrecht Faculty in 1938. As a "lapsed" Roman Catholic and an agnostic, Van Baaren did not study in the conservative Utrecht Faculty of Theology with the aim of becoming a minister, but with the ambition to embark on an academic career in science of religion and Egyptology. After

Van Baaren was trained as an Egyptologist, but among his many publications was only one (popularizing) book on Egyptian religion, *Mensen tussen Nijl en zon* (Van Baaren 1963). Increasingly, he became interested instead in the religions of what was then referred to as "the primitives", and as a result it was the anthropology of religion, including the works of Evans-Pritchard and Geertz, that delivered him his tools for analysis. In his famous, programmatic book *Wij mensen: religie en wereldbeschouwing bij schriftloze volken* (1960, e.g. 9–22), Van Baaren criticized Van der Leeuw's notion of primitive religion and introduced instead the more neutral term "religion of illiterate societies". This was part of his attack on Van der Leeuw's essentializing and normative idea that there exist two distinctly different mentalities, the primitive mentality and the modern mentality, of which all humans have some combination.

Van Baaren was strongly opposed to what he saw as prejudices within Van der Leeuw's system. He attacked not only Van der Leeuw's notion of a primitive mentality, but also, for example, his emphasis on dynamism – the idea that the experience of an impersonal, divine power is the core and origin of religion – and the idea that therefore God was a *Spätling* – a latecomer – in the history of religions. Van Baaren went through a long process during the 1950s and 1960s in which he abandoned his phenomenological training and re-invented himself as an anthropologist of religion. And moreover, Van Baaren was, from his youth onwards, an agnostic, and therefore took from the outset a completely different outlook on the world of human religions than Van der Leeuw. Van der Leeuw was a theologian, and he was interested in developing PoR in such a way that it fitted into the training that he had to give students in the Faculty of Theology.

The Rise of the Phenomenology of Religion at Leiden University: C. P. Tiele's Evolutionism and Chantepie de la Saussaye's Typological Phenomenology

We are already discussing the decline of PoR in the Netherlands. We need to do that, but perhaps we should first take a step back and look at the emergence of PoR in the Netherlands, around such figures as Chantepie de la Saussaye. If we then go through the history of PoR in the Netherlands we will get to Van der Leeuw and Van Baaren's revolt against him.

---

graduating in 1945, Van Baaren became Obbink's research assistant, which enabled him to prepare his PhD thesis.

The Dutch phenomenologists of religion – beginning with Chantepie and including Van der Leeuw himself and later Bleeker and Hidding – were professors of the history of religions who needed, in addition to their historical work, some comparative mode of studying religions. It was to this end that Chantepie included, in the first volume of his famous *Lehrbuch der Religionsgeschichte*, a section called "Phänomenologischer Teil" (1887, 48–170).[12] What he here offers is no more than a system of categories that were understandable for theologians. Look here [Platvoet points to the table of contents].

I see such categories as magic, sacrifice and prayer that theologians would be familiar with. These categories are either part of the Christian tradition (such as prayer) or of the form of Judaism that Christianity reacted against (such as sacrifice).

Exactly. Chantepie took these Christian terms and turned them into comparative categories that helped identify similar elements in other religions. Later phenomenologists, whenever they encountered something that did not fit in the established system, simply added new categories, such as taboo and mana. The idea was that when the outside world, studied by anthropologists of religion, taught us new things, we might add a few new categories, but mostly the phenomenological system worked with categories that were intuitive and useful for modern theologians for comparing Christianity to other religions.

So Chantepie's phenomenology was a tool for comparison?

It was a tool for comparison and no more than that. But it is important to stress that Chantepie developed his typological phenomenology in opposition to Tiele. Tiele also compared, but his strategy was genetic, ordering religions from lowest to highest, the latter being adoration of God – his own idea of the ultimate, supreme religion, to which the history of mankind would necessarily develop, by laws discovered by him. As a result, all humans would ultimately, at some time in the future, adhere to this supreme religion.

So in Tiele's view we have not only comparison, but also an evolutionary – even a teleological – aspect which is given a normative interpretation, with Christianity – and in particular his own liberal Christianity – as the highest and best?

---

12. For a long time this book, which was also translated into English and French, was an international standard work for teaching history of religions within the new discipline (Stausberg 2007, 309–310).

Absolutely. And for Tiele, this evolutionarily inspired history of religions was so natural that he thought that it might replace dogmatic theology, and that his own science of religion would eventually incorporate even practical theology (cf. Platvoet 1998a, 120). But all the "seminary things" that could not be incorporated into his new system – apologetics, polemics and dogmatic theology – would have to be thrown out of the university.

Tiele, by the way, was one of the architects of the university law of 1876 that established the *duplex ordo* system into the Dutch faculties of theology (cf. Platvoet 1998a, 115–126). During the 1860s and 1870s, Dutch politicians were debating heatedly how to structure the theological faculties, and most of the influential figures were rich Arminians, including Van Heemskerk.[13]

The minister of education who saw the law of 1876 through Parliament?

Yes. Ultimately, Tiele's radical ideas were not accepted and there was a compromise. Practical and dogmatic theology [the "seminary stuff"] were given a place at separate divinity schools adjoined to the faculties of theology, thus installing the *duplex ordo* system. And then a new discipline was introduced with the 1876 law, namely the general history of religions (*de Geschiedenis der Godsdiensten in het algemeen*), which included both the historical and comparative study of religions.

Of all the non-Christian religions?

Yes, but in the service of the Christian religion.[14] And also philosophy of religion was introduced as a new subject, as the *duplex ordo* replacement of dogmatic theology – formerly called *doctrina de deo* and natural theology. Now a new kind of trinity was introduced with history of religions, the comparative study of religion, and philosophy of religion. But mind you that the comparative study of religion did not yet go under the name PoR.

Chantepie developed his systematic form of comparison against Tiele's evolutionary type of comparison. Originally, Chantepie, after having earned his doctorate at Utrecht University had been appointed Professor of the History of Religions at the University of Amsterdam. Contrary to the old state

---

13. The Arminians (*Remonstrantse Broederschap*) constitute a small, liberal Protestant church, whose members have been very influential in Dutch religious, cultural and political life. The Arminian ministers were trained at the Arminian Seminary, which in 1873 moved from the University of Amsterdam back to Leiden University from which Arminian theologians had been expelled in 1619. From 1877, Tiele held a double appointment as professor at both Leiden University and the Arminian Seminary.

14. This is most visible in the case of Judaism: Old Testament Israelite religion and Hellenistic Judaism were carefully studied, but Rabbinic Judaism was in practice excluded from the new discipline.

universities in Leiden, Utrecht and Groningen, the University of Amsterdam had been a so-called Athenaeum Illustre, an academic institution without the right to grant academic degrees, and had only very recently, in 1877, become a (municipality) university itself with the right to grant the doctorate degree. Therefore, when the chair in Ethics became vacant in Leiden in 1899, Chantepie gave up his chair in Amsterdam and moved to the more prestigious Leiden University where he became a direct competitor of Tiele who held the chair in the History of Religions there.

Just to get it straight: when we compare Tiele and Chantepie you say that only Tiele operated with an evolutionary scheme in addition to the typological approach of Chantepie. But that is not to say that Chantepie was less normative. Would you even say that Chantepie was more normative in the way that he saw Christianity as more true than the other religions?

Absolutely. You see, the phenomenologist Chantepie (Pierre Daniël Chantepie de la Saussaye) was the son of another famous Chantepie (Daniël Chantepie de la Saussaye) who had briefly – 1872–1874 – been a professor of theology in Groningen where he had been the front man of a new theological modality in Dutch reformed theology, the so-called ethical-irenic modality. The modalities in the Dutch Reformed Church began to form around this time, and all the professors of the *duplex ordo* faculties of theology were linked to one of the modalities. They had to train ministers for a particular modality, for in the early twentieth century the modalities had become so strong that you could not obtain a ministry unless you were a member of the association of the ministers of the modality to which a particular congregation belonged. The ethical-irenic modality was one of several reactions to the liberal or modern theology of the likes of Tiele, Abraham Kuenen (1828–1891), and others, that reigned in Leiden. Utrecht was dominated by the right-of-centre confessional modality, and Groningen had the middle-of-the road ethical theology which was open to comparative science of religion, but against what they called the rationalism of modern theology (see Platvoet 2002, 85–86). Chantepie brought this middle-of-the road theology to Leiden, and when Van der Leeuw studied in Leiden, from 1908 to 1913, he had two mentors, namely Kristensen who supervised his dissertation[15] and Chantepie who formed his theological views.

---

15. Like Kristensen and Van Baaren, Van der Leeuw was an Egyptologist. He defended his dissertation, "Godsvoorstellingen in de oud-Aegyptische pyramidetexten" ["Conceptions of God in Ancient Egyptian Pyramid Texts"], in 1916.

Gerardus van der Leeuw in his Dutch Context

To what extent did Chantepie's ethical theology influence Van der Leeuw?

To a very large extent. As I said, Groningen was the centre of the ethical modality and when Van der Leeuw obtained the chair for History of Religions at Groningen in 1918, he came there not only as a historian of religion and as a phenomenologist, but also as the new front man of ethical theology. Van der Leeuw even became the president, in the same year, of the association for ministers of the ethical modality, and was later president of the Ethical Association (*Ethische Vereniging*). Willem Hofstee (1997, 46) tells this story in his biography of Van der Leeuw.

So we have arrived now at Van der Leeuw, whom most scholars of religion probably consider the most influential figure in the Dutch PoR. You have written on Van der Leeuw's work and a couple of things struck me reading that. You emphasize Van der Leeuw's tendency to reconfessionalize PoR and to stress that Christianity is more true and pure than the other religions. Furthermore, and related to this, you identify two additional axioms in his work, namely that man is religious by nature, and that God or the divine or *das Ganz Andere* exists and that religion is the human response to that postulated unseen "reality" (e.g. Platvoet 1998a, 130–133). What I am wondering now is whether these two axioms were already present, either explicitly or implicitly, in the work of Tiele and Chantepie. Or whether they were additions of Van der Leeuw.

I do not think they were additions. Certainly Tiele developed a view of religious evolution that necessarily had to end in the type of religion that he himself confessed. So Tiele was, contrary to what Donald Wiebe (1991) has claimed, just as inspired by his own theology as were Chantepie and Van der Leeuw (see Platvoet 1998a, 144n55). Even those phenomenologists of religion who were not trained as theologians – Kristensen and Hidding – were still inspired by their personal theological views and considered Christianity the supreme religion.[16]

It has often been pointed out that Van der Leeuw's PoR introduced two Husserlian concepts, that of *epoché* and that of eidetic vision or eidetic intuition. That is true, but for Van der Leeuw *epoché* was merely jargon that meant nothing else than "try to be objective" and describe religions as the believers practise and live them without condemning them. And then, after

---

16. Kristensen studied history of ancient religions; Hidding studied Oriental philology. Even so, Hidding (but not the Lutheran Kristensen) occasionally functioned as a minister in the Dutch Reformed Church.

you have done this historical work, move on to comparison, either in the evolutionary way (as Tiele did, and Hidding does this again)[17] or in a more systematic way (like Chantepie) that uncovers an intuition – an *eidos* – or a structure or essence as Van der Leeuw calls it – of a phenomenon that can be further worked on by the philosopher of religion – philosophy of religion here becomes the *duplex ordo* variety of dogmatic theology – or by the theologian. Both Kristensen and Van der Leeuw still accepted this tri-unity of history of religions, the comparative (or phenomenological) study of religion, and the philosophy of religion. With the law of 1876 these three disciplines were tied closely together at Leiden University – and the University of Groningen – with both Tiele and later Kristensen being appointed at Leiden to teach all three.[18]

Van der Leeuw, however, effectively replaced philosophy of religion with his own ethical theology within this tri-unity, and he did that explicitly already in his inaugural lecture in 1918 (cf. Platvoet 1998a, 130–133).[19] So throughout his academic career as an Egyptologist and historian of religion at Groningen, Van der Leeuw joined history of religion, PoR and his own ethical theology together.

I should add that some decades after Van der Leeuw's appointment in Groningen, the ethical modality started to crumble. Van der Leeuw remained a theologian, and developed a very personal, Christocentric theology in reaction to the huge problems in European politics that he witnessed – Hitler, the Second World War and so on. It was this personal theology that influenced his history of religion and PoR.

Would you say that it was Van der Leeuw's theology that delivered the ontological axioms for his PoR, such as the religious nature of man, the reality of *das ganz Andere*, and the superiority of Christianity?

Yes.

---

17. We return to Hidding's evolutionary PoR later in the interview.
18. Tiele's initial appointment to teach general history of religions required him to teach both the history of the individual religions and comparative science of religion. In addition, he was charged, from 1891, with teaching philosophy of religion (actually, the "history of the doctrine about God"). Tiele's successor, Kristensen, had a similar appointment, but ignored the philosophy of religion and was formally relieved from it in 1925 when he was given a new commission to teach history of religions and PoR ("*De Geschiedenis der Godsdiensten en de Phaenomenologie van den Godsdienst*"). Cf. Molendijk (2005, 34–35).
19. Curiously, and in contrast to Kristensen, Van der Leeuw's formal appointment did not mention PoR. His initial commission (which was identical to and probably inspired by Tiele's) was to teach history of religions and the history of the doctrine about god (1918), and this was supplemented with encyclopedia of divinity (from 1922) and Egyptology (from 1926) (Hofstee 1997, 42–43).

Was it also an additional aim for Van der Leeuw, as it was for the Danish phenomenologist of religion Edvard Lehmann (1862–1930), to separate the gold from the dross in the inferior, non-Christian religions (as Lehmann put it)?

Yes. Lehmann was one of the phenomenologists of religion that inspired Van der Leeuw.

Because his theology later in his life was not tied to any of the major currents in Dutch theology, Van der Leeuw had very few students and was, academically, and certainly as a theologian, quite a lonely figure. He of course wrote a great deal, and in 1940 he became also a confessional, church-appointed professor of liturgy and played an important role in the liturgical renewal in the Dutch Reformed Church. Also in other ways, he played a role in the management of the church, and he became minister of education after the Second World War (1945–1946) for the Labour Party (*Partij van de Arbeid*). But his PoR did not have any real effect in the Netherlands outside Groningen, and even there he had very few students. It contributed to his academic isolation that the church in 1923 appointed [Theodorus Lambertus] Haitjema (1888–1972), a Barthian, as Professor of Dogmatics in Groningen, and that Hendrik Kraemer (1888–1965), also a Barthian and a missiologist, succeeded Kristensen in 1937 as Professor of History of Religion in Leiden. Karl Barth became *the* great source of inspiration for the church-appointed Dutch dogmatic theologians in the 1920s, 1930s and 1940s, and therefore the PoR which Van der Leeuw developed, and the theology by which it was inspired, remained a minor affair in a remote corner in the Dutch theological world. Van der Leeuw's PoR did not find any resonance in the Netherlands.

Was that because Van der Leeuw's PoR, with its emphasis on experience, focused on the human response to the divine, whereas Barth and the Barthians focused on God's revelation that comes "*Senkrecht von Oben*" ["vertically from above"]?

Yes. And Van der Leeuw explicitly excludes that element, revelation, from his phenomenology as something the phenomenologist cannot say anything about.

Van der Leeuw's Limited Influence on the Next Generation

So perhaps Van der Leeuw's influence was stronger outside of the Netherlands than within?

Absolutely.

Even so: is it really the case that Van der Leeuw had so little impact in the Netherlands? You say that he was a lonely figure in Groningen. But surely he was not the last phenomenologist of religion in the Netherlands. You have mentioned Bleeker (in Amsterdam) and Hidding (in Leiden) who both belong to the generation of phenomenologists after Van der Leeuw (and who had formal appointments as phenomenologists of religion). Did Van der Leeuw not influence these scholars?

Hardly, though the teleology that Van der Leeuw formulated, for the general course of the religious history of humankind, was found also in the work of Bleeker who talks of the *entelecheia* of religion: the energy inherent in religions that drives them to their final and full destiny. Bleeker here comes into problems with the principle of *epoché* [to which he explicitly adhered but here seems not to follow] because he tries to discern the historical logic through which imperfect and impure forms of religion necessarily develop into the perfect religion (e.g. Bleeker 1970, cf. Waardenburg 1972, 183–190 and Cox 2006, 126–136).

The same goes for Hidding. Hidding was the only one in Dutch PoR who seriously tried to develop a philosophical anthropology as a substrate for his PoR. Also for him, the evolution of religion necessarily leads up to the religion of love, which is Christianity (cf. Waardenburg 1972, 190–196).

Both Bleeker and Hidding were influenced by Van der Leeuw, but they were not his students. The one student that he did have, Fokke Sierksma (1917–1977), rebelled against him. Sierksma was considered too radical in his criticism of his phenomenological upbringing to succeed Van der Leeuw – and he was even rumoured to be an atheist, although he was not one in my view (cf. Platvoet 1998b, 334–338).

In an article, you describe Sierksma as a "post-Christian believer."

Yes. And then there is Van Baaren, who eventually succeeded Van der Leeuw in Groningen [in 1952]. He started his rebellion against Van der Leeuw by writing his dissertation (Van Baaren 1951), which he defended here in Utrecht, on the topic of revelation – a topic that Van der Leeuw considered beyond the bounds of the study of religion.

Did Van der Leeuw's PoR at least not influence Bleeker?

No. Bleeker was formed by Kristensen and was a modern or liberal minister [where Van der Leeuw was ethical/mainstream] in the Achterhoek [the easternmost part of the province Gelderland]. There he started to write little booklets on PoR, but developed a system completely independent of that of Van der Leeuw. He of course knew Van der Leeuw, and he must have read Van der Leeuw. But you see, there was virtually no interaction or correspondence between the two. So in the Netherlands there were important individual phenomenologists, but there was no Dutch school of PoR.

Even if there was no single school, does it not go too far to say that there was no institutionalization of PoR at all? Were there perhaps more than one Dutch school of PoR?

No. Kristensen's teaching on PoR, as later translated into English by Carman (Kristensen 1960), is more of a deconstructive phenomenology than a constructive one like Van der Leeuw's. When Kristensen looks at categories used for comparison, he deconstructs them in order to show that whatever we think to be true of some category in general, does not hold up in lots of individual cases in the history of ancient Mediterranean religions – which was his main area of expertise. He asks us to be acutely aware of all the historical differences. So Kristensen remains a deconstructionist historian of religion in his phenomenology.

Would you say that Kristensen is more empirical then?

He is much more empirical.

But he is still a phenomenologist in so far that he finds it useful – necessary – to have certain comparative concepts, even if they mainly help us highlight differences between similar historical cases?

Yes, but Kristensen limited himself exclusively to ancient religions. He could not do anything with primitive religions, he said, for that material was so far removed from his expertise that he could not understand it. And he did not trust at all the reliability of whatever data had been collected about them.

For good reasons!

For good reasons, yes. But Van der Leeuw, by contrast, used this material uncritically to build his own dynamistic system around notions of mana or the power, this impersonal divine force that Van der Leeuw considered the primitive starting point of "religion" in the evolution of religious history. Kristensen restricted himself to the researchable religions, on which he had what he called secure data.

Van der Leeuw founded the NGG, the *Nederlands Genootschap van Godsdiensthistorici* (now *Nederlands Genootschap voor Godsdienstwetenschap*; the Dutch Association for the Study of Religion) in 1947. The association still cherishes his memory and every other year hands out the Gerardus van der Leeuw Dissertation Award. Of course the NGG was founded only three years before Van der Leeuw's death in 1950, but I still wonder whether the association played any role as a platform for PoR.

Not as far as I am aware of. Van der Leeuw's limited influence on his Dutch colleagues is perhaps also due to the fact that he was quite content with his relative isolation in Groningen. He refused all offers for positions elsewhere. In fact, he was happy not to have many students; happy that he only needed to teach a little bit and could write a lot.

"Phänomenologie der Religion was a Historical Accident"*

But there is another thing that we have not yet touched upon, and that is that the very term *Phänomenologie der Religion* was a historical accident.

What do you mean?

See, Van der Leeuw had published a booklet in Dutch in 1924 called *Inleiding tot de Godsdienstgeschiedenis* – in English *Introduction to the History of Religion*. This was Van der Leeuw's first introduction to the science of religion. But everyone knows this book only in its second edition from 1948 where it is called *Inleiding tot de phaenomenologie van den godsdienst* – *Introduction to the Phenomenology of Religion*. It was Van der Leeuw's German publisher, Ernst Reinach, and his editor, Friedrich Heiler, who persuaded Van der Leeuw to use the title *Einführung in die Phänomenologie der Religion* for the first German edition in 1925. This German translation was the first academic publication to carry the title "Phenomenology of Religion". And Heiler wrote a preface in which he did two things. He says first that the book is appearing in a new series edited by him (on *"Christentum und Fremdreligionen"*; "Christianity and the Non-Christian Religions") aiming to enhance the *Frömmigkeit* (piety) of the readers, and he points out, second, that the Dutch professor Gerardus van der Leeuw ends his book with a confession of his belief in Jesus Christ. Heiler really overdid it. He continues to cite, at the end of his preface, the entire credo in Latin. He really turns his preface into a laudation of the Christian inspiration of PoR by Van der Leeuw.

But is that unfair? Is that not the position which Van der Leeuw himself takes in the book?

It is, it is. You can find it in several places. But Van der Leeuw brought with him from his *duplex ordo* theology that he must be restrained. He confesses his own Christian belief therefore only guardedly. He would never confess it as explicitly, as exuberantly, as Heiler did it for him. It would be helpful to compare the different editions and translations of this book and see how they differ and how explicitly Van der Leeuw's theological inspiration is presented in them.

But the other thing that is important in this booklet is that Heiler added a footnote to his preface, stating explicitly that Van der Leeuw had made him add that the title, "Phenomenology of religion", did not imply any Husserlian inspiration. His work was inspired rather by Dutch comparative science of religion. He even mentions Tiele here and says that the book is an introduction to Dutch science of religion (*godsdienstwetenschap*) in the way Tiele, Chantepie, Kristensen and he himself practised it.[20]

If there was an influence from philosophical phenomenology at all on the PoR of Van der Leeuw it was not through Husserl directly, but through Heidegger and Scheler and other pupils of Husserl. Even in Van der Leeuw's *Phänomenologie der Religion* (1933), a book well over 600 pages, Van der Leeuw mentions Husserl's name only once and does not refer to any publication by him. Furthermore, Van der Leeuw only developed a (minor) interest in philosophical phenomenology after 1925.

Only after it had been suggested by Heiler to call his approach phenomenological?

Yes, only then did he begin to study Husserlian phenomenology.

So the term phenomenology is an add-on to an already established Dutch tradition of comparative science of religion?

Yes, exactly. Van der Leeuw stands in the Chantepie tradition, except that he replaces philosophy of religion with his own theology, and adds an evolutionary aspect that Chantepie and Kristensen avoided, but which he takes from Tiele. Non-Dutch scholars, such as Jim Cox, can hardly be aware of this curious history and therefore tend to over-emphasize the Husserlian influence on Van der Leeuw, for all publications that enable one to understand Van der Leeuw's theological position and context, were published in Dutch.[21] Also Wim Hofstee's biography of Van der Leeuw is in Dutch. The only published book that discusses Van der Leeuw's theological context and which is available

---

20. The crucial footnote reads in its entirety: "Zum rechten Verständnis des Titels sei beigefügt, daß der Verfasser dieses Buches das Wort "Phänomenologie" nicht in Sinne der Philosophie von Husserl und Scheler gebraucht, sondern im Sinn der vergleichenden Religionshistoriker wie Tiele, Chantepie de la Saussaye, Edvard Lehmann, die darunter die systematische Darstellung der religiösen Einzelphänomene wie des Gebets, des Opfers, der Zauberei, Askese usw. verstehen" (Van der Leeuw 1925, n.p.).

21. Platvoet is here thinking of Chapter 4, "The Decisive Role of Dutch Phenomenology in the New Science of Religion", in Cox (2006, esp. 118–125, 128, 135–136). A similar critique could be directed at Jonathan Tuckett (2016) who sees Van der Leeuw as a Husserlian because he bases his analysis only on *Phänomenologie der Religion/ Religion in Essence and Manifestation* without taking into account *Inleiding tot de Godsdienstgeschidenis/Einführung in die Phänomenologie der Religion*.

to non-Dutch scholars is *Religionswissenschaft und Kulturkritik* (Kippenberg and Luchesi 1991), based on a conference in Groningen.[22] Fortunately, Richard Plantinga's unpublished doctoral dissertation on Van der Leeuw (Plantinga 1990) is now available on the Internet. Plantinga is an American, but of Dutch descent, and he reads Dutch as well as German and French, the three languages in which Van der Leeuw published. So, he has been able to study Van der Leeuw in his theological context. His dissertation gives a very good introduction to the theology of Van der Leeuw's phenomenology.

So that is an important corrective to Jim Cox's history of PoR.

And to others as well. It was Eric Sharpe (1975) who first claimed that Van der Leeuw was a Husserlian, and perhaps this is where Cox gets the idea from. But let me stress again: Van der Leeuw drew on Husserlian phenomenology only because it was intellectually fashionable, and he did so only superficially. For Van der Leeuw, *epoché* and eidetic vision were merely Husserlian jargon for things comparative historians of religion did anyway. I mean, *epoché* is the restraint to try not to bring any prejudices into one's work. For Van der Leeuw this meant (only) restraint from *confessional* theology. It did not prevent him from bringing in the one, big unprovable assumption that all religious people share, namely that there is a transcendent power and that one *must* respond to it and therefore *must* be religious.

So Van der Leeuw did not consider the existence of a transcendent power to be a problematic assumption?

No, he was too much persuaded of its for him obvious truth.

Also the notion of eidetic vision was mere jargon. What the phenomenologists wanted to do was to systematize the wide array of historical data in such a way that it could be fitted into the philosophy of religion or into their own theology.

The Development of a New Methodologically Agnostic Mainstream in the Dutch Science of Religion

This is perhaps a good time to return to what I would consider a core development in Dutch science of religion, namely that from the 1950s you begin to get a new type of scholars appointed to the chairs in history of religion at the *duplex ordo* universities. Until then, almost all professors of history

---

22. Hans Kippenberg had been Van Baaren's successor in Groningen, but had moved to Bremen (and been succeeded by Jan Bremmer) by the time this conference was organized.

of religion, with the exception of Kristensen and Hidding and a few others, had first worked as ministers in a parish (*gemeente*) of the Dutch Reformed Church before becoming professors, and even as professors they remained connected to the church and were set on developing their science of religion in such a way that it served the training of ministers of a particular modality of the Dutch Reformed Church. From the 1950s onwards, however, you have Sierksma, Van Baaren, Waardenburg and later myself, who all studied theology to pursue an academic career as historians of religion. In this group you also have the first post-Christian scholars of religion, Sierksma and Van Baaren. These are the first signs of change, signalling the replacement of PoR by a new, methodologically agnostic approach to the science of religion in the 1960s and 1970s.

As I describe it in my article "From Consonance to Autonomy", there were several important stages in this development. First there was the confrontation between Sierksma and Van der Leeuw. Sierksma was working on a dissertation on Greek religion, hoping to become the successor of Van der Leeuw. But he increasingly came to doubt the phenomenological framework of his teacher and voiced his critique in a series of letters to Van der Leeuw, written in 1948, that were later published together with Van der Leeuw's replies (cf. Platvoet 1998b, 336–339). Following this methodological clash, Sierksma changed the topic of his dissertation to a methodological one proposing depth psychology as *the* future instrument for the study of religion, both historical and comparative, to replace the phenomenology of Van der Leeuw (Sierksma 1950).

Van Baaren went through a similar development. He was an agnostic from the 1930s onwards, and he moved away increasingly from the Egyptology in which he had been trained to the study of preliterate religions, especially their art, and especially in Papua New Guinea. In addition, Van Baaren became inspired by the methodological discussion within the anthropology of religion involving scholars such as Evans-Pritchard, Geertz and Spiro, and he used that as a stepping-stone for breaking down the huge statue of his predecessor, Van der Leeuw. It began with his dissertation on revelation (defended in 1951) – a topic you could not touch in Van der Leeuw's opinion – and he continued in his inaugural address on magic (in 1952) – where he stated that he, as a Roman Catholic, experienced an enormous amount of Protestant prejudice against himself, against Roman Catholics and against the religions of illiterate peoples. In a series of later publications, Van Baaren further developed his criticism of Van der Leeuw. In 1957, he published an article (Van Baaren 1957) on the ethnological basis of Van der Leeuw's phenomenology in reaction to the appearance, in 1956, of the third edition of *Phänomenologie der Religion*. In this article, Van Baaren laid bare how weak and prejudiced Van der Leeuw's use of ethnological data really was. A decade later, in 1969, Van

Baaren published the article on "Systematische Religionswissenschaft" that we talked about earlier, and founded the Groningen Working-Group for the Study of Fundamental Problems and Methods of Science of Religion.

A collection of papers from the meetings of this working group was published in 1973 (Van Baaren and Drijvers 1973) and this book very clearly demonstrates the shift taking place in Dutch science of religion. Van Baaren, and most other contributors, such as Han Drijvers (1934–2002; then Lector and from 1976 Professor of Semitic Languages), here take a definitive turn towards regarding religion as a part of human culture and history. Not every participant in the group shared this view, though. The philosopher of religion in Groningen, Hubertus Hubbeling (1925–1986), took part in the discussions, and in his contribution to the 1973 collection, he argues that philosophy of religion is science of religion *plus* the question of truth. But Van Baaren says in his article: no, we do not touch the truth question at all. We make the *epoché* permanent.[23] Van Baaren's article in this collection marks the end of Dutch religiously inspired PoR.

So this 1973 book by the Groningen group is more important than the long article that Waardenburg published on Dutch PoR in 1972 in *Numen*, based on the discussions of the Utrecht working group that you participated in?

Yes, this is the methodological revolution – the change of paradigm. Waardenburg's article is a piece of research history. It does not present a new alternative.

I see. So the 1973 book is also where the breakthroughs by Evans-Pritchard, Geertz and Spiro are first taken into full account and are used to deliver the final blow to PoR?

---

23. Van Baaren writes: "Van der Leeuw uses this term [*epoché*] to indicate a modest suspension of judgment. The scientific validity of theological statements is kept fully intact; it is only for the time being put in brackets (*eingeklämmert*) [...]. The point of view defended here is not that theological pronouncements concerning the truth or untruth of a religion should be put between brackets for the time being, but that they should be crossed out definitively from the language of science of religion as irrelevant" (Van Baaren 1973, 48). Already in his PhD dissertation from 1951, Van Baaren had banned questions of the truth or falsehood of revelations from the province of science of religion: "Phenomenologically seen, each religion starts with a revelation. The decision whether this revelation is true or untrue is outside phenomenology's province. It must be left to either theology and faith, or to philosophy of religion, because God as he is can never be an object of science of religion which is concerned only with God as humans experience him" (Van Baaren 1951, 11). On Van Baaren's dismantling of Van der Leeuw's PoR in general, cf. Platvoet (1998b, 339–343).

To deliver the final blow, yes, and to establish a new, agnostic paradigm: religion as culture, religion as part of human history. This paradigm considers religious claims to be postulations, that is, claims that can be neither verified nor falsified. They may be true; they may not be true. As scholars of religion we have no instruments to discern whether religion is true or false, and therefore we must take an agnostic position as scholars of religion, whatever our own personal position might be.

And another crucial difference between the phenomenological and agnostic approaches is their mode of comparison. Phenomenologists compare everything and believe that their intuition helps them cut through the bewildering amount of data, but the result is that their work becomes unreliable. By contrast, in my PhD dissertation (Platvoet 1982), I propose that we severely reduce comparison to enhance its reliability. I therefore compared only three place- and time-bound case histories, each of which was first minutely researched historically and contextually.

The Demise of the Phenomenology of Religion in the Netherlands and Waardenburg's Unsuccessful Attempt at a Phenomenological Revival

You have told me that in the Netherlands PoR collapsed around 1970. Why did it happen so abruptly?

Only the methodological collapse was abrupt. After 1973, PoR simply became obsolete. It had no influence anymore on younger scholars and students, although it lingered on nominally in the title of courses and professorial chairs for some time. This was because the old phenomenologists did not convert to agnosticism, but continued as phenomenologists until they retired. Here in Utrecht, for example, Hoens and Zandee disappeared as professors of religion only in 1982 and that left me, Koos Waardenburg and Ria Kloppenborg (1945–2003) as the new generation. And I was the only one of this new generation who explicitly propagated the new paradigm. Koos Waardenburg kept quiet about it, and Ria Kloppenborg, as a Buddhologist, was not interested in these issues. But when she came to England in 1993 and was invited to give a BASR lecture there on Buddhism and witnessed the discussions among phenomenologists and agnostics she remarked "Oh, but we have solved this twenty years ago, over here in the Netherlands." So she was in complete agreement with the new paradigm, but felt no need to actively teach it.

In Groningen, Van Baaren was succeeded by Hans Kippenberg who developed a discursive science of religion that was, as far as I can see, also a neutral, agnostic form of science of religion.

Lammert Leertouwer (1932–) came from Groningen to Leiden in 1978 when in 1977 all of a sudden the unhappy Sierksma had died. When he had been passed over for the Groningen chair that Van Baaren got in 1952, Sierksma had been appointed *wetenschappelijk hoofdambtenaar* (Senior Research Fellow) in Leiden without a teaching commission. The position of Sierksma in Leiden had always been a very problematic one, because his psychoanalytic approach to the study of religion was strongly resisted by other members of the Leiden Faculty of Theology. So he went actually into a form of academic exile, though he could read and write and publish as he wanted and could conduct seminars for older students. He was given a lectureship only in 1972 and a full professorship in 1973, but he then died prematurely in 1977.

So it depends on the change in personnel when a new paradigm actually begins to be taught to students. It takes time. And this paradigm change was never carried out in Nijmegen or at the Free University – though [Dick] Mulder (1919–2014) came close.[24]

Even Koos Waardenburg was a kind of neo-phenomenologist. But as an Islamologist he was also very much focused on facilitating and participating in the dialogue between religions. And whenever you are into religious dialogue, you are close to a religionist position. But I see hardly any influence of any form of Waardenburg's neo-phenomenology on the wider discipline of Dutch science of religion, just as Van der Leeuw's phenomenology did not have much influence on it.

I am surprised that Waardenburg did not have more success with his attempt at a phenomenological revival. Like Van der Leeuw, Waardenburg was an internationally esteemed scholar. But then again, my own teacher in Leiden, Ab de Jong, who studied under you and Waardenburg in Utrecht, has told me that whereas Waardenburg invested enormously in achieving international fame – he received almost two bags of mail every week, and for a while he had no mail slot, for none was large enough – he did not invest much time in his students. In that light it may not be surprising that he had no academic heirs.

But what about Waardenburg's international connections? You told me earlier that he had worked in the United States and that he had actively propagated a new form of PoR after his return to the Netherlands. Had he gone to the United States to work with the phenomenologists of religion there?

---

24. Dick Mulder was Professor of History and Phenomenology of the Non-Christian Religions at the Free University Amsterdam from 1965 to 1984. Though a Professor of PoR, Mulder too only taught about, but never practised, phenomenology as a specific approach to the comparative study of religions.

Waardenburg first started studying Law at the University of Amsterdam in 1949, but switched to Theology in 1950. Having graduated, with majors in PoR with Bleeker and, I think, in Philosophy of Religion sometime in the mid-1950s, he undertook further studies in Islam and Arabic at Amsterdam, Leiden, and with Louis Massignon at Paris. He obtained his PhD on 7 July 1961, at the University of Amsterdam by defending his thesis *L'Islam dans le mirroir de l'Occident*, supervised by Bleeker. After a UN commission to produce a two volume survey of the universities in the Arab world, he moved to McGill University, in Montréal, Québec, Canada, as a research assistant to Wilfred Cantwell Smith from 1962 until 1963, and then, until 1968, to a teaching post at the University of California at Los Angeles. In 1965, he and the Utrecht professors of science of religion Hoens and Zandee met during the IAHR congress at Claremont. This encounter eventually resulted in Waardenburg being appointed at Utrecht University in 1968 to teach Islam and PoR.

Was Waardenburg's "new phenomenology" inspired by Eliade?

No! It was not. Waardenburg was well aware, of course, of Eliade's contributions to the PoR. But he distanced himself from Eliade's approach and emphasized the empirical character of his own approach. In his book *Religie onder de loep* (Waardenburg 1990), for example, he discusses Eliade's programmatic *The Quest* (1969) and then goes on to distance himself firmly from the Eliadean school. But on page 215 he remarks in a footnote that even though the hermeneutical approaches of Gerardus van der Leeuw, Joachim Wach (1898–1955) and Mircea Eliade (1907–1986) may be "outdated", they "still force us to reflect [on them]".

What, then, was new and different about Waardenburg's neo-phenomenology as opposed to that of Eliade and Van der Leeuw? Or, what did Waardenburg think was new?

Waardenburg distinguished sharply between "classical phenomenology" (from Chantepie to Eliade, with Van der Leeuw as paradigmatic) that aimed to uncover objective and general facts and laws about religion, and his own "new-style phenomenology", which was inspired by Wilfred Cantwell Smith and focused instead on understanding the subjective meaning that religious data, and religions, have for concrete humans. He called his "neo-phenomenology" therefore a "hermeneutic science of religion".

Waardenburg's aim of understanding the subjective meaning of religion was considered so unexceptional and unobjectionable by his Dutch colleagues in the study of religion that they failed to see the necessity of formulating a new approach dedicated to this aim. No-one therefore joined Waardenburg in developing the "new-style phenomenology of religion" he was so assiduously propagating. Already in 1973, the Groningen Working-Group definitively parted ways with Waardenburg's new-style phenomenology by ignoring his programmatic contribution to *Religion, Culture and Methodology*. In the epilogue, Han Drijvers and Lammert Leertouwer (1973) raised six critical questions against his approach and asked whether Waardenburg's approach, concerned as it was (in their words) with "subjective meaning and ultimate sense", had really "left traditional phenomenology behind?" For Drijvers and Leertouwer, Waardenburg's research of the faith of believers by means of *Verstehen* ([experiential] understanding) and *Einfühlung* (empathy) seemed to imply a theological *parti pris* [taking sides].[25] They declared Waardenburg's approach one of a kind with that of Van der Leeuw.[26]

You worked together with Waardenburg. Did his phenomenological inclination have any impact on how religion was taught and researched in Utrecht?

Waardenburg and I rarely taught undergraduate classes together, so I hardly have any personal recollection from sitting in on his classes on how his phenomenology affected his teaching on religion. But it is clear from the summary in the 1982/1983 and 1983/1984 calendars of the UU Faculty of Theology, that he devoted the full, 24-hour compulsory course Introduction to Science of Religion for undergraduate students to his new-style phenomenology. However, Professors Ab de Jong (Leiden) and Wouter Hanegraaff (Amsterdam) both attended that course at Utrecht in September/October 1984 when less than half the classes were taught by Waardenburg and the remainder by me. During the symposium for my 80th birthday at Leiden University on 8 June 2015, both drew attention to the significant difference between Waardenburg's classes and mine.[27] Whereas those of Waardenburg

---

25. As they put it, Waardenburg's approach, moreover, reduced the cultural context of religion to such an extent that it "no longer admits of regarding religion as a cultural variable" (as did the Groningen Working-Group) (Drijvers and Leertouwer 1973, 167).

26. As Drijvers and Leertouwer (1973, 168) point out, Van der Leeuw regards religion "as the human answer to a power revealing itself", whereas Waardenburg views it as "human self-expression answering [ultimate] questions after life and reality." The difference in wording reflects theological developments of the decades that separate the two, but they remain equally theological.

27. Wouter Hanegraaff (1961–) has since 1999 been Professor of the History of the Hermetic Philosophy and Related Currents at the University of Amsterdam. Ab de Jong (1966–) has since 2009 been Professor of Comparative Science of Religion at Leiden University. Hanegraaff and De Jong are among the most influential Dutch scholars of religion today, and their methodology is strongly influenced by Platvoet. The seminar that Platvoet refers to was organized by Ab de Jong, Corey Williams and myself.

on his new-style PoR were quite consonant with the views of the theologians at the Utrecht Faculty of Theology, De Jong and Hanegraaff felt that my approach was empirical, agnostic and anthropological, with religions being investigated as non-verifiable/non-falsifiable postulations that were to be re-searched exclusively as parts of the cultures and cultural histories of human societies.

However, I did witness Waardenburg as organizer and lecturer in the graduate seminar on the history of Dutch Science of Religion in 1969–1970, and in the one or two other MA seminars we conducted together in the 1980s. In one of these, I challenged Waardenburg's notion that "religion" necessarily requires, not only a trans-empirical "transcendent" reference (cf. Waardenburg 1973, 122), but that any and all religions must also always have absolute truth or value for believers.[28] Waardenburg was upset when I pointed out that by far the greater number of the religions of humankind – preliterate, folk and recent – did not claim such an absolute validity, but were adoptive and adaptive and pragmatically promoted plural religious allegiance. I added that it was therefore incorrect in terms of empirical evidence to extrapolate the special cases of Christianity and Islam, as religions with uni-versal aspirations, to the very definition of "religion" and through it to require "absolute validity" from all religions. Waardenburg, however, never dropped "absolute validity" from his definition of "religion".[29]

You said earlier that Waardenburg mostly kept silent about methodology. But we have also discussed his not very silent methodological clash with the Groningen Working-Group. Does that mean that Waardenburg ad-mitted defeat and gave up promoting his neo-phenomenology?

Waardenburg actively promoted his methodology among Dutch colleagues in science of religion until 1974, for example by organizing two national sym-posia at Utrecht: in 1973 on "Science of Religion in the Netherlands"; and in 1974 on "Dialogue with Islam". From 1975 onwards, however, he no longer organized any such nation-wide initiatives to gather Dutch scholars of reli-gions at Utrecht in order to provide Utrecht, and himself, with a leadership position in Dutch science of religion. It is my educated guess, in retrospect, that the reception of his contribution to *Religion, Culture and Methodology* in the epilogue was crucial in causing him to abandon any ambition and hope

---

28.   Cf. Waardenburg (1973): Religion has "absolute justification, foundation" (ibid., 130) and "supreme truth and value" (ibid., 132) for its believers.

29.   Cf. Waardenburg (1990, 32): "a cultural element may be qualified as religious when it has – as judged by the researcher – 'ultimate' meaning and an 'absolute' validity for the humans in question" (cf. also ibid., 36, 241, 245, 251, 252).

that he might become the new Van der Leeuw.[30] He realized that Dutch science of religion had become hostile to any PoR, classical or "neo". This hostile climate is what he likely referred to in his 1997 article on PoR in *Theologische Realenzyklopädie* (Waardenburg 1997).[31]

Clearly PoR is passé in the Netherlands. Has it all been for nothing, or has PoR brought us something of lasting benefit?

It has brought us the aim of trying to be objective. It has brought us, together with colonization and exploration, knowledge of other religions than Christianity. It has brought us the world. And it has forced us to confront the world and its religions, past and present. But to make sure that future ministers could handle the confrontation with the non-Christian religions, PoR insisted on the superiority of the Christian faith. It opened up to the other religions only in a religionist and Christocentric way.

Would you then say that, at least within the Dutch context, PoR was a necessary step in the emancipation of the study of religion from theology?

I think so, yes. Especially, from the point where professors were appointed to teach only history and PoR, and not also philosophy of religion. Tiele taught all three. Van der Leeuw taught only history and phenomenology and replaced philosophy of religion with his own theology. This made it easier for Van Baaren to explicitly exclude philosophy of religion and its truth question altogether from his systematic science of religion. So yes. PoR was a step on the road, perhaps a necessary step. But now it's merely history.

Commentary – Two Phases in the History of Dutch Science of Religion: The Phenomenological Phase (1877–1973) and the Culturalist Phase (1973–)

As Platvoet presents it, the history of the science of religion (*godsdienstwetenschap*) in the Netherlands can be divided into two very

---

30. Before abandoning this project, however, Waardenburg proposed the principles for a new-style phenomenology once more a few years later in Waardenburg (1978).

31. Waardenburg writes: "Ein Wissenschaftler, der von sich überzeugt ist und der sich in der akademischen Szene bewähren will, würde es zur Zeit kaum wagen, als Religionsphänomenologe in Erscheinung zu treten" ["A scholar [of religion] who is convinced of his own worth [as a scholar of religion] and who wishes to prove his mettle in the academic scene, would hardly dare to present himself as a phenomenologist of religion [in the Netherlands at that time]"] (Waardenburg 1997, 731; quoted in Molendijk 2005, 27n12).

distinct phases: a "phenomenological" phase and a "culturalist" phase. The phenomenological phase began with C. P. Tiele's appointment as the first Dutch Professor of History of Religion in Leiden in 1877 and ended roughly one hundred years later, in 1973, with the publication of *Religion, Culture and Methodology* by the Groningen Working-Group for the Study of Fundamental Problems and Methods of Science of Religion led by Theo van Baaren. During the phenomenological phase, all professors commissioned to teach history of religion within the faculties of theology at the four Dutch public universities of Leiden, Groningen, Utrecht and Amsterdam, operated within a religionist and theological paradigm characterized by three main tenets. First, it was held to be self-evidently true that God exists, and that religion is the human response to this fundamental fact. Second, Christianity was recognized to be only one religion among many, but was still considered the supreme religion to which all other religions could only aspire. Third, the history of religion was considered to have two principal tasks: the historical study of individual religions, and the comparative study of religious phenomena across traditions.[32] The three tenets reflected both the personal convictions of the professors during the phenomenological phase and the fact that they earned their bread by educating future ministers for the Dutch Reformed Church within the *duplex ordo* system.

Within the boundaries of the phenomenological paradigm there was of course also room for individual differences. Indeed, within classical PoR we may distinguish between three approaches: (1) the strictly *typological* approach that distilled general categories (e.g. prayer, sacrifice) through comparison and which could be either bold (Chantepie) or cautious (Kristensen); (2) the *evolutionary* approach that attempted to discover the laws of religious evolution (Tiele; Hidding); and (3) the *typological-evolutionary* approach that combined the systematics of typology with the genetics of evolutionism (Van der Leeuw; Bleeker).

Waardenburg's neo-phenomenology, which was developed when the study of religion in the Netherlands was about to transition into the culturalist phase, can be seen as half-continuous with classical phenomenology. Waardenburg no longer considered Christianity to be self-evidently the truest religion, but he retained the view that universalist and exclusive religions (= Christianity and Islam) constitute the most truly *religious*

---

32. All Dutch scholars of religion during the phenomenological phase recognized this double task of the history of religion, regardless of whether their formal teaching commissions included only history of religion (Tiele, Chantepie when in Amsterdam, and Van der Leeuw), or both history and PoR (Kristensen, Hidding and Bleeker).

religions. In addition, whereas Waardenburg avoided making explicitly religionist claims by shifting emphasis from the objective truth of religions to the subjective experience of religious believers, his insistence that religion concerns – and that only religion can address – "the ultimate", inscribes his neo-phenomenology into a theological discourse (albeit now Tillich-inspired through Cantwell Smith).

In sketching the history of the phenomenological phase of Dutch science of religion, Platvoet points to a number of curious facts that have been overlooked by previous, Anglophone scholarship. First of all, Platvoet reminds us that the first so-called "phenomenologists", Chantepie and Tiele, were not formally commissioned to teach PoR but saw themselves as historians of religion. It is not until the mid-1920s, 45 years after Tiele's appointment in Leiden, that the very term PoR appears in official teaching commissions (Kristensen) and book titles (Van der Leeuw). Crucially, Platvoet asserts that the introduction of the term PoR into Dutch scholarship did not change anything about how the Dutch went about studying religion: They continued to compare and look for essences, and to do this in the service of the Christian religion. Without engaging in depth with Husserlian phenomenology, Van der Leeuw employed the jargon of *epoché* and eidetic vision to claim some of Husserl's prestige for his own work (and later Dutch phenomenologists of religion seem to have continued along this track).

Platvoet also points out that while the Netherlands was home to many famous, individual phenomenologists, there was no Dutch "school" of PoR. Even if Tiele, Chantepie, Kristensen, Van der Leeuw and Bleeker worked within a common religionist-comparativist paradigm, they operated in self-chosen isolation and did not attempt to develop a shared research agenda or to found a scholarly association for PoR or anything of that sort. When Waardenburg tried to organize a national platform to support his neo-phenomenology, his colleagues had left phenomenology behind and it was too late. The failure to develop a successful academic infrastructure for PoR (both classic and "neo") may help explain why both Van der Leeuw and Waardenburg had few students and little impact on the study of religion in the Netherlands.

For 45 years, from 1973 till the present day, Dutch science of religion has found itself in a post-phenomenological, culturalist phase. Platvoet argues that the Groningen Working-Group not only destroyed the old paradigm, but also introduced a new paradigm, inspired by the anthropologists Edward Evan Evans-Pritchard, Clifford Geertz and Melford Spiro, and that this paradigm became the new mainstream. Like the phenomenological paradigm, this new, culturalist paradigm can be characterized by three broadly shared tenets. First, it views religion as a part of human culture and therefore as something that should not be studied in isolation (as *sui generis*), but always in relation to other aspects (Van Baaren speaks of "functions") of culture and society, such as social order and art (Van Baaren 1973, 36–37). This principle, which we may refer to as the culturalist principle, was formulated in explicit opposition to the essentialism that characterized Van der Leeuw's PoR. Second, the new paradigm dictates that religions should be studied as human postulations or projections – for as scholars of religion, we may never know whether culturally postulated superhuman beings really exist or not. This second principle, the principle of methodological agnosticism, was formulated in opposition to the religionism (or "methodological supernaturalism") of PoR. Crucially, however, the culturalist paradigm shares its third principle, adherence to the comparative method, with the phenomenological paradigm. Even the iconoclastic methodologists of the Groningen Working-Group recognized the value of the phenomenological ambition of understanding and theorizing religion in general, and Van Baaren therefore did not want to replace PoR merely with historical and ethnographic studies of individual religions, but called for a *systematic* science of religion aiming to study religion as such (1969, 1973). In essence, the ambition of Van Baaren and the Groningen Working-Group was to salvage Chantepie's typological phenomenology, free it from any religionist and theological biases, and develop and refine it, for example by taking into account the reliable data on the religions of illiterate peoples that were now becoming available but had not (to be fair) been available to Van der Leeuw. In Van Baaren's own words, "science of religion as a systematic discipline is based on the material collected by history, sociology, anthropology, psychology, etc., and tries to classify these materials systematically, to understand and to explain them" (1973, 45).

In reality, however, the mode of comparison actually practised by the members of the Groningen Working-Group was of a less systematic and more cautious kind, reminiscent rather of Kristensen than of Chantepie. It was also this cautious form of comparison that Platvoet practised, and which he theorized as "limitative comparison" (Platvoet 1982) and taught to his students. Dutch study of religion can still be characterized as culturalist, agnostic and cautious. Reviewing Dutch scholarship on religion from the 1970s till today, one finds a culturalist-agnostic methodology applied (mostly) to historical and ethnographic studies of single cases and (occasionally) to comparative projects of a limitative character. A systematic science of religion *à la* Van Baaren, involving large-scale comparison and the ambition to explain religion, still has to be developed in the Netherlands (cf. Davidsen 2020).

Markus Altena Davidsen is Assistant Professor of Sociology of Religion at Leiden University, the Netherlands. For his doctoral dissertation, "The Spiritual Tolkien Milieu: A Study of Fiction-based Religion" (2014), he received the Gerardus van der Leeuw Dissertation Award from the Dutch Association for the Study of Religion. As editor he recently published *Narrative and Belief: The Religious Affordance of Supernatural Fiction* (2018, Routledge).

Acknowledgements

The interviewer wants to thank Jan Platvoet warmly for his constructive comments on the edited text and his generous suggestions for the note apparatus. Both of us also want to express our gratitude to Ole Davidsen and Ab de Jong who provided valuable feedback on an earlier version of the text.

References

Bleeker, C. Jouco. 1970. "The Conception of Man in the Phenomenology of Religion." *Studia Missionalia* 19: 13–18.

Chantepie de la Saussaye, P. D. 1887. *Lehrbuch der Religionsgeschichte*. Freiburg im Breisgau: Mohr. (2nd edition, 1897; 3rd edition, 1905; 4th edition, 1925.)

Cox, James L. 2006. *A Guide to the Phenomenology of Religion: Key Figures, Formative Influences and Debates*. London: T. & T. Clark International.

Davidsen, Markus Altena. 2020. "Theo van Baaren's Systematic Science of Religion Revisited: The Current Crisis in Dutch Study of Religion and a Way Out." *NTT Journal for Theology and the Study of Religion* 74(3): 213–241. https://doi.org/10.5117/NTT2020.3.002.ALTE

Drijvers, Han, and Lammert Leertouwer. 1973. "Epilogue." In *Religion, Culture and Methodology: Papers of the Groningen Working-Group for the Study of Fundamental Problems and Methods of Science of Religion*, edited by Theo van Baaren and Han Drijvers, 159–168. The Hague: Mouton.

Hofstee, Wim. 1997. *Goden en mensen: de Godsdienstwetenschap van Gerardus van der Leeuw 1890-1950* [*Gods and Humans: Gerardus van der Leeuw's Science of Religion*]. Kampen: Kok Agora.

Kippenberg, Hans G. and Brigitte Luchesi (eds). 1991. *Religionswissenschaft und Kulturkritik: Beiträge zur Konferenz The History of Religions and Critique of Culture in the Days of Gerardus van der Leeuw (1890-1950)*. Marburg: diagonal-Verlag.

Kristensen, William Brede. 1960. *The Meaning of Religion: Lectures in the Phenomenology of Religion*. Translated by John Braisted Carman. The Hague: Nijhoff.

Molendijk, Arie. 2005. *The Emergence of the Science of Religion in the Netherlands.* Studies in the History of Religion 105. Leiden: Brill.

Plantinga, Richard J. 1990. "Seeking the Boundaries: Gerardus van der Leeuw on the Study of Religion and the Nature of Theology." PhD thesis, McMaster University. Retrieved from https://macsphere.mcmaster.ca/handle/11375/8338 (accessed 22 July 2018).

Platvoet, Jan G. 1982. *Comparing Religions: A Limitative Approach: An Analysis of Akan, Para-Creole, and Ifo-Sananda Rites and Prayers.* The Hague: Mouton. https://doi.org/10.1515/9783110821819

Platvoet, Jan G. 1993. "De Wraak van de 'primitieven': Godsdienstgeschiedenis van Neanderthaler tot New Age" ["The Revenge of the 'Primitives': History of Religion from the Neanderthals to the New Age"]. *Nederlands Theologisch Tijdschrift* 47(3): 227–243.

Platvoet, Jan G. 1998a. "Close Harmonies: Science of Religions in Dutch *Duplex Ordo* Theology, 1860–1960." *Numen* 45(2): 115–162. https://doi.org/10.1163/1568527981588359

Platvoet, Jan G. 1998b. "From Consonance to Autonomy: The Science of Religion in the Netherlands 1948–1995." *Method & Theory in the Study of Religion* 10(4): 334–351. https://doi.org/10.1163/157006898x00141

Platvoet, Jan G. 2002. "Pillars, Pluralism and Secularisation." In *Modern Societies and the Science of Religions*, edited by Gerard A. Wiegers and Jan G. Platvoet, 82–148. Leiden: Brill.

Sharpe, Eric. 1975. *Comparative Religion: A History.* London: Duckworth. (2nd edition, 1986.)

Sierksma, Fokke. 1950. *Phaenomenologie der religie en complexe psychologie: een methodologische bijdrage* [*Phenomenology of Religion and Complex Psychology: A Methodological Contribution*]. Assen: Van Gorcum.

Stausberg, Michael. 2007. "The Study of Religion(s) in Western Europe (I): Prehistory and History until World War II." *Religion* 37(4): 294–318. https://doi.org/10.1016/j.religion.2007.10.001

Tuckett, Jonathan. 2016. "Clarifying the Phenomenology of Gerardus van der Leeuw." *Method & Theory in the Study of Religion* 28(3): 227–263. https://doi.org/10.1163/15700682-12341361

Van Baaren, Theo. 1951. *Voorstellingen van openbaring phaenomenologisch beschouwd: proeve van inleidend onderzoek, voornamelijk aan de hand der primitieve en oude godsdiensten* [*Conceptions of Revelation Phenomenologically Considered: An Introductory Essay Based Principally Upon Primitive and Ancient Religions*]. Utrecht: Schotanus & Jens.

Van Baaren, Theo. 1957. "De ethnologische basis van de faenomenologie van G. van der Leeuw" ["The Ethnological Foundation of G. van der Leeuw's Phenomenology"]. *Nederlands Theologisch Tijdschrift* 11: 321–353.

Van Baaren, Theo. 1960. *Wij mensen: religie en wereldbeschouwing bij schriftloze volken* [*Humans like Us: Religion and Worldview among Illiterate Peoples*]. Utrecht: Erven J. Bijleveld.

Van Baaren, Theo. 1963. *Mensen tussen Nijl en zon: de godsdienst van het oude Egypte* [*People between Nile and Sun: The Religion of Ancient Egypt*]. Zeist: W. de Haan.

Van Baaren, Theo. 1969. "Systematische Religionswissenschaft." *Nederlands Theologisch Tijdschrift* 24(2): 81–88.

Van Baaren, Theo. 1973. "Science of Religion as a Systematic Discipline: Some Introductory Remarks." In *Religion, Culture and Methodology: Papers of the Groningen Working-Group for the Study of Fundamental Problems and Methods of Science of Religion*, edited by Theo van Baaren and Han Drijvers, 35–56. The Hague: Mouton.

Van Baaren, Theo and Han Drijvers, eds. 1973. *Religion, Culture and Methodology: Papers of the Groningen Working-Group for the Study of Fundamental Problems and Methods of Science of Religion*. The Hague: Mouton.

Van der Leeuw, Gerardus. 1924. *Inleiding tot de Godsdienstgeschiedenis*. Haarlem: De Erven F. Bohn.

Van der Leeuw, Gerardus. 1925. *Einführung in die Phänomenologie der Religion*. Munich: Ernst Reinhardt Verlag.

Van der Leeuw, Gerardus. 1933. *Phänomenologie der Religion*. Tübingen: Mohr. Translated by John Evan Turner, *Religion in Essence and Manifestation: A Study in Phenomenology*. London: George Allen & Unwin, 1938.

Waardenburg, Jacques. 1972. "Religion between Reality and Idea: A Century of Phenomenology in the Netherlands." *Numen* 19(2–3): 128–203. https://doi.org/10.2307/3269741

Waardenburg, Jacques. 1973. "Research on Meaning in Religion." In *Religion, Culture and Methodology: Papers of the Groningen Working-Group for the Study of Fundamental Problems and Methods of Science of Religion*, edited by Theo van Baaren and Han Drijvers, 109–136. The Hague: Mouton.

Waardenburg, Jacques. 1973–1974. *Classical Approaches to the Study of Religion*: Volume 1: *Introduction and Anthology*; Volume 2: *Bibliography*. The Hague: Mouton (= *Religion and Reason* 3–4).

Waardenburg, Jacques. 1978. "Toward a New-style Phenomenological Research on Religion." In *Reflections on the Study of Religion*, 113–137. New York: Mouton.

Markus Altena Davidsen

Waardenburg, Jacques. 1990. *Religie onder de loep: Systematische inleiding in de godsdienstwetenschap* [*Scrutinizing Religion: A Systematic Introduction to the Science of Religion*]. Hilversum: Ambo. This book was first published in German in 1986 under the title *Religion und Religionen: Systematische Einführung in die Religionswissenschaft.* Berlin: De Gruyter. https://doi.org/10.1515/9783110852196

Waardenburg, Jacques. 1997. "Religionsphänomenologie." *Theologische Realenzyklopädie* 28, 731–749.

Wiebe, Donald. 1991. "Phenomenology of Religion as a Religio-Cultural Quest: Gerardus van der Leeuw and the Subversion of the Scientific Study of Religion." In *Religionswissenschaft und Kulturkritik: Beiträge zur Konferenz The History of Religions and Critique of Culture in the Days of Gerardus van der Leeuw (1890–1950)*, edited by Hans G. Kippenberg and Brigitte Luchesi, 65–86. Marburg: diagonal-Verlag.

Afterword

The Meta-theoretical Landscape of Phenomenologies of Religion

SATOKO FUJIWARA, DAVID THURFJELL AND STEVEN ENGLER

In planning this interview project, we expected to find a variety of uses of the term "PoR", and this did indeed turn out to be a key finding. By letting interviewees lay out their own "emic" definitions of PoR, we in effect conducted a survey of divergent perspectives. The resulting picture is so diversified that, arguably, PoR should be seen less as a single approach than as a largely empty signifier, receiving different meanings depending on context and meta-theoretical stance.

That said, although there are many differing definitions of PoR in these interviews, it is possible to draw out general themes. We offer the following meta-theoretical map, using three scales or axes. The first two sketch an area within which different views of *what PoR is* can be situated: in terms of overall purpose (descriptive versus essentialist) and degree of complexity (robust versus selective). The other allows us to compare views not of the nature of PoR per se but of its intrinsic significance (meaningful versus worthless). An additional factor, beyond these three scales, is PoR's relation to other theoretical perspectives in different national and institutional contexts. These four dimensions of PoR's variation are not normative: they are attempts to describe this book's main finding: that scholars of religion have a wide variety of views of PoR. One of the findings that we attempt to describe is the range of normative stances that scholars themselves hold towards PoR.

From Descriptive Taxonomy to Essentialist Empathy

The interviewees' ideas about the overarching purpose of PoR occupy a spectrum from descriptive to essentialist extremes, with the former emphasizing taxonomy and the latter the apprehension of essences. Though there are middle-ground positions, scholars' views tend to cluster at the two extremes. Where some consider PoR to be the pre-theoretical and inductive production of a neutral taxonomy of religious phenomena, others, whether they approve of this endeavour or not, see it as aiming to understand the essence of things religious. Connected to this dichotomy are several others that characterize the goals of PoR at a more fine-grained level (Table 1).

Table 1. The descriptive–essentialist scale.

Taxonomical	Essence-capturing
• Inductive	• Intuitive
• Empirical	• Empathetic (*Verstehen*)
• Historical	• Philosophical
• *Epoché* as scientific neutrality in general	• *Epoché* as a means of understanding
• PoR as initial stage	• PoR as goal
• PoR as pre-theoretical data processing	• PoR as an anti-reductionist movement

The majority of Nordic scholars have tried to confine PoR to its taxonomical version, emphasizing PoR's pragmatic value. On the other hand, some scholars in other regions find the essence-capturing part of the PoR attractive, but hard to put into practice. They either "selected" some of the elements of the essence-capturing PoR or applied it in a "moderate" way. For example, some maintained the attitude of *epoché* in the sense of being neutral as much as possible while dismissing the goal of essence-capturing. Others replaced essence-capturing and empathy with the understanding or interpretation of what a certain symbol means to the people they are investigating. In other words, they changed universalism for context-conscious interpretation. (Some Nordic scholars also replaced classic, universal taxonomies with more modest, for example, regional, taxonomies.) In some cases, interviewees seem unaware that they have made a selection. For example, Chung found PoR attractive by contrasting it with the World Religions approach. However, the first half of Mensching's *Die Religion: Erscheinungsformen, Strukturtypen und Lebensgesetze* (1959) was organized thoroughly according to world religions because he attempted to grasp the essence of each of them. PoR is not necessarily incompatible with the World Religions approach while, as Cush argues, the latter is also not inherent in the former.

From Robust to Selective

Some scholars see PoR as a highly complex theory, combining most or all of a long list of characteristics. Others emphasize only a small number of features from this list. Our distinction between robust and selective PoR describes this spectrum, from complex to simple views. Each type has many variants. If we think in terms of a family resemblance view of PoR, this scale describes the difference between family members that have most or all of the family's list of defining features and those that have only a few. Robust PoR (for example, philosophical or hermeneutic phenomenology and continental PoR, along with classic and empirical PoR) is characterized by the methodologically rigorous use of most or all of a list of related principles (Table 2). Selective PoR is based on a small number of these principles. It is both narrower (developing fewer principles) and broader (interpreting those principles less rigorously, applying them to a broader set of phenomena).

Table 2. The robust–selective scale.

Robust	Selective
• Focus on intuition and experience	• Emphasizing a small sub-
• Focus on what presents itself to consciousness	set of these
• Seeking universal structures or essences	
• Descriptive	
• Comparative	
• Historical	
• *Epoché*	
• Empathy	
• Antireductionism	
etc.	

This distinction does not imply that robust PoR is more proper, true or legitimate. It is primary in the genealogical sense that it offers certain archives or models, some elements of which are emphasized more than others in specific forms of selective PoR. Perspectives at the robust end of the spectrum are almost exclusively theories used and championed by scholars. Perspectives at the selective end include a larger proportion of straw-doll conceptions used by critics of PoR.

Here are three examples that illustrate this distinction. Robust PoR's antireductionism (allowing phenomena as phenomena to reveal themselves in their own terms) has informed selective affirmations of the *sui generis* nature of religion. One feature of some types of robust PoR is an emphasis on essential structures in subjective experience. A selective emphasis on this feature informs Ninian Smart's typological emphasis on a transcultural list of religious dimensions. Philosophical phenomenology's ontological *epoché* (bracketing the issue of whether that which appears in consciousness has independent existence) and empirical PoR's epistemological *epoché* (bracketing assumptions and interpretations in order to focus on the description of subjective experience) inform selective claims that scholars should bracket the issue of the truth or falsity of religious worlds. In each case, one of a larger family of features comes to play a larger – because narrower, selective – role.

Tables 1 and 2 help to explain why some of the interviewees refuse to be identified with PoR. They dissociate themselves from a robust version of essentialist, essence-capturing PoR. Their own work is often a selective from of PoR, which foregrounds only certain characteristics of these more robust versions. Likewise, we can also understand why scholarly views of an iconic phenomenologist like van der Leeuw are ambivalent. He has been believed to represent a robust essence-capturing PoR, but, according to Platvoet, this was not the case: van der Leeuw's approach was selective. Given that not even van der Leeuw held a robust essence-capturing view of PoR, it appears likely that there has never been such a thing as robust PoR in the Netherlands. Indeed, this is Platvoet's view.

From Valuable to Worthless

Where the two scales above allow us to compare different views of PoR in terms of theoretical characteristics, two others allow us to compare assessments of PoR. The first looks at the *intrinsic* assessment of PoR. It captures interviewees' normative assessments of PoR, from positive to negative, from appreciation to critique. A number of more specific value-laden dichotomies are connected to this general assessment (Table 3).

With the advent of post-modernism, post-structuralism, post-colonialism and other critical discourses in the late twentieth century, PoR lost its ground. In this context, when PoR is attacked, it is often the robust essence-capturing version of PoR that is *said to be* targeted. In fact, critics tend to criticize one or two specific aspects of PoR, as suggested by the right-hand column of Table 3. In effect, they offer a selective critique of a selective view of PoR. (The taxonomic mode of PoR was simply left behind as outdated.) Insofar as the above tables reflect the range of actual usages of "PoR", it seems that critics have been

Table 3. The valuable–worthless scale.

Valuable	Worthless
• Rational	• Irrational
• Scientific/philosophical	• Theological/religionist
• Empirical	• Subjective
• Firmly grounded in experience	• Lacking external validity
• Verifiable through introspection	• Not falsifiable
• Down-to-earth	• Jargon-laden
• Meaningful	• Boring
• Useful	• Trivial/empty of practical significance
• Essential for understanding others	• Projection of scholarly categories

attributing a misleading prominence to robust PoR. Robust essentialist/ empathetic PoR has served as a scapegoat, a screen for the projection of meta-theoretical anxieties. In fact, criticisms tend to attack some version of selective PoR, singling out a reduced set of characteristics for critique (e.g. "sui generis" views or essentialism). In the name of attacking the bugbear of robust PoR, critics reject a strawdoll, selective reduction of it.

Another important finding is that different views of PoR are strongly shaped by national and institutional factors. In countries where university departments of the study of religion are closely related to those of philosophy (as in Japan), scholars are more inclined to emphasize the philosophical aspect of PoR. In contrast, where departments of the study of religion adjoin those of history or ethnology (as in Scandinavia), scholars shun philosophical PoR. The imaginary fault lines between rational, scientific West/North and emotional, faith-rooted East/South that we mentioned in the introduction of this book may reflect not cultural – or still less innate cognitive or functional – differences but historical contingencies in the development of academic institutions.

These factors are also reflected in generational differences. Some interviewees saw it as crucial to distinguish between phenomenologists and historians of religions, but to their younger interviewers these approaches often look alike (see, for example, the chapter on Italy). Though rivals in some contexts, mid-twentieth-century phenomenologists and historians of religions had something in common: they framed their research using a set of categories like sacrifice, initiation, cultural hero, Supreme Being etc. This commonality may derive from their historical role in the generations that rejected the earlier evolutionist scheme. The interviewees also belong to an era when humanities scholars were more or less conscious of certain "big questions" of humankind. What has been called PoR embraces not only the elements of the three scales presented above but also more amorphous factors like these. Our interview project could vividly capture the characters articulated by each interviewee and interviewer.

The Changing Role of PoR in Conference Proceedings

One way to trace the changing role of PoR in the study of religion is to look at the programmes of international conferences in the discipline. We have reviewed the programmes of past World Congresses of the International Association for the History of Religions (IAHR), the largest and most long-lived international organization of the study of religion (Table 4). This reveals a change in the way PoR has been assessed and featured. PoR moves between what may be labelled a relational position with respect to other approaches in the study of religion and a substantive position where the specific characteristics of PoR itself are highlighted – e.g. elements such as taxonomy, essence or *epoché*, whether robust or selective. Where a substantive view of PoR looks at characteristics internal to PoR, a relational view defines it in contrast to other approaches.

The programme of the 1960 Congress in Marburg contains a section titled "Phenomenology etc." among seven sections. As all the other sections are dedicated to the historical studies of individual religious traditions, it would appear that any presentation that did not fall under them was pushed into the seventh section, namely, thematic studies with various or vague methodologies. This relegation of PoR to the category of a generic "other" is relational: PoR was viewed in Marburg less in terms of what it is, than in terms of what it is not. The President of the IAHR at that time was Pettazzoni, who had succeeded the first President, van der Leeuw, and who according to Casadio, positioned himself over against PoR. In this light, it is understandable that "Phenomenology" was treated as a residual and relational category.

The structure of the Marburg programme also treats "Phenomenology" as an umbrella term for research that looks at more than one religious tradition, usually thematically. This usage coincides with what Anttonen recalls in his interview:[1]

> Basically, from the point of view of scholarly traditions of comparative religion in Anglophone countries as well as in Germany, phenomenology of religion is identical with the term "comparative religion". Why a distinct

---

1. This paragraph was originally included in the interview given by Anttonen. It was cut due to the word limit. We cite it here, given its relevance in this context.

Table 4. Relational views of PoR in IAHR Congress programmes.

1960 (Marburg)*	I Primitive Religion II Orient, Judaism III Buddhism, Japan IV Greece, Rome IVa Iran V Islam Va India VI Christianity **VII Phenomenology, etc.** VIIa China	1990 (Rome)	I Oceania, Africa, America, Mesoamerica II East Asia, India III Iran, Egypt; IV Greece, Rome, Hellenism, Pre-Christian Europe V Judaism VI Christianity in the first centuries, Christianity in modern times VII Gnosticism, Manichaeism VIII Islam IX Buddhism X New religions XI Methodology of comparative research **XII Phenomenology of religion** XIII Anthropology of religion, Philosophy of religion
1975 (Lancaster)	I African Religions II Near Eastern and Mediterranean Antiquity III Buddhism IV Christianity V East Asian Religion VI Indian Religion VII Islam VIII Judaism IX Celtic and Germanic Religions X Methodology **XI Comparative and Phenomenological Studies** XII Iconography XIII Psychology of Religion XIV Sociology/Anthropology of Religion XV Philosophy of Religion	1995 (Mexico City)	No mention of "phenomenology" in any of the 88 sessions in the Proceedings.

*I–VII represent sections which were at the same time room assignment.

label of "phenomenology of religion" appeared on the scene in the first place was, according to Hultkrantz, that comparative religion "was too weighed down with an association with Frazer and the old unlimited evolutionism" and because of "van der Leeuw, who in his turn was swayed by the philosophy of religion".

(Anttonen, citing Hultkrantz 1970, 75)

PoR remained a section heading in the programme of the 1975 Congress in Lancaster. The order of sections remained the same, from historical studies to other studies, but the latter group was more articulated. PoR was no longer a sole residual section, and it was linked explicitly to "comparative studies" as a category. It is also noteworthy that was explicitly distinguished from philosophy of religion. PoR was still framed in relation terms, but less so than in the 1960 Congress.

In the proceedings of the 1990 Congress in Rome, PoR was separated from both "comparative research" and philosophy of religion (the latter grouped with anthropology of religion). There were thirteen sections in total.[2] Interestingly, one of our anti-phenomenological German interviewees, Antes, appears as the author of the first paper in the "Phenomenology of religion" section.

Arguably, these usages of "PoR" in the programmes and proceedings of the IAHR Congresses are relatively unprovocative. Scholars involved in organizing these congresses did not think it would be problematic to identify scholars with PoR, even if they did not explicitly identify themselves with that approach. It may be the case that participants were prepared to be categorized in a way different from their own academic identities because of some practical reasons, for example, papers had to be divided into several sections evenly. But that cannot be the only reason.

A "relational" usage shares its fate with the structure in which it functions. Any attempt to divide research within a broad field like the study of religion is forced to treat certain approaches or areas in relational terms: treating each in substantive terms – dividing things according to the highly specific characteristics of each – would create an untenably large list of divisions. The presence of PoR as a category in the Congresses from 1960 to 1990 tells us that PoR was both defined relationally, in contrast to historical or area studies, and in somewhat more substantive terms (at least after the 1960 Congress), insofar as its value as an umbrella category reflects a sense that various sorts of research shared in some sub-set of its characteristics. That is, a selective view of PoR informed its value as a programme category: a robust view would have served to include on a very small number of papers sharing the same longer list of characteristics.

In this respect, relational views of PoR in the context of the IAHR ended with the 1995 Congress in Mexico City. There were 88 different sessions, but no mention of "phenomenology" appears in its proceedings. It was not only PoR that disappeared. The previous approach to structuring the Congress programme was abandoned. The change became clearer

---

2.　In the programme book of the Rome Congress there are nineteen sections, but its structure is repeated in the proceedings: from historical studies to other studies, with "Methodology of comparative research" and "Phenomenology of religion" as two different sections.

in the 2000 Congress in Durban. With an increased number of papers on cross-methodological and interdisciplinary topics, it became impossible to structure the programme according to the "histories of individual religious traditions and the rest" style.

This look at the history of IAHR Congress programmes suggests that, the study of religion had an assumed "centre" in most of the late twentieth century, and that PoR claimed to be that centre. We can see the erosion of that claim in the increase of competing methodological and theoretical approaches over the decades. Pettazzoni wanted the historical studies of religions to be the centre and tried to make PoR marginal. However, in the twenty-first century, the study of religion no longer has such a distinct centre or periphery.

Satoko Fujiwara is Professor of the Department of Religious Studies, Faculty of Letters/Graduate School of the Humanities and Sociology, at the University of Tokyo. She received a PhD in the History of Religions from the Divinity School of the University of Chicago. She is Secretary General of the International Association for the History of Religions (2020–). Her publications include "The Reception of Otto and *Das Heilige* in Japan: In and Outside the Phenomenology of Religion" *Religion* 47(4), 2017 and "Japan" in *Religious Studies: A Global View*, edited by Gregory D. Alles (Routledge, 2008).

David Thurfjell is Professor in the Study of Religions at Södertörn University, Stockholm. His research circles around themes pertaining to Shi'ite and Pentecostal revivalism, religion as a means of social mobilisation and the discourse surrounding religion and secularity in northern Europe. Among his publications are the monographs *Living Shi'ism* (Brill, 2006), *Faith and Revivalism in a Nordic Romani Community* (Tauris, 2011) and *Godless People* (Norstedts, 2015).

Steven Engler is Professor of Religious Studies at Mount Royal University in Calgary. He studies religions in Brazil, as well as theories and methodology in the study of religion/s. See http://stevenengler.ca

References

Hultkrantz, Åke. 1970. "The Phenomenology of Religion: Aims and Methods." *Temenos* 6: 68–88.

Mensching, Gustav. 1959. *Die Religion: Erscheinungsformen, Strukturtypen und Lebensgesetze.* Stuttgart: Schwab.

Index of Institutions

Index of Professional Associations and Journals

Index of Names

General Index

Lightning Source UK Ltd.
Milton Keynes UK
UKHW021829250321
380997UK00003B/108